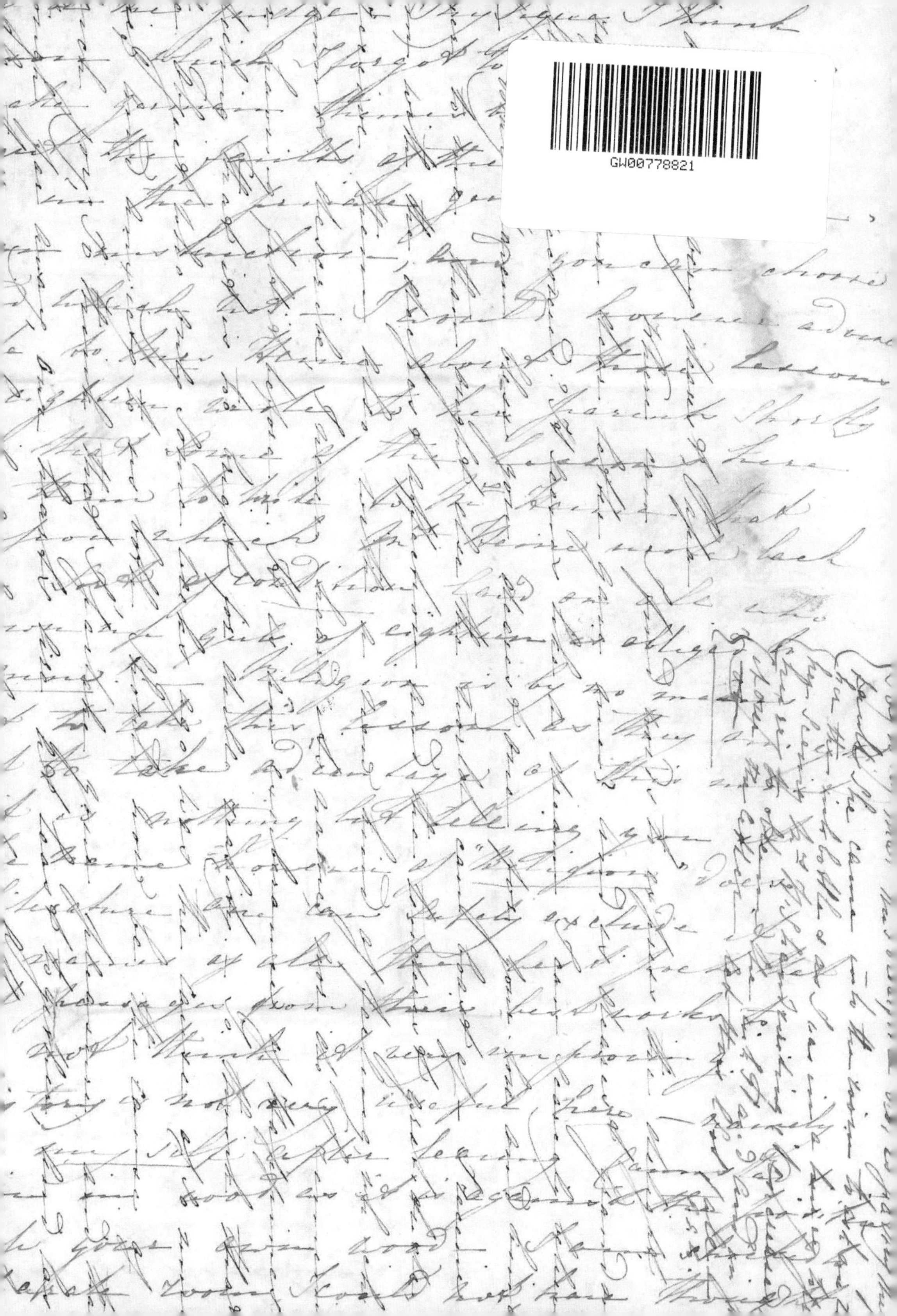

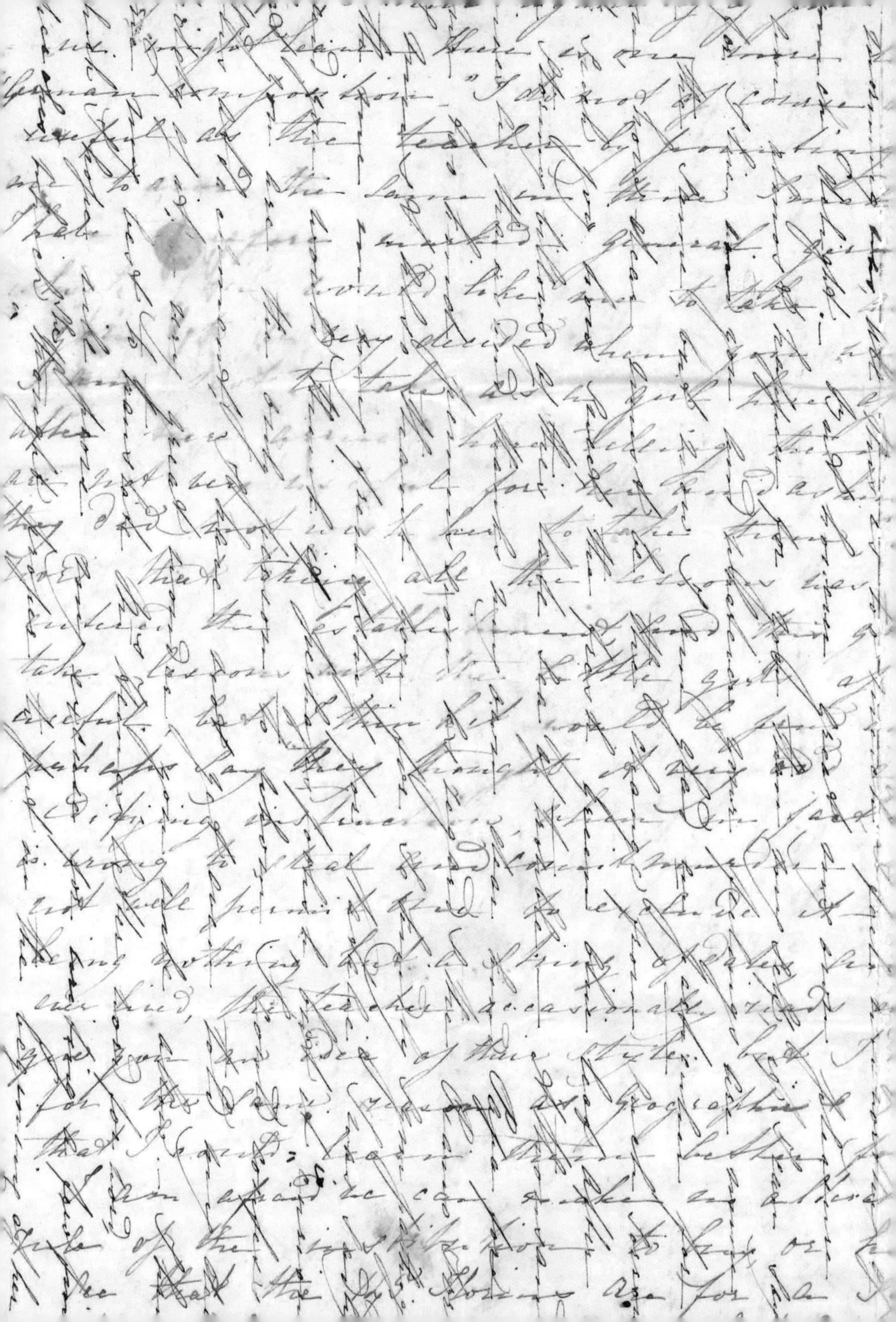

me. [illegible] here is one more
German composition [illegible] I do not of course
understand as the teacher by [illegible]
are to give the same [illegible]
[illegible] marked General [illegible]
[illegible] would like me to take
[illegible] very decided [illegible]
[illegible] take [illegible] girl [illegible]
[illegible] telling the [illegible]
are just [illegible] for [illegible]
they did not wish her to take [illegible]
for [illegible] taking all the lessons [illegible]
[illegible] the establishment [illegible]
take lessons [illegible] the girls [illegible]
careful [illegible] would be [illegible]
perhaps [illegible] they thought [illegible]
[illegible] instance [illegible]
is wrong to steal [illegible]
[illegible] permitted to [illegible]
being nothing but a string of tales [illegible]
ever lived, the teacher occasionally tried
give you an idea of this style. [illegible]
for the same reason as geography [illegible]
that I could learn [illegible] better [illegible]
I am afraid we can make [illegible]
use of the [illegible]
see that the [illegible] for [illegible]

In the bosom of her Father

Cover Image: Edward Bulwer Lytton by Henry William Pickersgill, circa 1831 (Detail)

In the Bosom of her Father

The Life and Death of Emily Bulwer Lytton

Complete Illustrated Edition

In Two Volumes

Volume Two

Mary Letitia Greene
and
Henry Lytton Cobbold

Letters transcribed by Clare Fleck
except Rosina letters, transcribed by Steve Carpenter

Part Four

~ Letters from Germany ~ Aged 15 to 16 ~

Stuttgart in 1845

Traditional Stuttgart dress

CHAPTER 21

~ *Cannstatt Letters - The Institute* ~

Stuttgart – Pop 285,589 – Hotel Marquardt; Royal Hotel; Hotel Continental. Stuttgart, capital of the Kingdom of Württemberg, pleasantly situated on a plain close to the River Neckar, with forest covered or vine clad hills all round, is one of the most attractive towns of Germany. The modern quarters are handsome, and the old parts have retained many of their picturesque features. It is a favourite summer and winter residence; there is an absence of smoke, and in winter considerable sunshine. Printing and bookselling are prominent in the business life, which is also largely engaged in making pianos, furniture and fancy wares. *Bradshaws Continental Railway Guide 1913*

* * * * *

Emily's letters from Cannstatt - the greater part of what we discovered in Box 88 in the Knebworth House archive - could fill a volume of their own. I am tempted to print them complete as a separate book. Here is a text that teenage Literature and History students ought to read alongside Dickens and the Brontës. My daughter dropped out of English Literature A-level faced with Dickens' *Hard Times*. Emily's letters would have been more relevant to her teenage sensibilities.

This is not to deny that Emily's life has the irrelevance of privilege when weighed against the great majority of her contemporaries, but the anxieties and deprivations of separation are at the root of all growing up, and Emily's correspondence with her father is uniquely rich and real. It is also the work of one great writer, and another who would have become one.

I give you here extracts from most of the surviving letters. I have edited repetition and detail - and even that is painful to me, as it is often the minutiae of daily life that is most fascinating from the foreignness of a far away future.

You are therefore at the threshold of seven chapters of intimate father/daughter letters. I quite understand if that is too much for you. If you want to finish Emily's story before bedtime, please do skip upstairs to Chapter 28. I am happy for you to do so - when time is precious, I am well-known for using the fast forward button, even in the most engaging of stories. In the previous chapter, Miss Greene tells you what happens in Cannstatt in the years 1843-1845. These following seven chapters tell you what is happening in Emily's head and Emily's heart.

* * * * *

In these letters, we see a deeply loving - albeit absent - relationship between a father and his daughter, that, tragically, they cannot recreate when they are reunited in person. Edward Bulwer may not be the best father to his children - but neither is he the ogre that biography and legend has cast him. And I present this correspondence as my primary evidence.

Although it is one of the magical features of these letters that the writing is tight-packed on wafer-thin paper and cross-written - as though to gain entry to Emily's mind you must crack a labyrinthine code - I have taken Clare's magnificent transcriptions, broken them up, spread them out, and edited them into a format that I hope is as easy on the modern eye as possible. In laying Emily's personal and private teenage thoughts bare, in Minion Pro text, I trust you will give kind context to the sometimes saccharine and gushing 15-year-old style of her writing, which I have not sought to make easier to read.

The style itself tells so much - especially of how Emily thinks she will best please her father. How she will win and secure his attention and love. Sometimes she is apeing the romantics of his poetry and novels, and other times deliberately practising and developing the florid manners of French, German and English courtesy and letter writing. If at times you find it cloying, I ask you to consider that Emily is a child of the age of *The Old Curiosity Shop* (1840) - and we forgive Dickens for that. Don't we?

* * * * *

Sunday 17th September 1843. ...How are you, dearest Papa? I am so very anxious to know if the good effect of the Baden baths still continues, and that you do not feel the worse of [sic] ***your journey.***

When you left me on Wednesday evening the wretchedness began to grow very abject indeed, and instead of letting me go to my room the black-haired girl took me, as a great favour, into Mrs Heine's room, where I was obliged to be gay and merry with them, at least in appearance, for inwardly the 'amari aliquid' was rising very fast. ['amari aliquid' is Latin for 'something of bitterness' - from a Lucretius quote, no doubt a favourite of her fatalistic father, 'from the midst of the fountains of pleasures there rises something of bitterness which torments us amid the very flowers'.]

Courtesy of the Stadtarchiv Stuttgart (B 294)

However after supper I sought the Balmy [i.e. Balmy Rest = sleep], ***and the next morning those four friends of whom I before told you, came to me after breakfast to chaperon me to those horrid gymnastics, and pointing to the roof***

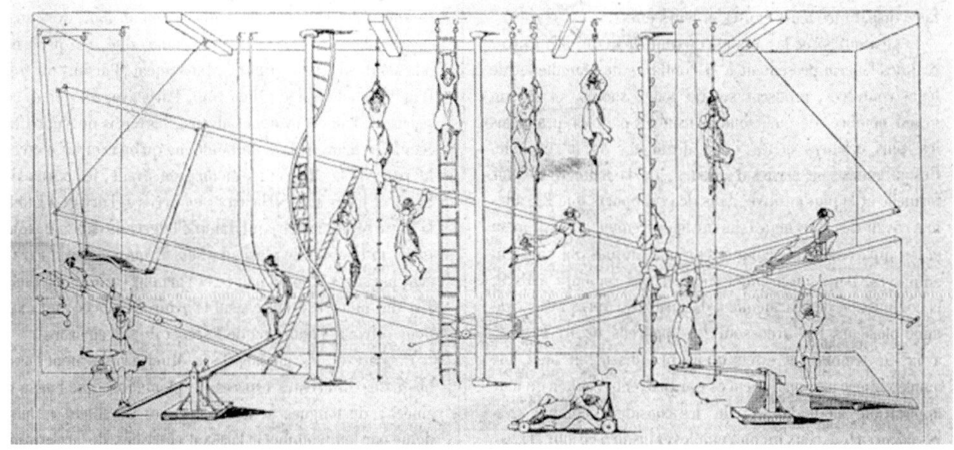

Gymnastics - from the brochure of a similar institute in France in the late 1830s

of the house where a girl (my complete idea of red-haired Grissel) [In Shakespeare's *The Taming of the Shrew*, Griselda is the annoyingly perfect wife]***) was hanging herself. They uttered exclamations of the most enthusiastic admiration, and then told me she was "such a sweet girl". To which I quietly replied "so!" (a most convenient word here). But when they told me she should like to know me & if I pleased they would introduce me to her, I felt a strong inclination to say "Gott bewahre"*** [God forbid], ***but checked myself in time.***

* * * * *

However to do the poor place justice, I like it on the whole much better than I expected. The people, I mean Mrs Heine, etc. etc., are very kind in their way & I have not been disappointed in the Italian. But I have not yet found anyone to love. My four friends (the best in the school) I might perhaps in time be induced to like, but I have not yet discovered the Fraulein Angelina Angelica [a reference to Byron's housebound Venetian love?] ***that you spoke of.***

Indeed I do not see much of any of them, for I prefer staying in my room and as I do not yet lie down [in treatment, on the 'Streckbett'], ***I have plenty of time to amuse myself with those delightful books you were so kind as to give me to read. I am now reading*** *Eugene Aram* [Edward's 1832 novel of a scholar driven by passion to murder in 18th Century Norfolk] ***and whatever original beauty it may lose by being in German I am quite charmed by it.***

I have got a green gown and have gone through the exceedingly painful ordeal of doing one or two of the gymnastics for the first time. I do not think I ever did any thing in the whole course of my life more thoroughly disagreeable - for independent of the thing itself, Doctor Heine came with me to show me what to do, which of course drew the eyes of all those girls upon me. And, as soon as he was gone, I was obliged to go on with my awkward feats amidst the jeers and titters of the rest (excepting the Italian, who rolled her dark eyes and told me not to mind them). The novelty, however, is now wearing off and they content themselves with a condescending stare from the tops of their ladders etc. etc.

A great many girls have left since I came [presumably, it being the end of summer], ***and though the prettiest are gone, the most good natured are left.***

Miss Jones [another British girl] ***does not attend the school, but lives with her mother in apartments in the other part of the house. I drank tea with her the other evening, but I suppose she is like me and does not prepossess at first sight, for I did not see anything loveable in her.***

* * * * *

Sir George Shee [The British Minister in Stuttgart] ***was kind enough to call on me yesterday – he was very good natured indeed. He wrote a note to Dr Heine this morning to ask if I might go to church to a Dr Parsons here, an English clergyman. I did not go, as I thought I would ask you first if you would like it.***

Mrs Heine told me to ask you if I should learn dancing, or rather take dancing lessons, & she says she wishes to have your reply soon. They have bought me a great many things such as sheets towels etc. etc., all of which I thought they would have provided themselves.

As you say, this place is just like the world - at least what I fancy the world must be. I am the only one that has a room to myself & am looked upon by my friends as people in furnished lodgings look upon those that have a house of their own. The little corner you spoke of I have made as pretty as I can, and have arranged for writing and working, two of my favourite occupations. Reading, I have reserved for the delightful time I am to lie down for four hours a day. I am writing now in that nook.

How did you find dearest Grandmama and Teddy? quite quite well I hope.

Three of my friends (the names of whom I do not know therefore I am forced to call them 'friends') are gone to Stuttgart, as well as the governess - and I have luckily, politely got off the invitation to spend a day with 'mes parens' ['my parents'].

I am very sorry the governess is a governess, for I like her very much. She is very good natured and kind, but I see very well that it would not exactly do to make a great friend of her because of the other girls.

Dr Heine has just been here - tomorrow I am to lie down for two hours. I asked him about the water Dr Broom ordered for the spots and he said I should try one other bottle, and if it still had no effect to give it up.

* * * * *

The library here is a small bookcase with some tattered books in it – mostly translations from the English or French. And the other governess is a sort of house keeper for the second class – so you see my suspicions were partly well grounded!

Dearest dearest Papa I think of you so very often, think of your being so delicate, and wish that it were possible for me to take all that ever makes you poorly or unhappy on myself. It would be such a pleasure to think that I could spare you one pang. I think one the chief reasons that I like this little room so much is that I can come away from the crowd of girls and think of you, and be with you in thought, tho' you are far away.

They only go out to walk once in each week, and on that day they do not do any gymnastics - at least only one hour, but that they look upon as nothing at all! You may fancy my horror at finding myself walking with, and forming, one of those jabbering creatures - and I then remembered with shame with what contempt I used to look upon the schools that I used to see walking out in England.

Courtesy of the Stadtarchiv Stuttgart (B 312)

Cannstatt Spa in 1845

We had to pass a fashionable promenade - a base copy of the one at Baden - not the one that I saw with you, but another quite at the other side of Cannstadt. There were some people there drinking the waters. I have looked everywhere for the view that they have shown in the prospectus but have not as yet been able to discover it.

* * * * *

Throughout the correspondence, Emily and her father keep up a playful exchange about Edward's dogs, June & Parson Black, and what appears to be a German pen-friend for the two dogs, befriended (or imagined) in Baden Baden, Baron von Stealbones. ***I can fancy June's extasy*** [sic] ***on your return. I wish I could have seen him. Pray do not forget to give him the note from Baron von Stealbones. If you send me his answer, I can forward it. Be so kind also to give him my love and my respects to Parson Black. I am very anxious to see June's answer. I suppose he will allow an old friend like me to read his letter.***

* * * * *

We make 'visits' every evening, when 'the toil of the day' is over, which I think is one of the most amusing things they do, except that it is very like child's play. For after I have made them 'une visite de céremonie', they come about ten minutes after to me - more I think for their amusement than anything else, for they bow & curtsey etc. etc. I think as yet Mrs Thomson's ring is quite safe, that is to say, I do not think I shall ever give it from love - though perhaps it may go at Christmas as a matter of course.

There is one girl whom I am very very sorry for. The news came yesterday that her mother is dead. She has not come down to breakfast, dinner or supper - but sits the whole day in her room, and when one passes the door one can hear her sobbing.

I have received this instant a visit from Mrs and Miss Pfizer [the family of Bulwer's German translator and publisher] - *they were very goodnatured and staid* [sic] *a long time. The post has just come in, but as the letter carrier has not yet been here, and as the Doctor says I must go into the garden, I must for the present relinquish the very delightful occupation of writing to you. In the hope of receiving a letter from you tomorrow morning, I will not yet therefore bid you farewell for good (as the saying is) but only say 'au revoir'.*

* * * * *

I have not indeed been disappointed - how can I thank you enough, my own darling Papa, for the rapture which your delightful long charming let-

ter gave me, just received. Your very kind and excellent advice I shall most thankfully take and adhere to in the smallest particulars. You may guess I have not been attracted to mere form and face for (excluding the Italian) the one of my four friends that I like the best is a short stout girl with ugly features but good natured countenance & projecting teeth!! But she is very '_________' [indecipherable].

You tell me to write to you once a fortnight - if you only knew the delight it gives me to write to you-! if [only] the amari aliquid the toil did not rise! [Lucretius's 'amari aliquid', Latin for 'something of bitterness', becomes Emily's expression for home sickness - although home sickness is a term that needs reworking for Emily. Perhaps we should say, loved-one sickness.]

Be assured I shall not set my face against the Gymnastics. Anything that gives you pleasure gives me pleasure too, and I receive no pain when I confer pleasure.

You are kind enough to say you miss me – ah! If you could only know how I miss you – every thing reminds me you are gone – the gossip of my companions (I have not as yet found one 'friend') is so different (mais cela va sans dire [but that goes without saying]*) from your delightful conversation – in fact everything. I try to make myself as agreeable as I can and endeavour to make no enemies by my manner. And as I have not yet received a music lesson, I shall give double attention to the mental music, as you so prettily say.*

With regard to Dress, I have turned my plaid one, and it will do extremely well as a common winter one - and I have seen some pretty ladylike stuff [material] *which is very cheap which I think I shall get for a best one. I also think I shall not require a new bonnet, but shall get my Tuscan* [straw] *one cleaned with a dark velvet ribbon and lining to match.*

I have laid in a store of paper, pens etc. etc. with some of the money you were so kind as to give me. Those little things are very cheap when you buy them yourself, but uncommonly dear when you trust to others for them. I have got some new shoes which will last the whole winter, but as they are not very ornamental I have got Mrs Heine to pay for them.

* * * * *

Today is Monday so I can fancy you at Craven Cottage with your long

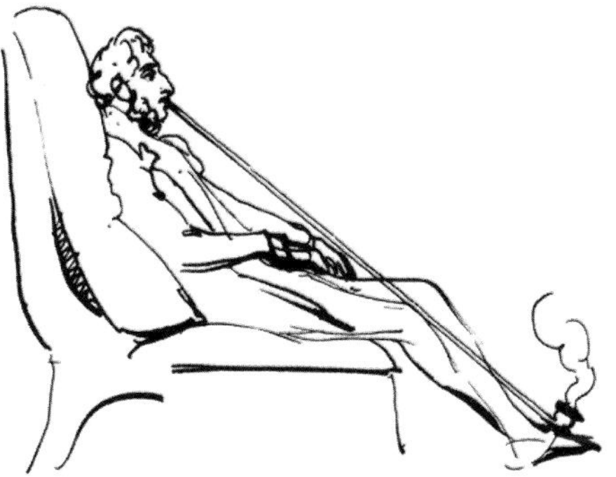
Edward and his long cherrywood pipe

pipe (I wish I was there to light the flame of Genius) and giving June his breakfast & bestowing on him the caresses which, poor thing, he has so long been deprived of.

Do not fatigue yourself, dearest Papa, to write to me when you have other things of more importance to do – but only remember what delight a few lines give to one who loves you so dearly, so very dearly as I do, when you have time. You certainly did not suit the action to the words when you said in your delightful long letter that you were a "horrible correspondent", but I cannot of course expect such a long one every time. But when I do not get a letter from you, I shall torment you with another scribble, and so on, till you are obliged to say "well this is rather too much". I laughed very heartily indeed (the first time I laughed since I came here) at the Villiersehen Wőrte [not clear what this is]. *It is excellent.*

I began my cure today, but it is to increase as I become more accustomed to it.

And now dearest Papa, as Mrs de Weling says, "you have my annals" since you left. Indeed, I did not intend to speak so much of myself when I began this letter as I find I have done, but I must trust to your goodness to forgive me. Ever believe me, your own fond attached affectionate, Measy

* * * * *

Dear Sir Edward, writes Miss Greene, *Emily's sweet letter & the conversation we had this morning has put my mind quite at rest as to the points I was uneasy about, but I have thought over with great alarm at the idea of Lady Bulwer's being so near her – when Emily was quite a child, she was (L.B.), we all know, very jealous of her, & when she hears that she has been travelling about with you, & that you are so fond of her, she will not stop at saying anything. To myself she has said, years ago, such diabolical things as to your opinion with regard to your daughter - the recollection of which made me shudder. Pray put Md Heine upon her guard to protect the dear girl from her,*

& believe me to remain yours sincerely, M.L.Greene

* * * * *

Sunday 24th September, 1843. My dear Mrs de Weling, Pray excuse me for troubling you so often with letters but I could not resist writing you a few lines to tell you where I am and what I am doing... Papa is gone back to England after leaving me with Dr Heine at Cannstadt – it would not be the truth were I to say that I felt anything else but very unhappy at parting with dearest Papa, but I know I am doing what he pleases and wishes me to do in staying here, and doing everything that lies in my power for my figure.

It is not however mere shape that Papa cares about so much - but all the Doctors he has consulted about it say that, if the defect is not now cured, in six months a disease might commence which would be miserable. They are all very kind here and the treatment very gentle. Of course there are a great number of disagreables, but that I have made up my mind to - and endeavour to - bear them as well as I can.

Papa gave me all his own works that he allows me to read before he left, but they are all translated into German - as he says he would not let me read more English novels unless he had the satisfaction of thinking that I was improving myself in a foreign language and at the same time amusing myself. I have plenty of time to read them, as they lie down here four hours a day on a

Emily's set of her father's novels in German as translated and published by Gustav Pfizer, now on the shelf of Edward's Library at Knebworth House

sort of bed made for the purpose.

We do great many various sorts of gymnastics and bathe three times a week in a particular sort of water. There are also a great many other things which we do - or rather which are done for us - and which I cannot exactly tell you in a letter.

I have a very pretty room with a beautiful view, but when we talk of beautiful views here, we must not think of Neuwied, or woe betide the Cannstadt _________ [indecipherable].

I received a very great treasure the other day in the shape of a letter from my dearest Papa. It is full of such kind advice as to the choice of companions etc. etc., and then such kind encouragement steadily to continue all that will be of such benefit hereafter in saving me from a life of wretchedness and disease. I miss dearest Papa very much indeed, for, independent of everything else, he is such a witty, clever and kind companion that however kind others may be, one still feels that he is gone. But I have nothing to complain of. The cure is rendered as agreeable as it can be, and both Mr Heine and Mrs Heine are very kind in their different ways. And the girls too are very kind and obliging in their way...

I cannot any longer trouble you with my chit chat and bad writing, so begging you to remember me to 'Tessy' [the maid] *and to give my dearest Anna many loves and kisses from me, I must remain your sincerely attached and grateful, Emily Elizabeth Georgina Bulwer*

* * * * *

Tuesday 26th September, 1843. My Darling Emily, You see, I begin high up in the paper, to have a long talk with you. Blessed is he who invented letters, which 'waft a sigh from Indus to the Pole' [from Alexander Pope's *Eloisa to Abelard* (1717)] - *& now carry from London to Stuttgart my fondest & tenderest prayers for my Measy. Your delightful & long letter was a great relief to me - and came as a great pleasure – for I think I see in it the faint dawning of a reconciliation with the 'Poor Place'* [he is quoting from her letter]. *I fancy your taking to your corner after the "Toils of the day"- & receiving your visitors, whose ceremonious courtesies are I suppose by this time indicated with warm greetings.*

But the Gymnastics. Oh – by this time you must adore the Gymnastics – I imagine to myself your graceful activity & already see you at the top of the ladder looking down in your turn, on some newly arrived Novice.

With regard to the English church - how are you to get there? & how can you go alone? You don't answer these points & all I can say is that I have no objection provided you have a female companion & a conveyance. Not being on the spot to decide how far these are practicable, je me fie a votre discretion [I trust to your discretion]. *Much will depend on your own feelings & whether the church you go to at Cannstatt is agreeable to your own devotions. If so, I conclude it must be most convenient.*

With regard to Dancing, I don't fancy you will learn much there, and you seem to me to dance well as it is, but probably Dr Heine recommends it as an exercise, & probably the girls generally learn it. Judge for yourself, & accept or decline it according - 1st, as you think it is considered a help to the Gymnastics & good for the shape; 2nd as you feel inclined to it as an amusement. In short, the cure must be the first object, & next on all things, my darling, your own inclinations & wishes. Your straw bonnet won't do alone, you must have a warm winter one.

* * * * *

Now for my annals [which, after general news, come to the dogs] *...on the very day I arrived* [in Town, from Craven Cottage], *imagine my consternation, June vanished – whether lost or taken no one could say – I was afraid he had gone to see his cousin at Baden. However Bills were printed, advertisements issued, rewards offered, & finally he was returned with much cost & after great trouble. My man servant wept bitterly & says he "will never be the same man!" so great were his sufferings – True, I was very unjust to him, & said if June was not found he would remind me too much of my loss & I would discharge him!*

How June went is still a mystery – at present his only amusement in Town is in perpetual war with a settlement of fleas who have effected a colony on his back.

My catarrh continuing, I was forced to consult a Dr who pooh poohed poor Dr Brown's powder & set me to injecting iced water, which greatly relieved the catarrh but has brought on a cough – so I am obliged to suspend operations. In fact I have had little time to think of myself, for my dear Mother has been ill still – and I am very uneasy about her.

* * * * *

No sooner had I arrived in Town, when lo, a note from Miss Greene saying she should be up on Saturday & wanting me to give her a rendezvous at Mrs Thomsons. Since I don't see the necessity of making Mrs Thomson au fait upon our family matters, I preferred calling on Miss Greene in her lodgings.

We have had two interviews. At the first she was a little unreasonable - & I could not make her understand or conceive that we had done for the best in placing you at Cannstatt. She seemed to fancy it was some gratuitous cruelty of mine & would not regard the necessity of your cure as a serious matter – said it was all in the mind, & that you would be straight if you were happy... that is, with her. She also offered to go to you – which I declined for the present.

Our second interview was more satisfactory & she seems now reconciled to the arrangement - thanks chiefly to my reading her your letter, in which she could see at least how frank & familiar our correspondence was, & that you had the good sense & charming self denial to accommodate yourself to present disagreeables for future benefit. She is going back to Carrington [north of Nottingham, when the 17th are barracked] *& will write to you. In replying to her (without of course asking you to disguise anything) it will be well to make the best of things & at least let her see that you agree with me in thinking that the Cure must be attended to - & that some such Institution was necessary. We have parted very good friends – in spite of a 'tiff' at first. She is extremely attached to you certainly. She says Bonnie is grown beautiful.*

* * * * *

I reserve for the clean envelope something I must call your attention to. Your letter is beautifully written in style as well as sentiment - the only fault my critical eye can discover, is in your affectionate wish that I am not the worse of my journey. It ought to be 'for' my journey, dear. Rather ungracious not to overlook the grammar for the sake of the sentiment – but I blame those Authors –

Not a word from Madame von Weling [whom he is parodying with that expression and the earlier use of the word 'dear'] *in reply to my last.*

Here follows June's letter: "Cousin Stealbones. I suspect you are an impostor! You write English too well for a German. The Family of the Stealbones always had a bad character & are supposed to have acquired their fortune by smuggling. The little property I have is honestly acquired... [etc.]"

* * * * *

On a separate sheet, Edward adds the following - giving his young daughter again the onus of managing the shame and intrigue of his private life with her new guardians. *And now comes my disagreeable intelligence – Lady Bulwer is at Geneva, and she wrote to some people here that she was going to Germany to see you. Now this may be a bravado – still it is as well to be prepared. What I fear most is the indecent exposure of some violent scene. I therefore think you had better at once try & make sufficient friends with Madame Heine to approach the subject. Try & do so naturally – by saying that if any persons should call & ask to see you, you would request to know first before you were sent for, who they were, their names - & if you don't know the names, if they came from me. And then you could bring out that I was separated from Lady B - & would not permit any communication from her.*

This is unpleasant, but is certainly necessary, just to put them on their guard against being taken by surprise; & you on your guard against being suddenly & unawares called into the presence of those you should avoid. It will be necessary also that, if any scene should occur, you should be kept perfectly clear from it. The Heines would only have to show my note (that I gave you) to anyone & say civilly that their instructions were peremptory - & then they must fight it out.

If however you don't feel your way with Madame Heine & have not grown familiar with her – perhaps I had better write. I will do as you wish. But you see, some preparation is necessary. Write by return of post, & tell me what you would like best. I think it very doubtful any attempt will be made, but unless the Heines are prepared, you see, they would not make any opposition -

& you would be exposed, my poor child, to all sorts of annoyance, which your relationship could not allow you to resist.

But, at all events, if you think you could speak to Madame Heine yourself more easily & naturally than I could write, & prefer that plan, you must impress upon her at first that the conference is strictly confidential, & that I as well as you make it a particular request that nothing should transpire to the girls or the other teachers, or anyone in fact – upon the plain ground, everywhere recognised, that family matters are sacred. Your own good sense & reflection will shew you which is best to be the oracle – you or I.

And now God bless you my own Darling - & believe in the fond love & anxious forethought of your most aff. Father, E.L.B.

* * * * *

Thursday 5th October, 1843. My own dear dearest Papa, Thank you, thank you, a thousand times for your dear long letter - it is so kind of you to spend so much time upon giving me perhaps the greatest pleasure I know. You do not know, my dearest Papa, the pain it gave me to hear you had not been well. I beseech you not to do much and do not confide too much to Doctors - they are like governesses and always find fault with the treatment of the one who had gone before, however right that one might have been.

Dear Grandmama has too been unwell - pray give her my fondest love and tell her how sincerely I hope she will very very soon recover.

I shall inflict upon myself the pain of answering the disagreeable part of your letter first. I have considered and reconsidered your question and have at length decided you had better be the speaker on this occasion. To be sure, I might say it more naturally, and it would be less formal and formidable than if you wrote it - but then Mrs Heine lives in a different part of the house altogether, and I seldom see her but on matters of dress, lessons, money, etc. etc. She does not possess that quality, charm, which lures one to confidence, and if I ask for a private conference (for I never could introduce such a subject in the midst of calculations of gulden, kreuzers, etc. [Württemberg currency]*), I am afraid I should not be, after all, able to tell her it is true. Paper does not blush, and* [Emily accepts] *if blunders are made in conversation, they are forgiven - nay even tears and confusion are overlooked - but still, I think as*

matters stand, it would be better if you were to write. How willingly would I spare you the pain and trouble, but all I am afraid of is I should not do it well - and then better not do it at all.

* * * * *

As for the subject of my last letter it is now all cleared up so I need not say more about it. I wrote a long letter to dear Aunt Mary yesterday.

Emily is referring to her distress at Miss Greene's initial letter declaring she is coming immediately to Cannstatt, ***now that your Papa has left you*** - before Miss Greene is given the comfort of seeing Emily's first letter. The worry of Miss Greene upsetting the balance of the life she is just getting used to, is made worse by another letter that crosses in the post, a rare note from Teddy [from 18, Oriental Place, Brighton], ***I have reserved my best and greatest news for the last - only the other day I heard from Dear Aunt M & she proposes going to Germany to see you. She is already gone to London...***

Her father writes later, ***I have just had your letter, enclosing Miss Greene's. But I hope long ere this you will have received mine which will set your mind at ease - a thousand thanks for your confidence and, believe me, I fully appreciate your good sense & good feeling – how like Miss G, to write off in that fidgety flighty way before she had even spoken to me on the subject!.... So Irish!***

* * * * *

I am very much ashamed of my bad grammar - it was indeed very like a hausmaid to say "worse of your journey", but forgive me.

I am by no means the experienced and nimble performer at the gymnastics that you suppose - but hope to be so soon, not from love of them, but that I think they have already done good, not to the shape but to the general health.

The English Church is held in the Parsons' [family] house just over the way, so I can go alone and need no companion. I suppose it would be only civil to go once or twice as I was introduced to the Parsons family the other evening at the Jones.

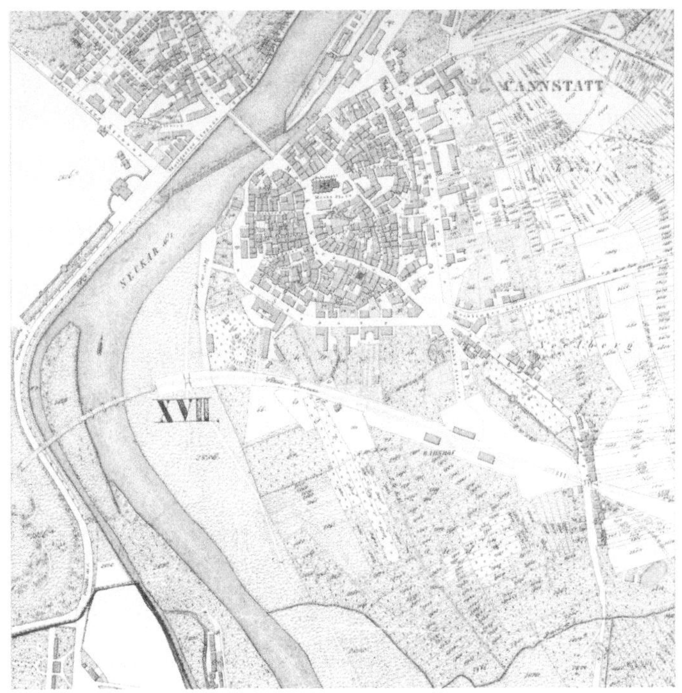

Map of Cannstatt in 1825...

It is very very kind of you to confide in me. Be sure, dearest Papa, I shall do all can to make you not repent your confidence. I have not yet told Mrs Heine about what you say to the dancing lessons. I myself think it would be best not to take them unless Dr Heine particularly wishes it...

Mrs Heine has bought blankets,

...the Institute is the four clustered buildings on the south side of Bad Strasse, with gardens stretching out to the east and down to embankment, built for the railway and to help with flood defence.

sheets, towels and a quantity of other things and, finding that I was going to write to you today, she desired me to tell you she would be very much obliged to you if you could name some banker in Stuttgart where she could get money, when she wanted.

This, my dearest Papa, I tell you as a message from her. Wherever I go I find it is my fate that people should lay out money upon what they term "absolute necessaries" and then the people in the next place say, "what a pity so much money should have been spent on such and such a thing - if only I would have been there, I would have shewn them, etc. etc."

She also desires me to tell you that the music mistress gives singing lessons, but not good ones - that those, in Stuttgart, are very dear, and if I go into Stuttgart every time, a conveyance will be necessary; and if a teacher comes out here, he will also charge extra for the time taken coming, and the means by which he comes. She therefore desires to know your wish. I think it would be more advisable to give up singing as long as I'm here. I can pay double attention to it after I leave this place.

* * * * *

You quite astonished me when you said you were at Craven Cottage the Monday after you left me. Dearest Papa take care you do not do too much. I often think you spoil your own health, poor Papa. You must not work too hard - I entreat you pour l'amour de moi [for my sake] *forget the Muses now and then, and think of yourself. Think of your own dear health and try hard to shake off that naughty cold. It, like everything and everybody else, loves you and does not wish to leave you - but you must drop its acquaintance and rid yourself of its unfortunate visits...*

I am delighted dearest Teddy is so much better and envy him his visit to your friends the D'Eyncourts, of whom I have heard you speak so much. As soon as I have received his letter I shall write him a long one in reply in which I shall not fail to bring in my "power not knowledge" speeches together with a host of "dears"!

I received a long letter from Madame de Weling yesterday in which she spoke of herself as a being born to sorrow and crushed by disappointment and cares - but still clinging to all that is just and honourable [etc.]... There was a

postscript at the end desiring me not to yield to morbid sensibility and visionary sorrows! In fact the whole letter was fit for a novel - what a pity you have ceased to cull the flowers of fiction!

* * * * *

This - generally happy - tone of Emily's correspondence continues for the first two months at Dr Heine's Institute. The 15-year-old English girl is making the best of her lot, and by her own charms and with the comfort of her father's letters and books, appears to be thriving as best she might.

There is a reassuring humour to many of her day-to-day tales, which suggests reasonable contentment - and she particularly enjoys word play with her father around recurring themes that only they hold in common. Madame de Weling continues a source of fun. ***I received this day a letter from Aunt Mary - your definition of her (much as I love her) is very good, a worthy excellent person, but wanting tact and delicacy. Only fancy! she tells me that had I remained with the "the last of the Baronesses" (as she terms Madame de Weling)*** [a play on the title of Edward's new book, *The Last of the Barons* (1843)], ***it was her intention to have applied to the Queen Dowager*** [Adelaide, the German widow of William IV] ***to have written to the Schloss!! This, as she justly called it, "would have been a move that would have astonished the people!" If it had really taken place, how terrible it would have been. Poor little Neuwied would have bubbled and boiled and seethed as if indeed water and fire were mixing, and the sea of disagreeables last spring would have brought forth another sea this winter - the very thought makes one exclaim in ecstasy, hurrah for the gymnastics!***

* * * * *

It is not long before the link with her Neuwied life becomes unnecessary. ***I am going to try if possible to drop Mrs de Weling's acquaintance, I mean I am going to try to discontinue writing to her. There will be no use in keeping up a correspondence with one I do not love much and who most probably does not care much for me.***

Edward's impression of Sarah de Weling, as given to Miss Greene, is 'vulgar'. This use of the word 'vulgar' has happily tipped off the top of social parlance today - along with the similarly distasteful term 'nouveau riche' - but we may read its use here as suggesting 'pushy' and 'of airs', as well as having a pre-occupation with money. Emily has adopted it from her father's colourful vocabulary, and is grown-up enough to sense - what we would call politically incorrect - comic potential, particularly in the notion that it manifests itself in physical appearance. Emily continues the paragraph on Madame de Weling - ***How very difficult it is to discern vulgarity in a foreigner! I am quite sure the ugly girl I before told you of is very vulgar, and yet because she can talk German with surprising rapidity, and cannot understand one word of English, I persuaded myself she is not vulgar. I confess I have been rather disappointed in her, but still am constant to the Italian. She is not pretty (at least not what I think pretty) but she has a rarity – a mild black eye.***

* * * * *

Catty comments - usually with comic intent - about the other girls, are also consistent in the recurring word play between daughter and father. ***There are a great many going and a great many coming. It is almost painful to see how little those that remain sorrow for those that go. They bid, it is true, a very warm farewell, but it is with a broad grin... then they rub their hands &, with a steadfast eye on the uppermost rung of the ladder, they endeavour to recall cats, monkeys and the dear departed one.***

But a truce (as Mrs de Weling says) to my ill-natured observations on the girls and gymnastics, and let me do both justice - if the former do not regret your absence, they do at least enjoy your presence, and are very good natured; and if the latter spoil your hands, they improve your figure and make you feel a glow of health and a gush of happy spirits, which enables you in your turn to be good tempered.

* * * * *

Not surprising in a 15-year-old girl - and the daughter of a Regency dandy who is all but a byword for it - is vanity, and a self-consiousness of her physique and complexion. These concerns appear with regularity. ***I have been***

observing for the last few days with the greatest complacency that my hands were getting very much emaciated - but one morning, as a punishment for my vanity, I awoke with them covered with blisters from the gymnastics! I have adopted the lemon, the wax, the rubbing, the close cuting and all the other

A ladies class at a German gynmasium - 30 years later, but the girls' expressions match

tortures you recommend...

Imagine my mortification and horror! The blackhaired creature has just been in here and tells me with a grin of delight that she has just read in the newspaper that "the celebrated Sir E.L.Bulwer passed through Stuttgart some weeks ago for the purpose of placing his daughter in Dr Heine's celebrated establishment"! So now I suppose all the world knows that I am here, and for what! Is it not very provoking?...

I do not wonder in the least at hearing dear Bonnie is now beautiful, when I saw her last she gave every promise of being a very pretty girl - she has such a beautiful complexion such nice coloured rich long hair such beautiful eyes and such a fine skin...

[My skin] I think is much better. I have discontinued Dr Broom's water and in the Spring am to drink a water which Dr Heine hopes will entirely remove it [the acne]. *He makes a round about once a fortnight to all the girls, and when he comes to me I never fail to ask him (as you told me) about "NOSE AND COMPLEXION"; I am afraid that he must think that I possess a far greater share of vanity than is ever in general imparted to our sex; or even than Mrs von Weling thought to give me...*

* * * * *

Here follows Professor Stealbones letter to John June...[etc.] *Professor Stealbones' broken English is certainly more apparent in this letter, which as far as I am forced to pay the toll I have taken the liberty to read... But that Stealbones is a German, there is not the least doubt - and the reason he wrote his last letter in such good English was that he has an old English cat which he keeps, I believe, as upper hauskeeper & is, I believe, a descendant of the famous Jacobine* [a faction of the French Revolution] *celebrated in the annals of Catkingdom for her warlike achievements. This cat had early learned to write and spell her own language, and the Professor having first barked what he wished to say in German, Puss mewed it then in English. And afterwards, with considerable pain in the paw, wrote the letters you were kind enough to take to their respective owners.*

* * * * *

Emily's confidence seems to grow in each weekly letter. Her father's preoccupations therefore settle - away from an anxiety over her health and well-being - into the familiar worry that an unnecessary amount of his money is being spent in her name. He also returns to his permanent obsession, his own work. He is, this autumn of 1843, preparing *The Poems and Ballads of Schiller*, a poetic translation of the German poet and dramatist Johann Christoph Friedrich von Schiller (1759-1805). This is suitably Bulwerian bravado for an English author who does not speak German.

Friedrich Schiller

Emily jumps to assist. This is exactly the fantasy role this 15-year-old daughter of England most renowned writer is preparing herself for. The first task is to relay a question to Herr Pfizer as to what Schiller means by the allusion 'Goldkind' - literally 'golden child'. Alongside swiftly relaying the question to Stuttgart, she even braves her own opinion. ***I have read [the quotation] a good many times and have come to your conclusion that the golden children must mean tears, but humbly entreating Schiller's ghost to pardon my boldness and presumption. I must say I think 'perlenfl__'*** [indecipherable, 'beads or spots of ___', possibly 'pearls of truth'] ***a better comparison than golden children, however we shall hear the Pfizer explanation soon...***

She becomes bolder in her responses to her father's literary work. ***I was quite vexed - nay, I was almost angry that that beautiful speech of Madeline to Walter*** [in Edward's *Eugene Aram* (1832)] ***should be profaned by being translated into German. Only fancy, in a most touching address of Walter to Madeline they have made him begin "geliebtes Mühmchen"*** ["beloved coz" - in the original it is "sweet cousin"] – ***could anything be so unpoetical? So like the Germans.***

But, as we might expect, anything direct from her father's pen is never less than canonical. ***The more I read her annals the more I am delighted with Madeline, her letter to Eugene Aram is so very beautiful - how true that is, that one often can write things one cannot speak. When I read it I was on the verge of exclaiming with Mr Ward, "O Bulwer, how can you know the wom-***

an's heart so well!!" We can almost hear Rosina laughing all the way in Geneva.

Assuming Emily means Robert Ward (1765–1846) - he was an English barrister, politician, and novelist. Wikipedia quotes Prime Minister George Canning (1770–1827) that Ward's law books were as pleasant as novels, and his novels as dull as law books.

I have often thought (tho' the thought has never shaped itself to words) how much better I can write to you how much and how dearly I love you, than I can tell you so...

Alas! The rub of their relationship. That leaves us these beautiful letters, and ultimately the tragedy to come.

...But may not the reason be this? When I am with you I am too much engaged with your 'presence' to think of my own feelings; and when you are gone your void teaches me to discover how very much I love you and then I hail, and bless, pen, ink, and paper, as a means of telling you so.

The reclusive scholar, Eugene Aram, is hiding a dark secret... which is revealed when his love Madeline's cousin Walter uncovers the fate of his long-lost father. Edward Bulwer Lytton's ***Eugene Aram*** *(1832)*

* * * * *

Emily knows from witnessing consistent disputes with her guardians over money and economy, that this is her father's most fragile fuse. Not a letter is sent from Cannstatt that does not worry about - or seek to justify - money spent. The warning letter to the Heines about Lady Bulwer turning up - once decided better written than spoken - when it arrives, comes within the convenient distraction of a stiff note to Madame Heine about Emily's mounting expenses.

I now come to the disagreeable part of my correspondence – the letter for Madame Heine which - after you have read & if you approve of – wafer [seal] *and present (let the wafer be dry). But don't scruple not to give it (& let me know if I can express otherwise, the scarce expressible grievance) should you think it can be improved.*

When I settle with Madame Heine, I can replenish your exhausted finances, which have not, I fear, sufficed to prove the value of your resistance to the 'petites frianderies' ['little treats'] *of which Madame Heine spoke with so intimate a sense of their allurements.*

God bless you my dearest Emily. I fear this letter will be rather a golden child to you. But in this world one cannot even call to one's own Father without paying for it. 'Der Erde gott – Das Geld' ['The Earth God - Money']... *everywhere* [a quote from Schiller]. *No wonder that I constantly inculcate* [instil by persistent instruction] *on your youthful mind the value of money - without it, what are we! Poor creatures – whom a shopman terrifies and even the postman scares... ever & ever, Yr fond Father E.L.B.*

* * * * *

Saturday 4th November, 1843. I have this evening for the first time worn the machine! It hurts a little every time I move, but I suppose that will go off. I am wound up every day like a watch which I should think would make me grow very much. As yet I can perceive no alteration, but I should think it would be too soon to expect any. I must now bid you good night, dearest Papa, and, as tomorrow is Sunday, I look forward with delight to a long talk with you.

Sunday Morning. As for the 'petites frianderies', I have not yet been tempted by them. Mrs Heine gives pocket money - 7 Gulden at a time - with which I pay for candles, gloves, letters, etc. I shall at the end of three months enlarge upon the lessons and tell you which I think useless. She has previously promoted her continuation of music by praising the music mistress - s*he teaches* *the language of music, which is always the sign of a good teacher* - and, *as for dancing lessons, Dr Heine looks upon dancing as a part of the cure more than as an accomplishment, and wishes me to take the lessons with the rest.*

I take the greatest liberties with your name when talking with all the teachers. I hope you will forgive me, but you know that you yourself say that "Character must be kept up at all sacrifices!" I have ingratiated myself in the music mistress's particular favour by pronouncing an enthusiastic "O Ja" when she said she was sure you were an admirer of Beethoven. And the governess is always quoting passages from your books in favour of the different things that she teaches; the other day when showing me a new embroidery stitch, she said, "I am sure your father would like you to embroider well, you know in speaking of needlework in one of his works he terms it 'a pretty excuse for thinking'" to which I replied "oh yes, to be sure" - though I have not the most distant idea to what she alluded. At any rate the speech is worthy of you, for I never work without thinking much more about you than the pattern. [The quote is from *Ernest Maltravers* (1837)]

The dancing master made his appearance last Wednesday. He is the most ridiculous man I think I ever saw. He was flourishing about the room to show us certain steps - upon reaching the wall he suddenly started back and remained some moments in a most theatrical position, with his head thrown back, his mouth open, his arms gracefully extended, one foot in the air, the front of the other scarcely touching the ground and his body bent into the shape of a half moon! When suddenly - amongst the titters of his spectators - he uttered a cry resembling a wail and, pointing to the wall, a poor little harmless spider was seen nearing her web! Off the man-of-steps bounded - and in a succession of 'Pirouettes' gained his umbrella, which he applied to the unfortunate spider. Then holding it at arms length, he minced out of the room - and returned with his upper lip curled and repeating ________ [indecipherable - looks like, "fie Doric!"] *so many times that the girls could restrain no longer their risible faculties with all their might - which greatly disconcerted their dancing 'Erzieherr'* [tutor].

* * * * *

Emily's claim not to have yet been tempted by 'petites frianderies' is, we may guess, just jest. *Each girl here gets, every morning at breakfast, three lumps of sugar in a large basin (there are no cups here) of coffee. Most of the girls take out the three lumps of sugar and drink dreadfully bitter coffee for their breakfast in order that they may have the sugar in the evening - when they burn it in the candle and make what they call Bon Bons. With these Bon Bons they give parties and serve up their refreshments on a drawer turned upside down. I now and then go to these parties - but, you may be sure, never partake of their refreshments.*

I have accustomed myself to drink bitter coffee like the rest, but do not spare the sugar from a desire to give parties with it, but from pure avarice - and take the greatest delight from seeing my store daily increasing. Fancy then! my anger and amari aliquid [something of bitterness] *on hearing the Doctor pronounce the cure for my cold to be "beaucoup de l'eau sucreé"!* [lots of sugar water!] *I found him more crooked than ever on seeing my snow white sugar mountain disappearing and diminishing, and to make a horrid drink which I most heartily detest. However, with the assiduity of a spider, I have recommenced amassing - and have made a new resolution that, in case of catching another cold, Dr Heine shall be last person to know of it .*

* * * * *

Although Henriette Heine, the doctor's wife, is the daughter of a Stuttgart burgher on the Catholic Council, it is clear that the religious pressure, in this German scientist's house, is not as intense on Emily as it has been in her previous Scottish and Irish homes. Amongst my favourite tales of these happy first few months at the Institute is that the first Sunday morning she takes herself to the English church across the road, there is no one there - because it is raining.

A great many girls are gone to Stuttgart today, as it is Sunday - as I, at the first, refused all their invitations, I receive none now, to my great joy. I now love Sunday so much, because that is the day I generally write to you, as I have so much time and, as I said before, when I write, I fancy I am again with you.

The girls here cannot understand my not wishing to go to Stuttgart with them, but they little know the circle of golden memories and gay joyous thoughts that haunt this little room where I can think of, and write to, you. I

Courtesy of the Württembergische Landesbibliothek Stuttgart

The road to Stuttgart, a few years later in 1863

am quite sure that mere artificial circumstances can have little influence on internal happiness - can anything be less elegant than this room? - [yet] could anything be happier than the time I am now spending in it, when I forget that I am here, and think that I am with you.

I know this boarding school feeling so well. I was fortunate to have my own room for the second half of my ten years at boarding school. One's dreams live beyond the light of that room's window, but its darkness and its blessèd peace give it the comfort of a womb. And here, expressing that same comfort within loneliness and mal du pays, is one of the richest lines of Emily's letters:

My pounds are from you, my crowns from Teddy, my shillings from Aunt Mary, and my sixpences from Bonnie. No letter from England is a penny.

* * * * *

Like her grandmother's, and her father's, Emily's anti-social nature - shyness, romantic melancholy, whatever - only goes so far. She does pay visits to the two British families, the Parsons family and the Jones family. ***Mr Jones is a very curious person indeed, yet was I am sure (when a young man) thought by his aunts a very talented though reserved youth! He tells me about seven***

times in the course of ten minutes that you have "written a great number of beautiful works"!! as if I did not know already and that it was very great news.

The Parsons, she prefers. ***They are very nice kind people and I like them very much, particularly Mrs Parsons, who I think must have been a beauty when young.*** Emily is included on their family outings to the Theatre in Stuttgart. ***We went*** [on 30th October] ***to the Opera to see Mlle. Evers in*** *Lucia von Lammamour* [a telling misspelling of Lammermoor - the opera by Donizetti based on the novel by Sir Walter Scott] ***for the last time*** [21-year-old Katinka Evers (1822-1899) is moving to Italy to further her singing career]. ***It was really beautiful, and as I had never seen an opera before I was agreeably surprised - as I had fancied it was little better than a Concert, which both you and I find so tiresome.***

It was most touching when Lucy appears, quite quite mindless, with all her beautiful hair streaming over her shoulders, and fancying that she is happy - till the sight of her cruel Brother reminds her of her misery (and like the first morning in a strange place) she recollects by degrees a few of the events that have caused her wretchedness and, at last, the whole dreadful catalogue, and falls senseless to the earth.

'Lucy of Lammamour'

Mlle. Evers is a beautiful actress and as it was her last night she did her best. When the opera was over she made her farewell speech and wreaths and bouquets were showered upon the stage. Sir George Shee was there also and enquired very kindly after you. Mrs Parsons has lent me very kindly Sir Walter Scott's *Bride of Lammamour* [sic] ***to read.***

* * * * *

Emily appears in these initial letters to be bearing up well. Despite the rigours of the treatment and the unsettling strangeness of the environment it must be more fun being in the company of girls her own age than cooped up with Madame de Weling and her young child. Yet, after two months, she still has no close friend or confidante. This is about to change. With all the trouble it brings, we might wish for these simpler times.

My opinion of the tall Italian remains the same, she has neither altered for the better or worse. As for the ugly girl whose name is Idah, she daily loses ground as my favourite, and I find that she is generally disliked. I take German lessons with Juta, the tall Italian, which saves money as we each pay the half of the price.

It is impossible for me to tell you how I dread taking a part in this play. I never did such a thing before and, as I do not possess Teddy's talents for acting I am sure I shall do some dreadfully foolish thing which will prove a fertile cause of merriment for [these] laughter-loving young ladies during the winter - no very pleasant look out! Particularly for me, who have such a silly dread of being laughed at.

But in all my little companions I find none able to make me forget Teddy - and, amongst all the others, I look in vain for 'a you'. I often wish I could change places with June [his dog], *were it only for an hour, that I might breath the same air with you. He always is with you, and I will not say that he is insensible of his blessings - no companion of yours could be that. But I will not wish to rob June of his master, for I must recollect that were he separated from you, he could not write to you, and I can always talk to you by pen, tho' it should be at the risk of being scared by – Der Erde Gott!* [Money!] –

My frock has been made up and has an extremely pretty body and frightful sleeves, but is quite good enough for this place - which is called by the girls 'Buckel Palais' or 'Hunch Back Palace'!

A severe example of spinal irregularity at 'Buckel Palais'

A very good name don't you think?

* * * * *

I hope dearest Grandmama is, by this time, quite well… should I write to her?... only when I write a question, I miss your answer, and that makes me sad for it reminds that a wide space is between us...

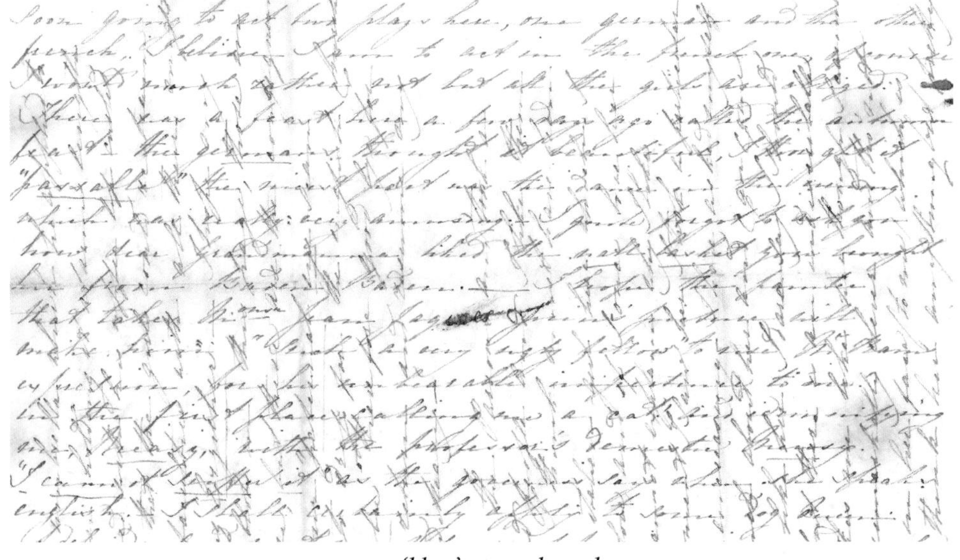

'blots' - tear-shaped

I hope, darling Papa, you will forgive the blots in this page - those in Mr Stealbones letters were on purpose, but these were …an accident, so pray do not let your parental eye scan them too much.

I am just going to dress for the English Church, being at present in ma robe de chambre [dressing gown]- ***therefore goodbye for the present… pray remember that you are made 'the household god of thought'*** [words from his poem *Eva; a True Story of Light and Darkness (1842)*] ***by one who is ever and ever and ever your own fond and affectionate***

Measy.

The lovestruck young teenage slave Nydia meets Ione - the obsession of the man with whom she is obsessed - in Edward's sensational novel ***The Last Days of Pompeii*** *(1833)*

CHAPTER 22

~ *Cannstatt Letters - Falling In Love* ~

There is one little italien [sic] ***girl here which I think I shall really in time be forced to love - and if I once love her, I shall love her the best of all here. I cannot explain why I like her so very much, but from the first moment I saw her, I took a particular liking to her, which has been daily increasing. I have asked myself thousands of times what I like so much about her, and can come to no conclusion; if I saw another like her, I dare say I would not take the same fancy to her; but there is an indescribable fascination in herself which makes me like her, though I cannot say why. Though only 12 years old*** [actually 11] ***she is remarkably clever, and tho' not pretty she has something in her face (to me) which is better than pretty, but most people think her anything but pretty.*** Emily Bulwer. 4th November, 1843.

* * * * *

Saturday 18th November, 1843. My own very dearest Papa, The time you yourself allotted for my writing to you has arrived; fourteen days have rolled away since our last conversation and now I come to unloosen to you a grief and to beg you to forgive the fault that occasioned it.

You must know the teacher has been changed and we have now got another which (with all respect be it said) made rather a ridiculous impression upon us in his first lesson. And now comes my part of the story, and I am brimming with shame to tell it you, but you must know it or my mind would not be at ease. My dear little favourite, of whom I before told you, came to spend the evening the other day with me in my room, and to amuse her I very naughtily, very foolishly, very imprudently and very absurdly made a most nonsensical story of which this unhappy teacher was the hero, and a very odd girl in the school was the heroine. The silly nonsense was committed to paper

and carefully deposited in a drawer.

No sooner had this effusion been carefully put aside, than the bell rang for the rehearsal of the French and German Theatres and my little friend and I went down together. As the last time the French play had been acted first, & this time the German one was to take the precedent, the French actors and actresses (my friend and myself included) went to the other side of the room for the purpose of having a full view of the play. Natalia (the little girl's name) placed two forms together which formed what she called a little house. Now as she represents a gardener in the french play whose name is Gervais [suggesting the play is *L'Homme Habile, ou Tout Pour Parvenir* (1827), a comedy by Jean-Baptiste-Rose-Bonaventure Violet d'Épagny (1787–1868) - how could he not write comedies with that name?], *I put my hand round her waist and very incautiously said (for one of Mrs Heine's numerous sisters was close by) "Now, chèr petit Gervais, 'Raum in der kleinsten Hütte für ein glücklich liebend Paar'"* [A quote from Schiller's poem *Der Jüngling am Bache* - 'Even in the smallest hut there is room for a happy loving couple']. *Upon which she very innocently said "da hast du gung Bett"* ["because you have laid on (as in 'provided', but an appropriate double entendre in the circumstances) a bed"]. *As one only says 'du' in German to relatives or very intimate friends, it directly drew Miss H. Camerer's attention, and she enquired if we had yet attained to the privilege of 'du'-ing. Poor little Natalie answered, "Not in the real, only in the ideal."*

That evening passed away and the next came, and it brought my little friend with it. We repaired to the drawer to reread this detestable stuff - but it was no where to be found!! My heart began to beat and Natalia's cheek to redden, but at length all our fears ended in a laugh and we thought no more of the story or the sudden absence.

The next morning, as I was lying on the Bed and strapped down in such a way as it was impossible to move, or even turn my face away, who should walk into the room but..... Mrs Heine! She enquired very gravely if I was well, and then after a few moments silence she took something out of her basket and holding it up, she asked me if I knew what it was? Judge my horror on seeing the very book in which the absurdest of absurd compositions was written!

I spare you her admonitions and my feelings. Both are easier to guess than to describe. I could not excuse myself in any one thing. I felt that all she said was perfectly right and that I deserved all that she could possibly inflict. But when she talked of Natalia being a child, and one easily led, and that it was the duty of one so old as I am rather to help one so young to do right, than teach her to do wrong...I cannot express what I felt - to be accused of teaching the only one I love in this place to do wrong was more than I could bear, and the reflection that there was truth in the accusation added fuel to fire.

After she had exhausted her wrath she left the room. To end the long story short – I went in this evening to Mrs Heine to beg her pardon and after hearing a long lecture on the impropriety of such conduct and being assured a thousand times that we are all as God made us, she forgave and promised to forget.

I retired with a foreboding that my dear little Natalia had also suffered through me. My foreboding was right - on going into her room I found her disconsolate. But upon my telling her the result of my interview, she also went to Mrs Heine, and was also forgiven, and now the storm has blown away; and I would have spared you this long childish story, my dearest Papa, but I could not be happy till I knew you knew it, and shall not be quite happy till I have your forgiveness for doing that which, if I had thought for a moment, I might have known you would have disapproved.

* * * * *

In November 1843, aged 15, Emily sees Liszt play. She gets into trouble at school. And she falls in love.

Doesn't every teenager?

Every teenager does not get to see Franz Liszt (1811–1886) play - in that one evening Emily's life was particularly blessed - but substitute whoever it was you saw when you were 15 (for me it was Kate Bush at the Hammersmith Odeon) and you'll know what I mean.

You probably also made up some stupid story about a teacher, or an unfortunate classmate who you were too blind, or pumped by peer pressure, to understand you were bullying.

And I bet you fell in love.

You may differ from Emily in that you probably didn't fall in love with an

11-year-old girl. But consider a few mitigating factors in this case. Firstly, Natalie Ritter de Záhony (1831-1895) will be 12 on Christmas Day. Puberty plays a different hand to all girls, and the difference between a 12-year-old and a 15-year-old can be, randomly, very pronounced or very slight.

The two dearest playmates of Emily's life to date have been her brother Teddy - a month older than Natalie - and Aunt Mary's great-niece, Bonnie Wilkinson, two and a half years younger than Emily, and not much more than a year older than Natalie. For the last year, her only companion has been 5-year-old Anna de Weling.

We see in her letters - particularly of this period - that amongst the many burdens that Emily places on her own shoulders, in the distorts of her troubled youth, is to see herself as the premature matriarch of her little family triumverate - she, her father and her younger brother. She is that all-too-common teenage mix of being both very old and very young for her years. No one puts it better than Gallagher & Lyle in the 1970s song *Fifteen Summers* - although your heart strings still need tuning, you want to play the whole recital right away.

The unfortunate misalignment for Emily is that these momentous moments of her childhood take place while she is emotionally alone, and - in this month of November 1843 - receives not a single letter from her father.

The explanation for Edward's silence comes in December. But we must put ourselves into Emily's gym shoes. This difficult confession to her father - the mortification of her fantasies and emotional bullying being exposed to Madame Heine, her first time in trouble at senior school, blended together with the confusion of an intense and hormonal 'pash' (as such a crush used to be know in the boarding schools of England) - and all in a month of rapturous Liszt piano - is greeted by, morning after morning, empty post bags.

* * * * *

I like to follow an illustrious example, therefore 'begin high up in the paper to have a long talk with you'. Emily writes to Edward, after another week of not hearing from him, on Sunday 26th November. ***You say yourself, 'Thought is the Muse, versification is but her dress' - if this be the case, the Muse must begin the letter, but in what dress she is to appear I know not... In***

short, I have a question to ask you, my dearest Papa, and I do not know how! I do not know if I should say! Is anything the matter? Or is it my infatuation which makes the time seem so long? Or what can be the reason I do not hear from him? etc. etc. Pray write soon and tell me the answer to this enversified thought...

What a thing Thought is! I think it is a sort of deity... At least when I think of you, Thought creates you - and you may be, for all I know, in the midst of some gay and beautiful circle, enchanting those around you with that voice 'whose music to the ear, becomes a memory to the soul' [from his *Eva; a True Story of Light and Darkness*]***; or you may be holding a tête à tête with June*** [his dog]***; or you may be lighting the flame of genius*** [his floor-length cherry-wood pipe]***; or you may be preparing surprises for your publishers by drawing caricatures on the pages of the book you are now writing. You may be doing a thousand things.....and yet.....you are with me, and I see and hear you once again. Thought is omnipresent when I think of you.***

I think also of my dear Brother.....It seems such a long time since I saw him. I often wonder if he thinks as often of me as I think of him. But that is a selfish thought, for how is it possible that he, who has so much to do, should think of any one person as often as I, who have nothing else to think of but you and him?...

* * * * *

I have also heard Liszt! [Liszt, then 32-years-old, plays the last night of the Stuttgart leg of his Autumn 1843 tour that Tuesday, 21st November.] ***I was (like everyone else) perfectly enraptured and such is the power of imagination I fancied he must be, in his personal appearance, something like what I fancy your idea was of .....Eugene Aram! Pray do not say "She shall not read my books if she compares my heroes to strolling players." You may be quite sure I would not do any thing so profane, but Liszt just looked like your description of the student.***

Liszt in 1843

Bye the bye, talking of *Eugene Aram*, ***what is***

the name of Houseman's child? In German it is Hannchen, but that is so un-English that I am at a loss to find out with what name Dr Pfizer has thought fit to take such a liberty. This should get a rise out of Edward if nothing else in her letters does. Tellingly, Emily doesn't hear from the Pfizers for some time after imparting this criticism to their English client. In Edward's original 1832 novel, Houseman's daughter 'Jane' dies (so like Emily to bring up the untimely death of a daughter). My friend Joachim Mathieu defends Pfizer, telling me that 'Hannchen' is an affectionate form of "Hanne", the female form of "Hans", the German version of 'John' - therefore a good translation for Houseman's daughter 'Jane'. But slipping this aside into her letter, Emily confirms to her father that his desire for her to learn German is starting to be useful.

Courtesy of the Deutsches Literaturarchiv Marbach

Gustav Pfizer

The description of the stricken father in the original English version of *Eugene Aram* is worth including here - we will hear its like again:

"I tell you, ye hell-hags," shrieked his harsh and now straining voice, "that ye suffered her to die. Why did ye not send to London for physicians? Am I not rich enough to buy my child's life at any price? By the living--! I would have turned your very bodies into gold to have saved her. But she is DEAD! and I - out of my sight - out of my way!" And with his hands clenched, his brows knit, and his head uncovered, Houseman sallied forth from the door...

* * * * *

But Edward would do well not to take his German translator too much to task, as his own translation of celebrated Württemberg poet Friedrich Schiller is just hitting the shelves - and Edward speaks a lot less German than Dr Pfizer speaks English. ***Aunt Mary spoke of [your translation of Schiller] with***

rapture in her last letter. I was exceedingly amused by the effect it produced on her opinion of Schiller. Before, it appeared her letters were full of exhortations "to beware of all German books, particularly Schiller", as they might "turn my mind in no time" – they are now filled with points of admiration after long enthusiastic sentences in favour of Schiller's beautiful *Glocke* [Bell, as in *Das Lied von der Glock* (1799) - The Lay of the Bell] ***or whatever the poem may be that she is at that moment reading.***

*Schiller's **Lay of the Bell**, translated by Edward as published in an 1860s American edition*

Mrs Wilkinson has read your translation of Schiller and her judgement is, in the words of the Irish lady who had her picture taken, "I think it more like than the original"!

Since little Natalia and I have become such good friends she came to me with a Book in which a quantity of Latin and Greek phrases were introduced and begged me to tell her what they meant... she only wished to see if I knew as much as her Brother, who she said used to tell the meaning of everything said in that Book.

* * * * *

Here we have the first mention of Natalie's closest brother, Carl Ritter de Záhony (1830-1889). Emily doesn't appear ever to meet Carl - unless he is part of an early family visit to the Institute - but in the daydreams of these two schoolgirls he will feature prominently. In their imaginations, Emily will set Natalie up with her brother, Teddy; and Natalie will set Emily up with her brother Carl.

Natalie, and stories of Natalie, now feature consistently in Emily's letters. They are slipped in amongst the other news, like the distracted thoughts they are:

Pray be so kind as to tell me, dearest Papa, if you know any thing of an italien family – the name – Ritter di Zahony? It is Natalia's surname and she says two of her brothers were a long time in London and from all I can judge she seems to be of some noble family...

Natalie is, I believe, to open the concert as she plays beautifully for her age and has great musical genius...

You know you told me that I should be writing to you what a delightful place this is, but as Lucretius says etc. etc. it is just the reverse – in the middle of this amari aliquid [bitterness/homesickness] ***there rises on fonte leporum*** [a fountain of delights (the same Lucretius quote) - I first took these two illegible words to be 'Ponte di Lacrime', as in 'the Bridge of Tears', or Ponte dei Sospiri, as in 'the Bridge of Sighs'. I had noticed, in a close up, that the Institute is about to get its own 'Bridge of Sighs' to connect a new wing] - ***namely – Natalia! Pray do not think this sudden friendship very rid[ic]ulous, I own I wonder at it myself, for I never liked any stranger so soon or so intensely to use Miss Vincent's expression*** [not clear who Miss Vincent is, but there is an actress/singer called Miss Vincent who perfoms in Edward's West End plays].

The Bridge of Sighs?

And then, puzzlingly, Emily adds, ***My dear little friend is an orphan, it is true she has a stepmother, but both her father and her real mother are dead - poor little thing, her unhappy situation only makes her more interesting.***

This last bulletin is not true. Or, at least, so evidence that we will examine later suggests. But it may point to something more telling. Emily's new little friend may be the greater fantasist.

This, in some ways, is proved to be true by later events. And, importantly, may mean that the 12-year-old is more the bad influence than the 15-year-old.

* * * * *

When I first came here my endeavour was to select friends, or rather companions, from among those girls who seemed to be the favourites of the others - by this means I thought that, even if they should not like me for myself, they would not dislike me if I made one of the retinue of their favourites, and that they would admit me into society. Thus I only made political friends.

When I found myself pretty much on a footing with the grandes dames (for I assure you there are grande dames here), I began to feel the want of a friend - someone whom I could love not merely for the advantage of knowing them, but for themselves. I fixed upon Nathalie (as her name is in the original). I had long watched her though never spoken to her, and wished very much to become acquainted with her - though not in the same way as I had become acquainted with the others, as she is so young.

I conspired to introduce myself and not withstanding the late erruptions [sic], *we are now great friends – so now, my Darling Papa, I can now safely tell you.....I have a friend - that is to say, I love one person more than I thought I ever would when I saw that long row of grinning girls the first evening of my arrival.*

* * * * *

Tomorrow will be the last day of eleven weeks in my almanack [making it the end of November, 1843] - *it is a great delight when I can say one other week is past, and I am very much obliged to you for shewing me how to mark their flight...*

I think, my dearest Papa, you must have been thinking of Dr Heine's institution when you composed [in *Eva; The True Story of Light and Darkness*] –

"Few are the joys that life bestows
On him whose life is but repose
One night from year to year"

- for indeed day here is turned into night as one spends almost the whole of it in bed...

My sugar is daily increasing and, though I have not the most distant idea for what I am hoarding it, every fresh lump gives me as much pleasure as if it were a pound – are you not ashamed of having such a foolish child?

My tooth ache, thank God, is gone, without the tooth being obliged to be extracted.

Dr Heine says the spots are better, but I do not think so myself.

As for the principal thing, there is no alteration, and I fear it will be but slow work. If, in the course of a few months, Dr Heine thinks that it arises from a strained sinew, there may be hope of an entire cure - but I am afraid I shall not be so fortunate. I have not the least dread of an operation, though almost everyone else looks upon it as a masterpiece of cruelty.

As for the gymnastics I am still extremely awkward in them, as they hurt the hands very much indeed.

I have just, this moment, heard that the eldest of the Milanollos is dead: only think how dreadful, from the unkindness of her father who broke her heart!! I would not at first believe it, but they say it is quite true.

Teresa and Maria Milanollo

Again, Emily slips in a story of an abused daughter dying. The Milanollo sisters - Teresa (1827-1904) and Maria (1832-1848) - are celebrity violin child prodigies from Savigliano, Piedmont (now northwest Italy), whose concert tours throughout Europe have been a sensation. As you can tell from the sisters' dates, this gossip is also not true. And again, we may guess it comes from Natalie - the sisters are touring near her home town at this date. The younger sister, Maria, does die aged only 16 - of consumption - but not until 1848.

* * * * *

Mr Jones was full of news today that one knew ever so long ago, as he generally is. After warning me not to eat too hot soup as it spoiled the teeth, he asked me if the gentleman whose name was Mr Henry Lytton Bulwer was any relation to us. Upon my saying he was your brother, he cried out "thought so, thought so, knew he was your father's Brother."

"He is going to Madrid, do you know that?" "O no Papa" cried Mrs Jones (for she always calls her husband Papa) "not to Madrid, to Spain" (not a very good proof of her geographical 'Kenntnisse' (plural of ***knowledge) - "Very true, my dear," returned Mr Jones, "very true, to Spain - and as I was going to say before, I think him a very proper person, could not have chosen a better, what do you think Miss Bulwer?"***

In these sort of predicaments - in which one wishes to say "yes", and yet a plain "yes" is not quite the thing to say - I have observed the old gentleman delights in pleasing me, yet he does not at all seem to consider them as predicaments, but as very great compliments.

Throughout these early letters of Emily - for the first time in her life without a personal guardian and an on-the-spot mentor - there are examples of her fishing for her father's preferred etiquette. This is particularly on matters relating to her colourful and complicated family. Henry Bulwer's diplomatic career was far-flung, and ultimately one of distinction, but we know - and Emily knew - from Miss Greene's judgmental asides, that her rumoured-to-be sexually-adventurous uncle was, to many, a figure of gossip.

And her mother, of course, even more so. On almost her very first day at the Institute, Emily is sought out by a local 'Polish Countess' - very 'exaltée' - who is full of difficult questions about her parents, and invitations to tea. The two English families - the genial Parsons and the comical Joneses - Emily has sufficient Cheltenham upbringing to be gracious to, and enjoy; but she struggles on her regular encounters with the Polish Countess, who ***I am positively persecuted by... shall I go or not? I am afraid in the end she will be offended...***

Why will her father not write?

* * * * *

You told me to scold you when you did not write, that I could never do - if I was ever so angry - as I know you have so much to do, and so much to think of. I forgive your silence and conclude that no news is good news.

My own dearest Papa, what I would not give to be able to see you now and then? To be sure, I think of you all day, and dream of you all night, but it is only your shadow, not yourself - and I try to make myself like this place, because I know you wish me to do so.

In writing to Aunt Mary I always try to (as you told me) "make the best of it", so that she seems by her letters to think that I am in Paradise.

I should like very much to give Mrs Thomson's ring to Nathalie at Christmas – but unluckily I imprudently wore it the first evening I came here and, when I became a little more acquainted with the girls, they timidly requested to see the "splendid ring" I wore the first night they had "the pleasure of seeing me".

I was reluctantly forced to display this "splendid ornament" to their admiring eyes and, as if to utterly destroy all chance of ever possessing it themselves, they questioned me as to the donor, and the hair at the back. To all these 'simpli interro qui' [Latin: individual interrogations] *I was forced to reply, and so I can not give the ring now to anyone here.*

Besides, I have also thought that were I to give anything which they regard as so costly to one, and not to give something of equal value to all my friends, it would create jealousy. So perhaps it is, after all, as well to relinquish the pleasure of bestowing it on Nathalie. But I think it would be well to give it to Mrs Parsons who has really been very kind, and who would think that the ring is new, and the hair mine - Besides it will do away all obligation.

I have been much disappointed with the governess, whose face is by no means an index of her mind, as she is anything but good-natured and actually listens at the door!!

Fondest love to G'mama and Teddy, and my dearest Papa, may I beg of you never to think of me in any other light than as one who loves you dearer and more faithfully than she loves any other creature (except Teddy) in the world. When you can find time, remember the delight a few lines from you would give me.....your own Measy.

* * * * *

At last, a letter arrives - on Saturday 2nd December, although postmarked in England on 25th November. *My dearest Emily, You may well suppose that only some occurrence of unusual importance delayed my writing to you – alas, I have been constantly engrossed with my Mother's illness, which fills me with the bitterest grief & anxiety. Much as I have suffered throughout life, I do not think I have ever had so deep a sorrow & so heavy a heart.*

You must excuse a short letter from me under such circumstances... indeed I find it difficult to turn even to you – my Mother's sickbed haunts me. Night & day I see before me her pale face..... She has still so much vigour of mind, & had lately such energy of frame, that it is difficult to think of her as old, or prepare oneself for the worst..... I feel that, with her, lies half of my own life..... She has not only been a parent, but a friend, soother, confidante & benefactress..... I seem to watch a setting sun – with the feeling that when it is sunk, the whole world will be grown dark. But I must not sadden you with my sadness..... what must be, must. And God gives us the Faith of another World, & a happier life.

You reproach yourself, my dear child, too much for your little indiscretion. [It is unnecessary] For me to say more than that it is necessary for you, above all persons, to be on your guard against that tendency to ridicule common to the young & the levitous – because in our unfortunate circumstances with regard to Lady B, a rejoinder may be so bitter & unanswerable. You must enter life with a firm resolution not to make an enemy. That which is amicable, is also politic; & after all, nothing pains us more than to feel we have pained another's vanity - without provocation.

You will do well to make the amends to the girl & to the governess – by some little presents. Ask Madame Heine for what money you want – till she sends me her account and I can, in settling that, replenish your own purse. You may be sure that if I have good news to communicate I will write immediately – two or three weeks will probably decide. Yrs most aff E.L.B.

Edward's monument to his mother in Knebworth Park

CHAPTER 23

~ *Cannstatt Letters - The Death of Mrs Bulwer* ~

Source of my life, upon its morn and noon
Shedding the light that dwells in parent eyes
Now in the shadow of its eve, I rear
Towards griefless stars this monument to thee
Emblem of memories raised by Christian hopes
Far above graves:- mark, how serene in Heaven
The upright column leaves the funeral urn.

Edward Bulwer Lytton, on a monument to his mother in Knebworth Park

* * * * *

My beloved and darling father, your letter has this moment arrived. I conjure you, by all that is most holy and most sacred, to take comfort. Believe me, I know your feelings – by placing myself one instant in your situation, I feel that this earth is a hell, and peopled with sorrows and afflictions. But, my poor dear Father, your agony has been too great, your sorrow has been too acute, your hopes too much blasted, your dearest ties too much severed for this one dear rock on which you cast your anchor to be taken from you.

Dearest dearest Grandmama, if I love her so much, how immense must be your love! But it is that love that has so magnified your fears. Oh! as there is a god in heaven, he must have pity on you - you who have been so injured, so afflicted. And if prayers of one who has nought to love but you, and the dear one for whom we now sorrow, will be heard by the All Powerful, night and day will the angel of Prayer be on the wing, bearing my earnest petitions to the Almighty Father.

Oh if I were only with you. But as you love her, as you love all that is dear to you, do not be so very sorrowful - her dear affectionate heart will grieve the more to see your sadness. She is indeed a Sun, a bright and glorious one, but not a sinking one. If a cloud veils it for an instant from the eyes of its adorers, it is not for ever lost to sight - and when the cloud is passed it will only shine the brighter.

Never did I feel the bitterness of being so far from you as now. What would I not give to be able to say one soothing word to you! I see you before me - you, the talented, the worshiped, the adored; I see you with the characters of that deep melancholy that runs through your letter stamped on your face, and, my dearest Father, if it were not wrong to talk of myself at such a time as this, I would say that I wish to die.

Do look on the bright side - for there is a bright side. I know but too well how disponding Grief makes us. I know how the heart is torn when wounded in its tenderest nerve, but in this instance I am sure your fears are too great. This earnest entreaty is not made by one unacquainted with an aching heart, or by one who knows not what it is to weep for the creature one's soul holds dearest – it is made by one who, like you, has a parent who has unrivaled sway over the affection. Who is the All in All. It is made by one whose heart beats twice for every throb of yours. Grant then my prayer and be led by Hope, for she is a gentle guide. And must you really have a heavier heart than you ever knew before, and all that I can do is shed tears for you far far away - but be it so! What are my sorrows to yours?

But perhaps (and oh! how much confidence I place in that dear 'perhaps') before these few lines reach you, the dear sufferer will be able to smile again and bid you banish fear. I will not write more. I know you will think every minute lost that is not spent watching the dear object of your present cares (would that I could help you!). Never mind my being anxious. Do not write to me. I shall endeavour to practice my precepts, and hope for the best – you have the tears, the prayers, and the bleeding heart of your devoted child.

* * * * *

I know you join with me in genuine feeling for my relations at the imminent death of my great-great-great-great-grandmother. However, I also know you are going to struggle with the maudlin and florid nature of some of the letters in this chapter. But I am not going to shy away from including them. They represent Emily - for a brief moment in time - absolutely hitting her stride in her relationship with her father. She nails exactly what he wants to hear.

My dearest Emily, Your most feeling and affectionate letter is just arrived and I do not lose a day in replying to it. Nothing can be more dear to me than your sympathy, & the warmth with which it is expressed in so trying a time. [It] brings you closer & closer to my heart. I rejoice in your letter for the beautiful disposition it displays - as well as for the comfort it gives; from hence I shall remember it fondly & gratefully. I bless you for feeling so tenderly for me & with me.

I bless God for bestowing on me in my daughter so gentle & so pure a friend. And now in the fullness of my heart I hasten to call on you to share my delight when I say that my Mother has rallied, almost, as it were, miraculously... For the first time for weeks she has been moved to her dressing room - the fever is abated, the cough is better - and I begin to entertain some hopes, tho' with fear & trembling. The truth of it is, we have a long winter before us, which is a great obstacle in the way of recovery.

* * * * *

In this temporary respite to the grief, there is time to *turn therefore with hope and cheerfulness to business – In the first place, forgive me my dear child for not having before attended to your wish about the piano forte. In my last letter it escaped my memory. Certainly you must have one, but wait till I send you some money, when you will pay for it yourself. Avoid as much as possible bills with Madame de Heine.*

2ndly, I am enchanted to hear you have found the comfort of a friend in Natalie, of whom you give such a charming description. I hope she [knows] something of English, or that she will let you teach her – upon what you say of her position, she may probably visit you hereafter in England, if your mutual affection continues, & to enjoy England she should know the language.

3rdly, Henry is appointed at last Ambassador to Madrid and has just gone. At any other time this would have pleased us all much, but the neces-

sity for his leaving at such a time only added to our pain.

4thly, I enclose you Madame de Heine's bill & letter - I cannot read German [hand]written characters – I will get you to translate both for me, & send me a literal translation as soon as you can – marking such [items] as are unnecessary & you think can be avoided in future. The total is extremely high – but I suppose much is made up of bed furniture, which won't occur again.

It does not seem to include even the Doctor's fee - is the account in Württemberg florins? Be so good, also, to obtain one of his printed prospectuses. Don't send it to me, but copy out what he says there is the price for the first class and also copy what he maintains is included in that sum. I wish to see what the additional charge is for a private room - not that I shall abridge that poor little comfort for you. You can very easily obtain the printed prospectus as I might wish to give it in London. Meanwhile tell Mrs Heine with my compls that I have received her note, that I do not read the written German characters, but will get it translated and attend to it in a few days… God bless you, my dear child. Most aff yours E.L.B.

* * * * *

Emily replies on Sunday 17th December with long emotional expressions of delight that Mrs Bulwer has rallied, *such a sunbeam of a letter as yours of this morning was; all this is too much, I feel unworthy of so much delight…* We'll step past these effervescences, and go straight to her translation of what is effectively Madame Heine's 'End of Term' report - except that, at this school, the term does not come to an end.

...I am happy to be able to tell [you] that Miss E has accustomed herself easily and quickly to our mode of life and is also well and happy.

Dr Heine says the means that have been hitherto employed for Miss E's improvement have had not only a beneficial effect on her whole constitution, but, as previously remarked, an improvement in her carriage. Miss E's complexion is also improved.

Miss E is an amiable, clever and good-hearted being, but requires careful guidance. She is very fond of reading, but has not much pleasure in real learning - as, for instance, in French. The curate Mr Nagel gives her, together with a very cultured young lady here, instruction in the German language, and he is very well pleased with Miss E's themes [essays].

In the execution of female work, Miss E is not very forward. She brought a large piece of worsted work with her, which is not very nicely worked but which I wish her to finish before she begins another. Of course the time for work is, through the cure, not very long; and all that I have to observe is that she writes too many letters, which takes up her time from learning and is not very good for her carriage.

Miss E has a very good music teacher and as she is talented & industrious I do not doubt that she will make good progress. If Miss E will take no lessons in singing, it would be better for her to have 2 music lessons a week, as the teacher gives all the music lessons in the institution. She charges so extremely little. Miss E has, as yet, had no instruction in singing. One lesson from a good teacher from Stuttgart would, at the very least, be 4 florins.

Miss E is fond of dressing herself prettily, but has however, as yet, not much care for her clothes, and, as her dresses and linen were in rather a bad condition when she came to us, I was obliged (see enclosed account) to (against my custom) pay out a good deal of money.

As Christmas now approaches and - as it is, in general, the custom with us in Germany to give presents at this time, which we do all assembled round illuminated trees and which gives the boarders much pleasure - if I do not hear from you before the 20th December, I propose taking upon myself to give Mlle votre fille something in your name on 25th December which I hope will give her pleasure. With the assurance of the continued care of the personal, as well as bodily benefit, of Mlle votre fille, I remain very respectfully yours, Henriette Heine.

* * * * *

Having translated her own review, Emily is quick to add editorial: *She says I write "too many letters" - now, with the exception of occasionally writing a few lines to Aunt Mary and Teddy, I write to no one but you, and only then every second Sunday, so it cannot interfere with my learning as she intimates.*

In the second place, 'my feelings have been much hurt' by the following sentence: "Miss Emily is very fond of dressing herself prettily" – I cannot re-

member ever having given reason to say so of me, and thus by a repetition of Madame de Weling's assurance that I had a sufficient share of vanity, you will, I am sure, think me very conceited.....I beg you to lend a deaf ear to this peculiarly wounding aspersion.

As to the present which Mrs Heine declares it her intention to give at Christmas.....A few days ago she went round with a large paper on which she wrote the names of all who wished for anything at Christmas. I said I wished for nothing, which was the truth - but when she was gone, the other girls assured me it was much the best way to say something, as otherwise she would be sure to get something very expensive. I therefore endeavoured to think of something useful, cheap, and something also that would make an effect - as the girls told me, if one chose any thing which looked poorer than the presents of the others, she would be sure to make up the deficiency. I therefore fixed upon a black silk apron.....not that I wanted it in the least but thought it was better than running the risk of her buying some useless and expensive thing.

I now see by her letter that she is determined to give me something besides. Now I think if you would be so good as to tell her in your reply your extremely kind intention of allowing me to have the Piano Forte when I receive money from you, and give her to understand that that is your Christmas present.

* * * * *

So much for her letter - and now for her bill, the total of which is indeed enormously dear, but I think I can put you in the way of rendering the next more moderate...

You are quite right in suspecting that all the lessons would be classed under one name in the bill – that of General German Instruction... and under this head is comprehended Geography, History, Arithmetic, Natural History (at least what they call natural history, but what is not so really) and the lessons they dignify with the name of, Physique [a Frenchified version of what would now be called Physik in German and Physics in English]. *Arithmetic is for me (being English) decidedly useless. As for Geography and History, I think I could learn them much better by reading for myself after I leave this place, than by the lessons given here – but this I leave entirely to you.*

Natural History is not about animals, as the name would lead one to suppose, but about stars, how worlds were formed, and such sort of things, & as I am rather at a loss to discern if it is really useful, I must again beg of you to be the judge. Physique, I think we might leave.

There is one more lesson which I forgot to mention viz 'German Composition'. I do not of course make German themes [essays], *but I think it is useful - as the teacher, by pointing out the faults of the others, teaches one to avoid the same mistakes I make in the private German lessons. I have therefore marked 'General German Instruction' and you can chose which you would like me to take, and which not.*

I would, however, advise you to be very decided when you write to Mrs Heine about those lessons I am not to take, as a girl here of eighteen wrote to her parents shortly after her arrival here, telling them that some of the lessons were not very useful for her and asking them to write to Mrs Heine..... whereupon Mrs Heine wrote back word that taking all the lessons were a sort of condition laid on all who entered the establishment, and this grown up girl of eighteen is obliged to take lessons with the little girls of nine!

Religion is by no means useful, but I think it would be prudent to take this lesson as they might perhaps say they thought it very odd not to take advantage of this most edifying instruction, when in fact it is nothing but telling you not to steal and commit murder. The name 'Essentials of Religion' does not well permit one to exclude it.

Literature, one can safely exclude, it being nothing but a string of dates and names of all the best poets that ever lived. The teacher occasionally reads out passages from their best works to give you an idea of their style, but I do not think it very improving.

For the same reason as Geography, History is not very useful here – namely, that I could learn them better for myself after leaving Cannstadt.

I am afraid I can make no alterations in wood [heating costs], *as it is against the positive rule of the institution to buy or keep your own wood.*

I am shocked to see that the 145 florins are for a separate room, I could not have thought it would have been so expensive, but I am quite ready to give it up if you wish...

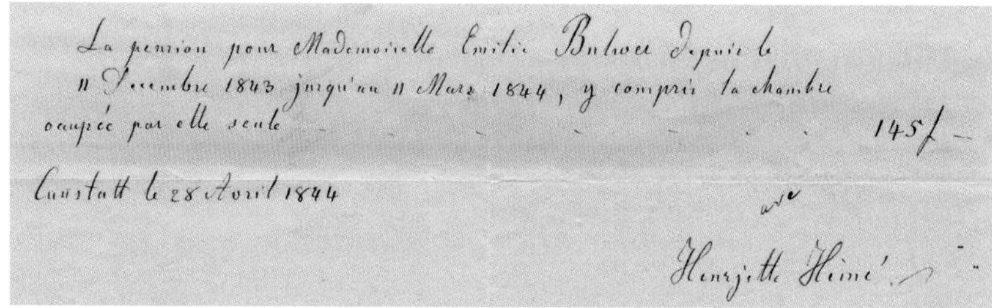

La pension pour Mademoiselle Emilie Bulwer depuis le 11 Decembre 1843 jusqu'au 11 Mars 1844, y compris la chambre occupée par elle seule - - - - - 145 f -

Canstatt le 28 Avril 1844

Henriette Heine

It is not given up - the following quarter's bill for 145 florins for a single room for Emily

* * * * *

And now that these mercenary matters are at an end, let me again return to your dear dear letter... I am so glad, so very glad and so very grateful that you so kindly sympathize with me in my friendship for Natalie; some weeks ago I had begun to teach her English, and she has just taken three lessons with great zeal and apparent pleasure - when she was siezed with a bad cough which confined her to her room and, for a long time, to her bed... and she is still, I am sorry to say, suffering from the effects of it.

Her peculiar beauty is her smile, which seems to illuminate her whole face which is thoroughly italien – the form perfectly oval; her eyes are a sort of brown, I do not mean those sharp piercing dark brown eyes which one sometimes sees (and which to me at least are peculiarly disagreable), but a very soft light brown, and shaded with long black silken lashes.

I can only explain the sensations your letter produced upon me by a line I once read in some italien book and which I still remember. It is this, "Fu stupor, fu vaghezza, e fu diletto"! ["It was stupor, it was desire, and it was pleasure" - apparently a quote from the 16th Century poet Tasso, which continues, "if it was not love, that moved his villainous heart" - not the most appropriate quote really.] ***I do not know who wrote it, but it is at all events very expressive...***

I have just obtained a prospectus and find that the charge, in the first class, for board (I mean that long string of meals which you probably remember), bathes, neccesary machines & attendances is – 500 florins a year. The extras which he mentions are, Doctor's fee, lessons, washing, fire, and candles. Do not mind me if you think the charge for a private room too high - if you wish me not to have one longer, only say so, and what you wish I shall like.

I suppose this letter will reach you about Christmas Day – may it be a very happy one for you all, but may the returns be still happier. Whatever Mrs Heine's presents may be, I shall nevertheless be a little unhappy at being unable to tell you [in person] all I wish for you. However I hope my fondest hopes may be all realized for you, and when enjoying the peculiarly comfortable, happy feeling which I think an English Christmas generally brings with it, remember that there is one in the 'ferneland' [far-off land], *whose fondest wish is your happiness and brightest delight – your love... Farewell, dearest dearest Papa, ever your own fond, Measy*

*****

As Miss Greene has already told us - on Christmas Day - the following note arrives, dated Tuesday 19th December, on black edged paper:

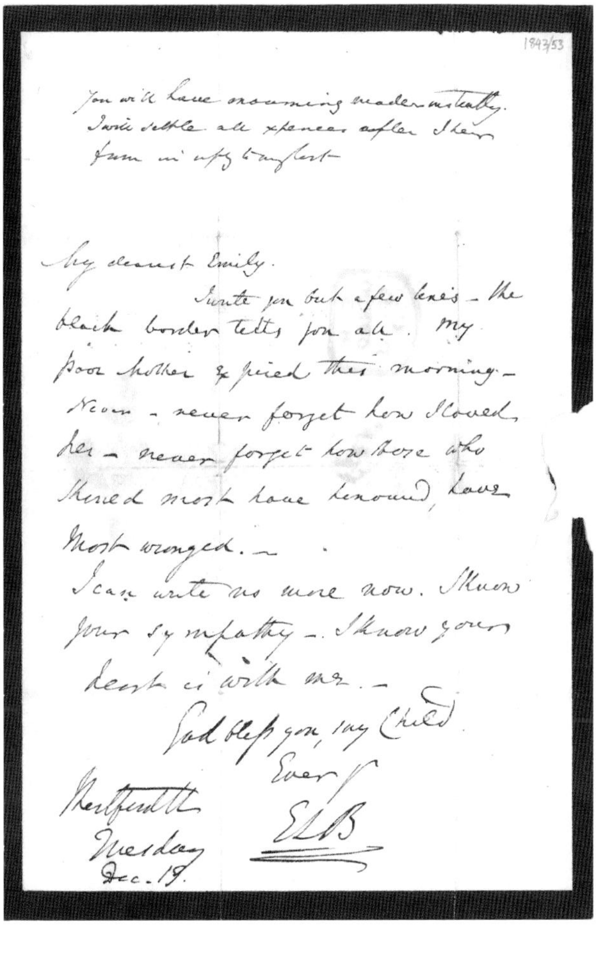

My dearest Emily, I write you but a few lines – the black border tells all. My poor Mother expired this morning. Never, never forget how I loved her – never forget how those who should most have honoured, have most wronged.

I can write no more now. I know your sympathy – I know your heart is with me. God bless you, my Child. Ever yrs E.L.B.

Her previous letter has not yet arrived. As, at the top of the page, is added, ***You will have mourning made instantly. I will settle all xpenses after I hear from you in reply to my last.***

* * * * *

Dated Monday 25th December - Christmas Day - ***May Heaven be with you my Father! and Heaven <u>will</u> be with you, and the bright spirit who has quitted the cold cruel winter of time and entered the bright radiant Spring of Eternity will hover around you with its angel wings and whisper you comfort. Henceforth is an angel your guide, your guardian. Henceforth is your name in the song which Heaven's new inhabitant chants to the Almighty. Henceforth is your child's life dedicated to one holy, one sacred purpose – not to try to make you forget your past sorrows, alas that were impossible, but – to try at least to soften their memory, to try to replace (but ah! how feebly) all that you have lost. Henceforth am I the vestal of all that can bring you consolation, of all that can soothe this rugged thing called life.***

O! if I were only older, I could be with you and fulfill my vow better. In Heaven you have Her, and on earth you have your child. Dear as you are to me, sorrow makes you dearer, ten thousand times dearer. It seems as if the rivers of all other griefs flowed faster now, to swell this sea - yes, deeply, deeply do I feel what you tell me never to forget. It seems as if the last lingering moon beams that had before shed light over the ruins of all else, were now faded – but Father let me be your soother, and we will journey together till the portals of Heaven close on the toilsome past and disclose the welcome Future! May Heaven comfort you, may God bless you, is the tearful prayer and the earnest wish of your sorrowing and devoted child.

P.S. Today is the first day of the Holidays, all the shops are shut, and no one can lend me a sheet of other paper. Oh! what a mockery is happiness to the miserable!

* * * * *

Ten days later, on Thursday 4th January, 1844 - having had no further word from her father - Emily writes again, now also on black edged paper, ***My thoughts are too much with you, my own dearest Father, to let another day pass without writing you a few lines. Sleepless as my nights have been since***

I received your last letter, the past night has been one of peculiar pain to me. You are always before me; in the middle of the day, as in the dead of night, the thought of your unhappiness presents itself as a picture to my mind and renders me the most miserable of the miserable – Oh! I could bear everything else but that.

If I could only know you happy, or at least not unhappy, with what delight would I suffer the greatest sorrows; but there is at least one sweet thought, one gentle comfort left – though the fairest flower that gladdened your path seems now gone, it is but transplanted to fairer garden – though the dear friend who soothed the bitter from life is removed, the power of that friend is increased, is exalted - and when the dreadful thought rises that you will not see her more, O! turn from the mournful, and behold the joyous - reflect that you will ever now, as it were, feel her presence; reflect that angel eyes will look down from the arches of heaven upon you, that angel lips will bless you in the regions of bliss...[etc. It goes on. Extraordinary for a 15-year-old. But too much for these pages with the following still to come.]

My dearest Father, may I now be your friend & - I know it seems very presumptuous in me to wish to be your friend, but Heaven knows I do not mean it so – I know I have nothing to offer you but my love – but that love, how vast, how boundless? Father do not look upon me as child, I will be no longer a child – I will try (and one can do anything one trys to do) never to be childish more – I will sooth you, will comfort you, I will pray for you, I will bless you, I will love you – not as a child but as a woman. And Oh! Let me remind you of one who, young as he is, will never the less prove a friend, who when he is older will be able to show you his affection & his sympathy in other, but not less fond, ways than I can, and such a friend you will find in my Brother – He used to be my confidant long ago when we were children, and I know how deeply and how fervently his heart is capable of loving.

Oh! Do not think I tell you to be comforted from ignorance of the depth of your grief. I know it but too well. I know all that you must feel. I know all the bitter dreadful thoughts that mingle themselves with your sorrow. I know that in thinking on that dear life, how agonizing the reflection is, that it was embittered by so many wrongs, so many injuries. Oh! Believe me I know all this. I feel it perhaps as heavily as you do. But then, do you not think, that those who have suffered so much here will be distinguished by a brighter crown of happiness above? O! it must be so, or wherefore were we born? Why did the Almighty give us being if our life below was to be sorrow and we could not hope for greater happiness above? Yes, it is my deep sympathy for your afflictions, in the bitter sense of all our misery, that I entreat you to take comfort –

O ever tell me your sorrows my Father - perhaps in telling them, you may be relieved of some part of their load; let me know your sorrows, my Father, and reserve all that gladdens you for yourself. It is my only pleasure, the only thing for which I wish to live, to administer in however small a degree to your comfort and to your happiness. If I cannot do this, all that endears earth to me is gone – If I knew that I could give you no consolation in this world, how gladly should I hail the thoughts of another [world], for there perhaps my power to accomplish this one dear purpose might be increased. How powerful love is! even the dreadful dark grave cannot frighten it.

Not only are you now the beloved of an angel, but you love an angel! Your affection is transferred from a mortal, to one immortal, eternal; you now love an inhabitant of Heaven! We have read in fables, and the tales they tell to children, of mortals, who have been the favourites of some unseen spirit, and aided and comforted by this friend in all the trials and afflictions which encountered them, they felt less of their keenest and bitterness. And in smiling over these pretty stories who has not wished that they were true? But they are true - at least they have their meaning, and when you have the breath of invisible lips whispering you heavenly comfort, you will see and acknowledge their truth. And now, though I give you all the comfort that lies in my power, my tears are falling fast for you upon the paper - I can only write you two or three lines now, you shall hear from me soon again – My father farewell – for ever and for ever, Your fond, faithful devoted child, Emily

* * * * *

When we consider, in the closing pages of this book, the circumstances of Emily's premature death, we should remember this letter. For all its apparent spiritual maturity, it is a disturbing tract for a 15-year-old girl. Certainly it shows a measure of positive philosophy for which we must thank the Christian upbringing she has received from Miss Greene - but it also shows the measure of death-bliss and martyrdom that we must also attribute to the

Christian upbringing she has received from Miss Greene.

The word 'morbid' is the one that becomes increasingly associated with Emily in discussions between her father and Miss Greene. Such an epithet is a by-product of the trials and unhappinesses of her childhood, salted by the Bible-breasted guardians who have had her charge, and baked by the notion - whether true or not, she herself certainly entertains it - that she has inherited some of the madness of her mother.

Miss Greene, although not blameless as an enabler, is the most aware and most sensitive to this streak of morbid melancholy that runs through Emily - and more members of the Lytton family than just Emily. Maybe today we would call it manic depression, or perhaps simply the price of an overwrought, unbridled imagination - the sort of imagination that makes creative writing a Lytton family forté... or simply overwrought, depending on your view.

It is Miss Greene who recognises that there is a danger of it flaring at this moment - and she even turns a letter of condolence to Edward into a warning. She writes from 89 Bloomsbury Place, Birmingham [the home of the Wilkinson family, the 17th Lancers being at that time billeted in Birmingham],

Dear Sir Edward, Although I have felt great anxiety to hear that your health has not suffered from your late heavy affliction, I have forborne writing, not wishing to intrude on your grief - which you must feel the more deeply as the blow, when it did come, was comparatively unexpected from the astonishing rally she made towards the end of her cancelled life.

At such a time, any source of comfort must seem weak, but on reflection of her many excellencies, you will feel happy that your sainted Mother is now enjoying an eternity of bliss, where calumnies & falsehoods cannot reach - though even here they were powerless to injure.

I fear for the effect of this sorrow upon dear sensitive Emily, whose last letter to me after hearing she [Mrs Bulwer] ***was better, began with these words, "From the most miserable of human beings I am become the happiest." I watch anxiously for her next letter...***

* * * * *

Edward writes again on Sunday 7th January, with a black seal as well as black-edged paper, ***My dearest Emily, At length I can sit down to write to***

Mrs Bulwer, sketched at her death on 19th December 1843

you more calmly. I thank you from my whole heart for your last affectionate letter & indeed for all the warm feeling you have shown in this terrible bereavement. Hereafter I shall turn to you, as you so tenderly write to me, for solace in this loss - & for other affections... & in you, at least, I feel confidant I shall find some of my dear Mother's latest words more than realised – where she said, "may your children shew you the same tenderness & attention you have shewn me"... [I pass over his lengthy description of his mother's death - which if he were to heed Miss Greene's advice, he would too.]

...And it saddens me the more to think, how little of enjoyment, as far as we can perceive, that life, so full of value & noble virtues, was doomed to know. Her childhood was most melancholy; in the affection of her youth she was disappointed; in her marriage she was not happy; the succession to property in her widowhood was embittered with a thousand cares & toils, & the feverish anxiety of constant litigation; my marriage was a severe affliction to her.....Her last few years were perhaps the serenest – the most enjoyable! Thank God I was, then at least, a comfort to her. And she died when we loved each other most; when we had understood each other; when – but these regrets are idle – God orders for the best.

I turn with a kind of mournful solace to fulfill the the duties she bequeathed me – to preserve and honour her memory; to make the home that she loved so much one monument to her; to hold the property she left me as a solemn trust, & seek to emulate her active usefulness, her thoughtful benevolence.

* * * * *

I enclose a letter you will give to Madame Heine & force myself to speak of these matters. As in my letter to Madame Heine, I have sought to cut down the main expenses, & put things hereafter on a right footing. I could not well interfere with the small details for instruction – nor do I think that I could do so without engendering a discontent or ill will, of which you would be the sufferer. On the contrary, I entreat you to pay attention even to lessons which you do not think necessary – above all to French & indeed to all languages you can.....your intimacy with Natalie ought alone to familiarize you with Italian & will save you time and labour hereafter in that language.

With regard to singing, if it be really a good master, I would wish you to have him once a week. I have directed my bankers to lodge £20 with his correspondent at Stuttgart – to your credit, so that you can draw out when you go to Stuttgart what sums you want, from time to time. You need not draw out the whole at once. With this, I have informed Madame Heine you will pay for your own dress, candles, washing, letters & pocket money. I want that item of 'pocket money' entirely erased from the bill in future – you can now afford to hire your own pianoforte & you can repay Madame Heine for your mourning, which of course you had made, & you will have little other expense in dress, as you will remain in mourning for some months.

Tho' my dear mother's bequest will alleviate, [and,] with prudent management, ensure me competence [an income large enough to live on] - *provided at least Knebworth is our Home & I have no establishment elsewhere. Yet there are such heavy expenses & legacies to meet at present, that for the next year or so, I shall be much put to it for money - & tho' I can grudge nothing for your benefit, or your comfort, yet we must curtail the items in Madame Heine's bill which promote neither benefit nor comfort. You will therefore refuse all pocket money, even if she offers it, (as my instructions) & pay for every thing you can yourself.*

Mourning and half-mourning in an 1840s fashion plate

You will ask Madame Heine to inform you as soon as she receives intelligence that the money due to her is arrived, & ask her the address of the correspondent (no doubt the same corner shop we went to). For as soon as Madame Heine receives her money, you will find at the corner place the 20£ for yourself.

Teddy is very well, but his sympathy has not been like yours, & he has written to me less than I think his feelings should have prompted him to do.

And now God bless you my dearest child, get well as soon as you can & believe me your most afft Father, E.L.B.

One word with regard to correspondence: writing is certainly bad for you

– the position it requires injures even the straightest shape & must confirm bad habits. Once a fortnight is all I ask from you – you need have no other correspondence than Miss Greene also once a fortnight (not oftener), Teddy once a month - & if you like, Mrs Wilkinson or Bonnie once a month. One day once a fortnight will suffice for all of these - Letters too are very expensive, as you will find when you [pay for] them yourself, which I wish you to do.

* * * * *

For two full months following her grandmother's death, Emily spills out a torrent of pain and sympathy for her father. The letters are extraordinary - streams of consciousness written without the luxury of revision - at times deeply poetic for a child of her age, at times deeply disturbing for a child of her age. In the confines of this book - and with respect to you not being, I hope, in the same maelstrom of grief as the correspondents - I give you but a taste:

Sunday 14th January, 1844 - on black edged paper - *They say that time softens grief - O! may it be so with you, my poor dearest Father – with me, Time rather augments than lessens sorrow. The more I think of you, the more I reflect on your loss, on our loss, the more dread the thought becomes, the more agonizing the picture seems, which night and day I have before my eyes, of a heart so cruelly torn as yours has been, but still clinging to one who knew how to soften every care and solace every woe, and that one, that angel, that friend, that soother, to be gone - O! dreadful, dreadful.*

I can think on it no longer, and yet it haunts me like a spectre in the midst of the gay and lighthearted, as alone with my own sad thoughts I seem to hear the crash, I seem to see the shipwreck of your joys, I seem to behold the devastation which this dire event has wrought upon you, upon us all.

It is because I have never known what it is to call any one by the tender name of - Mother: it is because I do well know the bitter burning tears one sheds in secret and alone o'er the woe of being motherless, that I grieve so dreadfully for you who have all your life enjoyed the blessing, not only of a mother, but of the best, dearest tenderest of mothers, and now that mother is gone for ever. This because you have been father, mother everything to me, that my tears flows so fast at the thought of you, so kind, so affectionate, so

fond, so good, being so heavily afflicted.

And she knew sorrow, and you knew sorrow, and sorrow united you closer together. And I too have learnt to know sorrow in all its bitterness for you, and yet it also brings us closer together. Oh! her latest prayer has been heard, you shall at least find comfort in your children.

Oh Father by the love you bore, you still bear to her, measure my love to you. I remember long ago, one day at Knebworth when she and I were alone together and you were not there we talked a long time about you, and she told me how good you were and how much you had suffered, and she said when I grew up I must try and comfort you and make up for all you had lost. Dear gentle affectionate Being, I have often thought of her words since; as she spoke them I felt a sort of inspiration, and whenever I reflect on them I feel their holy influence come over me again, and it shall be my sweet duty to accomplish her wish as far as ever it lies in my feeble power.

* * * * *

Emily is striking all the right chords with her father, and it is a credit to her that she stands up for her brother, who - not unnatually at 12-years-old - does not find it as easy to participate in poetic paroxysms of pain. Not yet. In later life he will become a master of it ***Do not think Teddy does not feel for you because he is more silent than one would be led to expect. His character is a curious one and I have studied it well and know that he often feels the deepest when he says the least. Ah! yes he feels for you much very much... Believe me, you will find solace in him.***

* * * * *

I entreat you not to make the least scruple of telling me to share my room with another girl. Consistently, Emily repeats this offer in the name of economy - to the extent that, methinks, she doth protest too much. ***Do not think it will be a sacrifice for me - on the contrary it will give me pleasure to think I am doing what you wish. It might even save on firing and candles...***

And Natalie continues throughout this bleak period to be a resilient alternative to thought only of her father. *Poor dear little Natalie has a very bad cough and is confined to her room, and no one may sit with her, as when she is exerted in the least degree the cough comes on worse. With regard to Italian, I must tell you that Natalie came from Italy when she was 3 years old and has passed the other 9 years of her life in Germany* [Vienna seems more likely, but we will come to that later]. *She only knows a few words of her native language now, and even writes to her mother in German. I therefore fear if we attempted to speak Italian we should neither of us get on very well...*

In looking over your dear letters, I discovered to my great dismay that I had forgotten to (thank) you for so kindly forgiving my silly imprudence.....I will never never be so naughty again. I daily suffer from this imprudence as, though Mrs Heine has long since forgiven it, I do not think she has forgotten it.

I can see that she dislikes me. Every thing the other girls do to displease her, she lays upon me, and indeed I am innocent, as I have not the heart now to be merry and nonsensical with the others... But I am determined to regain her good graces; as you say I must enter life with a firm resolution never to make an enemy and, though I cannot with truth say that Mrs Heine is my enemy, yet I must endeavour to make her even not dislike me. Trying to please her will be a good preparation for trying to please others, and you said once that you wished me to learn early 'l'art de plaire' ['the art of pleasing']... *Mrs Heine will not have to complain of me again, or at least if she has, the fault will be in my innate stupidity and not in my want of attention.*

* * * * *

I now see that the paper is beginning to wane, and that the delightful time which I have looked forward to many days is now drawing to a close. Ah! when will the time come when I shall be able to look upon the correspondence as past, when I can be with you, when I can talk to you, when I can be with you. When I think of that time, however distant it may be, I feel that I would bear any thing, and every thing, for long long years, so that I might at last live with you and love you.

I tremble with pleasure at the very thought – it seems too much pleasure ever to be realised.

Sometimes think of me (whenever you think of anything but your dreadful sorrows) - think of me as loving you better than any thing else in the world, as feeling for you as tenderly as I am capable of feeling – think of me so, and you will think of me as I really am. Ever and always your fond and affectionate and devoted child, E.E.B.

* * * * *

My dearest Emily, I should long since have written to you [the letter is undated] *but that I wished to delay till I could give you some better account of myself. My constitution was so shaken as to betray some serious symptoms - but for the last few days I have greatly recovered.....and, when these final duties are discharged & my mind can turn to less saddening objects, I shall hope, by change of air and scene, to regain at last my average health.*

Bless you, my dearest child, for your letters – they have been to me most soothing – the most graceful I have received. For you seem to understand me – you do not attempt the usual cant of condolence – you feel that in such grief as mine, we do not want consolation - we want only sympathy; to praise my dear Mother – to own how much she was worthy to be loved & mourned. It is that which most diminishes the bitterness of the terrible tears wrung from eyes that have wept seldom.

But as yet you cannot even guess how much I had cause to love her - to miss her – to disdain ordinary comfort & to feel that in her grave lies buried all of youth, of early affection, of early tenderness & trust. My life now only can approach its decline. While she lived, I was still half a boy. I was always young to her. Now it seems to me as if I was grown old at once – as if my heart had turned grey. Do not fancy me ungrateful to you, or insensible to the great blessing left to me in such a child. But with you lies my future. With her - my past.

And so we see how in tune Emily is with her father, and how she comes by morbidness and melancholy naturally. It is in her Lytton genes. ***Blue devils***, as her father's character Pelham would call them [in his 1828 novel *Pelham*], or ***moods of black melancholy***, as Emily's niece and namesake Emily Lutyens describes the family blight [in *A Blessed Girl* (1953)].

* * * * *

This is my second visit to Knebworth since the funeral, Edward continues *– I am again in the old familiar parlour & again I shudder at the loneliness. What pleases me most is the idea - I think I expressed it to you before – to make this her home one monument of her. Before the windows of the principal rooms is an avenue she had just begun to plant. At the end of this Avenue I propose one day to place a monumental tower – it will be seen by us – (by those I trust who come after us) from every window. It will face the Home she loved & speak to us as a living thing.*

Avenue leading to Mrs Bulwer's monument

I mean also to fit up her room with all her relics and hoard all the furniture she loved best - & I shall place that room under your care. I mean to embellish the whole House, but according to her ideas – tho' perhaps in a more complete form of architecture than a woman can be suffered to have understood [an oft quoted line of Edward's - and one he has had his comeuppance for since, in most qualified architects also suffering to understand Knebworth House] *– and by an inscription stone to give her the due credit of it. Not a part of the House, while one stone stands upon another, but shall speak of her.*

"a more complete form of architecture than a woman can be suffered to have understood"

Knebworth House does still speak of her. But it shouts of him.

* * * * *

You & I, Emily, are almost the only ones in our family who understand the duty that remains to us. Edward is young – and his sex must be taught sentiment and reverence by grief of their own – but you, with your Woman's heart, feel all I ask for, by intuition not experience. My Brothers – Oh the hard tearless eyes of my eldest! I took him to the Deathbed – she had not been dead an hour – not a tear! & Henry, tho' kind, & far more feeling, is wrapt in ambition.

I say that <u>we</u> understand the duty left to us – that duty seems to me to vindicate in all things her name & memory. My Mother was too great, too frank, too unbending, to the mean hypocrites of the world to be generally understood. If I live she shall be– tho', alas, what matters it now!

Still, I remember when I myself was galled by calumny, how it comforted me to think one day might come when - if my children had my blood in their

veins - they would vindicate me. For there is no vindication to a parent's memory like a child! And what I hoped from my children I will seek to render to my parent, who indeed needs it less.

How, on all these points, I shall long to talk to you – consult your woman's delicacy - & feel every[thing - paper torn*] others might ridicule you will revere and hold sacred. If you could conjecture how much more dearly I love you for your letters, you would feel you hold the right key to my heart. Every one who loved my Mother becomes inexpressibly dear to me - while Death, which softens me to all else, renders it doubly impossible now to forgive any who have embittered that lonely life which had so little of enjoyment, stung that heart which was so acutely sensitive, assailed that character which in my eyes was the holiest under Heaven.*

And you will imagine how now it harrows me, how it startles me from sleep at night – how it haunts me at every turn – to remember that one such enemy I placed upon her path, & placed on her very hearth-

But all that is over now! – ribaldry cannot reach her, my homage cannot come to her ear.

* * * * *

It is not for her that I desire to embalm her name, it is, (I feel the selfishness) for mine. It satisfies a craving of the heart - it unites me to her thro' an idle superstition which makes me fancy she can hear & smile upon me still.

People nowadays love their parents so little – they seem to think it so in course that the old should die – that my love and my grief would seem maudlin weakness or affectation to most. Even your brother preaches to me about it.

But to know how different my relationship to my Mother is from the common household tie, one must have had my sorrows, one must have known a home desecrated & a trust betrayed - and then have suddenly come to the shelter of one pure faithful love, the reviving atmosphere of protecting, soothing, generous affection...[etc., for pages and pages.]

* * * * *

You know Emily now well enough to know the effect that such a letter has on her. Within tight continuous pages of heart-poured reply, there is much beauty, well beyond her years. ***You say you "stand alone in the world without a friend to whom you would own a fault, or from whom you would ask a favour" Alas! alas! alas! I cannot contradict it. The very relationship between us both forbids it, and even were I not your child, I have it not in my poor power to grant you any favour - and as for owning a fault, I should never be able to see that anything you did was a fault... but anything else you could expect and claim in a friend, look for in me – devotion, love, sympathy, tenderness, affection, in my heart you will find all; and great and deep as they all are, I shed tears that they are not infinitely greater and deeper.***

Emily's blue devils wrestle with her angels, in stark script before us - raw thoughts, that others will have at her own coffin side in four short years time.

We know not the infinite delights prepared to adorn her glad eternity. Dark and gloomy are the thoughts of Death and the grave. Still more dark, still more gloomy - how much more dreadful! how much more terrible! - the thoughts that the one we love most sleeps now the long sleep of death. The one we loved most lies now in the cold and silent grave, insensible alike to the ills the living suffer, and the joy which the living before produced.

Bright and radiant are the thoughts of heaven and eternity - how much more bright and radiant and glorious and beautiful when we know that the Being we loved most, and cherished most, is now a partaker in eternal joy and everlasting bliss with no wish but one – to see again and live again with all that the heart clung to below.

And yet, how hard it is to turn our thoughts from what is present, how very very hard to refrain from thinking that all we loved is there, there in the dark tomb, there where our love can no longer joy them [sic]***; and where the unkindness of others can no longer wound them, can no longer harm them.***

And then reason tells us that it is only the medium by which we loved which sleeps there, and that what we loved still lives and loves - but reason cannot calm the heart which still weeps on and cannot be comforted.

* * * * *

The maturity of these musings continues with more defence of the one whose "sex must be taught sentiment and reverence by grief of their own"... ***I know my Brother's disposition, and remember that long ago when I had any little childish sorrow he would sometimes chide me when I expected he would have said something kind - but this was always his manner when, in his heart, he sympathises deeply. He has not written to me.....but in a letter which he wrote to Miss Greene and which she forwarded to me, he expressed in the most affectionate terms his great love for you, and his deep sympathy for you at this dreadful time.***

Forgive him, if he has seemed to feel for you - and with you - less than one would have expected. Trust me it is only in appearance. He is only a child yet, and when he is a little older he will get into a happier way of showing the feelings of his heart, which I know are fond and affectionate.

* * * * *

And then, all of a sudden - like Alice taking her 'Drink Me' potion - Emily is a teenager again. ***A thousand thanks for thinking of dear Natalie, she is better – But it sometimes saddens me to see that she does not love me as I love her. But to deserve her love, one must be like her, and those that are like her must be rare indeed. She is so beautiful (at least I think her so) so amicable, so good –***

And more Natalie again - after another long spell of not having heard from her father - on Saturday 2nd March, 1844, ***I often wish you could see my beautiful Natalie. She is so unlike everyone else in the whole place. There is such a delicate refinement about her - at the same time something so gay and joyous. I do not say you would think of her as I do, for I really think my opinion of her may be a little inspired with the Elisir d'amour*** [the Elixir - or magical potion - of love], ***but I am sure you would like her.***

She is my Picciola [the little flower that grows in a prison cell in the 1836 novel of the same name by Joseph-Xavier Boniface] ***and, in her company only, are my sad thoughts a little lulled. She has such a sweet voice and sings the most beautiful little italien airs, which she remembers, yet quite beautifully - indeed she seems to me a being formed from songs and the sunbeams of italien skies. And for knowing her, I am indebted to you. It was you who first taught me to admire that nameless charm, that Anmuth*** [Grace], ***which***

so few people possess and which is so attractive; and, in her, it seems personified - and it was seeing that, which first led me to seek her acquaintance, and now she is so very very dear to me.

The flower in the prison cell - from the novel ***Picciola*** *(1836)*

* * * * *

Two weeks later, with still no letter from her father ***...I mentioned in a former letter how sad it made me to see that [Natalie] did not love me as I loved her - that to be sure I could never expect - but I meant that it made me sad to see that she only looked upon me as a common acquaintance; and now with the most inexpressible joy I must tell you that she really really loves me - my scarce permitted dream is realised, and to you, to you only, I tell it.***

I never told any one else of my affection for Natalie because it was more in thought than anything else - and to you only do I tell my thoughts, to others my deeds. I hardly ever could myself well define the reason for becoming so thoroughly attached to one whom I know, comparatively speaking, for so short a time [I would correct 'know' to 'have known', but her language - or mistakes - importantly reflect her state of mind] ***and perhaps you may think it foolish and childish, but then you do not know Natalie, you have not seen her.***

One thing, my dearest Father, I entreat you not to think – do not, pray do not, imagine that it is one of those friendships which books say schoolgirls form amongst each other, and which as soon as they are parted are broken and discontinued - indeed indeed this is not the case. I confess I know not the bewitching influence which Natalie influences over me - but this I know, that if she had not been here, I should never have cared much for any one here, even had the girls been twice as kind - and to do them justice they were all very kind.

Even if Natalie hated me, I should love her as fervently as ever. My reason for begging you not to think this is an idle school girls' friendship, is that I am afraid you do - because in a letter from Miss Greene she included one from Edward to her; and I copy out a few lines: "Did Emily tell you of the charming sentimental friend she found in the person of an italien girl? She is not a 'Serena' or an 'Amelia', her name is Natalie - is it not a very romantic one? She never told me of it. I suppose it is a great secret as she only told Papa"!

Now, I never would have written this to Teddy because he would never have understood me. If he once saw Natalie he would understand what I mean and I then could tell it to him. Perhaps to you, however, my own dearest Father, to whom my innermost thought belongs, I told it, but it would make me very unhappy if you misunderstand my real feelings...

* * * * *

Knebworth. Friday 8th March, 1844. *My dearest Emily, I am ashamed to have been so long without writing to you. But you were warned of my faults as a Correspondent and you must never be uneasy at some prolonged and ungrateful silence. Lately I have been moving about from place to place.*

I went to Brighton to see Teddy, but did not stay long for the place itself saddened me - my poor Mother having arranged to go there with me when she left Knebworth for the last time, & I had made with her so many little plans as to that excursion. Perhaps I was still more saddened by that vast division between the rising generation and the past, which the sight of Teddy occasioned – when contrasted with the form whose eyes I had so lately closed. And when, poor boy, he unconsciously said that he had been very happy at some place where he passed the Xmas holidays with Mrs Walker & I remembered that at that very time the one to whom he owes more than he can ever understand was on the bed of death......I felt that it was impossible to stay longer without letting my thoughts become unjust to him - because it was not his fault. It is the constitution of his age. I did not feel eno' for my own Mother when her mother died.

I was comforted, however, to see Teddy looking better & stronger than I ever saw him before. He has a good many young companions with whom he is popular.

After leaving Brighton I went for a day cab journey.....and now you find me here where I propose remaining some days. I am most anxious to get abroad, but am kept by the hope of parting with Craven Cottage or my house in town - both if possible, for I find them much too expensive now I have to keep up (as my poor Mother wished it kept) a place so large as Knebworth.

* * * * *

I do not expect to recover myself until I am out of England. My old friend Catarrh remains faithful, and I am yet more annoyed by a perpetual feeling in the heart – which is not so much painful as distressing. It often keeps me awake – it came on after her death (and) never leaves me for more than a day. The Doctors say it is not dangerous – but they do it no good with their exceptions. I am better than I was.....And now my dearest child from my health, let me turn to yours.

I am rendered very uneasy by seeing in a note from Teddy which I enclose to you that you have complained of being ill? What has been the matter? I find you now complaining of headache. Tell me all about yourself! & be careful for my sake – for indeed, my dearest Emily, I accept with my whole heart your tender wish to replace what I have lost - & find my Mother's love in my daughter's.

I am pleasing myself here in thinking how to arrange for your rooms etc. For when you come to me, you will rise into the dignity of châtelaine & I shall expect you to bring from Germany all the accomplishments necessary to keeping House and governing a family - cares for which Women have an inborn talent & Man an irresistible aversion. To keep keys & give out Roses and linen & look over washing bills – behold your legitimate destiny. Heaven help thee - and me - poor Innocents, with this large House & Household! If you do not by instinct acquire the arts of economy method & management we are lost! See then how useful you can be to me and how much I shall expect from you.

* * * * *

I rejoice to think you have so much comfort in Natalie - & really hope she will be suffered to visit you in England as long as she & you like. A girl wants a companion of her own sex and you are fortunate to find one in your fresh years of feeling. But again I beg you not to be led too much by the eye & the look. I observe that you dwell greatly on Natalie's countenance & refinement, & voice. But on her character you say little. And I fear therefore that the character may be less striking than the external gifts.

Is she generous & unselfish? Is she affectionate? Has she a good understanding, & above all a good heart & good principles? I felt jealous for you my child when you said in one of your letters that you feared she did not love you as much as you loved her. What is the matter with her? What defects? Why is she in the Institute?

And now - I wish you would tell Dr Heine that I should be glad to hear expressly from him what he thinks of your case what progress you have made, how much longer he thinks you will have to stay for your cure, & whether we hope that the cure will be complete or only partial. You have now been nearly 6 months and he can therefore form a judgement. Be good eno' to put these questions in writing & in German to Dr Heine, & tell him to send me his answer. At the same time you can give him the autograph which he wanted and which I enclose.

June, who is with me, desires his comforts and his love – He is rather triste today having got worried by a big dog yesterday.

Many tender enquiries after you are made by the Villagers here. They all look forward with pleasure to your reappearance amongst them. God bless you my Measy. Most affectionately yours, E.B.Lytton

P.S. According to my poor Mother's will, I take the name of Lytton after Bulwer – your name also in future is Miss Bulwer Lytton, which tell Mrs Heine.

* * * * *

This fantasy of keeping house for her father, as châtelaine of Knebworth, is a much more dangerous fantasy for the adrift teenager than any burgeoning romance with a 12-year-old schoolgirl could be. This is a promise that Edward will not be able to live up to. And this impossible dream, now deeply planted in his daughter, is to have devastating consequences.

To be fair to Edward, as he wanders the lonely passages of his new house, with only his dog June at his side, it is not likely that he would ever consider setting up his longtime mistress Laura Deacon as Knebworth House's châtelaine. But, Laura Deacon is to be replaced in the coming year with a much younger and more distracting alternative. Marion Waller is only five years older than Emily, and a whole new prospect for Edward's middle age. And she will enter Emily's story at the worst possible moment.

In response to her father's plans for Knebworth House, Emily enthuses,

How very very kind of you to think of me, and though I only hope you may not be disappointed as to the "inborn talent" for housekeeping, I shall be proud and delighted if I can ever be able to help you in the slightest way. I hope to learn the prudent management of money by these £20, and am beginning to see a little better now where and when I can spare, and where by spending I can save. Eight ponderous [as in awkward and heavy] ***Keys hang constantly at my side, as it is, and I am for ever in the midst of linen and washing Bills. I suppose at all events I shall not have to stay longer here than the July in 1845, and in the June of that year I will be 17 - within one year of being 18 - and you said once that, when I was 18, I could come to you!***

* * * * *

But as much as this affirmation that he wants her at his side is a delight to Emily, the report of his ill health and his criticism of her brother Teddy in the same letter is distressing ***...in the midst of my great joy in seeing your dear handwriting once more, some things in your letter have given me more uneasiness and sorrow.*** What becomes of her if he now has a heart attack? And what of the shocking things he says about Teddy? A scapegoat is needed to deflect blame from her brother. There can only be one. ***...remember how I was pained in the beginning of our great sorrow by certain letters which I received from Miss Greene in reply to some of mine, in which I wrote to her of my feelings, both with regard to you and myself. I could not and ought not to have been hurt at them, as they were meant to have been very affectionate and feeling, but to me they seemed so devoid of tact and sympathy, that it was almost with difficulty that I refrained from begging her to drop so dear, yet so painful, a subject all together in future.***

Now as Teddy writes so often to her, and she writes so often to him, I think she tells him to do and say things which perhaps his own feelings would forbid him to. Poor poor Father, what must have been your feelings! and what must you have thought of my Brother! and yet he used to be so kind and sympathising. I know not what to think, but my time and space are diminishing and I am still on painful subjects.

Never call your silences "ungrateful" - it was very naughty of me to have been so impatient. I was suffering from headaches, but now I am quite quite

well, and I beg of you never to be uneasy about my health, take care of yourself. Dr Heine sends you his best compliments. I gave him a written paper containing all your questions in German. I hope you will receive his sincerest thanks, both in his own name and that of his friend's, for the pretty autograph.

* * * * *

And now for my dear Natalie. I reproach myself for having given you an unjust representation of her. I am afraid you think her a great Beauty, with fascinating manners – oh voila touche [here is the key]. *But that she is not. Many cannot find anything pretty in her face, and her manners do not please all, and perhaps it is my admiration for her mind and heart that makes me think her so beautiful en defors* [on the outside]. *She is generosity itself; by generosity, I mean that generosity of sentiment and feeling, not giving presents (which, by the bye, is not allowed here). She is thoroughly unselfish. She is, I confess it, very enthusiastic - perhaps more so than a girl should be - but then her enthusiasm more resembles what you call 'that gush of goodness' than mere animation on any favourite subject.*

As for affection, her general charm of manner to everyone, made me for a long time uncertain if she looked upon me merely as a friend or as an acquaintance, and I discovered that her affections are not so easily won as I at first imagined. When, however, once really won, I feel confident that she will never withdraw them, and hope begins to dawn in me that she really loves me.

There is something peculiarly original, naïve, and unlike everybody else in her whole being. I know not where Edward heard of her as "a such sweet congenial soul, the only one amongst the vulgar herd" with "a romantic taste" and "dark hair" (by the bye, her hair is chestnut coloured) and I am sad that he looks upon a friendship I never told him of in so ridiculous a light. However I am very happy and very grateful that you do not disapprove of my loving her so much.

* * * * *

She is here on account of her right side, which projects rather more than the left, however, in other respects she is perfectly well shaped. To my great joy, it is her Mama's wish that she should remain here till she is quite cured, which will last till June 1845 – so that, at all events, she and I will remain an equal time here.

Her Mama is no stepmother as I first heard, but her own real mother - she must be, from all I have heard, a very rich grande dame du monde. At the same time [she] seems to be a good and fond mother. She lives at the present in Vienna.

You gave me such pleasure by saying you were anxious to get abroad, dearest Father, will you not come here then if you can? Oh! Do pray say yes. Natalie's Mama is coming to see her also in July.

I am glad your faithful June is with you, give him my fond love and tell him to be seinem Herrn treu [Faithful to his Lord]. *How kind of the villagers at dear Knebworth still to think of me – remember me kindly to all those to whom you introduced me when I was last there. And now I know all you have to do, and promise not to be naughty and impatient any more if I do not receive a letter from you just at the desired time. In the meanwhile, get rid of your Catarrh and your feeling at the heart, and remember that I am, your own fond child,*

Emily Bulwer Lytton

Pardonne mon gros tonnage

Dr Jacob Heine

CHAPTER 24

~ Cannstatt Letters - The Cure ~

My first greatest treasure is your letters. My second is your beautiful, beautiful books. Accustomed as I am from my childhood of hearing everybody speak of them with rapture, I never knew their real beauty until now that I have read many of them for myself. Upon closing each, I think it must be the most beautiful - and now that I have read four or five, I cannot say which one in particular has most enchanted me. The bewitching mysterious Zanoni [1842] *(which magical name looks still more magical in German characters, beginning with that awful ß – fancy a well-printed:* *and* The Disowned [1829], *in fact all the others are so beautiful that it is impossible to say which is most so.*

I have seen nothing of the Pfizers for a very long time. The music mistress asked me the other day to lend her Night and Morning [1841], *which, as I had not got in German, I was forced to write a note to Mrs Pfizer asking her to lend me a copy. This she did, at the same time sending me a note saying that she has had a very bad cough which has prevented her from coming to Cannstadt, but intends doing so the next warm [day]. There have been many fine days since she wrote but I have as yet seen nothing of her.* Emily Bulwer Lytton to Edward Bulwer Lytton - Sunday 24th March, 1844

* * * * *

Sunday 7th April, 1844 (but begun earlier - stretching the Cure rule of writing only once a fortnight). *As today is Good Friday and a very great holiday here, I shall take the opportunity of writing to you - or at least beginning a letter to you a little before the usual time. I am in such great hopes that the fine Spring weather will quite remove the naughty persevering catarrh. But what you told me in your last letter about the feeling in the heart keeps me in the greatest anxiety and uneasiness - and the more so because I think that it must much more depend on the state of your own mind and feelings than upon outward circumstances as in other illnesses.* She is sounding like Miss Greene. The patient becomes doctor.

I do so wish I could see you, even if it were only for a moment. When do you think you shall be able to leave England? Every place where you were when you were here has become dear and sacred to me, and I cannot tell you how unhappy I felt last week because I was forced to leave my room (that room in which you were twice) and what is worse, the window at which you stood and out of which you leaned, has been blocked up; and the corner which was hallowed by your head, and where I used to write to you and read and reread your dear letters has been, or rather is being, altered in order to join the old side of the House with this new wing.

I am now in a very large room where you never were, and which you never saw, some days till the old room is finished. And when I return the enchantment will be broken - the place where you stood will no longer be there. Though every stranger that enters this new room seems quite delighted at the "change", as they term it (the room being about a size larger than the one I had at Baden Baden!), it is anything in the world but a change for the better. In the first place, because you have never been here; and in the second place, I am just over Mrs Heine's black-haired sister's bedroom, and the first evening of my being here, dearest Natalie came as usual. Miss Anna [Camerer, Madame Heine's sister] *came up and after speaking a few words to me turned to Natalie and hinted that it was most likely that I would like to be alone, etc. etc. - in short gave her to understand that it would be more agreeable to her (Miss Anna) if Natalie did not come often!! Judge my horror! The consequence is that my dear Natalie has resolved not to come any more till I am again in the old room, for fear that if she came too often now, she might be prevented from coming when I leave this room.*

* * * * *

The time has come when it is Dr Heine's wish that we should be as much in the garden as possible - in fact do every thing we can in it, and till I return to the old room I shall always write to you here, in the garden house. You

The Gardens of the Institute - before the new wing is added

were here though only for a moment. Dr Heine told me to come to him on Sunday for a letter from him to you.....therefore I suppose he will answer all your questions in it.

Will you perhaps be so kind as to tell me (if you have no objection) how long he says I will have to stay here? I have just met Miss Anna who tells me that she was at a concert the other evening where she met an English gentleman of the name of Pringle, and he told her that he had read in the newspaper that it was your intention to come very soon abroad and to stay some time in the continent. Imagine my delight: it must be true or else it would not be in the Newspaper.

* * * * *

...Miss Jones, who by the bye constantly visits me, told me some days ago that her Mamma had read some advertisement in some magazine of a book, the title of which she forgot, written by Lady B   , and she then asked me if she was any relation of mine. Oh have pity upon me, my Father, and do not call me cruel and unkind because I tell you these things - believe me, I would bear them all and much more alone, and in silence, could my doing so spare you one moments pang. But I am afraid if I act by myself, without asking your advice in matters of this kind I may only do wrong, and therefore I give

you more pain than I can express. What I have to say must be said, and what I have to ask must be asked - so just pass over this passage in my letter as quickly as possible and do not let one thought rest upon it, but ever remember my love and my affection.

I answered as cooly as I could, that she had no doubt mistaken the name, there being a family of the name of Buller somewhere in England which name was often confounded with ours. She replied she believed the name to be Bulwer. [She] was not however quite sure, but would ask her Mamma (Thank God her Mama left the next day for Frankfurt). I should not have thought so much of it if she had not said Mrs Jones wished to know – the question was a natural one if it came from herself, as she must be supposed to know nothing of our family than just your name.

But what has so perplexed me is that old Mrs Jones asked such a question. I do not know if it was prompted by ignorance, or curiosity, or a wish to justify [if correctly transcribed, presumably meant in its religious sense] *or what, and I wish to ask you your opinion, and also to ask you if this, or some other question of the same kind, should be repeated, should I evade it as I did this time, or should I show that I feel hurt. If possible, dearest father, do not tell me to do the latter; perhaps that which has caused me the most wretchedness, since I have known the fatal secret, is to let strangers see that I know it.*

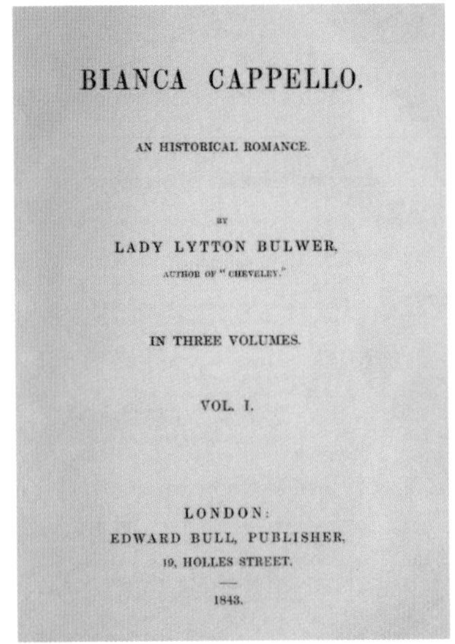

BIANCA CAPPELLO.

AN HISTORICAL ROMANCE.

BY

LADY LYTTON BULWER,

AUTHOR OF "CHEVELEY."

IN THREE VOLUMES.

VOL. I.

LONDON:
EDWARD BULL, PUBLISHER,
19, HOLLES STREET.

1843.

Based on Miss Jones remembering the name 'Bulwer', the advertisment was probably for Rosina's 1843 novel Bianca Cappello (above). Rosina follows this in 1844 with Memoirs of a Muscovite (below) using her estranged husband's new name

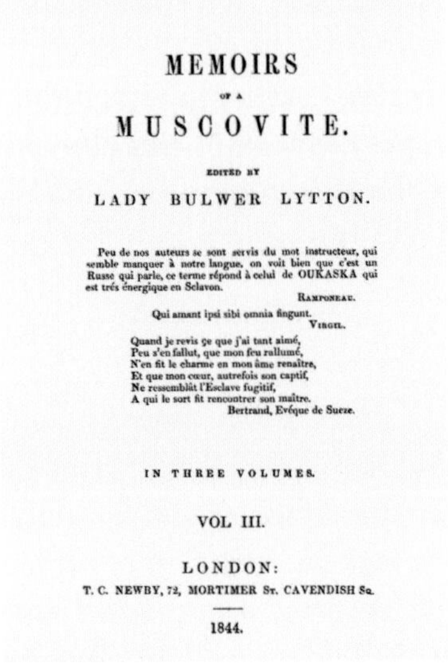

MEMOIRS

OF A

MUSCOVITE.

EDITED BY

LADY BULWER LYTTON.

Peu de nos auteurs se sont servis du mot instructeur, qui semble manquer à notre langue. on voit bien que c'est un Russe qui parle, ce terme répond à celui de OUKASKA qui est trés énergique en Sclavon.

RAMPONEAU.

Qui amant ipsi sibi omnia fingunt.

VIRGIL.

Quand je revis çe que j'ai tant aimé,
Peu s'en fallut, que mon feu rallumé,
N'en fit le charme en mon âme renaître,
Et que mon cœur, autrefois son captif,
Ne ressemblât l'Esclave fugitif,
A qui le sort fit rencontrer son maître.

Bertrand, Evêque de Sueze.

IN THREE VOLUMES.

VOL III.

LONDON:
T. C. NEWBY, 72, MORTIMER ST. CAVENDISH SQ.

1844.

* * * * *

And now forgive me, forgive me and forget that I have told you all this if you care. I should think you ought to dread reading a letter from me, for I generally have something disagreeable to tell you, or else some very very great favour to ask you; and this time (pray do not say "This is too much") I have both. As the Germans say, I have a dreadfully great favour to ask -

When you come here, could you, and would you, bring my dear Brother with you? I wrote him a letter at the time when my sorrow was so great both for myself and on your account - I told him, as I used to do long ago when we were together, every feeling of my heart. I told him that one of my greatest causes for grief was to think that you must pass the most agonizing hours which you perhaps ever knew without anyone who could soothe your grief and rob you of some of your sorrow by sharing it. I entreated him as a proof of his love to me, independent of all his own feelings, to show you that if much was gone, still something, however small, was left.

And I am sure he never received that letter. He never answered it, and indeed he says himself in his last letter that you sent me that he has not heard from me since he last wrote. There is so much that I long to tell him – and I am sure, my dearest Father, that the more one knows my dear Brother's heart, the more affectionate and sympathising it will appear.

And now dearest dearest Father, the last, but perhaps the greatest favour I have to ask, is that you will think of me as your very fond and affectionate - Measy

P.S. I dare say you have seen many beautiful violets this Spring and have let them bloom and die unheeded; knowing this I wonder at myself for being foolish and childish enough to send you the enclosed one. But it was the first I found this year and smelt sweet when I picked it; take it als ein Pflänzchen meiner Liebe [as a little off-shoot (literally, 'plantlets') of my love] - *I also enclose Dr Heine's letter. E.B.L.*

* * * * *

Monsieur! Ce sont mes nombreuses occupations... [translated from the French] *My busy schedule has prevented me, until now, giving you an update on your daughter. From your frequent correspondence with Madamoiselle Emilie, you will know that she is always in good spirits, has very good health, a fine bonny look, and her complexion has improved... the deformity is reduced; the left shoulder is higher; the right, and above the right hip side, are less highlighted; and the body has a better shape. Yet, Monsieur, please recommend to Madamoiselle Emilie that she be more exact and consistent, in the cure, as my remarks in this regard are not quite sufficient. Madamoiselle has the will, but she forgets easily; and it is necessary, to achieve the best result possible, for Madamoiselle Emilie to follow my instructions diligently.*

In respect of your question, Monsieur, of whether it is possible to cure the defect completely, I very much regret to be obliged to tell you that is impossible. The deformity had already been in place for too long and was too far advanced on her arrival here. The most that I dare promise you is an essential improvement if we continue the treatment for at least two years at the establishment. I hope, as Madamoiselle develops and is strengthened, so we will kept it in check for her future, and at the same time her shoulders and hips, so that nothing will be seen when she is fully dressed. On the other hand, if Madamoiselle interrupts the cure too early, it will risk the problem arising again as she is still young and visibly growing.

From my wife you learn, Monsieur, what lessons we fill the hours with when she is not undergoing the cure, and be assured that her education is not neglected; also we are able to tell you that Mademoiselle is attentive and enjoys all her lessons.

With my assurance, Monsieur, that we will do our best for the physical and moral wellbeing of Madamoiselle Emilie, I have the honour of being, Your most humble servant, Dr Heine

* * * * *

Monday 15th April 1844. *My dearest Emily, At last I sit down to write to you – with some contrition at a delay occasioned, as Dr Heine informs me his was, by "mes nombreuses occupations" – indeed I have been busier than ever, and little stationary, having been twice at Knebworth since I wrote. Some alterations are to be made there which I hope you will think improvements.*

To answer first, my dearest child, the point with regard to Lady B. on which you ask my advice. I can so far reassure you as to say, I think it little that you will have to be often annoyed by questions of that nature. Most

Knebworth House does not end up looking like this, but if Edward had had more money it might have done

people living in the World know that we are separated, and will have the ordinary good breeding not to mention the subject. It is only children, or very young or ignorant persons, who are likely to speak to you in any way of Lady B. Where more experienced persons happen to do so, you may be sure it is downright impertinence & should be repelled haughtily & even rudely.

I cannot advise you to tell or to insinuate any untruth, about the Lady Buller etc. – nothing wrong is ever politic in the long run. The answer would deceive very few people, and when it did deceive them for the moment, you wd only be exposed to their coming again, and blurting out, when least welcome, the discovery they had made that it was not Lady Buller but Lady Bulwer, besides Lady Bulwer is now Lady Lytton, or Bulwer Lytton.

What I would do in your case would be, if any one apparently ignorantly & innocently asks you any question about Lady B, or her books, to reply that you know nothing about it. If any person better informed, either through curiosity or other motive, speak to you – say as haughtily as you can "I suppose you know my Father & Mother are seperated, and I am surprised you ask any questions of a nature indelicate for you to ask & painful for me to answer."

In life you must learn how to rebuff insolence & if you do this once, you will be safe ever afterwards from the same party. This is all the advice I can honestly give you.

* * * * *

Now my dear love, as to a more important & anxious matter.....namely the cure, and your probable stay at Cannstadt.

The length of your stay depends on your cure, and Dr Heine informs that tho' you are sensibly improved, your cure is retarded by your want of attention to his instructions... Now my love, your cure really depends on yourself, on minute painful energetic attention to the smallest particulars. The greatest care in holding yourself in the way recommended etc. Without this, all the chagrin of your exile, etc. is thrown away – you make a sacrifice for nothing, & at the end of the time you will be little or no better.

What you want in your character is continuous thoughtful energy – a very common & a very womanly defect, but in your position, a very disastrous one. You must apply your whole heart & mind to the resolve to get cured. Write down all his directions. Put the writing in a conspicuous place where your eye will often turn. Keep constantly looking at it. It depends on yourself how long you stay & I cannot therefore answer that question at present, but I shall see you in the course of the Summer, & judge myself of your progress.

I fear I cannot undertake to bring Teddy, for when I get as far as Stuttgart I shall probably go on into Italy. It is my present idea to pass the Winter in Italy or Egypt. But I fully understand your affectionate motives in wanting to see your brother.

Will you give my compliments to Mrs Heine & say that in the confusion of moving furniture and papers, for an alteration in my House, her bill has got lost or mislaid. I am ashamed at giving her so much trouble.....but could she send another

My health is better, thank you for your tender anxiety but I still suffer from the heart & the catarrh never leaves me. I hope much of a residence of some months in Italy. God bless you my dearest child. Yr most affectionate father, E.B.L.

* * * * *

Sunday 21st April, 1844. Mrs Heine's bill enclosed. ***Father, dearest dearest Father forgive me oh! forgive me - though your words are as ever so kind and indulgent, I cannot but feel that in your heart you must be grieved and***

Compte pour les petites dépenses de Mademoiselle Bulwer.

Pour l'instruction allemande du mois de Decembre 1843 de Janvier et de Fevrier 1844	5/4.
pour les leçons allemandes avec Mademoiselle Bock, le 1er Fevrier 44	4. –
... 12 leçons de piano le 15 Fevrier 44	6. –
... les leçons de religion et de literature depuis le 11 Decemb jusqu'au 11 Mars 1844	3. –
jusqu'ici allait l'autre compte, et depuis ce tems nous avons encore dépensé:	
Pour l'instruction allemande du mois de Mars 1844	1. 40
... les leçons de danse	3. 24
... 12 leçons de chant à Madame Wallbach le 24 Avril	43. 12.
... 10 - - - allemandes avec Mademoiselle Bosch	4. –
... le bois du 2 Decembre 1843 jusqu'à la fin de l'hiver	18. 29.
	88/49.
	145
	233. –

Canstatt le 28 Avril 1844

Henriette Heine.

Emily's Account - April 1844

disappointed in me upon many points. What you say of my character is but too true, I want energy, but I want still more – perseverance. What Dr Heine says is just and true. The ardour which I felt in the commencement, to devote

myself entirely to doing all that lay in my power, to promote that in which you took so lively an interest, has lately been less vivid - my thoughts have been more on other things [playing the death of Granny card - although the game has, more likely, been Natalie]. ***But whatever disappointment and grief you may feel at my thoughtless want of steadiness oh! trust me, you cannot feel half so much pain as I do myself – to neglect anything in the smallest point to which you wish me so rigidly to attend, is a fault which to my own heart seems a crime...*** And much more of the same - until we get to -

...Italy is my Natalie's 'Vaterland' [Fatherland, in its West Germanic form] ***and I have a lot of superstitious presentiment that you will get quite well under its blue Heaven. Talking of Natalie, her cure is a much more rigid one than mine; she being obliged to lie down two hours longer than I am - and also to do other things that take up a great part of her day. So that, with the exception of Sundays, I hardly ever saw her but at evening - however that might have so far interfered with the cure, that I might not have held myself so upright as I should perhaps otherwise have done.*** [Stop sniggering at the back. Or if you are her schoolboy brother in Brighton.]

I now see but very little of her, as she never comes to me now; and if when I return to my old room she should renew the intercourse which formerly existed between us, that my grand aim and 'Zweck' [purpose] ***shall be – the cure – and that nothing else shall predominate over that.***

* * * * *

I am quite sure that the alterations that you are making in Knebworth must be great improvements, if the place itself can allow of improvements. [The laughter you now hear is that of Knebworth House's 21st Century occupants, custodians, architects and maintenance team.] We, of course, love Edward Bulwer Lytton's improvements to his house. No other house in the world looks like Knebworth House. Whereas you will find other fine examples of the Tudor (Knole), and Georgian Gothic (Strawberry Hill), versions of the house that his mother, and he, respectively, went to work on.

Much of our lives today are spent restoring, preserving and interpreting this unique vision. This treasure house of stories.

Edward Bulwer Lytton's improvements to Knebworth House... and (below) close up examples of some of his new decorative features - bats on barrels being a play on the family name, 'Lyt' for 'bat' and 'ton' for 'barrel'. The 1840s work, almost throughout, is inexpensive stucco layered on inexpensive red brick, and is now - where permitted, and when funds allow - replaced with more weather resistant materials. The two new examples below (left and right) are both cast. The original example in the centre shows the red brick beneath weathered stucco. On the left, post-Freudian sensitivities relating to modern public access has also led to tongue shortening.

* * * * *

I have this day received a letter from Miss Greene, in which she mentions her intentions of leaving Birmingham for London in some days. She also says that you promised that she should come here in Spring, and that she purposes reminding you of your promise. She however desires me to say nothing of it – You know, dearest Father, that I do not look upon it in the light of discerning secrets, telling all my thoughts and feelings to you. To you, I tell all that I tell to my own heart, and if I bore you with trifling petty concerns, it is only from my wish that you should know all that I know.

I suppose Miss Greene would think it hard and unkind (you know her way) were she prevented from visiting me some time this year, and I am sure I feel very very grateful to her for her affection. At the same time, I feel assured that (to use her own expression) "it would never do" if her stay here was prolonged to more than a visit. Strangers, particularly foreigners, would not understand her, and where she is not understood she is disliked.

This teenage embarassment at an overbearing and embarrassing 'parent' always summons images to me of the heartbreaking rejection of the ever-sacrificing, yet ever-overzealous mother Barbara Stanwyck in the 1937 film *Stella Dallas*. Stella Dallas ends up watching her daughter's wedding through the window, standing in the street in the rain, clutching the house railings.

However, of course you can arrange all this with her when she speaks to you herself upon the subject. Be so kind, dearest Papa, not to tell her that I should not wish her to stay long here. She would think me unkind and ungrateful, and indeed I do not mean it as such.

* * * * *

Never, dearest Father, think yourself bound to write to me in the midst of your "monstreuses occupations" – As long as I know that you are well or at least not ill, I will never be anxious again...

Sunday 28th April, 1844. Since I left off writing this letter last Sunday, I have left the large room in which I was during the time they were making the alterations......I am now in a little room facing the street on the same floor with the Heines. It is a nicer room than the other, having two windows and the other only one - and I feel obliged to Mrs Heine for wishing to give me a cheerful room, as she meant it kindly. But neither she nor any one else knows what attracts me to the other room - nor how indifferent it is to me if the room be gay or dull, if it be only hallowed by relics and remembrances. Besides Natalie (who is now in the large room, because her own room is being fresh papered) will be on the upper floor, and I am afraid that I shall see her but very seldom. And now my dearest dearest Father, I must bid you good bye.....

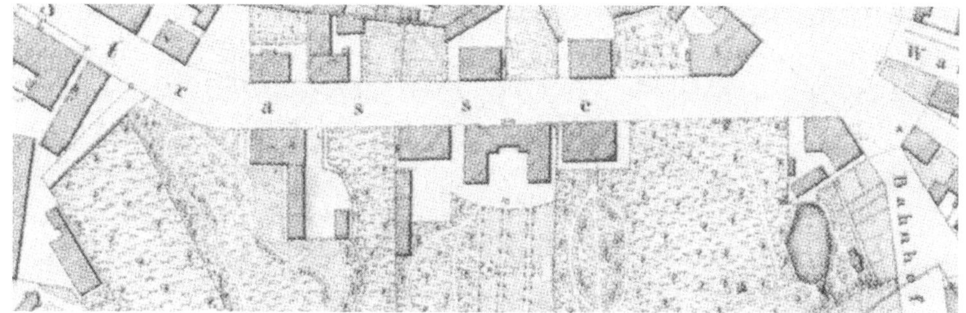

The new wing is to the right of the 'n'-shaped main building

* * * * *

Sunday 19th May, 1844. As today is a holiday and the girls have got leave to do what they please, I take the opportunity of at least beginning a letter to you. The Parsons, who receive English newspapers, tell me that the heat in England has been some degrees more than it has been here, in which case, I trust that you are now improving in health and that the catarrh is commencing to prove unfaithful. I also hope for many many reasons that all the business in which you have been lately engaged is becoming less weighty. In the first place I am certain you can not recover much in health as long as you have so much to do, and here is 'the central selfishness'! I fancy that the less you have to do in England, the sooner I shall see you here. Do you think that in your next letter you could tell me about the time when I might expect you? It would be delightful to be able to count the days and hours till that happy moment, to be able to think every evening that I am a day nearer you.

My dearest Natalie is looking forward with the greatest delight to the 10th of July as on that day her Mamma is coming to see her. I think you would love Natalie if you knew her. She is to me something which I never before knew or saw, and _______ [indecipherable] *seems more as if she had been known to me in some time which I cannot recollect, than as if she were someone whom I had never seen before. Of course the purest have their faults, but her little defects are those of a mere child. She reminds me now and then of my remembrance of poor Miss Landon.....The servant has just come to tell me a lady and gentleman in deep mourning are come to visit me - who can it be? I must go for a moment – au revoir-*

After an interval of some months Mr and Mrs Pfizer [Gustav Pfizer is Edward's Stuttgart-based translator and publisher] *have visited me for the third time since I have been here. They say that they could not come before on account of Mrs Pfizer having a bad cough. Dr Pfizer's father died last week which accounts for their being in mourning. Both enquired kindly after you.*

* * * * *

I have embroidered, or at least nearly finished embroidering, a pocket handkerchief which I had intended for you, but all the girls here say that no gentleman likes to receive an embroidered pocket handkerchief. I do not know if the German gentleman and the English differ or agree in this respect, at all events the handkerchief is not quite fine or well worked enough for you. It will soon be finished now, and perhaps you would be kind enough to tell me in your next letter if you would like me to work you another similar handkerchief, or something else in another style of work?

Would you perhaps allow me to give this regular first attempt to Natalie? Though nothing very pretty I think it will give her pleasure, but Mrs Heine would be sure not to let me give it to her if I could not tell that you had given me leave to do so. I think I told you in my last letter that I am now established "for good" (as the maids say) in a little room looking onto the street on the same floor as the Heines. I rather think Dr Heine has placed me here on purpose in order that he may be better able to see, himself, if I pay proper attention to the cure. But, dearest Father, be sure that whether I am near from [sic] *Dr Heine or not, I shall pay the greatest attention to all that he recommends for your dear sake.*

It is now some days more than three months since the goodnatured girl I told you of before saw the spine. I will beg of her to look at it tonight or tomorrow, and tell you what she says at the end of this letter.

There are great alterations taking place here both in the inside and on the outside of the house. There is an entire new staircase and the whole place in fact is getting to look much smarter, so that I think you will hardly recognise when you come.

I wrote a long letter to Master Teddy the other day. I do not know when he will think fit to answer it. The bell has rung for us to repair to the labours

of the couch so, with best love to June, I must beg you to remember me as your fond and devoted child, E. Bulwer Lytton.

Dearest Father, the girl has examined the back and says that the upper part of the spine is now perfectly straight – but the alteration in the lower part is but very slight. Mrs Heine asked me the other day if I ever used pomatum [pomade - then made with all sorts of horrors, like bone marrow and hog's lard]. ***I told her that my hair did not require it in general, and that I had found that if I once used it I was forced to use it always*** [the indenture of *Head & Shoulders* familiar to all dandruff sufferers]. ***She told me to tell you that she thinks it would be a good thing, and to ask you if you would like it. I have done as she wished. Your own fond Measy***

* * * * *

Tuesday 21st May, 1844. St Leonards-on-Sea, Hastings [where, he has told us, he has recently found *Hydropathy; or The Cold Water Cure*, by Thomas Smethurst M.D., whilst browsing in the Library]. ***My dearest Emily,***

> ***"If to your share some human error fall***
> ***Look to your heart and we forget them all"***

[after Alexander Pope in *The Rape of The Lock* - Pope's lines are:

> ***"If to her share some female errors fall,***
> ***Look on her face, and you'll forget them all."]***

Such is my answer to your frank and touching confessions of relaxed attention to the cure. I know well, my poor child, how wearisome it is to be constantly alive to the bodily ailments – to occupy the mind with the cure of the frame - & it does require some mightier inducements than those of self to go through this incessant drudgery.

Instead, therefore, of talking to you of all the inestimable advantages of health & appearance, which must result from your diligent perseverance, I only entreat you to have constantly before you my pride and happiness if you succeed, & my grief and mortification if you fail. As I carefully refrain from telling anyone why you are at Cannstatt, there are not wanting those who

will insinuate that I am very unfeeling to keep my daughter in exile. What a triumphant answer you will give me if you come forth as my sanguine hopes promise me you will, with no drawback to a shape that ought to be perfect & to the frank sweet intelligence of your winning countenance.

On the other hand – if all fail – I shall be exposed for ever to misrepresentation & calumny & exclamations of "Poor thing - see how she has been neglected. No wonder, since she was taken from her Mother & left abroad among strangers." Give me my living vindication my dear child! - Let this inducement sustain your energy - I am sure it will.

Oh! the bitter irony of this passage. This is exactly the view of Edward Bulwer Lytton that - to this very day - "there are not wanting those who will insinuate."

It is not for reasons he can predict at this time. It is not her physical condition on her return from Germany that will condemn him to this - but her mental condition.

And only Miss Greene recognises this danger.

* * * * *

I confide in you – Miss Greene writes me word that she hopes to see you by your birthday [27th June] ***& leaves England early in June. I have granted leave to see you, upon the condition not to take you out in the hours devoted to the cure, the baths, gymnastics, lying down, etc., but to see you only in the hours for lessons which do not so much signify - & 2ndly not to stay above a week at Cannstatt.***

I trust you to see that these conditions, especially the first, are rigidly kept to. I have given her every caution, also, to maintain your position & not to touch upon any of the old grievances which gossip only irritates.

I hope that she will be discreet, and, in that case, I am sure you will have great delight in seeing her.

I have delayed answering your last letter till I could give a better account of myself. I left London very weak and poorly & went to Tonbridge Wells, where I fell ill - left it, & come hither – a small place by the seaside thoroughly empty & deserted, but to which I feel grateful for the effect it has produced.

I now feel better & stronger than at any time since December, & tho I have little relapses and, at times, heavy dejection, I still think that I shall, please god [sic], *get up a somewhat shattered constitution. I am now taking these cares of the body I prescribe to you – breaking old habits of late hours, etc. & striving, might & main, to be well & strong.*

I know not how long I may stay here. I hope too, my dearest Emily, to get over to Cannstatt & see you, some time in June or July, & my next letter will probably fix the time. I hope that you are now reconciled to your new room and that Natalie's society is more restored to you.

Teddy sends me 2 letters for you, but the postage would be so heavy that I will send them by Miss Greene. They contain nothing but the brief laconicisms [short simple reports] *of most juvenile correspondents. He is very well, & in excellent spirits. I fear you read the word Egypt right. But Egypt now is a very easy journey & the Nile not much more dangerous than the Rhine, barring the crocodiles. I am glad Mme de Weling wrote to you, it is well to keep up all civilities with those one leaves behind. Adieu dearest Measy. God bless you & preserve you. Most aff yrs E.B.L.*

* * * * *

Sunday 2nd June, 1844 [notepaper topped with an image of Lincoln. It is odd that Emily sends her father from Germany at picture of his former constituency, whilst at the same time cross-writing to save postage costs] ***My own dear good kind Papa, It is impossible for me to tell you the delight your dear letter gave me . Thank you a thousand times for forgiving me my faults, thank you still more for accepting and believing my heartfelt promises for future amendment...***

...I do confess that I am afraid

that I shall never become what I would call perfectly straight. Amongst the numbers which have been placed in Dr Heine's care for anything the matter with the back, it is of the rarest occurrence that one ever goes away perfectly straight. His skill with anything the matter with the feet, is perfectly wonderful. But the change in spinal complaints is extremely gradual - to me, hardly perceptible.

You must not think, dearest Papa, because I say this, that I have in any way determined or made a resolution not to believe in the good effects of any part of the cure. On the contrary, I place a sort of blind faith in all Dr Heine prescribes, but I would not have you, my darling Papa, be too sanguine for fear that you should be disappointed in anything. You may rely upon me doing all I can to further everything that can crown your wishes...

* * * * *

Saturday 8th June, 1844 - an unusually instant response. *My dear Emily, Your letter has occasioned me great anxiety and since I received it I have been employed in enquiries as to the a* [sic] *new mode of treating those curvatures – which has been apparently very successful. This mode is entirely opposed to that of Dr Heine – no gymnastics, no exercise of any kind – it consists entirely of lying down on a plane of peculiar construction – nearly all day – and this would, in a case like yours, last for nearly or quite six months. At the end of that time, most merely lateral curvature such as yours seem generally cured. But such a plan must be so extremely tiresome & irksome, & I should imagine can never benefit the general health like one with fresh air, exercise & young companions, that I am loath to adopt it - even for the sake of your being in England – if there is any sensible improvement in the shape now.*

But I think at the end of nine months there ought to be a perceptible progress. Now this is what I want, clearly & distinctly, to know & this I expect to be the benefit derived from Miss Greene's visit. I wish, my dear love, that Dr Heine should examine your back in the presence of Miss Greene – that he should drop the line with a lead attached to it, to see where the spine goes out of a straight direction - that it should be specifically clear whether one shoulder which stuck out more than the other, is better – also, whether the hip which protruded is improved.

Now I don't expect that Miss Greene, who perhaps never marked you at the worst, can tell, without Dr Heine's observations & comparisons – but I wish this examination to take place immediately, & to have a letter from you & also from Miss Greene upon it. Don't say a word to Miss G about my having seen the new mode in London, as I cannot depend on her acct if she thinks this is the best chance of your being moved to England. Her affection would lead her and I must have your statement, with all Dr Heine says.

I am the more anxious about this, as I fear my visit may be delayed a little, for I am going to try the Water Cure with great hopes of its success in restoring my constitution generally – at Malvern Wells. And this may defer my coming to Cannstatt so soon as I should wish. My anxiety therefor [as with Miss Greene's 'shew' for 'show', I retain the archaic spelling] *is much increased if there is no improvement at all. I fear there will be no resource but this most tedious one of lying down constantly, and I own facilely* [easily] *that I do not feel so confident of the surgeon who tries this remedy, in spite of his success, as I could wish.*

But if there is an improvement, & at that a marked one – my mind will be generally relieved, for I never expected much, nor did Dr Heine, till after the first 6 or 8 months. It is not the shape alone that I consider of importance. It is the health & comfort of life that I regard more, & where the spine is much curved, especially in a woman, the constitution will be sure to suffer sooner or later & the illnesses & trials peculiar to women be seriously exaggerated.

Pray then, let me have, as soon as possible, a minute & detailed account – if the shoulder & hips are more balanced & even – if the curvature which, when I saw it, described an S, remembering what I drew [see image], *is straighter etc., & tell me all about your general health.*

* * * * *

I go to Malvern on Tuesday and take Teddy with me for his holydays. You need not correspond any more with the Miss Thomsons – it is not an acquaintance I wish for you to keep up. As previously mentioned, there is likely some secret here. It may be some personal history that arch gossip Mrs Thomson has knowledge of, or involvement in. It may be some knowledge of the new romance that is about blossom with Marion Waller. Or it may, simply, be some temporary tiff over Mrs Thomson's support of, and interest in, Teddy. The cause is not clear, but the irritation makes it stand out from the letter - and intrigue.

By the way, my love, & appropos of writing – you neglect your handwriting which promised before you went to Cannstatt, to be very elegant, and which is now progressively deteriorating into a very slovenly scribble. A good hand is so Ladylike & aristocratic an accomplishment, & the reverse in a Woman is vulgar & seems always to shew a slatternly character, that I entreat you to take pains & recover your old excellence here. All that a woman does should be neat & graceful. There is charm in a handwriting crossed when it seems in harmony with the character & that it is not very easy to analyze (sic) but which I dare say you may have observed in others. I have heard it constantly observed that such a girl must be of an elegant mind from the mere sight of a handwriting & when I myself get a letter from a strange lady my feelings of respect & attraction are very much regulated by the hand.

You will smile at this from such a horrible scrawler as myself – but I don't think it signifies so much for a man & even I am very much ashamed of my performances & wish I wrote better. [You will not be surprised to hear that this is one of our Archivist (and transcriber) Clare's favourite Edward quotes.]

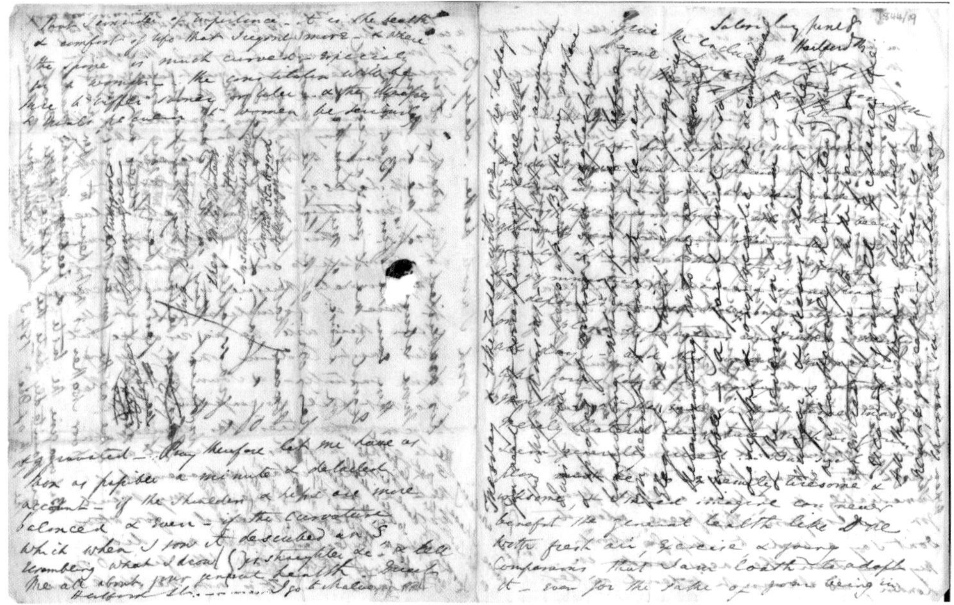

"I don't think (handwriting) signifies so much for a man"

Lady B has published her book [*Memoirs of a Muscovite,* (1844)] – *it is more abusive of me & Henry than even her first. But with regard to me, it runs a great deal on abuse of my books & person. Of the last, she humorously observes I have the face of a goat & the body of a grasshopper. That is the wittiest thing in the book. This work, beyond my mortification to see a person bearing my name degrade it so much, does not affect me as much as the former one – because my poor mother is not here to suffer from it. But imagine the taste & feeling which makes her pointedly date the preface of the book the 19th December 1843, the day my Mother died - and as all the newspapers stated the day, this could not have been accidental, but done on purpose.*

Give the enclosed to Dr Heine. Longing to hear from you. Most aff yrs E.B.L.

P.S. Since writing the above I have called on Mr Liston [Robert Liston (1794-1847)] *the celebrated surgeon* [primarily for the speed of his surgery pre-anaesthetics] *to have his opinion, and he so decidedly prefers & recommends Dr Heine's system that I am more than ever anxious to hear its results. He is very urgent that you stay at Cannstatt.*

* * * * *

Friday 14th June, 1844. *My own very dear Father. Your letter received an hour or two ago has caused me much unhappiness. To begin with the cure. I am so very sorry that I made you unhappy and uneasy in telling you my doubts and fears, particularly as the news with regard to the back, which I now have to communicate to you, are of the best nature possible.*

Dr Heine examined my back in Miss Greene's presence, as you desired, and he seemed quite pleased with my progress. The curve of the spine toward the shoulder blade which was, in the commencement, 8 lines, is now only 5, and the curve towards the hips (which Dr H desires me to tell you is now almost equal to the other) which was before 7 lines, is now 4, so there is a difference of 3 lines each way. Dr Heine says when I have done using the machines no fault will be perceptible, that the shoulders themselves are now equal, and that considering the time this cure has been hitherto, successful.

He shewed me the cast taken of the back at the commencement, and then I looked at the back in two looking glasses. The change is certainly perceptible.

When Dr Heine presses with all his might on the side that proceeds, the spine becomes straight for an instant, and the parts that come out, go, of course, in their right places again.

Miss G says the spine is much straighter now than when she saw it last, and she never saw it when it was at the worst, so it must be much improved besides. I am sure Dr H would not say what he did not think or what was not the case. He says himself that it is going on better than he had at first hoped for.

I cannot tell you how vexed I am to have caused you uneasiness, but my fears were confirmed by Dr H never telling me what he thought about my improvement. Of course I told no one about your seeing the new mode in London; my fears for the success of the cure are now banished.

* * * * *

I observe Miss G wishes much that I should soon leave, but when she speaks to me on this subject I tell her that my stay depends on your wishes, and your wishes will be regulated as to the cure. I think dearest Father I may safely tell you to set your mind at ease now that I know Dr Heine's opinion, only forgive me for disturbing you…

I hope sincerely that you may derive all benefit from the Water Cure. There was a lady at Neuweid who tried it, and from being the most delicate she became the strongest of persons. I trust it may be the same with you, and that when I see you again you may be strong and well.

Forgive me for writing so badly to you. I shall take the greatest pains in future.

My feelings are indescribable on this new attack [by Rosina]. [Inserted, in a different hand - presumably Edward's - *Oh! when is this to cease?*] *I hate and abhor myself for being the child of such a wretch. It is kind to look upon it as the effects of madness, but I cannot look upon it in that favourable light. One shudders at the bare name of murder, but is not this worse than murder? Is it not a perpetual constant frightful massacre? a living murder! One day your indescribable wrongs shall, and will, be avenged; a day is coming when the cruellest wrongs and blackest injuries will be remembered by God and revenged by* [torn]--- . *Your words, as I read them, served to freeze my blood*

and turn it to cold ice, and then it all [torn]--- ***to rush warm and vivid to my heart to make it beat still higher and still more ardently with adoration, on the one side and on the other – the deepest hatred. As people feel towards you, I feel towards them, judge then of my feelings.***

No, all this is never to be forgotten, but that most dreadful outrage to the commonest feeling which every human being (to say nothing of woman) is supposed to possess, will only serve to show the world the better, from what a hand this new assault has come.

This unhinged - almost Lady Macbeth - response goes a good way to supporting Miss Greene's concerns about Emily's mental state, and possibly the effects of the narcotics at her bedside - but, of course, it is one subject on which Edward is unlikely to recognise immoderation. He does, however, later censure her for it.

We should remember it as a useful marker of Emily's evolving feelings about her mother, which we will need to understand at the end of this story.

* * * * *

Miss G is most prudent and discreet, much more than I confess I first thought she would have been. It hurts and wounds me to hear her now and then insinuate that I have ceased to love her.

I cannot tell you how I envy Teddy. I do so long to see you and tell you all I have got to say to you and more.

I am glad you are going to try the Water Cure. I have heard much of it, but from my heart I pity you my dearest Papa for having to use so disagreeable a remedy. How long do you think you will be under it? Pray do write and tell me what effects it produces on you, and how you think it agrees with you. I only hope your constitution may not be too delicate to bear it.

My general health, dearest Papa, is, thank you, very good. What you say about the handwriting is very true. I have been neglecting mine shockingly lately, but will take pains with it for the future. [She is repeating herself, but I leave it in as, perhaps, evidence of Miss Greene's claim of her over-excited manner at this time.] ***Nothing is so ladylike, as you say, as a nice Hand, and pretty words embodied in pretty characters is like hearing a pretty person speak. In a man, however, I must say I think what is called 'a pretty Hand' is***

generally the sign of a weak character.

I forgot to tell you that I delivered your letter to Dr Heine and he returns his thanks and compliments, and will answer it soon but his "monstreuses occupations" must again plead his excuse for not doing so just now. Dr Heine says the cure will be much quicker and more perceptible now, as in the beginning it always goes slowly – and, with me, he had to wait some little time before he could impose the cure as rigorously as he does in general with others, because he says had he done so at first with me, it would have weakened instead of strengthened. He says also that it is a good thing the spine is as yet so flexible, as it renders the cure easier.

Thanks for Teddy's letters; Miss Greene desires me to enclose this note for you. When do you think I may expect you? How long does the water cure last before you begin to feel its effects? Did the air of St Leonards cease to agree with you? Miss G brought me the 3 little books which you had when a child. I shall take the greatest care of them till I am able to restore them to their rightful owner. Their titles are – "The [Moving] Adventures of old Dame Trot and her Comical Cat" [1807] ***"The Queen of Hearts"*** [presumably *The King And Queen Of Hearts: With The Rogueries Of The Knave Who Stole The Queen's Pies* 1805, by Charles Lamb]. ***and the amusing little book of the Conjurer and the Ring*** [The first two are juvenile picture books, but my best guess for this one is that it is an English version of Schiller's *Die Geisterseher* (*The Ghost-seer)* 1789].

I will not detain this letter longer so only beg you ever to think of me as your fond and devoted child, Emily Bulwer Lytton

P.S. Love to Teddy & June. I was again much annoyed by questions from the Polish countess with regard to Lady B. A countess professing to live in the world, as she does, cannot be supposed to be ignorant of the answers to her enquiries which were – if Lady B lived in Town, or Country; if I ever saw her, and the like. I suppose she is offended at my never having called upon her and wished to insult. My behaviour was, with all due respect to her rank and age, as you directed. No one heard what she said.

* * * * *

Thursday 13th June, 1844. Hotel Canstadt. Dear Sir Edward, writes Miss

Greene, *I arrived here on Tuesday 11th & drove immediately to see Emily. She seems in excellent health and her shape certainly improved, even from when I saw it - & I understand it was much worse when you took her from Mrs de Weling's. Dr Heine examined her back in my presence this day, in the same manner as Dr Cannon did at Cheltenham some years ago. He made me press my fingers down her spine, & I can truly say it is more straight than it was when I did the same thing with Dr Cannon.*

Poor Emily is much disappointed at not seeing you so soon as she expected but the hope that your visit is only just off, will [cheer] her up, and I hope a few months more steady attention to the cure will be enough & that you will then have the pleasure of taking her back to England.

I have adhered to 'my Bond' & propose leaving this [place] on Wednesday morning for Heidleberg if I hear that my brother has arrived there; if not I shall go to Stuttgart & remain with some friends of mine, with whom I travelled from England, till I hear he is there, & then go and meet him.

I like what little I have seen of both Dr & Mrs Heine very much – Emily is writing all the particulars of his opinion which she can describe, & she does this better than I do. Yours sincerely, M.L.Greene

* * * * *

As we have already heard from Miss Greene's account, when she gets back to England she switches this positive review to fears about Emily's state of mind. It is of note that none of the correspondence mentions laudanum. If Emily is taking laudanum at the Institute, it must be with Dr Heine's sanction and not thought unusual. Toothache appears the reason for its prescription. It is possible that Miss Greene knows that Edward takes it, and would not consider it unusual - although his new health regime eschews alcohol.

Miss Greene's letters go on to stress Emily's worries about her father's health, and I think it is right to assess that Emily's constant mention of it in letters is not simply courtesy, but that there is indeed - as Miss Greene fears - a paranoia of what would happen to her - now her Grandmother is dead - if her father was to die also. The concern, presumably, is that she would be back in the hands of her mother.

Dear Sir Edward, writes Miss Greene once back in England, ***I am very***

sorry indeed to find you are not well enough to come to town to speak with me – as it would be impossible for me, by letter, to convey to you my exact feeling about Emily, & equally impossible should I go to you [where Teddy now is]. ***I can, for comfort, confirm all I said of the improvement of her shape & bodily health, & that I am sure there is every cause to depend upon Dr & Mrs Heine's skill and conscientious care. I hope when you are well enough to be able to come to town, it will be time enough for me to have a conversation with you – but in the meantime excuse me for recommending you, when you write to Emily to make as light as possible of your illness & abstain from all subjects which may excite her – nor say you had this note from me.***

I made it a point to be calm and cheerful whilst with her, & assure you that even at our last meeting and parting, she was quite composed, and I have had two affectionate & pretty notes from her since. Yours faithfully, M.L.Greene

* * * * *

The 17th Lancers are back in Hounslow Barracks for a year in May 1844, so a letter written alongside this one, to Teddy, is addressed from the Wilkinson's current home, Belle Vue, Hounslow. Written across the top is ***When you write to Emily do not mention your Pap's illness.***

My dearest Teddy, I am sure you will be glad to hear from me that I spent an entire week with your dear sister. She is grown very tall & large & plays the piano beautifully - you would think it was 'Woodwards finger' that was flying up & down the instrument [the root of this in-joke is not clear, but may be an Irish expression after the Dublin-based baroque composer Richard Woodward (c.1743–1777)]. ***She also sings well & speaks German. She made many enquiries about you, some of which I regret to say I could not well answer, it is so long since I saw you.***

I took her several little presents which I thought she might like, amongst them a Dormouse, which arrived quite well, but so gay & lively, that he stole away the second night of his residence in his new abode in the little cage you may remember she had, & never was found afterwards.

I hope you will not be angry with me for one thing I took as a loan from you – your writing desk. She has also her own - one, which your Papa gave

her - but she has now so many letters & papers she requires a larger one & promises to take great care of it & return it to you directly she returns to England.

I hope you may be as happy with your Papa as she was when with him. She told me she never was so happy in all her life. I hope you will write her a nice long affectionate letter during your holidays. I also hope you will answer this letter soon & pray give me timely notice when you may be in Town, as I will be sure to go & see you. All your friends here desire their love, & believe me dear Teddy to remain as ever your affectionate, M.L.Greene

* * * * *

Monday 24th June, 1844. *My dearest Emily, Your account of yourself, corroborated by Miss Greene's, gives me the greatest happiness. I am indeed more delighted than I can express that you have made real & visible progress under a system, too, which must brace your general frame & - I hope & pray - ensure to you the best possible blessing of health. In fact, anxious as I am that the curvature should in no way detract from your appearance, I have felt still more anxious that it should be cured for the sake of your future health, comfort and happiness. It would be but poor comfort to me to think that by dress and management the defect might be made imperceptible, if it existed to any degree which, as you grew older, would affect your health, and embitter existence - as, unless checked & removed, it wd certainly have done.*

How thankful I ought to be that I noticed the defect so soon at Neuweid, & that Providence, whose agency in all that happens to us of good, it is so exquisite a happiness to recognize, led us to the right place for a remedy. Your account consoles me for my continued absence from you, & when I received it yesterday, gave me better spirits than I have known for a long time - or that I should have thought possible when I woke in the morning.

I wonder if you are wincing, as Miss Greene would, at this self-absolution and self-congratuation? We must remember that Edward is, at this time, in therapy himself - physical therapy, but the nearest equivalent of its time to psychological therapy.

And this new-found positivity, I am relieved to report, brings on a healthy fatherly response to his daughter's fantasies of her mother's murder. *And now, my dearest child, before I turn to answer your affectionate enquiries about myself - I must pause to blame us both, but myself most. While I feel deeply and gratefully your soothing affection to me & the burst of feeling occasioned by the new outrage offered to me & mine, from a quarter which ought least to conceive it; & while I cannot pretend not to wish & hope that in the severe choice between two parents, you may ever retain - & with justice - the decided preference for the one who longs to be to you both father & mother - I yet approach myself, with remorse, for indiscreet allusions & references which have led you into wrong thoughts, & expressions you may regret.*

No, my dearest Emily, never let the word or the thought of hatred to a tie so near escape you – never dream that I require, or that you should wish for me the terrible expiation of revenge. Justice I have prayed for – but where it comes best & ______[indecipherable] *to me is in the hearts of my children – in their love for me & trust in me.*

No revenge of any kind or degree would become me or my children. Kneel to God, who knows that all of us, even the best & holiest, have too many sins to permit us to be unmerciful to others. Kneel to God, I implore you, for pardon for the words and thoughts that escaped you in writing to me. Kneel to Him whenever these thoughts tempt you again – they are thoroughly & directly sinful. And the sin rests with me, if I induce or encourage them------------[sic] *it is eno' punishment to have forfeited the right to the natural love & respect of a heart like yours. And so let the curtain fall.*

The religious context of Edward's admonishment is surprising - from what Miss Greene tells us of Edward and Rosina's lack of godliness - but maybe reflects the aftermath of his mother's death. He sees his responsibility, at this moment, to take over as squire of her parish - this will fade when he finds a new girlfriend. But more relevant, perhaps, is firstly, the fact that he has been dealing with the trauma of her death, and secondly, her influence as a religious woman, and, the fact that she is his current deity... alongside water.

* * * * *

I have been rather more than a week under this treatment. I was prepared to feel worse at the first, under so startling a system, & at present can give no very satisfactory acct of myself. But my faith in the cure is confirmed by all I see &, what seems at first glance most dangerous – wet or lying in wet sheets, plunging the feet in cold water etc. - is really quite innocent & less disagreeable, after a little time, than could be supposed. My hope is to brace & strengthen the constitution so as to fit me for a hardy country life & to take pleasure in its active practical duties, and this result I yet hope to obtain.

But I fear it will be at least 6 weeks before I could leave this place with safety, for when the Water Cure is once commenced, it is dangerous to suspend it. Nothing but water cures the symptoms water produces. I am however greatly better, on the whole, than I was some months ago, & there is nothing now - as far as I can see - to occasion the least apprehension for me.

I am glad you agree with me about the elegance of good handwriting........

I do not quite understand what you mean by "it hurts & wounds me to hear Miss G now & then insinuate as [sic] *I have ceased to love her." Do you mean merely that she reproaches you with having ceased to love her – or that she hurts you so that you cease to love her? I hope the former – for she certainly has for you so true & devoted an affection that I should be very grieved if it ever failed of a due return.*

If the former – that is, if she accuses you of indifference, etc., you must attribute it to the jealous nature common to many affections, & forbear with it. And to the same cause must be ascribed any hints or remarks about myself, if she use them - which really arise chiefly or only, I am sure, from her wish to stand first in your affections. The love of the older party for the younger is often very exacting & jealous, & the younger does not often comprehend it. When I was a child, my dear Mother's feelings to me were of this kind, & I sigh now to think how little I understood them, & often felt teased & wounded by what in reality was the painful excess of love, & the fear that it was not sufficiently returned. Alas, the Young are often hard to the Mature.

* * * * *

Teddy must be dull here but he contrives to amuse himself. He has ridden out on a nice little pony once or twice, & begins to get familiar with the saddle. We anticipate pleasant rides with you, by & by, among the green lanes of Hertfordshire. He is very much improved in drawing & is now employed on a very pretty sketch from Nature. He is much stronger & healthier, tho' still

Malvern

delicate & the tonsils still enlarged.

Here the life is exactly like a school – we are under strict restraint, the accommodations are rather comfortless, & there is a queer set of people. One is roused at ½ past 5 for the wet sheet, & the food is thoroughly scholastic - roast mutton & rice pudding. I hope about the 3rd week to be much improved & will then report progress – meanwhile direct Hertford St - I shall leave the rest of the crossing [of handwriting on the page] *to Master Edward. Adieu my dearest love, God bless you, your most aff. Father E.B.L.*

* * * * *

Dearest Emily, I have been waiting to write to you till Papa heard from Aunt Mary about you. I am so glad to hear that your health continues good and that you are getting on so well in everything. Papa says perhaps next spring you may come home – that will be delightful. Do you know that I am come home for the holidays and am staying at Malvern with dear Papa – it is a very pretty place and there is a splendid view from the hills. I ride out

with dearest Papa sometimes on a little pony. It is capital fun here & just like coming to school. We all dine together and take milk & water for tea - as we are new boys we are allowed tea. Dearest Papa is, I think, getting better and I feel sure that he will soon get quite well and strong. We get on very well, and I pass my time very happily. But as the Latin proverb says "Nulla dies, sine lenea" [Not a day without a line drawn. Emily has been teasing Teddy, in her letters, with challenging Latin and Greek phrases, as though she has become very learned]. ***There are three Americans here, but they are very vulgar & I can only say, with Virgil, 'habcat sterquilinium'*** [produce manure] - ***at any rate they certainly do not add to our society. And now, my dear sister, believe me to remain your aff brother, E.R.Lytton***

Dr Wilson's Water Cure establishment at Malvern in the 1840s... and as it looks in 2016

Illustration from Emily's German edition of ***The Last Days of Pompeii*** *(1833)*

CHAPTER 25

~ *Cannstatt Letters - Bitter Sixteen* ~

"Alas!" said Julia... "does not sorrow fly to wisdom for relief, and they who love unrequitedly, are not they the chosen victims of grief?"

"Ha!" said Arbaces, "can unrequited love be the lot of so fair a form, whose modelled proportions are visible even beneath the folds of thy graceful robe? Deign, O maiden! to lift thy veil, that I may see at least if the face correspond in loveliness with the form."

Not unwilling, perhaps, to exhibit her charms, and thinking they were likely to interest the magician in her fate, Julia, after some slight hesitation, raised her veil, and revealed a beauty which, but for art, had been indeed attractive to the fixed gaze of the Egyptian.

"Thou comest to me for advice in unhappy love," said he; "well, turn that face on the ungrateful one: what other love-charm can I give thee?"

"Oh, cease these courtesies!" said Julia; "it is a love-charm, indeed, that I would ask from thy skill!"

"Fair stranger!" replied Arbaces, somewhat scornfully, "love-spells are not among the secrets I have wasted the midnight oil to attain."

"Is it indeed so? Then pardon me, great Arbaces, and farewell!"

from *The Last Days of Pompeii* (1833) by Edward Bulwer Lytton

* * * * *

On Thursday 27th June 1844, Emily turns 16. If she is attending a traditional English boarding school, she is at the end of the school year, comtemplating a long summer holiday with her family. She had one the year before. But not this year. This summer, Miss Greene has followed her father's strict instructions and remained in Cannstatt only seven days, and her father's promised visit looks increasingly doubtful due the restraints of his health and the Water Cure.

Emily has borne home sickness - though not having a home - for her far-away family. She has borne bereavement - though her pain is more for her father's loss than for her Grandmother, who she barely knew. She has borne the strifes of school life - though her displaced upbringing must have given her a better preparation for this than the majority of her contemporaries. And she has borne the cure - though endless days spent lying down and reading, however uncomfortable and physically unpleasant, are not too unnatural a sentence for a shy, dreamy teenager like Emily.

For all its trials, Emily's first year at Dr Heine's burgeoningly successful institute has not been the gothic nightmare that Lytton family legend has painted it. And in the relative terms of biographical pigeon-holing, Emily has not been 'unhappy'.

Around the time of her sixteenth birthday, this changes. Perhaps we should not be surprised. Most teenagers pass through a phase of hormonal melancholy and angst, and this will always be exacerbated by loneliness and the absence of physical family nurture. Don't the teenage children of all celebrity parents flirt with sex, drugs and rock & roll, and usually fall foul of one of the three? Emily is on a well-trodden primrose path dalliancing in the tempations of romantic love and stimulants.

* * * * *

The unhappiness that dominates the last three of the seven chapters of Emily's letters from Cannstatt is, on the surface, the result of lovesickness. The technical term - if you are inspired to look it up - is limerence. Miss Greene was once accused of it by her own family, over a young Rosina. A passing phase, therefore? In Emily, it takes a deeper root and has darker long-term consequences.

Why? Miss Greene blames, at this time, the dangerous opiates Emily is taking for her toothache, and, in the long term, having, too long, been separated from the good influence and nurturing of her 'family'. I agree with Miss Greene. It's sex and drugs. But, before we continue, let's just touch on rock & roll.

One of the greatest treasures, for me, found in Box 88, is Emily's piano book - a green, leather-bound book of handwritten piano pieces, embossed in gold lettering on the cover, Deutsche Gesänge [German Songs]. These are the exact pieces that Emily sat in her 'first class' room, playing on her expensive upright piano. Having this today is like having the contents of Emily's iPod.

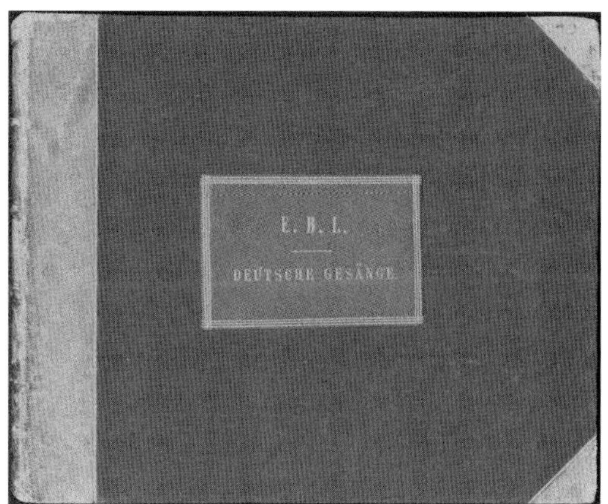

Emily's piano book

Abschied *- words by E. Schulze*

In summer 2015, I spend a mind-bending day in a sunny upper room in Barnes, London, listening to Emily in that sunny upper room in Cannstatt, Stuttgart, via the wizardry of my lovely "Woodward-finger"-ed (whatever that means) friend, Paul Smith. I listen to the entire contents of Emily's piano book, and immediately all my great-great-great-aunt's letters are thrown into three dimensions.

There are, of course, some straightforward 'practice' pieces - but amongst this collection of, now mostly very obscure, airs, are some really lovely romantic tunes. I am particularly struck by *Abschied* [Farewell], which is credited to the romantic poet Ernst Schulze (1789-1817), who died of tuberculosis at 28, having lost the love of his life when she was 18, also to tuberculosis. Wikipedia quotes from Schulze's letters and diaries published in 1855, ***I lived in a fantasy world and was on the way to becoming a complete obsessive.*** Emily's kind of guy.

Ernst Schulze

A number of Schulze's poems were set to music by Franz Schubert (1797–1828), but it is not clear to me whether this piece is Schubert - Emily doesn't take the time to mention it. Nor does she mention who wrote *Das Jagers Haus* [The Hunter's House] - a song about a beautiful daughter - but she does say ***as sung by Herr Pischek***. Herr Pischek was the pop star heartthrob of his day to Stuttgart girls, and it is very likely that Emily was taken to see him sing by the Parsons. If our emo teenager was allowed bedroom pin-ups - alongside her father - they would have been of Ernst Schulze and Herr Pischek.

Courtesy of the Institut für Neuere deutsche Literatur und Medien der Christian-Albrechts-Universität zu Kiel

Herr Pischek

I wish I could give you these songs as a soundtrack to Emily's letters, particularly the ones you are about to read - but I trust you to summon them up in your imagination, alongside an image of a mousy, acne-troubled, body-odoured and blood-leaking sixteen-year-old, shut away in an upper room of a far-off German clinic in the hot summer of 1844.

* * * * *

Saturday 29th June, 1844 - two days after her sixteenth birthday. The Saturday writing date - as opposed to Sunday - is indicative of impatience of thought. ***My own very dearest Papa, It makes me very sad to think how little agreeable this letter is doomed to be, but I shall be very glad when I have told you all that it is intended to contain. There is one thing which I have long wished to tell you, and have always put off doing so, thinking to see you soon. But now for some days past I have been, though not really ill, still very poorly and low, and subject to a constant bleeding at the nose, which tho' certainly a very unpoetical complaint to name, causes great debility - and since I have been so, it has pained me to think that I have never told you something which has long made me unhappy, and which I think is partly, if not wholly, the cause of my present complaint.***

I have long observed that Mrs Heine never liked Natalie and me being together, and some time ago she called Natalie to her and told her that she did

not wish her to be much with me because as I was 18 (!!!) and Natalie only 12. I had naturally read more than a child of 12 years, and therefore she thought it would be much better were Natalie to keep with the little girls, and were I to keep with the grown up girls.

Poor little Natalie said nothing [at that moment], however she told me that evening what Mrs Heine had said to her in the morning. I was rather at a loss to find out what objection Mrs Heine could have to my having read more than Natalie, but I was not long allowed to remain in doubt - as Mrs H came soon afterwards to me and told me to make a friend of one of the grown up girls and not of Natalie, because I had read many novels and she rather suspected that I was always talking to Natalie about Novels.

The light then broke in upon me [she has been reading too many novels], *I then saw clearer than ever, the imprudence (to say nothing more) of that first foolish step at the commencement, of which I told you long ago. I then saw how useless all our best after-efforts are, if - by thoughtlessness and imprudence - our first step has been wrong.*

It was however a comfort to feel how innocent I was in this instance of the charge Mrs H laid against me. I could not speak one word, nor did I attempt to justify myself – from that day I have never been thoroughly well, and yesterday I was forced to keep my bed all day.

Frontispiece of an 1840 English edition of Edward's **Ernest Maltravers** *(1837)*

* * * * *

Dr Heine does not allow me to do anything for the cure, or in the way of lessons. He says I must be kept very quiet, and attributes this constant bleeding to the shock occasioned by having a large back tooth drawn the other day. Others say it comes from singing. But, I confess, what Mrs Heine said, has made me very very unhappy, and I am sure it comes from nothing else but that.

Mrs H visited me yesterday and, because Natalie had been there a short time before to see me, she again told me how great would be her pleasure if I were not to be so much with Natalie. I thought this a good opportunity of telling Mrs Heine what was in my heart, and therefore made bold (as Teddy used to say) to begin. In the course of our conversation I entreated her to believe me, that since that unlucky day long ago, I had never spoken one word on any subject to Natalie which Mrs Heine would not have approved.

It cost me a great deal before I could force myself to say all this to Mrs Heine, for she is not the sort of person to whom one can easily open one's heart; however when I had finished speaking, she seemed not quite so disbelieving and, after a pause and some hesitation on her part, she frankly told me that since I had removed that obstacle to our intercourse - by assuring her that her fears were groundless - she found that she had only one objection remaining. This, however, was an obvious one, and [one] which I could not remove, viz: the difference of age! She further added that I could be kind to Natalie when all the girls were together, but that she did not wish me to show her particular attention in any way. [She said] that if I chose an older girl for my friend, she would have nothing against the friendship - that she did not wish me not to love, she only (!!) wished me not to love Natalie. She then went.

Emily's stray doodles...

...in her set of her father's novels all feature Natalie

Perhaps, dearest Father, I was wrong, but I confess I felt it a little hard, that for the sake of 3 [and a half, strictly speaking] *unlucky years, Mrs Heine should feel such a dislike to my being with Natalie. Though Natalie is a child in years, yet she is not so either in heart, sentiment or understanding; and how often in looking at her with admiration, I have hoped that you would not have disapproved my choice. I cannot help loving her better than any girl I have ever known.*

* * * * *

And now, my dearest Father, I feel indescribably happier since I have told you this. Pray forgive if I have bored you with it, but my only excuse is this – you are the only to whom I can tell my feelings in regard to Natalie. I never even mentioned Natalie's name to dear Miss Greene – not that I wish to make any mystery of it – but have you never felt that there are feelings and sentiments which one can only disclose to one?

Are the disagreeables never to end? But this letter is fated to be disagreeable.....I hardly know how to tell you.....On the receipt of the £20, I was very much in debt. Mrs Heine had laid out a good sum of money for mourning and things at Christmas (which by the bye I asked her not to do), and after having paid her for all these things, I had a great many dress makers bills..... so that in two months the £20 was much diminished... I will not suffer you to listen to all the detailed excuses of what has been necessary since, but they include: Summer mourning, a 'best' dress, a summer shawl for a concert in town *to which (Dr Heine) would like us all to go - this was looked upon, of course, more as a command than anything else...*

You will say I have been heedless and wasteful and extravagant - and you will not say the half of I say of myself - yet if you like I will send you my accounts. I do not think you will find anything in them I was either not positively obliged to buy or which Mrs Heine did not deem as necessary, except.....one bottle of Eau de Cologne – a luxury I should certainly never have indulged in had it not been that the Parsons used to take me to the Opera during the winter.

I know, however I reproach myself most dreadfully – so large a sum spent in so short a time.....it seems to say little for my economy that at the end of some months I have spent the whole of such a sum. However some of my expenses have been very great, and others - tho' in themselves comparatively trifling - always recur.

* * * * *

Dearest Father I cannot tell you how much pain it has cost me to write this letter, but the struggle is almost over now. You must forgive me for writing so untidyly and take the will for the deed as my hand trembles so I can hardly hold the pen.

One disagreeable remains still to be told, however I do not feel quite equal to the recital of it now and will therefore wait till you come, and when I shall be able to talk to you, my own dearest Papa.

How does the Water Cure go? Pray do tell me about your general health, above all about the evergreen catarrh and that naughty feeling at the heart. Poor little Natalie is subject to it too. Have the children – June, Teddy, and the Pipe accompanied you to Malvern? My fond love to all; and tell Teddy from me, that I hope he pays all due attention to the genial flame of the holy emotion. I am embroidering something for you……

Poor Miss Greene, not being able to find her brother, has returned to England. Luckily I had headaches the whole time she was here, so I could only use the cure in lying down, during which time she was allowed by Dr Heine to remain with me. I spent somewhat a triste [sad] *birthday in bed...*

* * * * *

After receiving his letter, she writes again the following day, Sunday 30th June, 1844. *How could I have been so extremely stupid and dull as to have written-"it hurts and wounds me to hear Miss G now and then insinuate* <u>*as*</u> *I have ceased to love her" - when what I intended to have written was "*<u>*that*</u> *I have ceased to love her", and as I did not reread the letter I was quite unaware of the mistake. Ah! no, dearest father could you for a moment suppose me for a moment ungrateful to one who has done so much for me and who loves me with such a devoted affection. It only saddened me sometimes to hear her sometimes insinuate that, if I loved her, I would persuade you to remove me to England soon - and when I pleaded your wish, she seemed hurt at her wish not being in as high consideration as yours.*

And I could not bear saying anything about my own health, etc.

It looked so selfish. However, of course, I never shewed her that this wounded me.

* * * * *

In my letter of yesterday how I longed to tell you my feeling on that point [her bitter vengeful comments about her mother] – ***but was, I own, afraid and ashamed to begin. Since that letter containing that sin has been posted, I have not known what it was to have one fanciful moment - and at night when I could not sleep, those dreadful dreadful words have, as it were, ranged themselves around my bed with their spectral faces and firey eyes till the rankling remembrances of the wild burning expressions of the bad passions of a black heart have paled away before the chilly cold hand of the most thrilling remorse!*** Here we have talk that shows ill influence from somewhere, and somewhere beyond 'novels'. Maybe it is bad company, peer pressure, some schoolgirl hysteria reminiscent of Arthur Miller's *The Crucible?* To me, it backs up Miss Greene's suspicions of the ill effect of medicinal narcotics. Above all, it illustrates a deep unhappiness that should concern any father.

Know you, that the earnest prayer with which I have besought a God of Mercy and Love to pardon me for the sake of Him who died for sinners such as I am. Oh! I am so wicked myself, I have such a bad bad heart! How could I speak in that way of any one, particularly one for whom I prayed every night and morning in the innocent prayers of childhood - of one who, whatever are her faults, is still my mother. Do you think God will forgive me? Oh! pray for me, dear Father, for you are good and I am very wicked. When I wrote that letter I was very excited. My separation from Natalie had cut me to the heart; it pained me to hear Miss G. talk so; I was far from well myself and this last outrage quite unstrung me, I hardly knew what I said, but since that moment I have been wretched.

I cried very much after reading your dear letter, you are so good and I so often so contrary to you with my bad wicked heart. And yet you are so patient with me. I love you very, very much. You are so kind to me and you never disbelieve me, and all here seem to disbelieve me except my Natalie. Oh! the morning after writing those words when I saw Natalie's gentle face, I felt how different her heart is to mine, and it made me very sad. When I am dying, those spectral words will rise up against me and – (o! horror!) they will mar the quiet of the peaceful grave. Oh! say God will forgive me, oh! say you will forget my dreadful sin, say o! say that hereafter the thought of my sin will not be connected in your mind with the thought of me - do, do say that you will not remember those terrible words, I did not mean them, indeed I did not. I have a very sad and a very heavy heart, but if you promise to forget and tell

me that God will forgive, I shall feel indescribably happier – Oh write soon my dearest Father.

* * * * *

Thank you very much for remembering little Natalie I feel very grateful to you for it. She is thank God quite well again and looking forward with delight to tomorrow as her Mama is coming to stay here some time.

You need not be uneasy about this bleeding as Dr Heine says it is not in the least dangerous – and I am much better today and hope to be able to begin the cure soon again. It is attended by wearing face ache. I have had one tooth extracted for it, but it has done no good. Every 3 hours I am obliged to take a cooling draught which has I think been of service. Is this a mention of laudanum? If it is, it is swiftly couched.

My poor Papa! How I pity you being obliged to use the Water Cure – for however stoically you may undergo it, I cannot help thinking it must be very disagreeable to have to take such a dewy repose on wet sheets – and your qualification of 'scholastic' to your life and diet, is not (at least in my opinion) a very great attraction.

The Knave of Hearts

When Kings and Queens a riding go,
Great Lords ride with them for a ſhow
With grooms & courtiers, a great ſtore;
Some ride behind, & ſome before.
Pambo the firſt of theſe does paſs,
And for more ſtate rides on an Aſs.

Pambo Knave of Hearts in Charles Lamb's King and Queen of Hearts (1805)

I envy dear little Ted very much, I am quite sure he never can be dull with you. So, he is promoted to a pony. Do you remember the day we all went out to ride together, and he went before like the valiant Pambo, Knave of Hearts, on an ass?... send my love to Teddy. I must beg you to have the kindness to tell me, in your next, some Latin phrases with their meanings, that I can tell him in my next letter. And now my dearest Father I must really at length bid you good-night and leave you to the 'Baling' [as in hay baling, or bundling] *on your cold damp sheets. I only wish I could endure the Water cure for you, and you could reap the benefits. Longing to receive a letter from you I*

must beg you to believe fondly gratefully and devotedly yours, E.B.L.

* * * * *

A note from Teddy in Malvern, dated Sunday 7th July 1844, is enclosed in her father's next. For all the distance between these long-separated siblings - in their respective clinics - it is a thing of wonder that, in 1844, a letter can travel from Cannstatt, on the riverbanks of Württemberg, to Malvern, in the Worcestershire hills, in a matter of days. ***Dearest Emily, I am delighted to hear from Aunt Mary that you are well, and that you play so beautifully on the Pianoforte. I hope that you were amused with the dormouse which Aunt Mary gave you – It certainly was very ungallant to leave so fair a mistress, but I suppose that it was a lover of freedom and preferred the German woods to your cage. I am become a great fisherman since I last wrote to you, and am quite an amateur of the 'gentle art'. There are some very pretty views here***

The view from Malvern in the Worcestershire hills in 2016

and I am very fond of copying them. Dear Papa has given me a beautiful sketch book which I shall always keep for his sake. There have been several departures here – I cannot say I felt very much inclined to go into mourning for them. I hope the New Boys won't be much worse. It has been raining cats & dogs all the morning and I am afraid it will continue and the patients will be more confined to the house.

Battledore and shuttlecock [a forerunner of badminton] ***have become all the fashion here. I am trying to get into the way of it, but I am afraid that success is hopeless. Since I began this letter, Papa has had one from you and tells me that you have been indisposed lately. I sincerely hope that you will***

soon recover, my dear sister, and you will be able to go on with the cure. I hope that the desk is convenient to you and that you like it and are able to keep all your papers in it. Pray keep it, dearest sister, as a small present from your aff. Brother, R.L.B.

* * * * *

My dearest dearest love, I am truly grieved that you have suffered in spirits from your separation from Natalie & fully sympathise with you – I can well understand how it has affected your spirits. At the same time, at all these places, it is common for the governess to interdict any strongly marked affection between girls, especially of different ages & sometimes very properly. I cannot but think, however, in your case, my Emily, there has been more than necessary rigour & I have been considering all the morning how best to help you.

I enclose a note for Madame Heine, which I hope may have the effect – you may read it, & if you like to give it, wafer it & be sure the wafer is dry before you give it. I have permitted myself the white lie, which I hope I may be pardoned, of saying I had not informed you of its contents. You will see also that I have put the matter somewhat different from what it really is, and placed it somewhat on her displeasure. This seemed to me judicious, as it prevents something of the jealousy governesses often have - moreover the appearance of too great an affection for Natalie will seem morbid & almost justify an attempt to check it.

The matter is really very difficult to manage for you & I have written what, at a distance, seemed most likely to attain your object - at the same time, you being on the spot, may be better than myself to judge if it be desirable to give it; if not write me a copy of what you would like me to write. At all events, before or when you give it, or perhaps better, just after, I advise you to go to Stuttgart & buy Mrs Heine & the sister whom you offended some little present – little but still handsome – a ____[indecipherable] *or a trinket – that conciliates. By this post, I order my Banker, to pay into your acct at Stuttgart (the same place as before) £20 – you had better not say any thing about this, but keep it there & draw out what you want – as it may be a day or two after receiving this before you find it & you may be impatient to make these pre-*

sents, you can borrow some florins from Madame Heine.

I wish, my dearest love, that the one annoyance about Natalie I may be as easy able to settle as the other about the money. You need not reproach yourself for want of economy, considering that you pay much to Madame Heine & have had mourning to buy, etc. – I think you have done very well. Mrs Heine is quite right in making you have a better dress – you ought to have all fitting your rank in life & at your age dress is a necessary as well an innocent pleasure.

At the same time, now that you are out of debt & pretty well set up, this £20 should last you, I hope, till you leave - & carry you well thro' the winter. Only received yours today & do not lose a post in setting your mind at ease as far as I can. Pray tell me the result & pray tell me also the other 'disagreeable' which I am very anxious to know. I do not apprehend much from the bleeding of the nose & it may be a relief of nature, but I am anxious to learn how it goes on. I am delighted to find you confide in me so trustfully, my dear child. Do so now & ever! Long letters are forbidden by the watercure [now its own word in Edward's vocabulary, although he later reverts to 'Water Cure'] ***so you must excuse note, E.B.L.***

* * * * *

Wednesday 17th July, 1844. *My own dearest kindest Papa, Your letter received this morning gave me the most inexpressible delight, how extremely kind of you, my dearest Papa, to take so much interest in my love for dear little Natalie. The letter for Madame Heine which you were good enough to allow me to read, is just right, and certainly calculated to obtain the desired object; if matters stood as badly as they did when I wrote last, I should have looked upon this letter as the most potent agent and have carried it to Madame Heine with the greatest delight, but you must know the present circumstances.*

Some days after I wrote last to you, the Countess Ritter di Zahony (Natalie's Mama) arrived and, as she took part of a large house just vis à vis to the institution, Natalie was with her mother every instant which was not devoted to the cure. One evening shortly after this arrival, Natalie came to me to tell me that she had acquainted her Mama of Madame Heine's dislike to our intercourse and asked her Mother's advice on the matter. The Countess di Zahony was kind enough to say that she beg of me to come over with Natalie now and then, at such remnants of time which were nor devoted to the cure or other employments, and that she would endeavour to show Madame Heine, as far as she could, that she wished her daughter to be with me.....and then, she thought Madame Heine would cease to object.

Accordingly the next [day], Natalie introduced me to her Mama, who went to Madame Heine to ask her permission for me to spend Sunday with Natalie, as Sunday is a day, which - with the exception of two hours devoted to the lying down - Dr Heine allows the girls to spend how and where they like. Mrs Heine was very gracious, and said if I thought you would have no objection she had none.....and therefore it was fixed that I would go on Sunday.

Of course I thanked Mrs Heine very much and very gratefully for the permission, and hoped that she did not discern any thing in my manner which looked like triumph, as knowing the jealous character of most governesses I was afraid she might think something of this kind – however I was much amazed when, on returning from Natalie's on Sunday, I did not find either the Heines or the governesses huffed as I had expected.

* * * * *

Now I think, my dearest Papa, were I to give the dear kind letter you were kind enough to write for me to Madame Heine now, it would only be (as Teddy used to say) "wasting the fruits of the land". I think that Madame H cannot well object to our intercourse as long as Natalie's Mama is here - but if, when she goes away, she should again object, may I not tell you ...and then you can tell me if you would allow me to give her your letter. I can never thank you enough.. for your kindness and sympathy. I long for you to see my Natalie. I think you will like her.

How extremely good of you to trust me with another 20£. Now that I am out of debt I feel confident of being able to make it last a long, long time... [more money matters follow]. *Thank you very much for telling me to give Madame H and her sister some present. At any other place this would have effect, but here the rule is that none of the girls are to give anything till they leave & then they must give something very handsome such as a piece of plate etc. etc. I must bid you good bye for the present I shall be back again soon..........*

* * * * *

Since writing the above I have met with a little adventure which has made me alter my mind, and which I must tell you. I met Mme H last night and she stopped me to tell me that she had lately felt very awkward about the invitation of Madame de Ritter, for, that she would not for worlds offend Natalie's Mama, at the same time she did not know if you would like it as you objected to my going to the Polish countess - and tho' she had no objection to my going with Natalie, she would wish me to say that you would not like it, the next time I was invited.

I informed her that I was confident that you would have no objection and that the reason that you did not wish me to go to the Polish countess was that she (Madame H) seemed not to like it - and besides you were afraid it might disturb the cure. But, as Madame de Ritter was kind enough to ask me only at such times as I was disengaged from the cure, I was sure you would have no objection. Mme H either did not hear me aright or did not understand me, for she walked away saying -"Yes yes, the next time she asks you, you must say your Papa would not wish it"!!

My dearest Papa you would do me a very very great kindness, if, when you next write to me, you would enclose a note to Mme H in which you would tell her, that I had told you that the mother of mon amie choisée (that was such a pretty turn) had been good enough to ask me once to come to her, and that I had asked you if you would like me to go - you could then tell Madame H that you had no objection in as far as it did not disturb the cure. You could then perhaps be good enough to tell her you had no objection to my being with Natalie.

Most of rest of the letter is taken up with how best to phrase this note - and anticipate Emily's observation that *Mrs H - in common with almost all Germans - has so accustomed herself to expressing her sentiments exactly as she feels them, that she has rather blunted herself to those little delicacies and politenesses in others which only serve as a dress to their real wishes.*

Forgive me my dearest dearest Papa, pray forgive me for writing to you in this way, which certainly does not (as the Housemaids say) become me!! - But I only tell you what I think, and of course you must do exactly as you please and as you think fit.

* * * * *

The other disagreeable is perhaps, after all, not worth telling you as it happened some weeks ago, but here it is. I have long observed that the Polish countess seemed offended with me and, some weeks ago, she was invited to a dance given on Dr Heine's birthday [April 16th]. *Of course I did not dance, and seeing me alone, she came up to me and began talking about you and asking me when I expected you. I said soon. Then she said all what follows in one breath, without waiting for an answer to any of her numerous questions –*

"And your Mother, when do you see her? Do you never see her now? Where does she live in general, in town or country, in England or on the Continent? Are you thought like her or like your Papa? Do you not sometimes wish to see her? When you return to England may you not go & see her? Do tell me where she is now?" - Here she stopped, fairly worn out.

Fancy my feelings, the eyes of all the girls were turning gradually upon me, and I saw that their curiosity was beginning to rise. A countess professing to be so much in the world as she does, cannot be supposed to be ignorant as to the answers to all those questions, and every moment the awkwardness of my situation increased. I felt extremely angry, and indignant at the same time. I knew there was a certain respect due to her age and rank, and still I wished to show her I was not insensible to her wish to insult me. I could hardly articulate a very haughty "Je ne sais rien" - when to my great relief, Madame Heine's sister called me away. Miss Anna then began to question me as to what the countess had been saying to me. Of course I did not tell her all, and only said she was asking about you. I felt all this most keenly at the time but perhaps it is hardly worth telling you.

* * * * *

The letter continues, and concludes, with more of Natalie – ***be sure that it is no school friendship... whenever and wherever I might have met Natalie,***

I should have loved her as much and as deeply as I do now; the usual pleasantries about his health, and hers - ***the bleeding has ceased and Dr Heine has obliged me to take the iron mud baths, which though very disagreeable have been of great service;*** and her amusement at receiving a note from the Banker - regarding the £20 - that begins ***"Milady"!... Only think! He addressed his note to me, "Milady E Bulwer Lytton"***

In contemplating the best qualities in a father that Emily might hope for in her current crisis, one might begin with those of a writer and a politician. In contemplating the less helpful, one might include haughty, over-egged, English pride, with a tendency to anger. Emily has for a father Sir Edward Bulwer Lytton - who replies, on Monday 29th July, 1844, ***My dearest Emily, I have just received your letter and agree with you that the invitation of Madame de Zahoney is a better and easier introduction to the subject than the previous one. I will therefore enclose another note to M. Heine.***

Apropos of these matters - in good society one never makes use of the word 'Countess' in speaking of people. If English, it is 'Lady'; if foreign, 'Madame'. With regard to the Polish Countess, you must not be taken in by these mere trumpery titles, to suppose that she is any woman of rank. We do not consider Polish Countesses in general to rank as gentlewomen. Many a Polish or indeed Hungarian Count or Baron is only a postboy. It is clear that she is a vulgar low-lived woman, and you owe her no respect at all after her impertinence.

If she or any one else speaks to you on the same subject again – your answer should be this "Madame est bien curieuse" [Madame is very curious], ***look her full in the face, get up, & turn on your heel.***

This answer will do for any one. To the Polish Woman, if again intrusive, you might add "est que c'est la mode en Polagne parmi les gens comme il faut, de jouer la role de mouchard en matiers de famille?" [is it fashionable in Poland amongst proper people, to play the role of spy in family matters?] ***& so taisez*** [silent] ***her from head to foot & leave her. She could not dare to complain of you to Madame Heine - if she did, you would repeat her questions and say you obeyed my instructions & that I considered such questions insults.***

My friend Manfred Schmid, Cannstatt resident and Stuttgart Archivist, has identified this Polish Countess as Countess Jaraczewska, whose only presence on the internet today is as the recipient of a letter from Goethe in 1823 (unless that countess is her mother-in-law) - but that reference might have impressed Edward momentarily.

* * * * *

In doing my dearest Emily all I can to renew your intercourse with Natalie & procure for you the pleasure it affords you – I must still make one or two remarks. I think all governesses right in general to limit the exclusive liaison between two girls, when it ends, as it generally does, to make them unsocial with others. And I am quite sure - tho' you say nothing of it - that you have neglected to follow my urgent advice: to make yourself popular with all, both girls and teachers; to practice upon all, that combination of charm, talent, tact & real virtue (for it is a species of benevolence) which is found in a prevenant, agreeable, open, social manner.

I am convinced that, if you had done so, 1st, that your intimacy with Natalie would not have been so obvious – it must have formed a great & invidious distinction between your manner with others in order to attract such peculiar notice; & 2ndly, I am convinced that if you had been extremely popular with all the other girls, Mad. Heine would not have ventured to make you an object of their sympathy, or have given you any annoyance.

* * * * *

Our position everywhere depends on our class in a great measure. I can also see from your letters - even from what you say so humbly about Madam de Zahony - that you are not sufficiently aware of your own rank. There is no foreign nobility in any way superior to your position & very few equal to it. As my only Daughter, & as therefore (till you marry) destined to be the head of my Household, & mistress of Knebworth, there are few daughters even of English ------[torn] *who would not envy your position. This consciousness in your own status, if you calculate it properly, ought not to give pride, but greatness & geniality of manner.*

Feeling sure of your own state, you ought to be sure that you reflect honour on any one you choose to know or be civil to, and feel pleasure therefore in being civil & frank with all. It is very true that, at first, many people will not recognize these claims in you, but you will not assert them long, before they wd be recognized.

So far as I am concerned, it will be to me not only pleasure but an advantage, to find in you, not a shy awkward girl, but an accomplished young gentlewoman able to do the Honours of a House, & this I certainly shall not find unless you follow my advice.

* * * * *

I don't object in any way to your intimacy with Natalie, but I expect that it shall not be so exclusive and prevent your mixing with others, & making yourself popular with them. If I were a schoolmistress & saw 2 girls always daundering about by themselves, I should immediately wish to separate them. It is not healthful & natural at your age, which ought to be social with all.

I suppose I must finish all my lectures at once - & I therefore must go on, to guard against morbid & vehement sensibility which, if allowed to grow up unrestricted will certainly tend to your unhappiness & that of all with whom you are connected. It is precisely this sort of sensibility which ends by unwomanizing the character. I do not here allude only to an excess of feeling with regard to Natalie, but to other matters. In your letter before the last, you indulge in exaggerated and incoherent outbreaks of remorse for expressions that tho' wrong were natural. With regard to the person who called them forth, it would be shocking if you did not feel profound horror of character – the relationship however will prevent you expressing it, & forbid you to say of the person what you must feel of the character. That is the resumé of the whole. The fact that it is Rosina that is thought the cause of Emily's irrational language and outbursts here blinds Edward - through shared susceptibility - to an inadequate fatherly response. On this matter he would do well to pay heed to Miss Greene's suspicions.

* * * * *

After a some money advice, Edward continues with more short shrift... *for really & truly in case you cannot learn the management of money, & the art of manner, etc. it will be a complete inconvenience to me & I shall be obliged*

to look out for some lady who can – serving you as a companion & me as a Housekeeper [and companion too? This clarification reveals thoughts on how to introduce a mistress into his 'legitimate' houshold]... he signs off, ***Yrs most aff. E.B.L.***

He adds as post script, ***What I say about a proper opinion of yourself is called for by such expressions as "I feel very very grateful to Madame de Z for not thinking me an unfit companion for her dear child as Mrs Heine does." Mrs Heine does no such thing.*** [torn]----- ***don't like to see you always with a younger girl than yourself & she may be very right, but you owe no particular gratitude to Madame de Z for any attentions shewn to My Daughter. It is Madame de Z whom I consider honoured of the two.. And I really must beg that you remember my birth, position and ancestry, when you talk so disparagingly of your own. O vous m'aviez fachée*** [you had made me angry] ***but it is all that morbid vehemence of expression & susceptibilty. Beware of it. For Heaven's sake don't let me remember you have Irish blood in you.***

* * * * *

You may say it is about time that her father got a little tougher on her, after wallowing, unhealthily, in her over-wrought sympathy at the beginning of the year. Or you may say, anger is a dangerous card to play our emo teenager in her current mental state. The good news I have for you is that - after a couple of expensively profuse cross-written pages of contrite Emily-guff ***(Thank you, thank you, dearest dearest Papa, for so kindly pointing out and warning me against my many and great faults. I fully feel the morbid weakness of my character, but I can do is beg you to forgive me and to forget the past and to promise you faithfully to do all in my power...etc.)***, Emily's core response, on Tuesday 6th August, is pleasingly resilient and mature, within the context, of course, of what her father might expect:

...Ah, dearest Father, think that I am morbid and weak & foolish, think that I often express the morbid & extravagant feelings of a woman & when I ought never to shape them to words, think that I am disorderly both inwardly & outwardly, & you will only think rightly and justly of me – but pray do not think that I am deceitful to you, pray do not think that where I am aware of a fault or an error I try to hide it from you. Whatever pain, whatever struggle,

whatever shame, it might cost me, I do not think that there is any fault that I should not disclose to you & beg your forgiveness. I now see & feel that it was wrong of me to part myself from the others, for the purpose of indulging in a grief which, tho' strong, you would perhaps term morbid & I promise you dearest Papa never again so far to forget your kind advice warnings.

I think (at least I hope) I feel & know what you mean by a prevenant manner, & tho' I am conscious of the want of it, at many times, & towards many people, I hope by constant practice & perseverance, at last, to get into the way of that happy art, that you may not have to find in me an awkward, ill-mannered girl, or one of whom you would have more reason to be ashamed than anything else. What thought could give me greater delight than that of being able to (in however small a way) to be of any service, or advantage to you; and what reflection could be more replete with pain amounting to agony than that, that I only caused you trouble, that I gave you no pleasure, was of no use to you, and that in me you were only reminded of past unhappiness?...

I will try as far as lies in my power to prevent you having to find fault with me for the same things again.

* * * * *

Pray, pray my dearest Papa forgive me for hurting and vexing you by any expressions beneath the honour due to your birth and rank – I did not think myself bound to pay any particular respect to that unfortunate Polin [Polish woman]*but I want to say, those around her & me thought she was entitled to it. Apropos of her, I shall behave as you desire, should the same thing happen again. With her I think it improbable, as I think she has had some désagrémant with Dr Heine.*

With regard to Madame di Zahony – she is always saying she esteems it [from the French] *"one of the happiest of her life's circumstances that Miss Emily has done her the honour to form a friendship with her daughter; and that her little Natalie is friends with the only daughter of a father, not only so celebrated, but so dear to all the nations of Europe, and all the* ____[indecipherable] *nations of the World! It's truly an honor, the memory of which will always be sweet to her."*

When I last wrote to you my feeling was that of pleasure at being again united with Natalie &, in my foolish heedless way, I expressed my feelings wrongly. I must therefore dearest Papa again, beg your forgiveness for it. There is a sensation - one which I think is peculiar to women - it is neither pride nor vanity, though to describe, seems like both, therefor is indescribable -----this, I have felt, when I have reflected that I may call you Father, and that this alone - even were you not of the high born and the noble, as you are - would be enough to make my position in being related to you the object of envy to so many.

This consciousness, though it has not given me the gentility of manner, which it ought to have done, has often lessened the almost insurmountable feeling of awkwardness & shyness which I so painfully experience when conversing with strangers for the first time. I shall however try to completely overcome this.

As for other rank, I think one must bear to see one's real rank in one's own country never thoroughly recognised in a foreign land. This has been proved to me by many little circumstances. However I will try to form my manners in the mould you wish.

* * * * *

...In speaking of Madame di Zahoney I made use of the word 'Countess' because I was at a loss to interpret her many names and titles, and thought to write them all in the term 'Countess'. I was not aware that the word was not used in English and will not make use of it any more. She has not visited me any more since I last wrote, as Natalie has been obliged to go nearly every day to Stuttgart to sit for her picture. This portrait, frustratingly, I am yet to find. To think that it hangs anonymously on some wall, or in some dealer's window in some European backstreet, haunts

Orphaned portraits in a Vienna window

me now whenever I am window shopping on a City break.

Almost all the nicest girls in the institution are gone, and new ones replace them – this reminds me of my nouvelle feats in the gymnastics – apropos – there is now only one ladder which resists my utmost efforts to mount it – every thing else I have by this time pretty well mastered.

Poor Mr Parsons died the other day in sleep - I believe the Parsons are going to return immediately to England.

As for myself the bleeding, tho' not nearly so constant, still comes at times.

Pray dearest Papa in your next letter tell me everything about yourself… fondly and affectionately yours, Emily Bulwer Lytton

P.S. Madame di Zahoney sent me a ring by Natalie

* * * * *

Friday 23rd August, 1844. Sudbroke Park, Petersham, Surrey. *My dearest love, I can assure sincerely that when I wrote last, it was with a strong struggle against the feeling that my letter would pain you & perhaps seem over harsh. But I was & am persuaded that it was necessary for you to rouse yourself thoroughly from the morbid susceptibility which is in your character - as in that of most amiable persons - & to look steadily & healthfully upon the world as it is.*

To face the world is like facing 'a Day' – you have the best of it while your eye is steady – but once sl___[indecipherable]… *and it will fly on you.*

I did not mean, my Emily, to accuse you of deceit, but merely of forgetfulness in not following my advice. It is not very easy to follow it… but I am glad that you perceive how necessary such rules are, to preserve one's equilibrium in a strange place.

* * * * *

…It is very true too that abroad, & even at home, you will find your position not acknowledged unless you can quietly assume it. We are every where, what we make ourselves. A highborn Countess may be a nobody & a parvenue with good manners - & that natural aristocracy of presence of mind

& elegance which impresses all society - may be the great power of the most brilliant circles. This is seen every day. To prepossess is to be powerful…..

Eno' of these worldly advices & suggestions, which do not come however from cold calculation, but from long experience - & from a conviction that the temper & the heart themselves, improve by the cultivation of external amenities.

* * * * *

I delayed answering yours till I could, in the first place, make some agreeable report as to my health. I left Malvern better in some respects, but much reduced & they thought me looking ill & thin in town. I went thence to Knebworth, practicing the watercure there – stayed a week & then came here to Dr Weiss [at Sudbrook Park in Petersham, just south west of London], *who was at Friewaldau* [now Jeseník in the Czech Republic], *near Priessnitz, the Founder* [who was born in the neighbouring village of Gräfenberg, now Lázně Jeseník].

Sudbrook Park Hydropathic Establishment

He made some alterations in the treatment, & I certainly now feel very much better, & stronger. I cannot however get rid of the chronic cold, I had when with you. The system does not seem to touch that. 2ndly, I wished to speak somewhat defending my plans, which are now these – to leave England for Ostend about Thursday fortnight, about Sept 12th or 13th; if I can then do without further stay at a Water Establishment, I will come straight to you – which will take about 3 days; if I am obliged to stay at one some little time longer I shall go to Boppard on the Rhine.

In the latter case, if Dr Heine does not think that a week's absence would interrupt the cure, I should much like to have you with me. You will ask him this, enquiring whether you cannot partially continue the treatment with me, and whether he can recommend a good female servant to accompany you – it would only take a day, by a voiturier [carrier] *to reach Mayence* [Mainz] *& in another day you wd be at Boppard. Agree to any arrangement of what is to be paid to the servant - it must be one useful & to save you trouble in travelling. Let me know this by return of post to Hertford St. I shall get it before starting.*

I am delighted to find Madame de Zahoney was pleased with your acquaintance with Natalie, & I hope it will continue despite your different nationalities. Does she speak any English?

For the rest, believe me, it will not be on my account, but your own, that you will make all the friends and secure all the affection you deserve. You require nothing but to let your heart be seen - or as your Uncle Henry used to say to me, "Put some of your goods in the shop window." I am very glad you are so active at the gymnastics – nothing like them.

...I am not surprised that the bleeding at the nose does not stop altogether yet. Perhaps it is better to go gradually, so long as it does not become a chronic habit – it may only be a salutary effect of Nature. God bless you, dearest Measy, Yr most aff. Father E.B.L.

* * * * *

Edward writes again two weeks later, on Saturday 7th September, 1844, It has been a year since he was with Emily in Cannstatt, leaving her in the care of Dr Heine. And - matching the staggered anticipation of his visit the year before, and a year later - his travel plans are once more delayed. *My dearest Measy, You cannot be more impatient to see me, than I to see you once more. Indeed the wish to judge of your progress myself, & to cheer you in your arduous and weary ordeal constantly haunts me. Even for more selfish reasons, I should be as glad as a schoolboy to have a holyday after all the dullness & dejection of this last melancholy year. But Heaven knows when I can escape.*

Since I wrote last, I have had a sharp attack which the Doctor thinks criti-

cal, & he says I shall be sure to have another, probably in the shape of a bilious fever, & that he considers it thoroughly unsafe for me to think of moving unless to another Water Establishment while this is hanging over me.

The worst of it, is that it is impossible to predict or scarce to conjecture when this will happen. He says within a fortnight – it may be sooner. When well over, I shall not lose a day in getting to you. You see, however, that you cannot expect me so soon as I had hoped, & that I can now give you no clue to guess the precise date of of my arrival.

* * * * *

This system is so unlike all others, that symptoms of damp brought on by hydropathy become highly dangerous if treated by any other mode, or unless indeed by very skilful Hydropathic hands - but are harmless and salutary when they are so treated. I may regret that I tried the system, but I fear there is no safety now but in pursuing in it, particularly till the crisis comes. The cold, which was a part of general chronic inflammation and more serious perhaps in its consequences than my Water [Doctor] supposed, is nearly well – if there is no relapse – but I am much reduced.

These illustrations of Priessnitz's Water Cure (above and opposite) show wet sheet wrapping, wet sheet unwrapping, wet sheet rubbing... and sticking your face in a bowl of cold water

Courtesy of the Wellcome Library, London

Courtesy of the Wellcome Library, London

However enough of me for the moment [well, at least for two sentences]. *I cannot tell you how much vexed I am for your & my sake too at this contretemps. But you must, like myself, practice patience. The only thing that consoles me is that I am pretty sure if I did go to Germany at once, the change of air, etc. would bring about the anticipated fever & lodge me at Boppard or some other establishment long before I reached you, & since Dr Heine objects to your joining me, we shd be as far from meeting as we are here.*

You must carry your thoughts on to the next year when your trial will be well over, and our meeting will not be a mere short visit.

Ever excuses for not being there. And ever looking for someone to chaperone his children *...I wish Natalie may learn English, for I hope hereafter, she & perhaps Madame Zahoney may be induced to spend some time with you, & as I only speak my own language, I should not otherwise become so well acquainted with her as I could wish.*

I grieve to hear you have suffered so much in your teeth. That is very important to your future ease & comfort. I wish you would mind & see the Dentist again – ask particularly what you avoid eating & drinking. Pray don't touch sweets, or acid fruits or German wine. You observe nearly all Germans have bad teeth, & this may arise from something in their food, which should be learned and shunned.

Miss Greene, when I saw her the other day, seemed to think they neglected your hair, which is growing less profuse – that is of less moment, & easily recovered – but pure sweet oil, such as they sell at the chemists, well brushed in, is the best thing you can use to preserve both the quantity & the fineness of texture. You may tell Mrs Heine I have ordered my debt to be paid to the Stuttgart agent according to her bill.

* * * * *

[Miss Greene] looked very well. She corroborates her former account of your improved shape. She is of course anxious for you to return as soon as possible – So am I....and I hope Dr Heine will be able to fix a time. At present we are both in the same boat - with our German Doctors - & can get at nothing definite or precise. Indeed this place [Sudbrook Park] *puts me much in mind of your mode of life - the same strange assemblage* [gathering of people], *the same cold fruits and water - not a drop of tea – cold water for breakfast & exercise, exercise, exercise all day! Weary work!*

I am enchanted to think that you have, in great measure, recovered Natalie & am so truly thankful that you have the luxury of a companion after your own heart. While I implicitly believe your assurance that you will avoid being so exclusively occupied with her and will be steadily sociable & gregarious with the others.

Allow me politely [to mention] I still see a melancholy decline [in your] handwriting, which is growing cat-like & German. Not as it used to be - honest, symmetrical & French in its character. Perhaps you will try to write more with a paw & less with a claw.

* * * * *

I am glad to learn that you are to play at a concert, it will serve to give you aplomb & presence of mind. In the world, shyness is never thought what it is, but called either pride or affectation. It will soon wear off with you.

June is particularly well & returns his compls. He has cut [slighted] *Parson Black* [Edward's other dog]. *Adieu – to you, I have written the longest letter I have accomplished since the Water Cure. You may depend on hearing from me the moment I am fairly launched, but don't reckon on me till I am absolutely out of all these traps. Since beginning this letter I have had symptoms that seem to auger an early coming on of the eventful crisis – but it is too capricious to be relied on. Most aff. yrs E.B.L.*

T.M.I.? Too much information? B.B.B. Bulletin from the Bulwer Bowels. But indicative of what makes these letters so unique and precious.

"Ha! Ownest thou thy wrongs, proud lord?"

The Last of the Barons (1843)

CHAPTER 26

~ *Cannstatt Letters - Taste of Future Relations* ~

The cushat [dove] ***would mate***
Above her state,
And she flutters her wings round the falcon's beak;
But death to the dove
Is the falcon's love -
Oh, sharp is the kiss of the falcon's beak!

from *The Last of the Barons* (1843) by Edward Bulwer Lytton

* * * * *

A month later, in the first week of October, 1844, Emily is once more saying goodbye to her father. It is not clear how long his visit to Cannstatt has been, but it can only have been very brief. Odd to stay for so short a time. He has made the effort to travel all that way to see her, with no other apparent reason - although he will stop at the Water Cure clinic in Boppard on his way home, and no doubt visits the Pfizers while he was in Stuttgart.

The following letters tell, sadly, that it is not a success. So why is the visit to Baden Baden with fifteen-year-old Emily so happy, and the visit to Cannstatt to see sixteen-year-old Emily not?

Emily has changed. To some extent this is simple adolescence - and the growing up we have witnessed - but there are deeper, more troubling issues. Miss Greene is right to worry about her.

Worse still, the unease of this visit foretells of the future relationship problems she will have with her father when she returns to England.

How can it be that the intense and deeply loving relationship we are witnessing between father and daughter in these letters can so quickly break down when they are together in person? Emily is first to ask this question.

* * * * *

Postmarked Monday 7th October, 1844, but written on the evening of Friday 4th October. *My own dearest dearest Papa, With a very heavy heart I take up my pen to write you a long letter, and to tell you everything j'ai sur le coeur* [I have on my heart]. *Do not, I entreat you dearest Papa, call me morbid and foolish, but hear me patiently to the end, for that which I am going to tell you comes from the bottom of my heart. If it did not, I should not have been so unhappy.*

That which pained more than any thing else this sad morning – which pained me infinitely more than any thing else which could be said or done about Natalie; which even pained me more than that which nearly broke my heart, your departure itself – is, my own conviction that I have considerably lost in your regard, in your esteem, in your affection.

I own the first day I came here, my dream by night, & my thought by day was the hope of seeing you once more - if it were only for a day - and of being able (tho' but in a small way) to cheer you and comfort you. And now the dream has vanished and I wake to a painful reality. You are come. You are gone. Not one of my hopes has been realized, not one of my wishes has been fulfilled. Instead of having given you the smallest pleasure, I have only given you the greatest possible pain.

* * * * *

You have undertaken a long journey at this unfavourable season of the year, at the risk of bringing back all that you have been labouring to get rid of, and all for me - & you think me insensible and ungrateful to so much, to so great, kindness. Ah pray pray do not think that, my own dearest Papa. As long as you were with me, my heart was too full, and I could not tell you how happy, how grateful I felt - and yet in the midst of all my happiness I felt at times very sad. I felt that if your complaint should come on again, I should

Courtesy of the Stadtarchiv Stuttgart (B 294)

Cannstatt - looking west

be the whole and sole cause of it, and I was continually making myself the bitterest reproaches.

If I looked discontented and soured, I can only say that I looked the reverse of what I felt. And if you thought my manner toward you was cold and not affectionate, I can only say it has been to me a subject of the greatest grief that my manner should so belie my thoughts.

And now that I am once again alone in my room - when I recall all the hours I spent thinking of you, and of what I could do which would give you most pleasure; when I remember the delight I felt on receiving your last letter announcing your proposed visit; when I think of the beating heart with which I read your little note saying that you were arrived; when I call you to mind; when I recall my own feelings on seeing, on hearing, you once again, after so long a seperation, and then.....this cruel morning. I feel that instead of pleasure, I have caused you only pain. I remember that we have parted - so oh! now indeed my feelings defy description.

You are kind enough to desire me to tell you when I am unhappy – I am unhappy now, in the bitterest sense of the word, But this unhappiness does not arise from my outward circumstances. It does not make me in the least unhappy that I am again in the middle of this quiet regular life. It does not cause me any chagrin that I again have the cure before me. On the contrary,

the prospect of carrying out my firm resolution of leaving Dr Heine 'pas le moindre chose à redire' [without a thing to complain about] *pleases me much.*

But when I practice to myself what you think of me, it is then when I remember our parting, and how ill you were rewarded for all your kindness and sacrifices for me - that pains me to the heart.

* * * * *

The only thing I can do now is to take the utmost pains to attend, in every way, to your kind directions and advice, and hereafter in the happy 'avenir' [future] *I hope to show you that I am not the cold and* _______[indecipherable] *being for which you may now take me. I will not tell you not to think so of me, for I would rather* <u>*convince*</u> *you myself that I am not so. And now if there is anything which you would like me to give up, if there is any thing which you would like me to do, if there is any thing however small in which I could serve you or give you any pleasure – do only tell it to me, dearest Papa, and in doing so be sure that you confer on me the greatest pleasure, the greatest favour.*

To say that I do not love Natalie would not be true – but I could, I would, give up this friendship, so dear to me directly (except for the reasons you pointed out to me) because in doing so, I should at once obviate all objections Madame Heine could make. And your good opinion and _______[indecipherable] *affection is dearer to me than all else. I know of nothing, dearest Papa, that I have reserved or concealed from you. I am, that my manner or looks should have led you to suppose that I am.*

A happy, preveniant [expectant] *manner is for me particularly essential – it is perhaps more necessary than the most elegant accomplishment - and I feel the want of it every day more and more. I know what it is, and can appreciate it in others - it seems however that for me it is almost unattainable. I know too, that in frankness & candour it principally consists. I will not however make you any promises, because Madame Heine told you I only promised and never performed - but I will endeavour this time to perform without promising.*

* * * * *

My anxiety to know how you are, to know how your cold is, and how you have supported the journey is very great – and when you have a leisure moment, a line from you will give me the greatest delight. Ah! how dreadful will be my feeling if you should again relapse. I am in a state of the most painful anxiety from which, however, I trust a few lines containing good news of yourself will soon release me.

* * * * *

And now, dearest Papa, I approach a subject on which I wished much to speak to you this morning, but I did not feel altogether quite able for it. What you said Madame Heine told you about the intimacy with Natalie is in some measure true, and especially in the commencement, but Madame Heine spoke to me, and I to Natalie on the subject, and had Madame H been constantly with us, she would have seen that we endeavoured to act in all respects as she wished.

Of Madame Heine, however, we all see but little - and if she chanced to enter my room and found Natalie there, she immediately suspected something wrong. If she happened to pass the girls in the gardens and Natalie and I were walking together, she generally came that evening and requested me to pay more attention to her wishes and give up this intercourse with Natalie. She charged the servants to watch when Natalie came to me, or walked out with me, and to let her know -

We parted! - it was Natalie's own wish as she thought it would put a stop to the constant 'désagréments' [unpleasantnesses]. *She selected another girl with whom she constantly was. I did so too. Occasionally I used to write her a little note – this I should perhaps not have done, and I own that it was very foolish and that I sometimes made use of exaggerated expressions, expressions forgotten as soon as written – but I fear Madame Heine must have exaggerated the whole case, or else given it some turn which has put it into quite a different light by the very serious manner in which you seemed to speak upon the subject altogether.*

Perhaps she may have meant it well – and perhaps it was her conviction that all she said was the case - be this, however, as it may, I feel that this painful and severe lesson has been for my good. The thoughtlessness and imprudence on my part has received a stern but effectual punishment. You must naturally have a very bad opinion of me, but while this fills me with the deepest grief and dejection, I do not ask you to change your opinion till you can say yourself - and from your own belief - that I have convinced you of the contrary.

You will however give me most heartfelt pleasure if you will tell me in your next letter what I can do that can further this. And only tell me if, by giving up Natalie altogether, I could do something towards it. It would cost me one struggle, one sacrifice, but only one - for in doing so I might perhaps receive your good opinion. You do not know how low and dejected these thoughts of having lost it make me.

In the fond hope of soon having good news from you, I beg you ever to believe me your most sincerely and devotedly affectionate child – Emily Bulwer Lytton

P.S. I have had a long conversation with Natalie – she has promised all. Madame Heine did not ask me yet what you said to me – so I did not mention it to her. If she does, I will say what you desired – And in all respects, dearest Papa, be sure that I shall follow your kind advice and wishes. E.B.L. Friday Evening

* * * * *

Postmarked Monday 14th October, 1844 - a week later - written on Saturday 12th. *My dearest Emily, I arrived in England late the night before last, and this morning I received your affectionate letter. I readily and sincerely believe in all you say. It would be want of candour not to own that I felt chilled and disappointed by what seemed to me a want of cordiality & 'abandon' in your reception & manner. At the same time it is probably that you have yet quite got over your old fear of me, & it often does happen that, after long absences, especially when the reunion is short & unsettled, a kind of gêné* [embarrassment] *& reticence exists – which tends to misconceptions on both parts of the real feelings entertained.*

I have no doubt, my dear child, that when we meet again under better auspices such misunderstandings will either not recur, or soon vanish under more general intercourse. For the present, therefore, let this subject rest, & be

Edward in 1844 by Theodor von Holst (1810-1844) - Holst's last painting

assured that my affection & love for you are in no degree diminished.

With regard to Natalie – there is every reason for me to wish that your friendship with her should continue, & any abrupt discontinuance or strongly marked alteration would be, as I before said, injudicious as well as unnecessarily painful. All I wish, and again you already know- viz; not to visit each others rooms, not to be found alone with each other, not to write, & to abstain from the warmth of manner - natural & innocent no doubt between young persons - but which you perceive is readily misunderstood. This done, nothing further ought to be excluded & I hope & trust that you will find no further annoyance in your intercourse with each other.

* * * * *

On leaving Heidelberg for the Rhine, I felt my cold severely, & by the second day I was so ill & prostrated that I was obliged to land at Boppard, where - after some consideration & reluctance - I transported myself to the water-

Boppard

cure establishment. The Dr there thought I had a sharp fever coming on, & insisted on my remaining two or three days, during which time by brisk treatment in the wet sheets, etc. the fever was certainly subdued, & I left much better – but the cold still continues, & is rather worse now than when I left Boppard. I have some hopes, however, that it may be rather a fresh cold than the return of the old one.

I go to Knebworth tomorrow & shall probably be detained there a fortnight or so. I have so much business during the two days I am here, that I have hardly found time for this hurried scrawl, but I would not let a post pass without doing my best to relieve your mind, & to assure you - 1st, with regard to Natalie, that tho' I spoke severely, it was not from displeasure or any conviction of impropriety on your part, but from the necessity to guard you against the misconceptions of others - which your own experience would not allow you to comprehend [if this was a sex lecture, exasperation & severity are indeed not the best vessels]*; & 2ndly, my dear child, my affection for you is too deep & strong to suffer any change from a little momentary disappointment which may be easily accounted for.*

What most vexed me was, perhaps, the feeling that you had something on your mind which produced secret discontent, & which I could only remove by winning your entire confidence. But for this, I should probably have spoken to you on the subject. All you can do to please me, is to persist as cheerfully as possible in the cure, & to be as happy & diligent as you can jusqu'au fin [until the end].

I am going to try & see the Dentist today & keep this [letter] open in case of any instructions on his part...

I have seen Mr Bigg the Dentist. He says that if the decay is in the centre of the tooth, they can easily be stopped – that they ought to be stopped – & that especially in young persons, [as] decay spreads to the other teeth. Where the teeth are close together, as they are with you, the decayed tooth should be filled so as to make a little division between that & the second one, & so prevent the spreading. Will you explain this to Dr Heine, & beg him in my name to be present when the Dentist sees you again. Meanwhile, for tooth powder, he recommends your brushing your teeth with magnesia, kept dry, which prevents acidity forming & preserves them from decay. Adieu, my dearest Emily, Yr most aff. E.B.L. Hertford St. Saturday

So. Don't give the impression of being too intimate with your girlfriend and brush your teeth. All Dads say that, don't they? Usually only when visiting Grandma.

* * * * *

Tuesday, 22nd October 1844. The rule of writing only on a Sunday has been abandoned. *My own very very dearest Papa, Your dear kind letter received yesterday gave me the sincerest delight - which was only damped by hearing that by feeling ill you were obliged to stop at Boppard, and that your cold continues. I, however share your hope that it may be a fresh cold which will soon leave you, and not your old enemy. I really cannot express what a 'soulagement'* [relief] *your letter has been to me, or how grateful I feel to you for its contents. Accept my warmest thanks for not thinking of me as I am afraid you did.*

What grieves me much - and what will continue to grieve until we meet again - is that, thro' any reserve or coldness of manner, you were so disappointed. I myself know no reason for it. All I know is that it was quite unin-

tentional and involuntary - but when I shall next see you, every thing of that sort will, I trust, have entirely left me. À l'égard de [concerning] *Natalie: I never visit her in her room now; her cough has returned, and she is confined to it, but I always see her when either the governess, or two or three of the other girls, are with her. I endeavour to be as little alone with her as possible, and foolish writing, etc. etc. is totally abandoned.*

* * * * *

How did you find everything going on 'at the great house!'? Feeling how much you must have to do just at this time, I feel still more obliged to you for dedicating so much of your time to me. I beg, however, not to write again till you are quite at leisure. I anticipate the greatest 'Freude' [pleasure] *this winter in the execution of your designs for cushions, etc. etc. - one large sofa cushion on white satin at which I have been embroidering very busily since you left is nearly finished, and I hope you will like it.* [This beautiful piece is now encased in the fire-screen in the State Drawing Room at Knebworth House] *The pattern is this – in each corner the most old fashioned Arabesque you can possibly imagine, something like the piece of stonework you pointed out to me in Stuttgart, and worked with gold thread, the arabesques stand out from the satin like the old fashioned embroidery one sees now and then on bed quilts, etc. etc.*

My aim has been as much as possible to imitate the old brocades - au milieu [in the middle] *are the arms and the supporters – the three crowns in all their glory, on blue velvet laid on (as it stands out more than work), the ermine below done with*

white chenil and black silk. The angels I have had painted on velvet, and also laid on, as embroidered figures never look gedichen [poetic]. *The work goes quicker than I thought for. If you should think of anything you want in embroidery, pray let me know - in the meanwhile I will go on making sofa cushions.*

I have had my dear little watch set to rights at Stuttgart, and it now goes extremely well. You cannot think how fond I am of it, and its ticking quite keeps me company when lying down. This image has a particular resonance. Emily stretched on her Streckbett listening to her life tick away.

* * * * *

I received a long letter from Teddy the other day – that is to say a long letter for him – he seemed well and happy and talked with much delight of an intended play which he is going to act, and for which he has had 50 bills printed. Thank you very much for seeing the Dentist about my teeth. I gave Dr Heine your message and he has promised to be present when the Dentist here pays his next visit. I have got the magnesia as you desired. When you next write to Teddy tell him I will write soon.

I feel now like one who, after a long journey, finds himself at the last platform of the last railway station, and knowing that within a certain time he shall arrive at his journey's end. This gives me fresh courage and renewed activity, and I anticipate real pleasure in doing all I can for the cure this winter.

Ah! pray, dearest Papa, love me always - on your love hangs my whole happiness and my only wish, and my most soaring ambition is to live for you, and to contribute, though only in a small way, to your comfort and happiness. I cannot tell you how very unhappy I was till I received your letter of yesterday, or how happy it made me. I most sincerely hope and trust that you will never again have reason to be disappointed in me. I am afraid tho', dearest Papa, you will be often disappointed in me in many things – but my manner or looks shall never again deceive you so far as to disappoint you in my affection, for true and devoted it ever shall be for you, my own dearest dearest Papa And never never think there is anything I would conceal from you - for to you I have always confided, and will ever confide, all I know, or think, or feel.

Mrs Heine has been thinking of changing my room. It is not sure yet, but I suppose if she does I shall come up to the old story [she means storey] *again.*

My letter must this time be shorter than I would wish, because I have been delayed continuing it by something Mrs Heine gave me to do, and I am afraid if I write more now the time for posting it may be gone. Talking of posting – I have enquired at the post office every morning since you went about your letters, but the answer always was that they had none. Did they forward any to you? And now adieu, my dearest Papa, ever believe me to be your affectionately attached child, Emily Bulwer Lytton

P.S. message from Mrs Heine re payment for singing lessons.

* * * * *

With relations back on track and emotions settled, you imagine, I'm sure, the subject of Natalie being avoided for a while. You are wrong. Unless you count two and half weeks 'a while' - and equate the idea of adjoining rooms with the waning of a romance. Maybe Madame Heine is testing her? It is hard to believe Emily when she says she has "no predominating wish about it". On Sunday 10th November, she trys her luck - *I also told you… that Madame Heine was talking of changing my room; the other day she called me into her room and desired me when I next wrote to you to give you the following message from her:- next to Natalie's room there is a room which I could have.*

In this case when we went to the Gymnastics, dinner, etc., Natalie would have to pass through my room. When I had a singing lesson or anything of that kind in my room, which could not be interrupted, the Governess would allow Natalie to pass through her room which communicates with the corner room (Natalie's room) by a side door. The room which Madame Heine intended giving me and Natalie's room are in fact like one large room separated by a door one can open and shut at pleasure.

Madame Heine desires me to tell you that she has no objection to my having the room if agreeable to your wishes. As for myself I have no predominating wish about it. If I remain in the room in which I am at present, well and good. My chief pleasure and delight here, I can enjoy the same in whatever room I am – namely – to think of, and write to you. If I am lodged upstairs I shall be nearer Natalie, and the close relationship of the rooms would pre-

vent any désagréament whenever Madame Heine should see us together. It is therefor for you to decide, my dearest Papa, and Madame Heine awaits your answer.

* * * * *

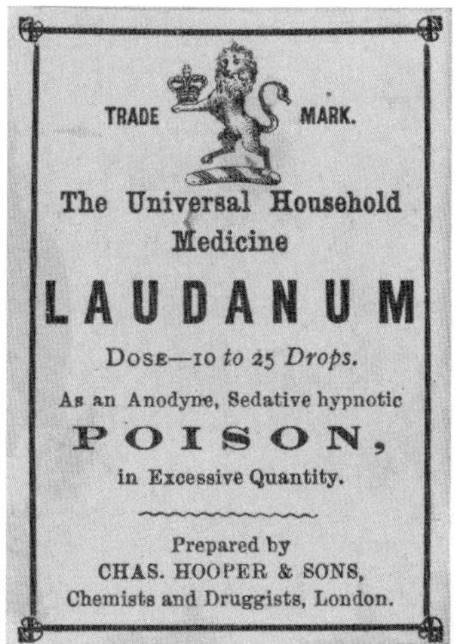

Prescription for toothache

Maybe it's the drugs. ***Yesterday I received a visit from the renowned "Hofrat & Zahnarzt"*** [Court Councillor & Dentist] ***Bop!*** [Bopp the dentist started a dental dynasty in Stuttgart, continued by his son Julius Bopp (1825-1884)] ***– the operation was very painful and lasted a long time – but I think that the teeth are stopped tightly and in the manner you desired.***

Maybe a Bop in the head equates to one on the head. In the same letter, she is mixing the titles of her father's novels, ***Whenever I have a leisure moment I transport myself to those happy days spent with you at Baden Baden by reading your matchless*** *The Last Days of the Barons*... But we must imagine her, swollen-faced, imbibing whatever medicine - and very possibly suffering an increase of bullying from the other girls, not only for looking ridiculous, but also for the fuss surrounding the recent visit of her celebrity father. She implies this in quoting from *The Last of the Barons*, ***the cry of – "sharp is the kiss of the falcon's beak"... I cannot help remembering the first fatal evening of my arrival here*** [the falcon looks of the older girls]; ***it is curious to note the various arts with which memory can recall to life the beings that peopled our past.***

There was another concert the other day at which I was obliged to play. Yesterday was Teddy's birthday, I thought very much of him. Pray tell him so with my affectionate love when you next write to him. And now, my own dearest Papa, I must bid you farewell... when your thought wanders over the long catalogue of those that love you, let it linger for a moment on the first name of that limitless list - it will be that of your devoted and affectionately attached child, E.B.L.

Emily does not get the room next to Natalie's. But her father's reply - written on Monday 25th November - is kindly supportive. ***If Madame Heine sees no objection to your being in the next room to Natalie, I will make no obstacle, tho' I am rather surprised at it, after all she said, & do not think it the wisest possible situation.***

I am grieved, my poor Emily, to think of the pain you suffered from the dental operation, mais il faut suffrir pour etre belle [but one must suffer to be beautiful], ***& I hope now, with the constant use of magnesia tooth powders, your trial in this respect will be over and your remaining teeth, which are beautiful, preserved till a good old age.***

The 'old house' progresses, but slowly. Part is suspended till Spring. I do not count on having all finished till you come, & your cushions on which you have the exact idea, will then be placed selon votre propre goût [according to your own taste].

* * * * *

Miss Greene has had the bad tact to write word to Mrs Thomson that you informed her (Miss G) that you were practically forbidden to write to Mrs Thomson or any of her family, which you much regretted. This brought me an angry letter from Mrs T.....you see how easily mischief can be made by indiscretion, which always distorts things.

Be guarded therefore in what you write to Miss G. You need not however trouble yourself to notice this to her, as it would only hurt her feelings - & some people never can understand when they do wrong, as some dancers never can comprehend why they soûler [spin] ***out of time. Besides I have promised Mrs T not to mention it to her – women always make such mysteries out of things.***

Teddy looks the picture of health & seems very happy at Mrs Walkers. I have been once more entering society since I have been here [he is in Brighton for 10 days] ***& it really is so agreeable a place, & so healthy, that I prefer it to London... & if I could get rid of Hertford St & the cottage, [I] would think of a house here when you join me. Society is more informal & friendly. In London all is talk – not conversation, all crowds – not society. The Granvilles (I mean Lord & Lady Granville not the Dr), the Cowpers, Lady Holland, etc. are here - & have small dinners which are agreeable eno'.*** This little aside -

which reminds of his grandfather's preference of living by the sea - I think, represents another clue that his relationship with Laura Deacon is over.

I am glad to hear Natalie ______ ____ ____ ____[indecipherable] ***her, my friendly feelings towards her, & again repeat & urge my hope that she may visit you frequently & long. Adieu dearest Emily yrs most aff. E.B.L.***

* * * * *

That Christmas, in 1844, there is the same fretting about money and presents as there was the year before - Emily doesn't have the means to look over what she wrote the year before, but the passage reads almost indentically. There are also the same reproaches about not hearing from him, and being worried about his health. These are - as though goading for a swifter response - accompanied by news of her declining health.

Still in Brighton - he writes on Friday 6th December - ***you, in turn alarm me by your own account of yourself – you say you are "far from well". Pray write & tell me what is the matter. You must keep up your spirits, my dear child, & if at any time your situation becomes too irksome & you think you suffer more than you gain, I will remove you. You have but to ask to come away, to do so.*** But just in case she should think of doing so, he continues, ***So confident am I of your good sense, & so assured that you will not, from annoyances merely frivolous, frustrate the good you have already derived & may continue to expect – if your mind is at ease. But I am sure that the cure must depend in much on being cheerful & contented. Do not fret about me, if I am a bad correspondent at times, & take no news for good.***

I told Teddy the other day that you were not well & he shed tears, the only time in my life I ever saw him cry – dear Boy, it delighted me to see he had so good an appreciation of you. He is looking well, & is in the midst of his half yearly examination. We are, please God, to go together to Mr D'Eyncourt's [at Bayons Manor in Lincolnshire, for the holidays], ***or after my visit to Kneb worth*** [leaving Teddy in Brighton in the meantime]. ***I leave this next week. The weather is most bitter & ungenial, but dryer & clearer within the last few days.***

* * * * *

I now come to money matters. And his response is almost identical to passages we have read before. ***I had hoped that your last 20£ would carry you at least over the winter... All Papas preach economy and I don't bore you with a lecture on that subject - but*** [will anyway...] ***in women especially, it is the foundation of most other virtues. It entails not only method & order & forethought, but the qualities of self sacrifice and self control in the little temptations of life which are often the sharpest - & enables us to be charitable & generous. There is no happiness & no dignity without it...*** [etc.]

Accept my dear love, my best wishes for a happy Xmas, & a hopeful new year. May the latter bring with it health, & peace & improvement in all things. Yr most aff Father E.B.L.

* * * * *

Emily is, naturally, jealous of Teddy - although Christmas at Bayons Manor is not a tradition that she ought to wish for, as tragic future events will reveal. She writes - in a letter postmarked Monday 9th December, 1844 - ***How happy dear little Teddy must be at the thought of spending the holydays amongst the descendants of 'the gallant Lord D'Eyncourt' of whom you have so often given me so charming a description.***

She should also - though she could never know it - beware of her relationship with the Thomson family. ***I confess I am surprised at what you tell me about Miss Greene à l'égard de Mrs Thomson. The matter stands so:- Miss Greene in all her letters desired me to write to her friend Mrs Thomson and asked me my reason for paying so little attention to her wishes? For a long time I took no notice of this. At length, however I told her that it was your's and Dr Heine's wish that my correspondence should be as limited as possible, and that therefore I feared Mrs Thomson must be excluded.***

Voila tout-ce-que j'ai dit [that's all I said], ***but in future I will be upon my guard, and shall not forget Miss Greene's talent for the 'Schmuck der Rede'*** [jewellery of speech]; ***and you may depend upon my not mentioning the case to her. As I find myself thus 'rampant on a field vert'*** [a heraldry expression, vert being French for green], ***I may as well proceed to tell you that in a letter received from Miss Greene some time ago, she offers to come and fetch me in Spring; now, unless this is your wish, it certainly is not mine, and I should not***

mind in the least having to wait months longer than March, till it was quite convenient and agreeable to you again to visit Cannstatt, rather than return under her escort.

Emily's pointed remarks about Miss Greene over the next six months - mostly unkind, at worst rude - are difficult to read. She gives one reason for it in a future letter - gossip in the school that Miss Greene is her real mother - however, in the subtext of her so-often-lobbying letters, it seems to be more about securing her father for herself when she returns. A teenage girl naturally rebels and draws away from an embarassing cosseting 'mother', but this disdain for Miss Greene seems political - more about Emily dissuading her father from a return to the pre-Germany family arrangements, and freeing her to be the unchallenged and unchecked châtelaine of his new 'old house'.

* * * * *

Thank you dearest Papa at not objecting to my being in the room next to Natalie - however I have thought over it myself and, as I think I can see, que ca ne vous arrange pas tout à fait selon vôtre grè [that it does not suit you perfectly according to your own liking - I leave the web translation unaltered as it is suitably silly - how can she not be wise enough at least to claim that she is making it her own decision?]. ***I will, if you please, decline your permission and remain ici bas*** [here below. And not in heaven]. ***I feel very happy that you think kindly of Natalie - she does more than return your friendly feelings towards her and always enquires with great anxiety after you. Thank you also very much, my dearest Papa, for so kindly hoping that she may one day come to England. She thinks herself that her mother may visit 'the Land of Lords and riches', as the Germans term England, in the July of 1847*** [which is, indeed, when she does come - it is intriguing that Madame de Ritter knows her travel plans so far in advance], ***but perhaps too sooner.***

As for the teeth, I never fail to use the magnesia toothpowder. And I have no doubt of its good effects. ...I generally lie down now an hour longer than the prescribed time every evening, and I also sleep stretched, so that I hope Spring may find me straighter and taller.

All the Eau de Cologne bottles that fall in my way - as well as all patterns for crowns, flowers, etc. etc. - undergo my scrutinizing observation, and by

the time I see you next I hope to have many little things (not broidered on a frame [previously discussed as being bad for the cure]***) which may be useful 'tant soit peu'*** [so slightly] ***for 'the old house at home'.***

We are all learning our parts for a french play which is to be acted soon. The name is *L'Avengle de Spa* [*The Blind of the Spa* by Stéphanie-Félicité, comtesse de Genlis (1746-1830)] – ***it is very uninteresting.***

As for myself I have not been quite well lately, but am now much better. We do the Gymnastics now in the house, as it is very wet out of doors - but after breakfast and after dinner we are out in the snow.

And now my dearest dearest Papa I must bid you farewell – Sometimes think of one who ever thinks of you........E.G.Bulwer Lytton

* * * * *

In her last letter of the year, two days before Christmas, she describes suffering melancholy that - exacerbated or not by opiates - substantiates Miss Greene's concerns. Natalie is not mentioned by name until the end, but sits as the elephant in the room. ***It is true that I have lately not been well, but it has been more an attack of the mind than of the body. An indescribable feeling of melancholy - for which I can give no reason - has, as it were, completely taken possession of me for the last few weeks. Of course I struggle as much as possible against it, but it seems as if the more I tried to get rid of it, the worse it came.***

An unaccountable despondency mingles itself with everything I do, or think of, and throws a gloom over all which renders me at times truly miserable. As I said before, I can give no reason for it – it does not come from anything external. It is more an internal sadness. For the last two or three days it has been, however, less frequent, and I have no doubt that it will wear off as it came on – by degrees.

* * * * *

I was most gratefully touched, my dearest Papa, by your kindness and confidence, and you shall never find either now, or (if God spares me life)

hereafter - when perhaps you will know me better - that I abuse either. Never for a moment could I think of asking you, my dearest Papa, to remove me - nor do I think it the least irksome to be here. On the contrary, I feel pleasure in forwarding the cure myself as much as possible and - as you found improvement - I could not respect myself if, for childish pretexts, I were to influence you to interrupt or break off the treatment. Therefore, dearest Papa, set your mind perfectly at ease on this point – the 'tristesse' I before mentioned does not come from the cure, or my situation here, and, as I before said, I am sure it will wear away. I have much freedom here, and many indulgences which I fully appreciate, and for which I am sensible and grateful. There is only one thing which makes me unhappy here and which cannot be altered.....et enfin 'Medio de Toute', etc. etc. [and at last, 'through it all' - I suppose, if transcribed correctly, as 'medio' is Spanish and 'de toute' French], *I have had many proofs (partly also through the governess, who tells me different things with the intention of warning me against doing anything which might occasion others to misinterpret my motives) that Madame Heine has not acted quite kindly à mon égard* [concerning me].

* * * * *

A lengthy moan about Madame Heine follows - skip to the next section if you will. You may feel, simply, she has a spoilt inability to get on with any female guardian. *She [Madame H] is seldom or never with the girls, therefore has not much opportunity of judging them, and whenever she has pointed out a fault to me, I have felt obliged to her for doing so, and have endeavoured to remedy it. But I have discovered that there are many things which she thinks, and says to others of me, that she has never mentioned to myself and has candidly owned to others, that she looks upon my disposition as one of the most distorted in the institution.*

The governess informs me that on her arrival that Madame Heine gave her, naturally, her opinion of all the girls & that she (the Governess) was startled and shocked at her picture of me - which Madame Heine perceiving, called upon the Dr and Miss Anna (her sister) to strengthen her assertions, which they did not fail to do. Amongst various other things, she declared that I seldom spoke the truth; that I spoke of 'choses que ne me concernment pas' [things that do not concern me] *to the other girls; and that when she (Mad-*

ame Heine) was near, [I] put on a schinheilig [falsely innocent] ***manner; that my greatest delight was to make myself remarkable; that my wish and aim was to simulate the heroine of a novel, and that I sacrificed everything that became a woman for the purpose!!***

The letter at this point become a jumble of anxieties that do not make sense - and again suggests her mind is intoxicated, for whatever reason - have a go at it yourself below if you fancy a challenge...

...but the gist is Emily's fear that Madame Heine has exaggerated ***in her conversation with you à mon égard*** [about me]... ***selon son gré*** [to suit herself].

It may be selfish, and I have no doubt that it is so, but still I cannot help feeling very unhappy that you should have seen my character in so unfavourable a light - and it seems now as if the flowers of my heart were blighted and withered, as if nought was left of the flame of my ambition but its whitened ashes. Be sure that I feel the selfishness in touching upon this painful subject, but I have shown you now, my dearest Papa, the canker worm that gnaws at my heart.

* * * * *

My dear littler brother! I was much touched by his affectionate remembrance of me, I will answer his letter of the other day as soon as I know his Lincolnshire address – pray be so kind as to tell him so, with my fondest and most affectionate love.

The room next to Natalie is now occupied and almost all the girls above

stairs have formed a sort of côterie [clique] *of their own of which Natalie is the soul. Her wit makes her admired, and her good nature beloved. She seems to like the merry life they lead together, and has become quite a little dame du monde* [woman of the world]. *She appears however to have forgotten me now – she but seldom visits me, and when she does, it is only for a few moments. Alas! I never found in her the affection which I have bestowed on her. In my story* [again she means storey, but it is poetic as is] *there are only children, so that in my leisure moments I am always in my room - and it is then, my own dear Papa, that I am most with you in thought – it is then that I most bitterly feel the grief I mentioned to you before. I do not think my feelings on this subject are morbid or vehement – tho' I feel that they corrode all happiness.*

* * * * *

Mrs Pfizer invited me the other day to dine with them and accompanied me to the best shops to make my commissions... Pray forgive me for writing so badly but I am in great haste......Ever believe me, my own dear Papa, Your fondly attached and tenderly devoted child, E.B.L.

P.S. My expenses till March, as far as I can foresee at present, will be:- the Piano Forte, Washing, candles, letters and I have to pay a somewhat heavy shoe makers bill amounting to about 12 fl, a dress maker's and a washing bill. Mrs Heine may desire me to buy some sort of camail [originally chainmail for protecting the neck and shoulders] *for the Winter & Spring, of this I cannot be sure – at any rate this will be the only article in dress which I shall have to buy till March, as I can wear my winter dresses till then...*

Accept, dearest Papa, my fondest hopes that the new year may bring you health and happiness. In great haste, your own Measy

***The Governess** by Richard Redgrave (1844)*

*This image has lived with me since I was a teenager as the front cover of the 1975 edition of **The Oxford Companion to English Literature** - endorsing my opinion formed in those years that English Literature is never better than when expressing suppressed desire and yearning*

CHAPTER 27

~ *Cannstatt Letters - Take Me Home* ~

Sunday 12th January, 1845. Miss Schaeffer, Governess at Dr Heine's, to Sir Edward Bulwer Lytton, ***Très honoré Monsieur!...***

...[from the French] ***I was told: treat these young ladies as children and beware making them my friends; I promised nothing, but to do my duty conscientiously. The first night I spent in Cannstatt I reflected on all I had been told about the young ladies, especially of Emilie. The next day I went to visit her; I was asked how I found her? I said, I don't make a judgement on seeing a person for the first time.***

Later, I went to see her more often than the others, because I found that Emily had - more than all the others - need of a genuine friend, and older than she, who treated her kindly. Soon I had made a friend. And since then I have had no reason to regret it. On the contrary, [times spent with] Emilie are happy times!

I regret having so little time at my disposal, and being often forced to leave Emilie when she's had most need of a friend around to distract her.

Monsieur must not believe (as Madame Heine does) that I am blind to Emilie's flaws, I assure you I am not - but, as she is my friend, I cannot stand it when people chitchat... The world does not easily forget the bad, but quickly forgets the good that is said of a person!

* * * * *

I also know, Sir, that Mme. Heine has told you much of the friendship between Emilie and Nathalie, and its intensity; permit me to tell you that I've never ever seen anything to shock. Their friendship is touching, especially that of Emilie's, which has more depth than that of Nathalie, which is a bit selfish.

For instance, if Nathalie is upset, Emilie surrounds her with the most tender care; if allowed to do so, she would care for the little one like a good mother cares for a dear child. It hurts me in these moments to tell her to leave and to go to her lonely room, but it is my duty to say it, and I do - though sighing as I do, that it upsets my dear friends. I find Emilie very proper, modest and innocent, and no one will make me believe ill of her.

* * * * *

Often, when at 11:00 I make my final check on her, I find her already asleep. I stay a while and watch over her; a peace that innocence alone can give, is then written in the face of my dear friend; at times I want to go look for Mme Heine and lead her to the bedside, but reason insists I stifle this desire and alone take in this vision I behold, that Mme would be unable to appreciate. She says to me, "vous êtes une personne exaltée" ["you're a fantasist", "you live in cloud-cuckoo-land", "you have airs" - take your pick], *because this is her favorite phrase. She would be wrong, because I am a quiet person - but one that can appreciate what is truly beautiful.*

Emilie is not beautiful, but her little face has no shortage of charm, and if a smile was more often on her lips, she would be prettier. But for some time Emilie has been dreamy and sad. She wants me to believe that this is my imagination, but it is not so. I know only too well that my friend often cries at night; I often rise to listen at the door of her room. When I go in, she tells me, "Miss, I am fine, so be quiet and go to sleep, because I am not sad"; I go - but I can not be quiet.

I did not tell Mme Heine in case the latter should scold, and I do not want [Emilie] to be told off. But all is well when she is, again, back happy and content. You'd not know to tell me why my friend is so sad? How do I want to console! Yet not knowing the source of her troubles! How can I watch her suffer longer without letting you know? You, who loves my friend so much - you will see her comforted and make her as happy as she deserves to be.

* * * * *

Her departure will make a great empty hole in my heart, when I contem-

plate it; Emilie speaks of it with delight! I console myself that she will be near to a father she adores and who she inspires me to esteem.

Sir, excuse the liberty I take in speaking so frankly to you, and giving you the trouble of reading a letter so ill-composed. Emily told me once that you do not much like people writing to you in German, which is why I do not write in my mother tongue. I remain, with best wishes for you and your Emilie, your devoted, I. Schaeffer, Governess at Dr Heine's, Cannstatt.

* * * * *

I wonder if Emily asks her governess to write this letter? There is a part of me that even suspects that Emily writes it herself, and "I. Schaeffer" is the name of another girl who can be trusted to pass her father's reply back to her! Or that she suspects - correctly - that her father will send a reply via her. Emily has art sufficient to be capable of such a schoolgirl deception, but I prefer to believe it is indeed her governess, of her own volition, who determines our heroine "very proper, modest and innocent".

Emily knows about the letter. She claims not to know its contents. But clearly the new governess is a friend who, to some degree is taking away the disappointments of her relationship with Natalie. From this first week of the new year, there is less pain over Natalie, and more looking to a brighter future.

* * * * *

Tuesday 7th January, 1845. ***Accept, my own very dearest Papa, my most heartfelt, most grateful thanks, for your dear kind letter – one cause of my unhappiness it has entirely removed. Of the others I will speak afterwards. In saying you are not influenced by what Madame Heine can say, you have indeed rendered me more happy than I can express. That she thinks ill of me, that she speaks unkindly of me to others, I can bear with the most stoical indifference - but I confess the thought that she had influenced your opinion was one replete with the most acute, most restless pain...***

Winter it may be, but Emily's prose is still in flower - so we'll jump to her acceptance that she ***confided perhaps too trustingly*** in Natalie - and that now,

My heart feels gladder and lighter than it has done for weeks.

I have - to use your own words - "calmly weighed the whole thing" and have come to the conclusion that I can over look all the désagréments passages [unpleasant bits] *which one must find in every situation (to use the maids' word), and which it would be more than foolish to take to heart. And that I can continue the cure with profit till March. Because in looking forward to this time, I can feel the presence of the end of all things.*

* * * * *

I can promise you faithfully not to fret till then - tho' I could not answer for a longer period. [How true the latter. How untrue the former.] *...The thought of seeing you in twelve weeks could make me callous to every désagrément, remove much of the bitterness from seeing myself forgotten by one* [Natalie] *who was once so fond, and whom I have loved with so tender a devotion.*

I can never feel again for any stranger as I have felt for Natalie. My affection for her has been a kind of wahn [madness] *and my heart seems now completely tired and worn out. May The Almighty be praised that he has granted me <u>you</u>, who are dearer to me than all else, & to whom I will dedicate my life. Perhaps Time may entirely efface my remembrance. And perhaps too, in after life, Natalie may remember me kindly now and then. In two years she is coming to England, and Fate may then bring us again together.*

And now, my dearest Papa, enough of these egoistical subjects. Be sure and tell me in your next letter how your dear health is, if you continue the Water Cure regularly, and if your cold continues to decrease. How happy dear little Teddy must be with you and at Knebworth. What would I not give to be one hour in his place?

* * * * *

The Governess is very kind to me, so much so that I am naughty enough often to wonder what can be the motive of so much affability. Only think, she asked me the other day for your address!! Therefore I suppose she intends writing to you! What can she have to say? I could not well refuse her the ad-

dress. So perhaps her letter may reach you before mine.

Curiosity was ever so greatly given to woman, and I own my share of it in this instance. It is no trifle when a governess asks you for the address of "Monsieur votre Père". The cherubs "Hoffnung" [Hope] *and "Freude"* [Joy] *vanish at the sound, and leave the field to "Tugend"* [Virtue] *and "Geduld"* [Patience], *who beg you with the grave politeness of a German (for I am sure Patience is a native of Germany) to await your....."Schicksal"* [Fate].

Thank you very much, my dearest Papa, for allowing me to ask Madame Heine for 20fl more. I have done so, but she has not yet given me the money.

And now, my own dearest Papa, I must bid you good bye. May God bless you in the prayers of your devoted and affectionate child, Emily

Courtesy of the Stadtarchiv Stuttgart (B 7374)

Across the bridge from Cannstatt

P.S. Madlle Schaffer, the governess, gave me some days since, a piece of her own work – a portefeuille [portfolio] *embroidered, on red velvet, in gold & mother of pearl. It is very handsome indeed. I keep it, my dearest Papa, for you – perhaps (if it should match the furniture) it might be of some use in the little writing room you described to me at Knebworth. My fond love to Teddy. E.B.L.*

* * * * *

Sunday 19th January, 1845. ***My dearest Emily, I answer your letter immediately. In the first place, I enclose a note to Dr H of my intention to withdraw you in March - according to your wish. You will give it to him. I have thought as anxiously & deliberately as possible over the best plan for you on your return. De voici*** [from here], ***I think the great thing will be to strengthen your frame and constitution, and if that be done, the cure will go on by itself. I propose on your return in March therefor, that you should have 3 months or so of the Water Cure.***

Here you are thinking, surely not? After three years of foreign governesses and metal stretching racks, he wants to wrap her in wet sheets in an English clinic? I can hear my own daughter intonating, "Daaad!"

I always meant this for you, as I know it will clear the skin entirely, develop the frame, & beautify the complexion. But besides this, it will strengthen the spine and the whole form, & certainly nothing else will be so likely to enable you to dispense with the cure safely, while growing.

I hope my dearest Emily, you will agree to this cheerfully – say nothing about it, as many people are prejudiced against it.

The months or April & May are best for the [water]cure. During this time your education must be, in a great measure, dormant – during the cure, intellectual effort is impossible. But I shall supply you with English Literature, in which you have much to learn. Teddy shall spend his June holy days with you.

When you have done with the Water Cure, you will have some little time for Masters in singing, dancing & music. After which, in the course of the Autumn, you will come to me, & I propose spending the following winter with you in Paris or Italy, to finish you & accomplishments etc. This is the plan I have chalked out.

A shimmering mirage of a prize at the end of it all. But, again, just a mirage. This is a prize Emily will not receive. A promise her father will not keep.

* * * * *

And he has still not got the message about Miss Greene. ***During this interregnum of the Water Cure, etc., till you come finally home to me, my wish is that you should be as happy as possible. I don't want you to be snubbed by any governess or stranger in that capacity. But a female companion you must*** *have &, on the whole, would not Miss Greene be the best?*

I propose asking her to go over to you, for I dare not trust myself to the German climate in March. Shall I ask her to go with you to the Water Cure? I consult you. Tell me what you would like? If not, I will try & find you some other lady of respectability to be companion - not governess. But I am so afraid of your being strange or uncomfortable, or in any way put upon, that it struck me Miss G might be most acceptable to you - but say frankly. Mrs Walker has recommended to me 3 sisters, old maids, who she says are most kind & Teddy says are "charming". I dare say I could get one of them to be with you till the Autumn.

So take your choice - Miss Greene, or some one else - & write, if you can decide so soon, by return of Post, as I should like to arrange before going abroad, wh I shall do early in February. My cold has returned, & I want a less [troubling] climate during the rest of the winter. So much for business. I delay conferring with Miss Greene till I hear from you.

* * * * *

With regard to Natalie – these disappointments [we] are all doomed to early in life - your heart, my child, will soon recover from the refroidement [cooling] *it has undergone. You must be as old as I am, & suffered as much, before the heart ceases to be elastic. You will find this out, croyez moi* [believe me].

Your governess has written me a very kind, well-meant note in your praise. Give her the enclosed reply, & in your next tell me if she is young or old, goodlooking or the reverse, & then perhaps I may guess at the motif you seem to suspect. If old or plain, she perhaps wishes to be your companion on leaving – if the reverse, her affection is most probably without any arriere pensée [forethought] *of interest, etc.* [Ha! LOL]. *You will do well in either case, not to check her advances, but to be as much friends with her as you think the custom of the place allows.*

Meanwhile, I again most urgently entreat you to herd with the other girls as much as possible & be as little alone. If you would do this, I should think it even cheaply purchased by the loss of your intimacy with Natalie. Think me not hard to say so!

Don't set your mind against the Water Cure - it is not disagreeable – I guarantee all good effects & shall _____[the cross-writing makes this indecipherable - I want it to read 'be with', but it looks like 'leave'!] ***you constantly during the process. Adieu ever yours, E.B.L.***

* * * * *

Tuesday 28th January, 1845. ***My own very dearest Papa... my most grateful thanks for all your kindness and confidence. I hail this plan of the Water Cure with delight! as I trust it may eradicate the eruptions*** [acne]. ***Thank you very much for so kindly considering my happiness and comfort while using it, but do not be faché*** [angry] ***if I refuse the proposition of Miss Greene!***

I feel most grateful to her for all her kindness to, and affection for, me - but do not compare love with the lady in your pretty poem of *The Lady and The Dogs* [from *Eva: A True Story of Light and Darkness, Other Tales and Poems* - this little fable poem compares the fickleness of woman to the constancy of dog], ***when I own that I dread the thought of again being with her! No, unless it is your particular wish that she should be with me, I would infinitely prefer one of Teddy's "charming old ladies", or any one else you please. I do not think I could be happy with Miss Greene.***

...Do not think me too éreintant [exasperating] ***if I ask you not to let Miss Greene fetch me – could not one of the old ladies do so?***

* * * * *

I gave your note to the Dr and, after having read it, he sent Madame Heine to fetch me, and had a long conversation with me, which he desired me to report faithfully to you - which I do here as concisely as possible:

If it is your decided wish that I should leave in March, he can & will say nothing against your arrangement - but he deems it his duty to acquaint you that no one leaves the institution before taking the cold baths; that in my case it would be almost dangerous to leave before doing so; and that it is impossible to take these baths in the early Spring.....That it would be his wish that I should remain till July or September, as otherwise my Übel [evil - also used for illness] ***might increase - but, as he said before, if it is your wish that I should leave, he will break off the cure by degrees.*** It is hard not to think that Heines' consideration here is financial rather than medical - three quarters of the way through the school year. However, the bill is paid quarterly - and the famous English author's good graces are presumably more valuable than 3 months of bedroom rent.

This is what he desires me to tell you with his compliments.

* * * * *

I gave Madlle Schaeffer your note. She is about 25 and decidedly plain.

Ah! my dear Papa with what delight do I look forward to next winter – a winter with you in France or Italy! how delightful!

Natalie has been extremely kind and attentive since I last wrote. She speaks much of you - you have quite won her heart. It is her mama's firm intention to come to England in July of 46 [Does she mean 47? Emily has previous said July of 47, which is when Madame de Ritter does come]. ***Almost every evening the girls are together and play at what they call "some spirited game" – so that I am only alone when lying down, and even then I am not alone, as my next neighbour is very talkative and tells me long stories.***

I know that when engaged in the Water Cure one may not write much, but do you think I might write a few lines now & then to Natalie? It would make me so happy, and besides it would keep up my German writing which I should

Courtesy of the Stadtarchiv Stuttgart (B 3901)

The Institute from the railway embankment

be sorry to forget. I have not said anything to any one of the Water Cure.

I am afraid, my own dearest Papa, that you will be vexed at my not wishing to have Miss Greene – tell me truly in your next letter.

I am in the greatest haste as you can see by my writing and can only assure you of my grateful love & fond affection, Your own Measy

P.S. I have discovered something with regard to what Madame Heine thinks, and says, of Miss Greene which is assez désargréable [rather disagreeable]. *She is firmly persuaded that she* [Miss Greene] *is my........... – you know what I would say – a very near relation! She says it is impossible that anyone who is not related could speak in terms si exaltés* [Mme Heine's favourite word - here we can leave its meaning as, 'so exalted'] *of me - and that if one can impose upon* [fool] *others, one cannot impose upon* [fool] *her* [Madame Heine]. *I trust this letter may find you well and your cold less........ your fond child, E.B.L.*

* * * * *

Wednesday 29th January, 1845. *Since writing yesterday, my dearest Papa, I have reflected that you may have some difficulty in finding any one except Miss Greene who would willingly accept the proposition of fetching me in March. Should this really be the case, and should you really not be able to discover any one in so short a time besides Miss Greene, I will remain here till July (if agreeable to you) - till then, I will continue to pursue the cure steadily and busily, and try to be as happy as it is possible to be away from you, my dear Papa. Dr H will think you have left me longer in compliance with his wishes. Should this be perfectly agreeable to you, do not make any scruples on my account - only promise me I may leave then, in July...*

Do as you please, my dearest Papa, I am willing, quite quite willing, to remain here if you like. Your very affectionate child, E.B.Lytton

For one so keen, supposedly, to come home, being willing to stay an extra three months just to avoid a visit by Miss Greene seems bizarre. Again, it suggests an alternative agenda - presumably Natalie is not leaving until July.

* * * * *

Friday 14th March, 1845 (from Malvern) ***My dearest Emily, I am very sorry to have occasioned you any uneasiness. I have indeed had a severe attack, apparently of influenza, but it was either brought on or agravated by the shock occasioned by the melancholy death of a poor friend of mine who destroyed himself in a fit of nervous excitement. I was tenderly attached to him & at that moment engaged in schemes for his permanent benefit, his circumstances being somewhat distressed.***

Samuel Laman Blanchard

The author and journalist - and biographer of Letitia Landon - Samuel Laman Blanchard (1804–1845) commits suicide with a razor on 15th February, two months after the death of his wife, overworked and plagued with money problems. Edward collects together a volume of his work, *Sketches from Life* (1846), and writes, in its introduction, echoing the apparent similar self-destruction of Letitia Landon, ***The predisposition to suicide has been pronounced by eminent physicians to be more frequently a constitutional tendency - a physical disease - than purely a moral obliquity of judgment or the result of mental operations... and [therefore] to be regarded with awe and pity, rather than by censure with which we should attach to a deliberate desertion of the obligations and ties of earth.*** Edward has thought about this.

He continues to Emily, ***I came hither to recover by dint*** [a blow or strike of a weapon] ***of the Water Cure & am now better, tho' far from quite well. I am strongly recommended to get to Italy as soon as I can, & hope to do so with advantage. I have not, meanwhile, been quite idle about you – but have been making all enquiries as to some proper lady to fetch you, & be with you. should I not return before you leave Cannstatt. As yet I have learned of no one whom I could trust – many who would receive you here are not willing to undertake a journey.***

The fact is, that July is a peculiarly awkward time – if you had left in March, I could have settled you at Brighton or elsewhere, perhaps at a Water Cure establishment, before leaving England myself; if in September I should be returned and ready to receive you at Knebworth. But in July, I am sure to be absent…it is of great importance that I should pass the Summer in Italy in

order to produce that permanent allevative which a warm climate in summer is likely to have. [And to spend time with my new girlfriend? This is possibly the first clue of a new relationship, with 22-year-old Marion Waller. More of whom in the next chapter]. ***However I hope to settle all shortly.***

* * * * *

Meanwhile, there are two things to be considered - 1st, your health; 2nd, your education. You have very much to learn before you enter the world, & require first rate Masters. If you are at Brighton from July till I come home about Sept., your studies wd be again interrupted & the time not long eno' for much benefit. Moreover, as I propose passing the winter at Naples, you could there get the best instructions in singing & music, French & Italian.

Now, as to your health, by which I mean principally the eruption. You say in a former letter this had vanished from the face – has it returned? And does it continue in the neck & shoulders. There is no safe cure for this but the Water Cure, & that will also strengthen & develop the whole frame. Perhaps that will be the best thing to do in the interim – provided as, I do not doubt, you still wish to leave in July.

Let me know exactly the state of the eruption & of your general health. I wish also that your back may be again examined, and to know if you have made progress since the last examination. Are you grown any taller and how are the teeth? On learning your answers to all this, I can best decide as to the Water Cure or not! Write as soon as you can. Look forward, my dearest Emily, to Sept. as the time for your real return to home, when I shall much enjoy welcoming you at Knebworth - & making you amends for your long exile and probations.

* * * * *

I heard from Teddy the other day, & about him today. He continues well – but has a sluggish inert physical indolence which vexes me much [more teen-age issues!]. ***I think of his spending the holidays at a Water Cure*** ["Daaaad!"]. ***I heard from Lady Murray the other day, she is going into Italy. Perhaps we may meet her*** [one of the unmarried daughters or daughter-in-laws of the 3rd

Earl of Mansfield?] ***The weather is intensely severe, snow nearly every day, nevertheless I fag at the Water Cure & hope to derive from it lasting benefit.***

You say nothing about Natalie – I hope all is well there. Does she still leave in July? If she stayed longer perhaps that might reconcile you to remaining till Sept. - but I don't want this, as I can manage somehow or other.

Miss Greene, if not gone, is going to Brussels, and evidently pumped hard to have you. But I got off very well.

If I get as far as Naples, I shall engage a house for the winter & an Opera Box. We shd leave England about the end of Nov & stay probably till the following April.

I hope Mrs H is less unkind & that your spirits are better. God bless you, most aff yrs, E.B.L.

* * * * *

The results of a post-winter examination of Emily's spine is not as positive as hoped. But Edward is sanguine, on Sunday 6th April, that ***it is possible that your general health being less strong may have had something to do with it, & now that the Dr thinks you are better, you may make more progress...***

I have no doubt of your deriving extraordinary benefit from the Water Cure, tho' I fear there will be scarcely time to try it this autumn, unless it be at Knebworth - if we could get a good bath woman. I am so glad you are an early riser and anticipate many charming walks before breakfast amongst the old haunts. Again, he softens the prospect of a bathing regime once she gets home, with a happy thought of early morning walks with him. He is conscious now of the need to keep her spirits up, as he has been advised by Miss Greene. Although there are still lectures on letting melancholy emotions get the better of her: ***Under other circumstances, [I should not] give in to your dread of seeing Natalie depart. I would either brace or nerve you to that trial, which is but a small preparation to the many severe ones you must anticipate in life. The mind must, like the body, render itself hardy, & grow exercised in struggle & endurance... But considering, my dear child, all you have gone thro in your solitary exile, I do not wish now to add to your pain, even with the motive of invigorating you by the ordeal.***

* * * * *

The subject of her travel arrangements remains the primary distraction of the next few months' correspondence. ***One cannot induce a Lady to go to Germany merely to bring you over, unless at some greater sacrifice of money than I can afford.*** Enquiries are made of the wife of Sir Alexander Malet, who has replaced Sir George Shee as the British 'envoy extraordinary and minister plenipotentiary' in Stuttgart, and of the Pfizers, ***in case any English family are coming over.*** He even suggests going back to Madame de Weling - ***she would probably be more kind & indulgent to you in the capacity of a visitor... and I could more easily get you from her house, than from the distance of Cannstatt.***

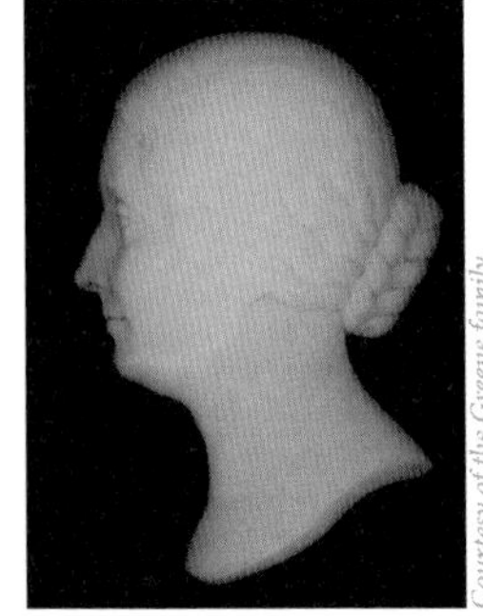

Mrs Wilkinson

Another suggestion is Mrs Wilkinson, who is in Brussels for a spell, as - unlike Edward, but like Patrick Brontë - she prefers to accompany her daughter to the Continent for her further education and language skills.

* * * * *

Monday 28th April, 1845. ***My dear Emily, I conclude from your silence as to my 2 proposals of M von Weling & Mrs Wilkinson, that you disliked both these alternatives... I shall bear your wishes completely in mind, & nothing but the sheer impossibility of managing it otherwise, will keep you in Cannstatt till September.***

I have had great troubles & anxieties, lately, which have rather tended to affect my health. Again, I am inclined to believe this relates to his shifting personal relationships, especially when he adds, a couple of sentences later, ***There is no news story that can interest you.***

He is leaving Malvern and returning to Knebworth - and again there is the rash promise of a better life for her there. His mother's room - that of the chateleine of the house - ***by the by, is finished, panneled in primrose & gold, with a pretty ceiling & all her pictures, cabinets & favourite furniture in it. I, at present, mean you to have that room - on the condition that it is kept all glass – the first neglect will be punished with summary ejectment. It is the pleasantest & largest room in the House.***

* * * * *

He is still not confessing his personal issues when, the day before his 42nd birthday, Saturday 24th May 1845, he writes, ***My dearest love, I am very grateful for your kind & affectionate letter, & tho' the time must come for me - as for all parents - when the affection of the tenderest child fades away into other & newer ties – such is the dispensation of Nature - I have at least the love now mine, & resign myself to what may remain of it.***

I have still great cause for anxiety & unhappiness...But…it is idle now to touch more on painful subjects… Fate does not weave her web for any of us only of gold & silver She is a Dark Embroiderer at the best.

When Edward slips into melancholy, he can hope for no better co-wallower than his daughter. As we saw the previous year, on the death of his mother, Emily strives and thrives to be his comforter. She responds - on Friday 30th May - ***My beloved and darling Father... Were I Fate, I would weave you such beautiful webs of such bright golden meshes, & spangled with such fragrant rosebuds, that you would never give me the title of a Dark Embroiderer. But I am not Fate, and I can only weave you a poor web of Love; but though its meshes may not be bright, nor its spangles so fragrant as those which others may weave you, it will at least, encircle you, when others have lost their lustre, and when the roses, so fragrant in the sunshine, are closed and faded in the evening dew.***

This reads as though she also suspects a breakdown in a personal relationship that neither she or we are party to. And if the loosening of ties with Laura Deacon and his other children is the cause, there is an unwitting and uncanny truth when she adds, ***And you must always call me 'your tenderest child' - and you must never doubt my love; but always remember, that your daughter loves you with no light love.***

Do not tell me your causes for unhappiness if, in doing so, you only awaken painful sensations in your own remembrance - but whenever you feel that by disclosing them you might render them lighter, do so, and if I can do nothing else, I can at least share them.

* * * * *

And shall I really see you in two months? And then how delightful the reflexions, that it is not only a meeting for a few days - as so many of the

previous ones have been - but a meeting which will endure for ever. [Alas!]

I cannot tell you how happy this thought makes me. I can hardly await the day which will restore you to me for ever, my beloved Father... The more I think of it, the less I can realise the happy thought of being with you. How happy, how delightful, will be the time when we will be able to talk over the past together, as a thing forever gone. Then you must tell me a great deal about yourself, and what your hero deeds were when a boy, and I in return will tell you some very ridiculous anecdotes and exploits of the Institution!

This will to be his companion, not simply his daughter, continues with a surprising reference to one of his previous paramours. These letters are so rich for analysis - it is increasing hard to believe that Emily does not know a lot more than we think she knows. ***I am writing so shockingly that even Lady Caroline Lamb would have thought the 'Shock'! too great, but I am in great haste. I have begun the cold baths, and feel better than I have done for some time. Good bye, dearest Papa, write soon and think kindly now and then of your Measy***

* * * * *

Wednesday, 4th June, 1845. ***My dearest love, Deep & grateful thanks for your affectionate & touching letter. I rejoice to think the time draws near when I can personally thank you...*** Although a short note - written in haste on his way to chair a public dinner (the 26th anniversary of the City of London General Pension Society, a thrilling prospect, I'm sure) - Edward does have time to address a tooth issue, ***if the tooth gives you pain, or if the dentist thinks it ought to be taken out, immediately let it be so – otherwise it had better wait the inspection of a London dentist. Germany seems a fatal climate to the teeth.***

When I read that Emily has toothache - since Miss Greene's visit - I immediately picture a vial of laudanum by Emily's bed. And maybe this explains the languid melanchoy of next letter, ten days later. As if she didn't have reason enough for languid melancholy.

The letter - dated Sunday 15th June - explains that ***before your letter arrived the dentist declared that it was of the utmost importance to have the tooth in question taken out immediately, and so frightened Dr Heine and*** *myself - by what he said would be the result of leaving the tooth, as it was, any longer - that Dr Heine insisted on it being extracted & promised to take upon himself the responsibility.*

Accordingly the tooth was taken out, and the inflammation I before mentioned is now certainly much better, tho' not yet quite gone. I am now drinking the mineral waters which I think do me good. [No mention of pain killers, but we should compare whether we would mention it if we'd popped a couple of ibuprofens.]

My most sanguine hopes with regard to the shape are more than realised and it seems, after having for so long a time proceeded but slowly, the cure was now getting on à pas de géant [by leaps and bounds]. *However the Dr says it will be necessary to take a machine with me to wear on the journey & during the morning. That will [be] rather disagreeable if I return to England with strangers.*

* * * * *

The greater part of her thoughts this Sunday, in June 1845, however, are whether - at the end of it all - there is indeed a place at her father's side when she gets home. Despite what her father promises, she doubts him - and she is right to do so. What we have, as a result, is an extraordinary love letter, which I have resisted editing, despite it being languid and over-written. It is a love letter. It is excused.

My own very dearest dearest Papa, You cannot think how welcome your dear letter was to me - indeed a few lines from you are always a long provision of joy and comfort to me through many low and tedious hours (for here the time goes by hours). Nor can I express to you how, with every minute, my desire increases to be once more united with you, my dearest Father. But it seems as if the time between this and then were fated to be spun out as long as possible - tho' before I tell you of my new disappointment, I must confide to you a secret and beg of you a favour.

You must know, my dearest Papa, that I have now had for many years a dear and secret wish – a desire which I perhaps never expressed to any one in the degree in which I have felt it. You, you alone, are the only person whom it regards, and you are the only who can fulfill it. Through many long years

I have cherished the hope that one day you would grant the earnest request which I am now about to put to you, and oh if you would only feel what I feel when I think you might refuse, you would, I think, pity me.

When away from you, I am never happy. As long as I was with Miss Greene (I confess it) my eternal thought was when will this end? You know when at Madame von Weling's I was not exactly in Paradise. Well, the reflexion which comforted me for everything else was that - at the end of whatever time might be fixed for my stay - there I should, at length, see you at the end, & be with you, though perhaps for a short time. And here, when I have known that you were ill, or unhappy, how much it has cost me to appear gay and happy, when my heart was sad, and longed to be with you.

You may perhaps smile incredulously on reading this, or you may think that I only feel this for the moment - but if you think so, it is because you do not know me. I have felt so for years. Lately I have had the presentiment (tho' I trust it is only a presentiment) that on returning to England I shall again be separated from you. Now, my dearest Papa, the favour I have to beg of you is not to separate me again from you.

You may perhaps think me very selfish in asking you this great favour, but remember the selfishness springs from my great love to you. And perhaps this [is] the chief & only reason of my having formed so few attachments hitherto - for so deep and earnest has been my affection for you, that every other feeling seems cold and dead beside it. It is true I have been much separated from you, and have seen and know you little, but may not the past be compensated by the future?

Perhaps you recall hours which I have passed with you, in which I might have seemed the reverse of what I have expressed – but trust me, had I loved you less fondly & devotedly, I should have been far more prévenant [attentive]. *The very deepness of my affection for you, together with my having been so seldom with you, occasioned the unhappy reserve which you took for coldness and lack of affection, when it in fact proceeded from the very warmth of my love itself.*

Let me live with you, let me see you a little every day, and you will learn to know me better. I will not push the point any further. I have now told you all which I have for years pent up in my heart, and I leave it with you to grant my request or no. As long as I myself saw the possibility of my wish being granted, I was silent, though even as a child I entertained the same desires – but I shall

now in a few days be seventeen. Is it then still impossible?

However, as I before said, I have now said my say – and pray, my own darling Papa, do not forget to answer my question in your next letter.

This passionate entreaty - this sweet, sad, love letter - from Emily to her father, answers so many of the mysteries of this narrative. All Emily has ever wanted is to be with him. She has set her heart on something he cannot give. And her heart can only be broken.

* * * * *

Postmarked Monday 23rd June, 1845. ***My dearest Emily, I recd yours to-day & write a hasty line in answer. 1st, to thank you, my own love, for your tender & affectionate wishes, & next to assure you that there is no ground for your presentiment that I can foresee. I have no idea of anything to separate us on your return & shall greatly enjoy the communication*** [this word is not clear, so a best guess] ***which brings us better acquainted with each other.***

Can he really think this? If he has grown apart from Laura Deacon and is not yet attached to Marion Waller, maybe it is his genuine belief and wish. If he is with either at this moment, it is cruel.

I wish to give him the benefit of the doubt, and believe his imminent relationship with Marion Waller, if it has begun, has not yet developed. I want to believe his wish to live with his daughter is sincere.

* * * * *

The struggle to find a way home continues. The day before, Sunday, 22nd June, Emily writes that she has had ***another visit from Mr Parsons*** [presumably a son of the late Mr Parsons, the English Clergyman], ***in which he told me that all his researches for a family returning to England had proved fruitless and that he had received a note from Lady Malet in which she asked him to tell me that, tho' there were many English now at Baden, they were all such curious people that she could not safely recommend any one there with whom I could return.***

There is only one plan which I can think of which remains, but even of

this I am doubtful. As Lady Malet said two ladies alone could not well travel together:- perhaps I could persuade Miss Greene to come to Stuttgart [i.e. not Cannstatt], ***where I could meet her and engage a servant of Mrs Pfizer's recommendation to accompany us from thence to Ostend, or wherever we would embark. This might remove the objection to my travelling with only one female companion... However I dare say there are some, which I do not perceive. I own, I am thoroughly bewildered and puzzled, for tho' I certainly came to Germany with Miss G, I am some years older now and tho' I am sensible of the care which she always tries to take, she is nevertheless eccentric at times.***

But in this perplexing dilemma I am not a little thankful that I can turn to a great mind, which - tho' it has peopled fairy worlds and called thousands into the beautiful Ideal [she is quoting from the last paragraph of his *Pilgrims of The Rhine* (1834)] - ***will not perhaps disdain to steer the little bark of my poor pigmy hopes & plans through the puzzling straits of the*** ______[indecipherable] ***Real.***

How happy, how delightful it would be, could you, without injury to yourself in any way, come yourself – but this cannot be, and it is only idle to think

Courtesy of the Stadtarchiv Stuttgart (B 262)

Cannstatt - looking north west

of or wish for it. Oh! when will the time come, when Night will only part us, and there will at length – at length - be an end to letters.....and separation.

* * * * *

You cannot think how triste & tediously the days pass now. Almost all the girls who were here during the winter are gone, or are on the eve of going. The spirited pleasure which a school certainly has sometimes power to give is passed, for the number of the girls with whom I associated has dwindled away to one or two, & they are also soon going to leave. The trifling gaiety of the institution is gone and all its thick repulsing chiliness is left.

With sensations that I cannot express, do I look forward to my meeting with you - with you, from whom I conceal nothing, whom I love so truly so fondly, so tenderly, whom I look upon not merely as a father but also as a brother, as my beloved and favourite brother.

The clock has just struck seven – seven, they say, is a lucky number but here at this time it is an unkind hour, for it tells me to lay aside my letter to you, to shake off light glad dreams, and to awake to the ___________[indecipherable] *of a french lesson.*

So farewell then, dear Papa, pray write soon to one to whose tedious and weary hours a letter is a sunbeam – and a letter from you a sunny era. Ah! could I truly say with certainty this day in four weeks I shall be with you – and could I then add - for ever !!! ....[sic] *Who does not like to build brilliant castles in the air? Would the one I have built were on terra firma. Remember me ever to be your fond and affectionate daughter, Emily*

The girls (yet remaining) gave me today the most beautiful wreaths & nosegays you can possibly imagine. From those with (whom) I most associate, I received a ring, & two very nice real old german Pokale [trophies]. *The governess Madmoiselle Schaeffer gave me a most splendidly embroidered handkerchief with rich real lace – together with some beautiful flowers.*

* * * * *

Friday 27th June, 1845. *My own very dearest dearest Papa, Today being my birthday* [her 17th birthday] *& a half holiday, you see me again at your side. I have also something to communicate to you which will of itself make up a little letter.*

The plan I proposed to you in my last letter touching Miss Greene will I am afraid not do – since writing to you last I have heard that whilst here, Miss Greene (as indeed I always feared) talked much to the Heines about our family affairs, which it seems has led them to some, however ridiculous, still very disagreeable suspicions - and it seems they expect that she should fetch me, and that it could not be otherwise.

Now tho' I candidly own all these suspicions are peculiarly disagreeable to myself, yet it is perhaps still more for your sake that I think it would not only be better & more prudent - but also more wise and more respectable - to avoid every thing which might give place to gossip. For, as being so nearly related to you, long after I am gone, one will talk about my having been here – and in a foreign land, and among strangers, one cannot be too much upon ones guard. Besides Miss Greene's eccentricity and love of talking, would not render her a desirable companion on the journey.

You see one cannot talk to the Heines about all this. They have of course never spoken to me upon these subjects. But if they talk to others about them, what is to be done? - nothing but to avoid every thing which might be a topic of the conversation or a subject to their suspicions.

* * * * *

Is this stressing of gossip about Miss Greene being her mother the true root of her antipathy toward Miss Greene's company? Or is Emily indirectly letting her father know that he has her confidence in regard to any liaison he has had, or may have? Could this be her way of reassuring him that he should not worry about her confidence, that she is grown up enough to keep his secrets?.....Or is it simply that Miss Greene talks too much?

* * * * *

In looking over all your letters the other day I came upon the one in which are contained the following words:

"...And wherever you may be, you have only to write to me 'Mon petit Papa' I am not happy here - come & fetch me - and your wish shall be my own"!! Now, if ever there was a time when I wished more than anything to say this to you, it is now. You do not know what I would give to say to you, "my dearest Papa, pray come soon to fetch me and let me live with you.

But then the thought that your health might be hurt by the journey and that this would then be thro' me, makes me shrink from availing myself of this, your kind desire... Somebody knocks, I must leave you for a few moments.

Her prayers are answered by this knock. It is a letter from her father saying he will come and *fetch* her... *indeed I might say this is the happiest moment of my life, for what has been my life? One long wish - and now this wish is realized!! When do think I may expect you? And would you like me to have my things packed up by the time you arrive?...*

I am so happy & so impatient to tell you so, that I cannot write any longer and therefore must beg you to believe me your own affectionate, attached and grateful child. Emily Bulwer Lytton

Write me a line when you are coming in order that I may be able to prepare your rooms at the Hotel – you must know I have latterly become a great Hausfrau.

* * * * *

Ah! Edward, how little you know yourself. A week later, he is back at Plan C. Monday, 4th July, 1845. *My dearest Emily, I am sorry there is so much difficulty in the way of your return, but does the objection to Miss Greene hold good with regard to Mrs Wilkinson? I think she might fetch you, & I think she would if you asked her...* etc. You've read it before. She's read it before.

He does eventually come himself. But something has changed. Something that summer has got its claws into him.

I am much touched, my dearest Emily, by your kind expressions & shall be delighted to see you again. Ever most aff yrs E.B.L.

Part Five

~ Early Adulthood ~ Aged 17 to 19 ~

A mystery painting that hangs high in a hallway of Knebworth House, assumed to be one of Edward's paramours - if it is, it is most likely to be Marion Lowndes, pka Waller, aka Angelo

CHAPTER 28

~ *Marion Waller* ~

When I think of all those past years how happy Angelo was, tears come in my eyes & I can hardly believe he is gone from us forever! I am sure no human being ever lived so bright & happy a life as Angelo did all those years. I would have gone through fire & water for him and he knew it. And I believe he loved me most of all who lived with him, for he told me so & wrote me a touching letter the Christmas before he died, telling me I had been the one he loved best.

~ Marion Lowndes (previously Waller) 1875

* * * * *

At some point in the 1840s, after the conception of the child Violet Beaumont in the summer of 1842 (as Emily sets off for Germany), Edward's physical relationship with Laura Deacon comes to an end. This woman, now in her 40s, who has borne Edward at least three children (Ernest, Gertrude and Violet - possibly five, including Georgina and the deceased Florence), and ***who is indeed to me a wife***, becomes his second not ex-wife.

For Edward is still married to Rosina. His first - and only - wife is living as Lady Bulwer Lytton in Geneva, writing bitter satirical books to supplement an annual allowance that does not keep her in a manner to which she was once accustomed. Rosina's exile on the Continent will come to an end two years after Emily's exile on the Continent - and she will go on to play one further dreadful part in this drama. She is not, we may be certain, back to reclaim her place from Laura Deacon.

* * * * *

Laura Deacon, as we've explored earlier, will later in life become Mrs Grant, and be discovered living in Maida Vale with two of her daughters, Gertude and Violet, in the censuses of 1861 and 1871, listed as an 'annuitant'. Laura will also play one more part in this drama - making an appearance at Knebworth in 1846, which we will also come to. But apart from this single episode, what contact Edward keeps with Laura after the birth of Violet is not known, beyond the monetary contact, and the inclusion of her three daughters - Georgina, Gertrude and Violet - in his Will. But then, what contact Edward kept with Laura before the birth of Violet is not known either.

For all the remarkable reams and richness of correspondence that Edward Bulwer Lytton and his family have preserved for us - cf. the preceding seven chapters - not a single letter to, or from, Laura Deacon survives. Maybe like Paul and Linda McCartney they never spent a day apart. Even if this were true, it is not the reason. The reality is that Edward's relationship with Laura Deacon has been carefully exorcised from the great man's story. Principally by the great man himself.

Unlike Rosina, Laura does not have the name to augment the annuity, so there are no lurid exposés from her. Even their novelist daughter, Gertude (aka Gerald) appears to keep well clear of biographical references in her romances. We know nothing about Edward and Laura's romantic relationship beyond the few lines in Edward's short-lived private diary, already quoted - how she left him flowers on the stairs for his birthday in May 1838.

* * * * *

The week I am writing this chapter in late January 2016, our server at Knebworth House is hacked. Every single file on its hard drive is locked by a virus called Cryptolocker. Worse, the virus is sophisticated enough to find the server's connection to its back-up drive - in a different building - and also lock every one of our back-ups. A ransom note is left on the server telling us, ***Stay calm. You can recover all your data by making a payment of 1072 GBP in Bitcoin currency in order to receive a decryption key...*** etc.

We pay for the best anti-virus software and have a sophisticated digital back-up system, so - hindsight is a fine thing - we have no off-line back-up of our files. Suddenly, we have lost 20 years of company letters and documents.

Stay calm. You are holding a complete book, so not all was lost. A personal back-up system saved my Emily folders - but every business document since Knebworth House moved from paper to digital was, literally overnight, lost to us.

* * * * *

There is a happy - if unethical - ending to this modern drama. Having consulted with the Police and security experts, we rationalise a business decision to pay the ransom and - remarkably - a decryption file is emailed from an untracable address in Poland, and all our files are, summarily, unlocked.

I lose of week of writing this book - and could now write a book on the murky world of bitcoins - but the overriding emotion left by this nightmare seven days - as I return to the rice-paper thin family letters of two centuries ago - is the fragility of information.

And the fragility of all the world's stories.

In the final week of January 2016, I knew that on Monday 23rd June 1845, a £5 bracelet was sanctioned as an appropriate leaving present from Emily to Madame Heine - but I no longer knew that on the Sunday of that same weekend in June, 1998 (Sunday 21st), 2514 people attended the Pets Pets Pets Show in Knebworth Park.

These little ink-lined pieces of paper - so personal, so rich in the minutiae of the past, so full of stories - held in my hand 170 years after they were scratched out in distant bedrooms, or in alcoves on long-recycled steamboats, are, quite simply, a miracle.

For, like the letters and papers of Laura Deacon, they could, so easily, have been plucked from a portefeuille and - in one quick toss into the fire grate - lost forever.

* * * * *

We do, however, have letters from Marion Waller. These are in the collection of Edward's son, Robert, who is left to see out the terms of his father's Will. In the mid 1870s, after his father's death, Robert enters into a cordial correspondence with his father's third great love - who, as a mother, calls herself Marion 'Lowndes' - concerning his many half-siblings.

It is testament to Marion's status in his father's life that - beyond the responsibility of her own children - she also takes on the responsibility of Edward's final two children, with a woman named Eleanor Thomson (a young widow he rescues as his housekeeper, and no relation, that we know, to the other Mrs Thomson of this story), who are orphaned by their mother's early death in 1869, and Edward's four years later.

On the surface, what happens to these two later children - a boy and girl, Edward and Alice - does not reflect well on Edward, and is a haunting echo of Emily's story. The daughter is placed in an orphanage, and - so far - her history is lost to us; the son, meanwhile, is taken in by Marion, loved as a child as far as we can tell (particularly by his half-sister Lucy Lowndes), and emigrates to Australia aged 18, where he lives until 1945, never telling his family about any relationship to Edward Bulwer Lytton.

There is more to this story than meets the eye - and maybe this book will have a sequel one day - but the precis does not look good. A son that is cherished - and daughter that is packed off to an institution.

* * * * *

It is because of these children of the 1860s, that I have Robert's correspondence with Marion Lowndes transcribed before me. The transcriptions are made from our archive by Edward Thomson's granddaughter, Elizabeth Thomson. Beth, who lives in Australia, knows none of the facts of her Lytton ancestry until, in the year 2000, she goes looking for a supposed cousin of her grandfather Edward Thomson - Arthur Edward Gilbert Lowndes.

Beth contacts King's College School and is sent a letter written in 1978 by Edward's biographer, Sibylla Jane Flower (Sibylla has been pursuing her definitive work on Edward for a much more serious length of time than my lightweight 17 years) - this reveals Arthur Lowndes as an illegitimate son of Edward Bulwer Lytton. On writing to Sibylla, Beth receives the startling news - for her family - that Edward Thomson is also a son of Edward Bulwer Lytton. That cousin of her grandfather is actually his half-brother.

Beth and her family visit us at Knebworth House in 2000, and we only have to see her face to know, instantly, that she is a Bulwer Lytton. As I have said before, Lytton genes are distinctive. It is a happy family reunion and another spur to me to understand more of the secret life of my great-great-great grandfather. Here is where many of the mysteries of Emily's life are hidden.

Courtesy of the Thomson family

Edward Thomson

When Emily returns from Germany in 1845, Laura Deacon, aka Mrs Beaumont, appears to be in France with her young children. It is another woman that will now keep Emily from her father's side, and cause the promises of his letters to be broken. This new relationship is just beginning - may not even begin until late 1845 - so we cannot say Edward knowingly makes promises he cannot keep. But we can chide him for his lack of knowledge of himself.

If it isn't Marion, it would be somebody else.

* * * * *

Before I study the correspondence in detail, I go looking for Marion Waller on the web. [Genealogy Alert. Skip forward five pages if you are not interested in the birth of the Shepherd Neame brewery - this is a Bulwerian tangent simply too random not to include.] The Marion Waller I find is a Marion Jane Waller of Alfred House, Preston, in Faversham, Kent. Alfred House stands on the Dover to London road, the old A2 - or as the Romans called it, Watling Street - England's front drive. I have a mental image of Edward, on a journey back from the Continent, stopping for the night in Faversham, and eloping with the Inn Keeper's daughter.

But Alfred House is not an Inn, it is the family home of Henry and Grace Waller, a prominent Faversham family. Of the Wallers' seven children, all three daughters make what would then be called a 'good match'. On the splendidly pink website FindAGrave.com there is a photograph of Henry and Grace's large white tomb in St. Catherine's Churchyard, Faversham. The tomb tells us that, in 1836, Henry leaves Grace a widow for 29 years. And that Grace dies aged 87 at her youngest daughter Marion's married home, Ospringe House - a few yards away from Alfred House, on the opposite side of the London Road.

And here is the rub - the third of the Wallers' prosperous son-in-laws, William Carter (1814-1889), marries Marion Jane Waller (born 11th September 1822) on December 4th, 1844 (a Wednesday - it suggests prosperity to be married on a working day), just a few months before our Marion Waller begins her acquaintance with Sir Edward Bulwer Lytton.

Marion Jane Waller cannot be our Marion Waller. But I am pleased I have purchased a copy of William and Marion Carter's marriage certificate, because it turns out to be an historic document. The list of witnesses at this Wednesday wedding in 1844 is a prescient foretelling of the modern incarnation of Britain's oldest brewing company. This ranks as one of the more bizarre discoveries of my Emily quest.

1844. Marriage solemnized at the Parish Church in the Parish of Preston by Faversham in the County of Kent

No.	When Married.	Name and Surname.	Age.	Condition.	Rank or Profession.	Residence at the Time of Marriage.	Father's Name and Surname.	Rank or Profession of Father.
59	December 4th 1844	William Carter	Of full age	Bachelor	Gentleman	Boughton Blean	William Carter	Gentleman
		Marion Jane Waller	Of full age	Spinster	—	Preston	Henry Waller	Gentleman

Married in the Parish Church according to the Rites and Ceremonies of the Established Church, by me, James [illegible] Vicar

This Marriage was solemnized between us, William Carter, Marion Jane Waller; in the Presence of us, G. [illegible] [illegible], Ths. Carter, Eliza [illegible], [illegible]

Marion Jane Waller's marriage certificate

Better still, it contains what is either the most extraordinary coincidence, or a clue to our Marion Waller's connection to Edward Bulwer Lytton.

* * * * *

[Severe genealogy alert - don't say I didn't warn you - none of these names are important unless you are writing a history of British beer or thinking of joining the Faversham History Society.] The eldest of the Wallers' prosperous son-in-laws - married to Marion Jane's elder sister Ellen Mary - is Henry Shepherd Jr. (1816-1875), of the Shepherd brewing company, that has been producing beer in Faversham since 1573. 28-year-old Henry Shepherd Jr. is listed as a witness on his sister-in-law's marriage certificate beside fifteen-year-old Eliza Neame, of the Neame hop-farming family of Faversham.

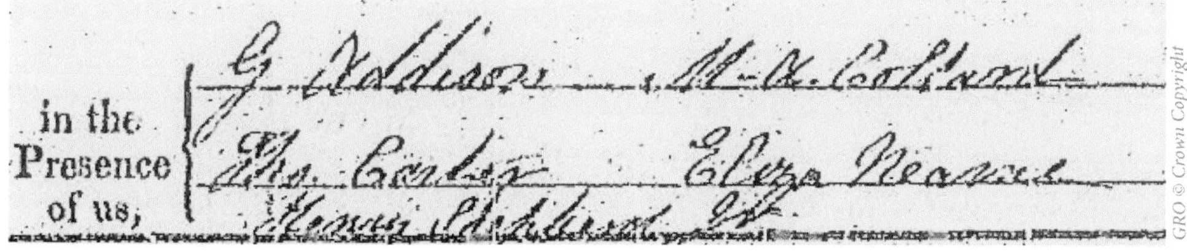

Eliza Neame (1829-1893) will go on to marry John Henry Mares (1820-1864), who four years after this wedding will go into partnership with Henry Shepherd Jr. Another sixteen years later, following the death of John Henry Mares, Eliza's younger brother Percy Beale Neame (1836-1913) will begin the process of purchasing the brewing company off Henry Shepherd Jr., creating what thrives today as Britain's oldest brewing company, Shepherd Neame.

Where will Percy Neame, the youngest son of a farmer, get the money to do this? By pooling the resources of his Neame relations, but specifically his mother-in-law, Mary Anne Collard (1817-1900), who is a third witness on this auspicious 1844 Carter/Waller marriage certificate.

A year and a half after this wedding, in June 1846, Mary Anne Collard swiftly marries Percy's cousin Harry Neame (1819-1848) - as an only daughter, Florence, is born three months later. Although widowed two years after, Mary Anne Neame, in 1857, inherits 50% of her father Henry Collard's £9000 farm. Percy Neame's initial investment in the Shepherd company comes seven years later - just before he marries Mary Anne's 19-year-old daughter, his first cousin once removed, Florence Neame, née Neame (1846-1934). Close-knit these Kent communities.

Henry Shepherd Jr., Eliza Neame, Mary Anne Collard... Here, as witnesses on one 1844 Faversham marriage certificate, we have all the ingredients of Shepherd Neame beer. The brewing company, the hops and the money.

Only one ingredient is missing. Water. Which brings us to a fourth witness on the certificate - the most interesting for our story - G. Addison.

Grace Addison is the eldest of Henry and Grace Waller's seven children, born in 1804. The prosperous son-in-law she brings to the Waller family dinner table is William Addison (1803-1881), physician to Princess Marie Luise Victoire of Saxe-Coburg-Saalfeld, mother of Queen Victoria; and a direct contemporary of Edward Bulwer Lytton; and, wait for it... author, in 1828, of *A Dissertation On The Nature and Properties of the Malvern Water,* on which subject he was the first to lecture at the Royal Institution. William Addison is practicing the Water Cure in Malvern when Edward visits in the mid 1840s.

* * * * *

William Addison is also a pioneering doctor of blood and nerve disorders, indeed he is busily identifying lymphoma alongside his contemporary Thomas Hodgkin (1798–1866), who is to give his name to a variation of the disease. About to become a leading light in this field is William Addison's wife Grace's cousin, Augustus Volney Waller (1816–1870), who will give the family name Waller to 'Wallerian degeneration', a process Wikipedia tells us ***results when a nerve fiber is cut or crushed.***

Marion Waller's brother, Augustus Volney Waller

Augustus is the son of Henry Waller's eccentric and radical elder brother, William Waller (1773-1829) of Elverton Farm, just a little further up the London Road from Faversham. When not tending his particularly fine Newtown Pippin apples [according to *Cobbett's Weekly Register, Volume 47*], William Waller is writing letters of esteem and support to imprisoned dissidents, and giving his children the middle names of his republican heroes. Thus his eldest, Augustus, takes the name of the radical French philosopher Constantin François de Chassebœuf, comte de Volney (1757–1820). As well 'Volney' rather than 'Chassebœuf', as Augustus is raised a vegetarian, living after his father's death with another of his father's heroes, Dr William Lambe (1765-1848), the similarly inappropriately named, father of veganism.

Like his brother Henry Waller of Alfred House, William Waller of Elverton Farm has seven children - with wife Jessie Eaglestone - and his youngest daughter is also called Marion. But because this Marion is William's daughter, her middle name is much sillier than 'Jane'. She is named Marion Wollstonecraft Godwin Waller - after other heroes of William Waller, William Godwin (1756–1836) and Mary Wollstonecraft (1759–1797), premium radicals and parents of *Frankenstein* author, Mary Shelley.

This, of course, is Edward Bulwer Lytton's Marion Waller.

* * * * *

After the Napoleonic Wars, Kent farmer and radical thinker (a rare combination nowadays) William Waller spends much of his time in Nice, then part of the Kingdom of Piedmont-Sardinia, possibly trading wine, and eventually moving his family there. After his death in Nice in 1829, the lease on Elverton Farm is brought up by the Collard family and William's wife Jessie remarries a local, Colonel Caesar Pian, and moves along the coast to the other Savoy hub, Genoa. It is only then that the seven Waller children are Christened, albeit with their atheist names.

Marion Wollstonecraft Godwin Waller, raised on the Continent and in early life frequently travelling abroad, is difficult to trace in English records. On the birth certificates of her three England-born children, Arthur in 1848, Lucy in 1851, and Evelyne in 1853, she is Marion Lowndes - and the father is, first Arthur Lowndes (Edward is writing the poem *King Arthur* at the time), then George (Edward's middle name) Lowndes, then Arthur Lowndes again for the third child, that dies in infancy.

Marion appears only late in life in English census records. In 1871, Marion Waller Lowndes is living at 32 Upper Gloucester Place, on the east side of Dorset Square. Her age is listed as 48, which suggests she was born in the same year as her cousin Marion Jane. 1823. This makes her five years older than Emily.

* * * * *

Information on the family of William Waller is so scarce that I am going to try your patience with one further discovery. Marion's eldest sister Cornelia Cullen Waller - presumably middle-named by her father after the Scottish physician and agriculturist and central figure of Scottish Enlightenment, William Cullen (1710-1790) - is married in Holborn, London, on 6th September 1841, apparently aged 21. We know about Cornelia because she and her chemist husband Charles Scatcherd Wilson Edwards emigrate to New Zealand in 1856 with their five children; including the fourth, Worley Bassett Edwards, who becomes a controversial New Zealand Supreme Court judge - the first educated solely in New Zealand - and therefore features in that country's encyclopedias and dictionaries of national biography.

Worley Edwards is supposedly extremely erudite, but eccentric and intolerent at having been banished by fate to the distant colonies. He might have settled back in England, having inherited some money from an uncle and aunt. However, he and his sister Florence invest the inheritance with their cousin Arthur Lowndes - who loses it, leaving them destitute. Their fare back to New Zealand is paid by Arthur's mother, Marion Lowndes - or rather by Arthur's father, Edward Bulwer Lytton.

In an unpublished memoir, Worley Edwards describes his relationship with his father Charles as 'difficult', and labels his mother Cornelia 'domineering'. The teenage Marion Waller isn't too happy living with Charles and Cornelia either - she joins them in their Great Russell Street home in the early years of their marriage, as she tells Robert in the following letter of 1875.

* * * * *

I left England when I was 4 years old and returned to it when I was not quite 20. My eldest sister married in London invited me over, & I left Genoa to go to her. But on my arrival I wished myself back, for I thought London a dreadful dingy place & lived a most miserable lonely life in Grt Russell St. I had to wait till I came of age to sign the Re-

Genoa

lease of the Trustees, but I do not think I ever went to bed in my little attic without crying myself to sleep. I did not like to pain my dear mother by writing all to her, but I began to save my money to go back to her.

At that time a book of His was lent me. From that day I lived in his works, but I am sure I shd never have written or seen him if I had not heard my sister say many ladies wrote to him to express their admiration. I pondered over those words, then wrote a little note to him telling him how unhappy & lonely I had felt in London (I knew no one & my sister was many years older & her husband old enough to be her father) & that I owed him the only happy moments I had spent in England.

I told him I was longing to return to Italy and that I begged for his autograph. I gave him an address to a Post Office. I put my note in a little nosegay, which I left on his doorstep. I did not expect an answer, but got one begging for an interview - that he was soon going to Italy himself.

But several letters passed between us before I took courage to call upon him in Hertford St., Mayfair.

There I first saw him, in his long dressing gown, seated at his writing table & surrounded with all the disorder of an artist, books, etc. etc. I thought I had never seen so handsome a man before - he suddenly appeared to me the beau Ideal of an artist & man of genius - and that picture will never be blotted out of my mind.

He received me & treated me so well & so respectfully that he soon put me more at ease for, perhaps you will hardly believe it, I was always a very shy girl. I called a few times after, but he always behaved well to me in his house. He promised to take me to Italy, and I was still so silly that I asked him how much it would cost me!

* * * * *

How tempted I am to answer that. This account is written thirty years after the events described, so we can forgive Marion some poetic licence and muddling of dates - but there are some straightforward facts that don't add up, that suggest she is an unreliable narrator. For a start she says her ***sister was many years older & her husband old enough to be her father*** - I think she means her new lover was old enough to be her father.

Cornelia and Charles's marriage certificate says that in September 1841 they are both 21 years old. Sibylla Jane Flower's research tells me that two other sisters - Stypatia and Augusta - separate Marion from Cornelia, and if Cornelia was born in 1819, four numerical years can seem a lot when you are still a teenager - but Charles old enough to be her father? By the 1870s, Charles Edwards is long lost to a farm in New Zealand, so Robert won't know any different. And it does divert attention from the reality that the real age difference here is between Marion and Edward Bulwer Lytton.

Whatever licence Marion's account takes, we are very fortunate to have it. It is a tantalizing glimpse into the secret world of Edward Bulwer Lytton.

* * * * *

The first thing the account is not clear about, is when this secret relationship started. This is relevant, because the earlier it began, the more unfair Edward's promises to Emily to take her to Italy with him for the winter of 1845/1846. Marion continues, ***Well - I think it was in March or April*** [no year given] ***we left for Paris Hotel des Princes - then went on to Turin, stayed a few days there then to Genoa. From Genoa to Leghorn by sea then to Naples.*** Then - after a brief description of their time in Naples (which we will return to later) - she begins an account of time spent in Rome, ***In Febuary 1846 we were in Rome...***

Is this two trips or one? If it is two trips, Edward is practising a grand deception on his daughter. I don't think (in this case) he is.

Although there is a break in Edward's letters in 1845, between 19th January and 14th March, I cannot believe that Edward travels to Naples in this time. On 14th March he is unwell, writing from Malvern, ***it is of great importance that I should pass the Summer in Italy in order to produce that permanent allevative which a warm climate in summer is likely to have.*** And ***If I get as far as Naples, I shall engage a house for the winter and an Opera box. We shd leave England about the end of Nov and stay probably till the following April.***

It is more likely that what Marion remembers as ***March or April*** is actually November or December 1845. Edward does not make it to Italy in the summer of 1845 - ***My plans have been so interrupted that I do not the least know if I am to get to Italy in July, or at all.*** Edward does leave for Paris in

December 1845 - with his mistress Marion, not his daughter Emily - and is indeed, as he planned, back in England by April 1846.

* * * * *

So when does he meet her? This lonely step-daughter of Colonel Pian. This bored fan living in Great Russell Street for whom the British Museum has lost its charm. This Kent girl from the Côte d'Azur who is to become, in all his lifetime, ***the one he loved best***?

If it is before 1845, she is embarrassingly young - and he is well to have kept his petite Mignon quiet.

If it is in the Spring of 1845, it could well be at Malvern, where she is a likely visitor to her Waller cousin Grace Addison, and Grace's Water Doctor husband William. The Addison connection is such a coincidence that it is tempting to think that meeting Marion in Malvern is, in fact, the ***great importance*** of his spending the summer in Italy.

But most likely, I think, is that the ***great importance*** of a more clement climate, and the concern of taking his daughter out of school and to Italy without a companion or a chaperone, is the reason that - at some point during that summer of 1845 - the great author is intrigued by a nosegay from a bright bi-lingual, probably tri-lingual, 22-year-old looking to return to her family in Genoa.

This is a happier explanation. The fault is, the selfish instinct that does not see how this love affair can only be to the detriment of his daughter.

* * * * *

As we have read in his letters of early 1845, 41-year-old Edward Bulwer Lytton is not a well man. I would be very interested to read Dr Addison's or Dr Wilson's or Dr Weiss's true, non-commercial, diagnosis of his symptoms. Edward thinks he has influenza in March, then throughout the year complains of skin and back problems. This may be allergies and writer's cramp - but it could also be his flesh and liver responding to some more serious blood-infections, or hepatitis.

In the coming years he is to complain increasingly of inner ear disorders. Nowadays we associate tinnitus with jet fighter pilots and rock musicians, but Edward's complaint is more likely the result of ear infections than decibels - lying around in wet sheets, I hear you cry! You could as well cry Ménière's disease or syphilis. The fact is, we don't know. The remedy we can trust Edward's doctors to prescribe is, more Water Cure - and himself to prescribe is, a smoke and some winter UV rays.

Our other unreliable narrator, his wife Rosina, has mentioned his fondness for brandy, but we may guess Edward's alcohol intake is reduced during the Water Cure years. Is he taking medicinal laudanum? He is still being bled by leeches in 1846 - it would be very unusual for him not to be taking medicinal opiates throughout his lifetime.

It is with this all in mind, that we must consider two character traits of Edward Bulwer Lytton that have a profound effect on his daughter's life.

* * * * *

Firstly, he wants a woman by his side. He is at his most miserable when he has no emotional crutch. His letters after the death of his mother refer to this, and the record of his love life - even glimpsed through its smoke and mirrors - strongly suggests that if he ever is out of female company, it is never for very long. And this need is especially strong - isn't it for all of us - when unwell.

Clearly there are times, during his correspondence with his daughter - especially after the death of his mother and during the chilling of his relationship with Laura Deacon - that he considers it possible that Emily could fill this role. He certainly teases her hopes and dreams with the prospect. But the philosopher should know himself better.

He should recognise the Mignon fantasy for what it is. A sexual fantasy. For, sure enough, every woman at Edward's side from Marion on, is a bright young thing - usually young enough to be his daughter; or towards the end of his life - in the case of Ellen Thomson, and his final paramour, Marie DeRosset (both of whom, like Mignon, die young and in tragic circumstances to be discussed later) - young enough to be his granddaughter. They are a call back to that lost love of his youth, the girl by the stream in Ealing.

They are all there to offer him a crutch - physical and emotional - but they are also, crucially, fulfilling the role of Muse. They are Nurse Nymphs.

Emily can not be that girl. There are disciples of Rosina who suggest that her father might have put her under sexual pressure. It is inevitable that you court the gossip of posterity if you cloud your personal history in smoke and spinning vanity mirrors. I don't believe this.

I do think Emily suffers sexual confusion in the intensity of her need for love. I have already mentioned it, that before I knew this story I wrote a screenplay called *Green For A Season* on this theme. I understand this confusion in childhood, and you only have to look at the end of Emily's story - which you already know - to see the ultimate length she will go to be Mignon to her father.

But the problem for Emily is the opposite. When Edward actually spends time with her, what he sees in her - haunting him, in a bad, not good, way - is her mother, Rosina. Fine in 1828. Not sexy post-1839. Rosina's allure is buried deep beneath the nine layers of Hell as far as Edward Bulwer Lytton is concerned.

We'll get to this in a moment, but first, the second character trait.

* * * * *

Edward, we have seen, is prone to losing his temper. He can be emotionally violent. Rosina is happy also to offer you examples of physical violence, although she is the only one in his long life to suggest this. But whoever is to be the Nurse Nymph at Edward Bulwer Lytton's side is going to have to be steeled to both his erotic and his erratic make up.

This flaw may be one of nurture - the spoils of an indulged childhood. It may be one of nature - the spoils of creative genius. I believe that in this case, mostly, it is one of narcotics and alcohol - the spoils of medicinal opiates and stimulants, brought on by the physical discomfort of persistent illness.

Either way, Emily - at this age, and with her history - does not have the emotional tools to deal with living with such a man. Within a few weeks, possibly a few days, of her return from Germany - during a conversation about her being sent away to school again rather than been taking to Italy and the Opera for the winter - Edward loses his patience with his daughter.

There is an unspecified lie on Emily's part, that is born and uncovered apparently through the meddling of Mrs Thomson. The result is a traumatic quarrel where Edward threatens the most damning of solutions, to return her to her mother, and - Miss Greene tells us - Emily attempts suicide by taking an overdose of laudanum.

In separation, deep and soulful bonds have been created between father and daughter through week after week, year after year, of heartfelt and loving correspondence. A few days in each other's presence, and all is dissolved.

* * * * *

I was going to call you Father, but I may not, will not, dare not, call you thus now; that I have lost your good opinion and esteem, is what I should have felt as my due – even if you had not told me so; that I [have] for ever lost your affection I know – & were it only from your willingness to give me over to my mother – yes! let me write the word in full & trample upon & mangle as much as possible those feelings which can so ill bear it – it is but a just punishment, and what I deserve...

...Life to me has lost its enjoyment – it must be alike to the criminal if he spend the last night allotted to him for existence in a prison or a palace [she is left on her own at Knebworth House]***; in both, his own feelings would be like his companions, the phantom visions of the past, & the pale & faint hopes for the clouded future, would render him callous to all external considerations. Had my crime been less heinous, I might perhaps have craved as a boon the neighbourhood of my brother now. I do not.***

Excuse her not making a lot of sense. Few suicide notes do. And consider laudanum her co-writer. The shame of the lie aside, the stark, horrible, dream-shattering reality facing the seventeen-year-old is that, after all these years, the instant she is back at her father's side, he wishes to send her away again.

Wherever I am placed I shall bear within me my own wretched feelings which will render me indifferent to all other circumstances. The more secluded the retreat, the more rigid the rules, the more unrelenting the disruption, the [more] grateful will it be to me; as the weary & broken-hearted looked formerly upon the convent, I shall look upon any place that will take me from

my own thoughts – as a place of rest from myself, and a preparation for a better life.

I know I have lost your love & your esteem for ever! I know you will never more regard me as your child, even as your weak and erring, tho' still fond, child... Oh! it is it is an awful thing to be alone with [the] thought that so young [a] one has betrayed a trust, deceived the kindest & most confiding of parents, forfeited forever his esteem and his affection, & to have nothing left one but the reflexion of one's own misery & despair.

* * * * *

You said the last part of your conversation last night would probably pain me the most. You said so perhaps because I lately entreated you not to let me leave you so soon again. That feeling was but for a moment. Now I am glad that it is so to be. It is well that we are to part. You will be released from one whom you can now neither love nor regard; and I may, in secret, cherish the fond remembrance of, & pray for, one from whom my own faults have banished me; but whom I shall as fondly love, & as proudly esteem, as I did when I was happier & better.

You were kind eno' to say that I was not to look upon our separation as a punishment – but I cannot help feeling that I myself am the barrier between us. I will not ask you ever to think of me with kindness. I know & feel you never can. All I ask is that, in your generous & just mind, when time shall perhaps have softened, not erased, the remembrance of my offence, that which I cannot help, & which is my misfortune, may not be mingled with that which I could have helped, and which is my fault.

May the All Powerful preserve and bless you, to whose kind heart I have often come in my childish & girlish grief. Your forgiveness I may crave, tho' I feel that forgetfulness is impossible... Again, thank you for the great kindness you have unfailingly shewn me may Heaven bless you for it, & may Heaven's angels watch over & preserve you when I shall be far away.....your sorrowing – tho' ever fond & grateful, Emily Lytton. 7 o'clock.

* * * * *

My dearest child, In the assurance of my sincere pity, & of the affection which - in spite of what may now seem harsh & stern, feels acutely all the pain my duty constrains me to inflict - can comfort you. Accept & lay it to your heart. Do not exaggerate your offence...If you will but resolve that it shall be a single & isolated act, not part of a disengenous habit, not a part of a system.. it is soon atoned for by you, & will be yet sooner forgotten by myself.

Nay, it may serve, though bitterly & roughly, to improve your character, to confirm your future happiness, to cement my love & esteem for you upon an unperishable basis – that of [a] conviction that, come what may, you will never again deceive me & what is more, that you will hold in horror deceit to all.

That which saddened & appalled me most, was not the deceit itself...timidity, surprise, many matters, might hurry & betray you into the first wrong step – but, as I said, it was the address & seeming candour with which the deception was carried on: when you said with an air of such simple truth, "should I have shewn you Caroline's letter if there had been the least foundation for it?" [Caroline Thomson (1829-1915) is Mrs Thomson's third daughter, a year younger than Emily]*; when, in repeated conversations, you declared yourself hurt & offended by allusions not merited; when, on my shewing you letters I wrote to Caroline & Mrs Thomson with your own copy to the former, & asked you whether in any way they could be altered to clarify your own feelings & impressions of what had past, & you replied, apparently with cheerful openness, that "they were what you wished"; when I shewed you Mrs Thomson's letter to me defending you, & you said you felt as I did "that the affront was in thinking you required defence".....you gave to a simple deception the character of a consumate practice in the art.*

* * * * *

Now as I before told you, it is easy to deceive me – this sort of facility you may observe pervades my whole character – even with my servants. I leave my money about, my papers in my table. Life to me would be worse than a jail if I were to be always on my guard even against my menial. But with those I love – with those I wear next to my heart – Trust is the very air I breathe, and the merest & dullest fool can be duped less easily than I can by one who sits at my hearth, Therefore I throw myself on the generosity of those I love or live with. Therefore my whole world seems to crumble at my feet when I find that I have been leaning upon treacherous breasts. But I do not, on fair & dispassionate consideration, apply to you the hard word of treachery. Deception is a much milder offence.

And for this, when I consider how much you have been estranged from those in whom you would naturally confide & had, as it were, prematurely to guard yourself among strangers; when I consider too, the timidity of your character, & the exterior coldness which belongs to my own manner – the difference of our sexes, etc., I can find excuse for your having, unaware, contracted something of that simulation which is the refuge of the weak amongst strangers. And secondly, for not having cured yourself of the habit, now you are with me.

But my child, my own beloved Emily, I implore, I adjure you to watch sternly, resolutely, incessantly, over this tendency – root it out utterly. All your admirable tendencies will fail you if this weed poisons all.

What a Father forgives, a husband hereafter never will pardon. Had you been my wife instead of my daughter, confidence indeed would have gone almost beyond retrieval. Not for my sake alone – For you future.....I implore you to let the pain you suffer be a salutory warning. A fault is soon forgotten & repaired. Be what has passed a fault only - never let it become a vice. A fault is an action, a vice is a habit.

And now, not only with complete, entire, & cordial forgiveness – with an assurance to take you to my heart as warmly as before, with a hope & trust that frankness henceforth will be the noble bond between us, & that you will adhere to the truth – as a ship to the star – I turn from the subject.

* * * * *

I come to the Plan which pains you so much. My poor child, it is no punishment. It has no reference to your fault. Before that occurred, I saw constantly before me the necessity, if I performed my duty, of your completing your education elsewhere. Do think calmly & rationally over the reasons. Do you suppose that I am untrue? That I am preaching the deception I have condemned, by inventing false excuses for a plan meant but for your good? How is it possible that you can have masters here, or at a Water Cure establishment if I go there, or in travelling if I go abroad? How, if I remain even stationary in a city, can you have Masters without some Lady to be with you & superintend – where at once can I find such a Lady? At your age?

Were you younger, a mere governess might do. Were you older, a companion. But blame me not, if I feel anxiously, fastidiously, the responsibility that I should thus delegate to some utter stranger; at a school, the method, the discipline, the machinery as it were, serve to produce all; that for a governess in the house, would require heart & principle & discretion - virtues so rare to find. A governess wants a governess; that is, a Mother to superintend her & direct.

Every friend I have consulted urges me to the plan suggested for the present. True, that before the late circumstances, I shrank from entering on the subject with you, but I should have done so at last. Those circumstances have but opened the way to the communication.

I suffer myself in it as much as you do. I deprive myself of a companion become dear to me. I condemn myself to be alone amidst wretched spirits & with failing health – perhaps too, in this, I throw back your own affection which may grow to me at this moment. Choose as I will, & with the greatest care, I shall feel nervous all the while. And yet I believe from my conscience that I am acting for the best; & certainly declare, upon my honour, that no angry thought, no chilled affection, no desire to punish, mixes in the slightest degree with the reasons that urge me.

* * * * *

And so, my Emily, oblige me! So, lend yourself, not sadly or despondently, but cheerfully to the sacrifice. I do not order you, I entreat you. It is a favour I ask, at your hands, to meet me willingly, & to soften my own pain – in this proposition. The trial & the separation will be but short, & as soon as I can find what I am sure will be best for both – some female free to reside with us .....in whom I can trust & you can love....your return will be holiday to both.

With regard to Edward – some recent circumstances related to his health make me think he must pass some time at a Water cure, & I am going to Stansted Bury [the practice of Priessnitz disciple, Dr Edward Johnson] *with a view to seeing if it will suit him. But I should like nothing better than your having as much of his [company] as may be possible. All other requests make frankly & fearlessly.*

And now, before ending this long letter, let me retract one sentence said in haste – about restoring you to your Mother, if you denied it. It was wrong, & without your letter I should have withdrawn it. It was the stung heart's cry of a moment. All, however, that I meant to say was that, if I seemed to you too hard & stern – if you felt that you could not live with me openly & fearlessly – if, in a word, I ceased in your eyes to be a Father in the true & tender character, & became but a guardian to be dreaded & deceived, you might feel your heart craving for your Mother – and – But no – even then I could not with my consent yield you up to her.....I said what I could not do.....My curse were better to you than her blessing. This then I retract & repent.

Will you now take comfort, my Emily, & be again my own dear child – looking perhaps with some natural repugnance (as a child will feel) to the mere thought of school – but letting the eye pass across it to the long holiday beyond. Look to the time when (this ordeal past) you will come forth, I trust, with new accomplishments & gifts – preserving what is best, correcting what is ill – justifying my father's pride, filling my father's heart, & feeling henceforth that in all the human errors to which you, as others, are subjected, you will find the most lenient judge in one too erring himself to be austere, too interested in your happiness not to advise you for the best... Ainsi soit il, ma mignonne [so be it, my pet], ***E.B.L.***

* * * * *

Neither Laura nor Marion are the answer to this dynamic. As much as Edward might wish them to be. Edward knows what the best answer is. But Emily has rejected it. So back to school it is.

Emily will come round to her childhood guardian once more. But never fully. She was sent to Germany to be weened of childhood ties. Independence and emotional detachment were expected of her. And she found them.

But, as her father is testament, even grown-ups need an emotional crutch. Until she finds a husband, Emily needs a mother.

She needs Miss Greene.

Geneva - Rosina's retreat for five years

CHAPTER 29

~ St. John's Wood - 1845-1846 ~

Geneva. Tuesday, September 30th 1845. Out of the blue, a letter from Rosina. ***My own dearest dear Emily, do not suppose because all these long, long miserable years have passed without you hearing from me, that you and my poor darling boy have been one moment out of my heart, or thoughts. No, my own dear Children – among the innumerable and almost unheard of cruelties and injustice that have been heaped upon me – the only one that has really rankled in my very soul, and imbittered past redress my most miserable existence, has been my separation from you, my children, and – with a refinement of cruelty worthy of the omnipotent tyranny of the darkest ages – having been prevented even the poor intercourse of corresponding with you!***

Had I even been the most criminal of women; instead of what is far more unpardonable in this world – only the most injured – such a brutal exercise of unnatural cruelty as that of being deprived of all the direct knowledge of the welfare of my children would have been unjustifiable; even in Moral! England – where men are allowed a carte blanche to be as ubiquitously vicious, and unprincipled as they please –

Emily you are no longer a child you will probably be Eighteen by the time you receive this letter (if indeed it ever has the good fortune to reach you) - it is therefore time you should know the truth. Had your father preserved a shadow of human feeling in his conduct towards me, you should never have known it from me; aware as I am that that truth is far worse than the blackest calumnies which his fecund and conscienceless imagination has so indefatigably and remorselessly propagated and invented of me.

Your lot is to live with your father and your duty is to bear with, nay more, to try and study, to soothe all his inequalities of temper; and to obey him in all things except where GOD has enjoined you a contrary duty. As with regard to myself – it is equally your duty, dear Emily, to remember that I am your Mother, and one who loves you, and my poor Teddy deeply, devotedly, anx-

iously, as only a Mother can love.

Naturally enough your father will surround you with his creatures, who with regard to me will not (to say the least of it) fail "To hint a fault, and hesitate dislike" [the expression continues, "Willing to wound, and yet afraid to strike" - popular after its use in the adultery trial of George IV's wife Queen Caroline in 1820] – ***and this it is, my dear dear child, which has made me, at length, resolve upon the painful alternative of telling you, as briefly as possible, the outlines of the truth of my most wretched life, since the day I became your father's wife and your Mother...***

* * * * *

This 5,000-word catch-up letter - full of horrible history and long-brewed bitterness - does not appear to reach Emily. It is put into the hands of two American sisters, the Temple-Bowdoins, who Rosina befriends in Bath and visit her in Geneva. They appear to deliver successfully a similar, shorter version, written on the same day, to Robert at Harrow School - but Emily's is re-

Harrow

sent a year and half later, with the bracelet that originally accompanied it, in a follow-up letter also written on a Tuesday, 14th December 1847, six months after Rosina's return to England.

I am now making a last effort to get this packet and Bracelet conveyed to you. It has been travelling about from one to another these two years, and last year the inclosed letter was opened to take out one that was in it for Teddy. For God's sake, my dear child, as you value God's blessing, do not send me back the bracelet as poor Teddy was made to send me back the watch I sent him, with an additional insult in the shape of a letter from your Father's infamous âme damnée [willing slave] ***that wretch Loaden*** [his lawyer].

I notice that Marion Lowndes in 1875 gives Robert back ***a little trinket which belonged to your sister and which I never wore, nor wished to receive.*** I wouldn't be surprised if this was the bracelet, intercepted with the letter. If Emily does receive the letter in December 1847 - after the trauma of previous deceptions of her father - I am sure she handed it straight to him.

* * * * *

In her two letters, Rosina tells how she has managed to pick up ***crumbs*** of Emily and Robert's history since her separation from the children in 1838 - or 1837 as she remembers it. Her memory loses a year - and a final encounter in Cheltenham - ***It was at Coventry, my poor darlings, that I saw you for the last time! two poor little fair unconscious children building castles with cards... My poor Teddy slept with me, and still his little voice wrings through my heart, still I feel his little arms twined around my neck, and see the big tears rolling down his innocent cheeks as he said between every kiss –"Oh only wait, dear Mamma, till I am big and nobody shall make you cry."***

She knows of Emily's time at ***an orthopaedic Institution!... this was indeed a blow to me! for, my poor child, it convinced me how grossly and culpably you must have been neglected - for when I left you, you were not only as straight as an arrow, but had a figure that was perfectly symmetrical.*** This she has learned from a former pupil of a governess she misnames, inappropriately, *Madame De Willing*, the mysterious Madame S____ de S____, who in the first letter is given a name, 'Stade' - but, still, I am unable to root out a Chargé d'Affaires named 'Stade' or his wife, and Rosina has forgotten the woman's name by the second letter.

One name Rosina has resolutely not forgotten is that of her childhood friend, ***that vulgar viper Miss Greene.*** Since we left Miss Greene, she has been living with the Wilkinsons, including a current extended stay in Brussels, where Bonnie Wilkinson is rounding off her education. Shunned, awkwardly, by Emily, and kept from disrupting Teddy's new life as a school boarder, Miss Greene's maternal instincts have retreated to the welcome always found at Mrs Wilkinson's home, and from her great-nieces, Bonnie and Rosie.

* * * * *

I next had a few lines from Emily from London saying she had had a prosperous journey and found her Papa looking quite well, and that she was to go with him to Knebworth in a day or two. Finding that she was at last safe at her Father's house, I did not answer this note till I returned to England at the end of 5 weeks, and was much surprised to find that Emily had not written Mrs

Knebworth House after Edward's 1844 alterations

Wilkinson, thanking her for her kind offer of going for her. She did send her a message through me to that effect.

Directly I was at all settled at Windsor [No.5, The Crescent. John Wilkinson's wanderings with the 17th Lancers are coming to the end - along with his 20 year commission - at the Cavalry Barracks in Windsor, and finally at Knightsbridge Barracks, both now home to the Household Cavalry], *I wrote to Emily and got a natural letter from her, full of descriptions of the beautiful place her dear Papa had made Knebworth, and saying that he was gone into Lincolnshire for Teddy to bring him to see her; and that she was so much occupied making preparations for their return that she had not time to write more.*

She continued for more than a week alone, and then wrote me a letter saying she had expected them that day but was disappointed - but that they were to come the next day. I heard again from her at the end of a week, when she expressed her admiration of Teddy's beauty and charms, but took care to keep in her expressions of love for him, or regret that he had returned to School; and both he and his Papa had left her again alone - thus [at the end of May] *4 years* [since they had been apart] *- five days was all they were allowed to pass together.*

* * * * *

From the account of Teddy's holidays having been so ingeniously managed that he had only from Monday till Thursday to spend with his sister, I became confirmed in my opinion that they too were to be separated from each other, in the same manner that I had been separated from them, in order to wean them from all attachments. However, they were again separated - and I got again most guarded, unnatural letters from Emily, and none from Edward (Teddy).

Sometimes Emily would tell that her Papa was again gone, and that she was very busy preparing for company; and in one letter she said she feared she would be ill for want of exercise, as she was not able to walk much and had no other way of moving; and wrote in very bad spirits, which I thought very natural left so entirely alone and disappointed in the hope of having her brother with her.

I wrote in answer, saying I was very sorry to find she was not in better spirits and begging her to keep up [her spirits], *as her Papa would soon be back; and upon the receipt of this, her Papa had returned and, as she has since told me, opened all her letters. Consequently she wrote me a very unkind letter, very unlike herself - asking me "why I always wanted to make her out unhappy" as she could not be happier than she was, and never mentioned Teddy.*

* * * * *

A month went on in this way, when suddenly she wrote to me that her Papa was taken suddenly ill and must go abroad and that she could "not any longer conceal from herself her deficiencies in English Literature" and some accomplishments in which she wished to excel, and that "her dear Papa had kindly consented to send her to a good English School."

This letter and plan I soon saw was all of her father's concocting, and determined to keep quiet. When, at last, I got a letter from him, professing the warmest regard and respect for me, and saying he was rather hurt at not having heard from me for so long; and saying that ever since he had been at Knebworth he had been daily and hourly intending to invite me and Mr and Mrs Wilkinson and their family to visit him there, but that first he had been prevented by people staying with him; and now by illness which would oblige him to go abroad. He then recapitulated what Emily had said about going to School - but I have his letter. This aside reminds us that, at this stage of the manuscript, Miss Greene is writing the account for her own purposes.

The same might be said of Edward's letter, and all its white lies.

* * * * *

About this time I came to London about some business, and called at Mrs Thomson's to apologise about keeping my trunk so long at her house - and what was my astonishment to find that she and two of her daughters had been amongst the first guests and companions introduced to his daughter. People whom he said were not of their rank. And that all Mrs Thomson's civility about Edward when he was ill was scheming to have him for her son Cockburn's companion when he grew up. And, as to the young ladies, I have his letter in which he regretted ever having introduced Emily to them as they were very unfit companions for her, but that it would teach him for the future to avoid all prim girls, and desired she might never write to them!

Emily never having mentioned the Thomson family having been at Knebworth, really shook my faith in her, and when I plainly asked Mrs Thomson and her daughters if she had ever spoken kindly of me, they looked cautiously at each other and would not answer. I asked no more questions, but went away sadly wounded at comparative strangers seeing that I had been so grossly slighted by one to whom they knew I had devoted so much. But most pain did I feel how ill they must think of her, and to myself I said "can my innocent and beloved Emily be false to me?"

* * * * *

I soon, however, again drove it from me, and gave her Father's influence all the credit; however, it has made me suspicious of everything, and I think that _______________[indecipherable, but it seems to read, *a whispering serpent is choking me* - if so, a reference to the divisive serpent of the Garden of Eden]. *I know from what she told me at Cannstatt, the pains he took to misrepresent and speak ill of me to her - divide and govern is certainly his plan.*

Since Teddy has met Emily, I find the tone of his letters changed to me, and I think she has been employed to shake his faith in me.

* * * * *

Upon Emily leaving Knebworth and coming to London for three days before she went to School, Sir Edward thought he must either honestly break with me - and say I was not to see his children - or let me see Emily after her return from Germany. So in November I got a note from him, inviting me and Mr and Mrs Wilkinson and family to go and dine with him to meet Emily, on the 5th, in Hertford Street.

As Emily will be only here for two or three days previous to removing for a short time to a very select school for the benefit of the best masters, will you come & dine here to morrow at ½ past 6. & I will be delighted to see Mr & Mrs Wilkinson with the Young Ladies if any judge it worth their while to come up to Town. I name ½ past 6 as the dinner hour, but you will find Emily expecting you at a much earlier hour.

There was also an unnatural note from Emily backing the invitation, and telling that there was a 9 o'clock train from London to Windsor and we were to dine at half past six. The Wilkinsons would not go - but I, of course, was too anxious to see and judge for myself what state Emily was in, in every particular. I went about 3 o'clock: her Father was not at home and she received me affectionately, asked why Bonnie did not come, and no more.

She struck me as being much better than when I left her at Cannstatt, but still odd. I found her reserve wearing off every moment; but still there seemed great mystery about her; except when she spoke of her Father, and she seemed then indeed to be frank enough about his conduct to her.

[Names are difficult to decipher in Miss Greene's handwriting, but I read Charles D'Eyncourt's niece's mother-in-law, Henrietta Hamilton] *Lady Boyne (1779-1854),* [Sarah Otway-Cave] *Lady Braye (1768-1862) and her* [widowed] *daughter, Mrs* [Catherine] *Murray (c1811-1875), came to visit her, it seemed they had been amongst the visitors at Knebworth, and when they came in, she proposed to me to shut the folding doors so as to prevent my meeting them. This I objected to, and she submitted.*

* * * * *

After they went away, and we were longer together, she spoke openly of her being turned away from Knebworth, and how much against her will it was that she was placed at School, though her Father had desired her to say it was all her own wish. She then talked of the reason why she nor her brother could ever live at home with her Papa, and I was sorry to find she knew a great deal about another family, which I hoped she would never know.

She then spoke with great bitterness of the short time she and Teddy had been allowed to be together after being so long separated, yet still did not speak of her dear brother with the warmth of affection she used to do.

Indeed, it seemed as if all her affections and feelings for anybody were crushed, and the love which I once thought she would have for her father seemed turned into bitterness and fear.

* * * * *

When he came into dinner, he and she seemed scarcely to speak to each other, nor did he remark [on] her not eating any dinner, which surprised me, as she had not eaten anything all the day whilst I was with her.

His first address to me was if the Wilkinsons would not come?; he seemed very ill, deaf and absorbed, tried to talk with me as we used to do, but seemed really unable [His departure for Italy is delayed by seeing the ear specialist Joseph Toynbee (1815–1866). The pioneering otologist will lose his life to experiments with prussic acid and chloroform as a remedy for tinnitus]. *He talked a little about Emily, and said how cold she was, which shewed itself so much when she met Teddy, who, poor fellow, was sadly thrown back by it.*

Courtesy of the Wellcome Library, London

Joseph Toynbee

Emily seemed to attend upon him at his tea and in other ways, just as I had often seen her mother do; and when he left the room and went down to his Library, her manner quite changed and she became frank and open.

She told me how very miserable she had been for the last three weeks at Knebworth, that it was brought forth by Mrs Thomson's want of sense and prudence; but she thought her father was only seeking for a cause to send her away - that he had said most brutal things to her and told her he would "send her to her Mother, whom she much resembled."

* * * * *

She wrote him a most pathetic letter, from her account, and was so completely out of her mind from terror, etc., that she took an overdose of Laudanum to make her sleep, which stupefied her so much that they were obliged to send for a Physician, who remained with her, walking her about several hours to stop the effect of it, and he told her maid that there was something very distressing upon the young lady's mind.

During all the time she was ill, her Father never came near her, but wrote her a letter in answer to hers, which she has since shewn me - and I should pronounce it a most beautiful 'specimen of art' written so plausibly that one in reading it would throw all blame upon her, and say he was a most excellent father. Which I daresay he persuades himself he is.

I have not heard all the particulars of the business which brought all this forth, but from what I have heard from Emily, I think that if she had had a sensible woman of the world for her relation, or friend, who loved and knew her, none of it would have happened; as it would not then have been brought up to a very severe judging father, who was looking for an excuse to himself for sending her away from him, as he had good reasons for going abroad, he said, for his health.

* * * * *

Marion Waller has taken Emily's place on the trip to Italy. Edward is about to leave his children alone, at their respective schools, for four months. Naturally he has the thought common to all parents (especially hypochondriac parents) of what would happen to the children if anything should happen to him. He needs Miss Greene back in their lives.

My dear Miss Greene, I am surprised you have not heard from Edward - He is a very bad correspondent to me. I will mention his neglect when I write to him. With regard to Emily, you need be under no apprehension with her religious instruction. It is a point on which I was very particular, & my recommendations have been from persons where assurances carry all weight – Lady Bloomfield, the Rev D Mayell & the Honourable Mr Noel – all of strong religious opinions & habits & all thoroughly acquainted with Miss Ridout. Bristol born Miss Susan Fortune Ridout (1793-1857) has been running a school for girls in Sussex Square, Brighton, having published two volumes of *Letters to a young governess on the principles of Education* (1837 & 1840). The census tells us that in 1841 her Brighton school has about 15 boaders aged between 10 and 15. By

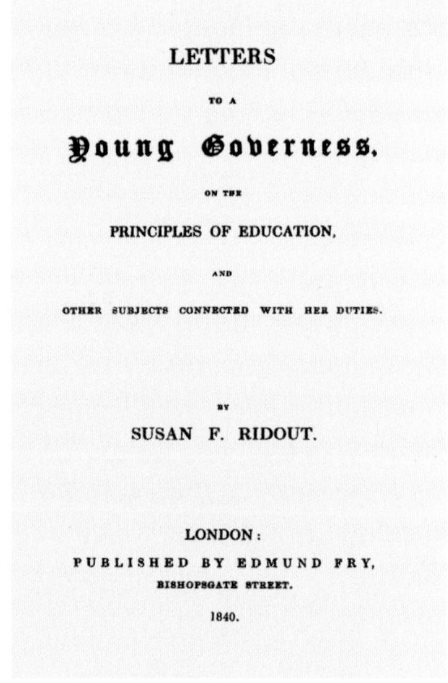
LETTERS

TO A

YOUNG GOVERNESS,

ON THE

PRINCIPLES OF EDUCATION,

AND

OTHER SUBJECTS CONNECTED WITH HER DUTIES.

BY

SUSAN F. RIDOUT.

LONDON:

PUBLISHED BY EDMUND FRY,

BISHOPSGATE STREET.

1840.

Miss Ridout's credentials

1845, aged 51, she has moved her school to a new residential boulevard built on land owned by Harrow School, Hamilton Terrace, running north from St John's Wood Road in north London. In the 1851 census, this school has only half as many boarders, but they are older, either 15 or 16.

The first Thursday in every month visitors are allowed to the pupils – if you like to call, Miss Ridout, 63 Hamilton Terrace, but I must request the greatest concern & reserve on all family matters, Lady B etc. I have requested your correspondence with Emily to be unseen - all other letters except between her & me, pass, I think very properly, under acknowledged inspection.

Hamilton Terrace, running north from St John's Wood Road, in 2016

* * * * *

However, God guided him in the choice of the place he left her at, and had the lady of the School been younger, and less stiff, and a little more agreeable, she might have been tolerably contented there - but the anxiety she suffered as to where her father would leave her next, prevented her.

I was permitted to see her, and to correspond with her without being read by Miss Ridout, and came to London to see her.....But I must first tell that at Christmas I got a letter from Emily saying that if I asked her and her brother down to Windsor to spend some of the holidays, her Papa had left her permission to go to Mrs Wilkinson or myself. I accordingly wrote to herself and Miss Ridout, inviting them.

Directly after he went abroad, Emily wrote to me begging that I would allow some of her correspondents to send their letters under cover to me, for forward to her, till she could settle something else. I, of course, did not consent to this breach of trust on my part, and even objected to forwarding letters from Teddy to her unless I read them, as I feared there might be some foolish, boyish joke about Miss Ridout, which would get them into a scrape.

There did soon a letter come from Teddy, which I read, and forwarded as it was a most innocent one - and said that such letters I would forward, and depended upon their honour that there should be nothing in them which their Papa or any person else could object to; at the same time telling them that I should much prefer not having to forward any.

Soon after this Teddy and Emily met, and I could see that she had talked of my having read his letter to her, as I received a most impertinent one from him, enclosed in one to her - which was left open for me to see - saying that he had done with "The Verdant" [i.e. The Lushly Green], *and had not sent her* [Emily] *the letter he first intended, as it would not do to give her* [Miss Greene] *a "handle against him", but that he would "manage to get rid of her"; this letter I forwarded to Emily and took no notice of.*

* * * * *

When Xmas came, both came down to Windsor, and we all went to meet them at Slough. She was just the same, at meeting, as she had been years ago. Poor Ted seemed cold and miserable, and greatly out of temper - which I did not at first understand, but found out after that he had lost a ring of hers, and that she had been scolding him the entire way down, and his honest nature could not conceal it.

They remained three days, and seemed very happy. Teddy became quite himself; and Emily, when alone with me, told me a great deal of how she at last managed to get away from Cannstatt, and other secrets - but avoided all going back to the subject to Madame de Weling and Neuwied. I saw in her that she was not yet the old Emily, particularly to Teddy, who seemed to feel bitterly the apparent loss of her affections, and deplored it sadly to me the few opportunities he and I had alone.

Every day we passed together seemed to melt away bad feelings and they

Windsor

seemed to be replaced by good ones, and they both left us. Emily went to Miss Ridout, and Teddy, at the end of a few days, went to Richmond to the Water Cure [at Sudbury Park, Petersham, in the care of Dr Weiss].

* * * * *

It appeared that the first Thursday in every month Miss Ridout's pupils are allowed to go and visit their friends, if in or near London. So upon the first Thursday of the next month, Emily asked me and the Wilkinsons to come to her in Hertford Street to dine - as her Papa had given her leave to do as she liked with the house before he went abroad - or to go to Windsor, but she would tell me when she saw me why she could not go to Windsor.

Again the Wilkinsons did not come, but I did; and spent a most happy day with both my dear children - as Teddy had come up to go to his friend Street's sister's wedding, as well as to dine with us.

I thought Emily very much herself this day. She told me there had been a great row at Miss Ridout's about her, as there had been a most impertinent

St John's Wood Barracks - home of the Foot Guards, who rotate between St Johns Wood, Hyde Park and Windsor Barracks

Wherever your Girls' School, in 1846, there's invariably going to be a brace of dashing young sergeants at a favour's throw

anonymous letter come to her dated from Windsor Barracks, abusing Miss Ridout in the most sensitive manner - calling her 'Sir James Graham' for opening the girls' letters, and proposing to her to run away with him on the Monday following, signed St. John.

Sir James Graham is the Home Secretary who has recently been made scapegoat for government policy of opening letters at the Post Office for intelligence. Frustratingly, Miss Greene does not name the Sergeant Troy behind this correspondence - but this in itself suggests an acquaintance or relation of the Greene family, possibly one previously with an eye for Bonnie Wilkinson.

The moment I heard this I guessed to myself who wrote this letter, kept it to myself - but have had good cause since to know that my suspicions were true.

This was why Miss Ridout would not allow her to go to Windsor - indeed, after I had heard it, she never was asked. As it was impossible that her time could have been more safely or innocently passed, and she never saw any person whilst there but our own immediate family. No people can be safe from anonymous letters or falsehood.

* * * * *

After this, I came to remain near Emily in London, and often saw her. And if she could be reconciled to School - or know what next was to become of her - I thought her very well placed, with a very good religious lady, where she had the opportunity of going to hear an excellent Clergyman preach any Sunday and Wednesday, besides going to visit and examine the young ladies upon religious subjects once a month. My mind became more at ease about her than it had been since I had been separated from her.

But now my fears about poor Ted's health commenced as I dreaded what effect the Water Cure might have upon his mind and nerves, as I had seen and known his father had been much excited and weakened by it. I therefore determined to go and visit him and a little circumstance about his letter determined me.

I went and found him everything my heart could wish, in health, affections, etc., he seemed happy and well fed, and all his good nature had been brought out and I spent a real happy day with him, each of us not wishing to allude to anything disagreeable; however, I heard some truths from him.

For reasons of my own I did not tell Emily I intended to go, till I had been there; but told her the next time I saw her, but was as usual much disappointed at the cool interest she seemed to take in him. The fact seemed she had been so entirely thrown upon herself, and such little interest shewn for her, that it seemed as if her whole nature was hardened for other people. This I recollect having warned her father to beware of as, if separated from everybody she loved, I feared it must injure her beautiful nature.

I recollect one answer she gave me when I talked to her about her love to Teddy, which was, "I have suffered too much from having my affections torn asunder not to learn to take care of myself - and I know I shall never be allowed to love Teddy."

The only thing which I saw to complain of about Miss Ridout was that she seemed too precise and particular (for Emily) in her manner, as to her laws. I believe they were both right and necessary. I heard something from Emily - and saw others - which made me think so, and also made me speak very plainly to her one day we were walking together.

* * * * *

My contentment about Edward was soon interrupted by a letter from him begging that I would go down to him as he had been delirious the night before and very ill. I accordingly went again to the house, and was shocked to see the alteration I found in him since the last time I had seen him - particularly his mind, which seemed in a shocking state of excitement; and I was told that he had been much worse.

He spoke in a most bitter manner of his Papa, and said things which I had not any idea he knew of. [He] seemed sadly anxious about what was to become of him, as no person in the world cared for him except myself. And talked in a wild way about publishing a poem he had written to make money, as his Papa gave him scarcely any.

After he had vented himself by speaking openly to me, he became more composed and I advised him to submit patiently to his Dr (against whom he seemed much prejudiced) and that his father would soon be home, when he would, I knew, settle all comfortably and agreeably for him.

He wished me very much to remain with him, which I might have been tempted to do, but that I feared being mixed up in the Party which was in the house. Besides, I feared interfering, as circumstances made me think that Sir Ed. wished gradually to separate me from all communication with his son - certainly, and I even fancied with his daughter - and ultimately so as to let them both feel and think that it was their own act. All this I shall yet know, but must, like himself, bide my time.

* * * * *

I left my dear boy much better than I found him, and promised to bring his sister down to see him if Miss R. would give her consent.

I accordingly did go to see him with her the following week, and we all spent a most happy day together. I found dear Emily most frank, innocent and open in her communication with me - both in our drive to, and from, Richmond - and she told me many things which I knew but imperfectly before, and all the how and why she was sent to Miss Ridout's.

She told me much of Mrs Thomson's conduct, which she says was the cause of all the scrape she got into. She certainly shewed great want of sense, but if Emily had had a Mother to deal with, or a man of honour, it would all have passed away as it was, nothing more than might be expected from a girl in terror of her life [she means her future, her future life], *without any knowledge of the world or anyone to guide her.*

For the first time she told me a great deal about Nathalie, and said she was sure her love for her was like mine for herself - but that all she suffered on her account almost drove her to madness.

All this she told me the day we went down to Sudbrook.

As Emily was not to go to Windsor in the Easter holidays, on account of the anonymous letter, she went down to Brighton with Miss Ridout [Brighton is Miss Ridout's former home].

* * * * *

Edward's letters to Emily whilst she is at Miss Ridout's [for the school year of Autumn 1845 to Summer 1846] are of the same sort as the Cannstatt letters, with the same admonishments of too much money being spent, ***£5 is a great deal for a girl to get thro' in mere pocket money*** - it turns out she has spent that full amount on a present sent to Natalie; interest in her reading list, ***ask Miss Ridout to let you read also some of [Oliver] Goldsmith's*** *The Citizen of the World* ***essays*** (the 1760s satirical perspective of a fictional Chinaman on British society and manners); and, again, entreaties to have ***a horror of concealment & of cunning*** and not to go ***into morbid extremes of susceptibility, avoiding melancholy thoughts & the false sentiment, which girls are too apt to indulge.***

There is also the following 'do as I preach' - which I add for the consideration of Professor Rice, lately of San Jose University, creator of the annual

Bulwer Lytton Contest for florid writing - avoid ***vague fancy & reverie*** for ***a florid style in both [thinking and writing] is apt to be contracted in Germany, & should be carefully watched & shunned.***

The big difference from the Cannstatt letters is that he now writes to her - as he did when she was alone at Knebworth for the summer - as a secretary or keeper of his household. ***Write to Mr Webb*** [the Knebworth Estate Manager] ***a line to say that I expect to be back in April – that I wish the gardener to know, in order to have vegetables, etc. for the end of that month; that the brown mare will be got into condition against that time, as well as the two bays; that the grey horse may remain out; & that I wish to recollect my instructions with regard to the chestnut mare. I shall hope to find the garden in good order & completed.*** And when she falls short on these instructions, he is quick to criticise.

* * * * *

As indicated by Teddy's distress, money remains a constant anxiety that Edward shares with his children. ***It is obvious that people [when] abroad are nervous & anxious about their affairs, & tho' I never worried you with much complaint of my own struggles, you must have known that I was much straightened in money matters, & therefore anxious to learn all particulars that related to them.***

In a particularly unfortunate incident, Emily loses a newspaper cutting - spotted by Mrs Wilkinson and given to her by Miss Greene - relating to his mother's estate. It turns out that it reveals nothing not already known or of benefit to him - but ***what I regret is not your mere want of worldly sense in the neglect, but your want of sympathy in what concerned me. Sympathy for another always awakes sense & judgement. The obvious***

The Will of the late Mrs. Elizabeth Barbara Bulwer Lytton, late of Knebworth, in the county of Hertford, and of Upper Seymour-street, Middlesex, was lately proved in Doctors' Commons by her son, Sir Edward George Earle Lytton Bulwer Lytton, Bart., one of the executors. It bequeaths to her eldest son, the house, No. 5 Upper Seymour street, with the furniture, &c. (except plate), he enjoying the Norfolk estate under the will of his father. To her second son, 1,000l. a year out of the Knebworth estate, he being well provided for by the will of his grandmother. To her youngest son, Sir Edward George Earle Lytton Bulwer, the estate and mansion at Knebworth, all the furniture, pictures, statues, books, wine, and appoints him residuary legatee of her personal estate. The plate at Upper Seymour-street, and the coins dug out near the Knebworth estate, to go with bequests of numerous articles of jewellery, rings, and pecuniary legacies to several of her friends. It directs that seven of her horses, which she describes, shall be allowed to run out their days, and be properly fed and provided for, but not to be shot or sold; that her dog named Fly should be taken care of by one of her servant, who is to be allowed 5s. a week for that purpose, and provided with an almshouse. Deceased died 19th December, 1843. Personal estate sworn under 25,000l.

Don't shoot my horses!

plan would have been to have sent it to Loaden [his solicitor], ***with whom you had corresponded – or to Mr Webb – or at least a copy of it - & have sent me another copy, taking the chance of its reaching me...***

These are things which it is necessary for your future happiness I should speak sharply about, because - putting me out of the question - there is nothing which so destroys domestic peace & confidence, in after life, if you marry, as a woman's inattention to the pecuniary matters which are entrusted to her - & on the other hand nothing more secures happiness than a woman's careful & thrifty management. And here speaks the Victorian husband enjoying the Mediterranean with his girlfriend. ***Economy in her is a far greater value than in a man, because it is always another's money that she is saving or spending.***

Nice - La Baie des Anges

* * * * *

I am being unfair. It is cheaper for Edward to live in Italy than in Society. And he does contradict himself with, ***At the moment I know a young lady equal in family to yourself who has only £30 a year to live upon, and does live***

on it. I hope he doesn't mean Marion Waller. She is currently earning supplementary overtime.

This habit, if unchecked, will end in his disgrace & probable ruin. I grieve to see the mother blood breaking out - the habit of borrowing – unknown-muddling away money – all ending at last in such shame!

Where he is being insensitive is in not appreciating how unsettling these lectures are to his displaced children. ***Suppose my dear child, I were to die tomorrow – all you would have to exist on would be about £55 a year – this is a secret, but it is a truth. It is my duty most urgently to force upon you every saving, & thrifty, as well as careful, expenditure - & so it must be for the future with regard to myself. Small as you may think these extra sums, they severely distress me.***

In order to procure you real advantages of Masters, etc., I go to the utmost possible I can - to more than I ought - for your schooling. The difference of £12 or £13 makes the cup run over & pinches me in much, necessary not only to my rank, but my comfort. I shall deduct that from some expense of my own that I had counted upon as absolutely required – for, as to any thing else, I have denied myself all the year. True that I have not spoken much of my affairs, but I have long since & often told you that I was greatly straightened.

* * * * *

So what of his ***absolutely required*** trip to the Mediterranean? He writes from Nice on 29th December 1845, that it is ***Delicious indeed - soft warm & sunny with a lovely sea & orange groves, but so exciting I cannot sleep & am worn out with wakefulness.*** Perhaps too much information.

Naples is less of a success. ***...the weather is not very genial, and I am completely cured of my Italian illusions, & shall try and settle peaceably in England on my return... The difficulty of getting good water is in itself a crying evil.***

More revealing, is Marion's account, 30 years later, to Robert. In Naples, ***he took apartments on the Chiaja & went into society, but not much. We took very long rides but we met one day the Duke of Syracuse & suite (Duke was civil to your father), but I got so uncomfortable & miserable that I never would ride out there anymore.*** [Prince Leopold of the Two Sicilies (1813–1860) is the king's brother. He is described in Wikipedia as surrounding himself ***with a court of artists, writers and musicians, who followed him from his palace on the Chiaia to his villa at Sorrento.*** Although a liberal, estranged from his fanatically pious wife, a Savoy princess, he represents a level of society gossip too much for Marion.] ***There it was he wrote*** *Lucretia* (1846). ***When we went to Pompeii we saw several people have his book as a guide. He tried to hire a villa on the hill, but as there was no fresh water to be had, he gave it up.***

In February, we were in Rome, took handsome apartments on Via dei Pontefici & lived very retired. As soon as he had done writing, we took very long walks on foot in the environs - he was pretty well & I was as happy as the day was long. We went to Frascate, 1st March 1846, then to Florence, 22nd March - I cannot quite remember if it was that year we went to Milan, lakes of Como & Maggiore. I think it must have been. At Como he saw at a stall a little book of Proverbs in Italian - it pleased him so much, that he bought it & made great use of it later in *My Novel* (1853).

* * * * *

When we returned to London he had sold his house in Hertford Street & we went to his other house, [19] James Street, Buckingham Gate - we were there in July 1846.

Whether it is now, or before they left for Europe, Marion tells Robert - in a letter of 20th February 1875 - ***The first time I saw you, you were near St James Park carrying a little boat, & your sister seemed to be listening with great affection to you. On arriving at your father's house in James Street I told him, I believe in these very words, I have just met a boy 'handsome eno' to be the V. of W-'*** [I read the Viscount of Westminster, Hugh Grosvenor (1825 –1899) who was Viscount Belgrave until 1845, when he was 20, certainly good looking, and the richest, ergo eligible, heir in the country] [I don't think Marion means the Vicar of Wakefield] ***& he then told me you were his children. From that day, forgive me, but I loved you both, yes loved you both as much as I have loved my children later. And had I had then any influence on your father, your sister would have been living with him - & had an English Lady of rank as companion & chaperone.***

St James Park in the 1840s

* * * * *

She [Emily] *returned from Brighton soon, and was the first to give me* [Miss Greene] *the information that her father was returned; and that Teddy had left Knebworth, and his Papa had placed him with a private Tutor* [Mr Miles] *in the Lilly Road* [presumably she means Lillie Road in Brompton] *for a few weeks, preparatory to sending him to Harrow. She begged of me to go and see her, as she wished to tell me the news, though she knew her Papa intended calling upon me after he visited her, the day after he arrived from the Continent.*

He did call here, and I soon found out that, what it was for, was to enquire about an advertisement I had given Emily cut out of a newspaper about Dividends of her Grandmamma's, and which she had lost. We talked little about either of the children. I told him how ill I had found Edward during the Water Cure.

Upon going to see Emily, she told me of some extraordinary communications of her father to her upon the subject of money and of his having told her she had but £6 a year, and Teddy nothing. She also told me that there had been a great battle between her Father and Teddy, and that Teddy had written a most insolent letter - but from what I could gather, full of truths - and I think frightened his father and shewed him what was in his son, and that he must pursue a different conduct with him to what he had hitherto done; as every time I saw them together afterwards, I saw the plan was to be very fatherly and very affectionate, in words at least.

* * * * *

Poor Teddy had not been many days in town after his leaving the Water Cure till he became very ill, and then I went, at Emily's desire, to see him at Mr Miles [his Tutor] *to take him to drink tea with her at Miss Ridout's.*

I found him in bed and in a high fever and in a most alarming state of excitement. The dear boy was most delighted to see me, and actually made me promise to return to him the next day before I left him, and I had the comfort of thinking that I was again of some use to my dear boy - as independent of procuring him proper drink and fruit, he found a safe person to whom he could open his heart to and unbosom his griefs and anxieties to.

Whilst sitting there one morning, his father came to visit him, and from his countenance (which I knew well) seemed 'more surprised than pleased' at seeing me there - but soon threw it off, and became quite kind. He seemed so very anxious about his boy, that he spoke of little else. He however did not forget to ask me "how I found out where Teddy was?", but never said he intended telling me, though living within a quarter of a mile of him.

For more than a week I spent several hours every day with him, and met his father again once or twice - but avoided the time I might meet him, as it left Teddy less alone to divide our visits; besides I did not wish it.

* * * * *

When Teddy was well enough to leave his bed, the weather in the day time was excessively hot, particularly in his room, where he was most exposed to the sun. I therefore thought it would do him good to take a drive in the Regent's Park in the cool of the evening. So ordered a fly to take him out with me. But upon going to Mr Miles to ask permission, I found that Sir Edward had given him orders to keep him at his studies. So, as I soon understood what they meant, I gave it up and disappointed my boy; but left soon without him to beg of his Papa to take him out to drive with him when next he called.

Accordingly the next day I heard from Teddy that his Papa had taken him out; he did not then say for how long, as the poor fellow always seemed at first ashamed to tell of any neglect. But I heard from Mr Miles that he had not been out for more than ten minutes, and that, up and down the dusty road in the sun. And that his father thought him so well, that he desired he should eat cold mutton and go into the School room to his lessons; to which Mr Miles added, the boy cannot go to lessons with the headache he has, as well as not being able to stand.

Soon after this Sir Edward called upon me and begged I would not interrupt Edward's studies, as he wished him to work hard the short time he had to prepare for Harrow. I promised not to do so, though I knew it would have done good to let him recover a little more. I only went to see him after the School hours, and one Saturday evening found him well enough to be able to walk, and brought him down here to enjoy the good air in the garden, and to take tea.

The poor fellow seemed very happy and revived every moment he stayed, and became more himself than I had seen him for some time - however, I took him back in about an hour. The next day his father came to again beg I should not take him out again to "disturb him". Nothing he would himself wish more than to have him, but that he wished him to work hard and be with the boys for his companions.

I, after that, went but seldom to see him and paid but short visits, and though Teddy wished me several times to go and see him, I saw he had got orders; as had the master, though he did not tell me so plainly, but I could see that what I had long suspected, that his father chose to separate me from him and prevent our corresponding, though he thought it not prudent to do it honestly.

* * * * *

One evening that I called and had a long talk with him, he said "I this day wrote to Papa, asking to have my tonsils cut out as I think it will put him in a passion, and I may get something out of him - perhaps he may take me to Knebworth for the holidays." Three days after, to my utter astonishment, I was walking down to see him when I met the maid with a note coming to tell me that his tonsils had been cut out the day before by the Doctor who had been attending him in his sore throat; and that his sister had been sent for to her school to come and hold him during the operation. This made me indeed think what had been told me was true, that Sir Edward liked doing cruel things to persons in his power.

In this manner I was left, till I got a note of two lines from my dear faithful boy, asking me to go down to him if I wished to see him before he went to Harrow, where he was to go the next day. I did go, and found him in a most unhappy and very excited state, and writing, as I always saw him when unhappy and wishing to drive it from his mind by employment.

I stayed with him a long time, as I saw it was of use to him to let out his thoughts to a person whom he must know would be faithful. I left him with a heavy heart, not being able, as I ought, to commit him to his Heavenly Father, who can over-rule all to his eternal good.

I went the next morning and found him much better and remained with him while he was sleeping: and the prospect of seeing the pretty school and grounds seemed to enliven him and he parted from me most affectionately and I have never heard from him since; and I will 'bide my time' to find out the means used to separate us! as I have my suspicions.

* * * * *

To return to Emily, I took her with me one evening to see poor Ted and we had a most happy walk home to Miss Ridout's - but found that we must not do so again, as my old good fortune followed me, as Miss Ridout got jealous. However she had the good taste to propose to me to take Emily and her companions to Confirmation - which I did, and God and myself only know my feelings upon that occasion.

As we drove home, I begged to be left at Mr Miles's - and upon enquiring from the maid how Master Lytton was, the answer was, very indifferent, and that he had had a bad night and was light headed. To my utter astonishment this seemed to make little impression upon Emily, and she drove off with the other two girls who had come from the school to be Confirmed with her, and whose manners did not at all please me.

This, like everything else, was soon explained to us, as - after my being for a longer time than usual without hearing from Emily - she wrote me a note, begging that I would go and see her at Miss Ridout's, as there had been a most disgraceful exposée of the conduct of two of the girls (one of those who had been Confirmed with her), but to come and I should hear all.

* * * * *

From the 1843 edition of the French novel ***Picciola*** *(1836)*

She told me a great deal of folly about these girls writing to young men, which had been discovered, and their parents written to, begging that they might be removed. One of the girls tried to draw Emily into the scrape also, but she got out of it, and whilst she was telling me the story I thought to myself, "the sharp things I said to you the day you took me out to walk, saved you."

The girls were immediately removed. Emily's Papa came and gave good advice to Miss Ridout, which she had the prudence and good sense to follow, and it was then arranged that Emily should remain till the Midsummer holidays, when she was to be removed for good. I say, this business explained Emily's conduct to me the day she seemed so inattentive to what was passing about Teddy's illness, for she was evidently engrossed with the other young lady. I saw this at the Church door, but took no further notice of it, than to take care they should not speak or have any communication with any person whilst they were with me.

This business, I think, did a great deal of good to Emily, and after that foolish girl was removed, I saw her several times and thought her much improved. It seemed as if she and Miss Ridout had come to a resolution to part friends. I don't know what Miss Ridout did - as the dividing system was well kept up there, and I allowed it - but Emily told me that though she thought her one of the greatest termagents [a violent, turbulent, brawling, or shrewish, woman] *in London, she could manage her.*

* * * * *

Did you notice that? Edward just won good parenting points off Miss Greene - his consistent, persistent, parenting critic. I'm so pleased. When you were about to be expelled from Senior School for inappropriate behavior I bet you wish you'd had a letter like this from your Dad:

Miss Ridout preceded you, as you know, in her acct. of the disagreeable & painful affair wh. has occurred, & tho' acquitting you of all other impropriety than that of mentioning to her what you knew, wished me to remove you. As I considered that you could not be removed on such a ground, and after such an occurrence, without the appearance of disgrace & the probability of great & lasting injury, I did not rest until I had seen Miss R & conversed with her on the subject.

And I am happy to say that she appears now to acquiesce with me in my views as to what is best for all parties. Nothing would have pained me more than your quitting just after such an event – your name would have been mixed up with the affair inextricably & for ever. To speak plainly it would be expulsion from school for disgraceful conduct. I even avoided seeing you today, that there might not appear to the others, or to the servants, any semblance of having you in to question, or appear as a party to so improper a

transaction.

I knew that I should not long be without your own version of the story & I trust you have been quite candid with me. No doubt Miss Ridout is right, that in strict performance of stern duty, you should have acquainted her with the first step that came to your knowledge, & however hard that may have seemed to the girl, it would have saved her all the disgrace she now endures, & all the future involvements, pain & discredit that may ensue.

At the same time I can well understand how difficult & how invidious such a task might have appeared to you and, I think that if you really & truly shunned all girlish levity on the matter; did not in any way enter into the impropriety; & warned & advised the girl to the contrary – that neither I nor Miss Ridout have cause for displeasure. Considering your imperfect knowledge of what took place, it is as much as could be expected from you – tho' not quite up to the mark to which a firmer & harder character might have come.

You need not, I think, my dear child, apprehend any further unpleasantness to yourself. I do not think Mr P, for his own sake, will stir much in the matter, & you, by your own acct. are quite clear of the whole. To leave Miss R at present would be an irreparable false step. I would rather not have you home even for a day – you must not appear to dread or to fly from any thing that can be said or done. The serious & proper manner in which Miss R has dealt with the thing raises her much in my estimation & now that the first excitement has cooled, I think she has every disposition to be just to others.

I pity the young woman, tho' her levity & folly are unpardonable. I pity far more her parents if they are persons of susceptible honor. No butterfly's wing suffers so much from the touch as a girl's fair name & honour from the breath of scandal. But where the scandal has been merited, deep indeed must be her shame. I know, my Emily, that I need not point out to you a warning & I feel confident that I shall always be your proud as well as most affectionate father, E.B.L. Tuesday night. [9th June, 1846.]

Tuesday again. A slow night, clearly, in the very separate weekly calendars of Edward and Rosina Bulwer Lytton.

I wonder if 23-year-old Marion Waller proofread it for him.

You've seen it before - but as the only surviving image of Emily as a teenager it offers a foundation on which to add a few years and picture Miss Bulwer Lytton in her late teens

Edward's Knebworth, illustrated for an 1870s edition of ***The Graphic***

...the sun shines so bright and gladly - and the sky is so clear blue and everything looks so green and fair that it reminds me of that happy time when you and I used to go out at Knebworth against each other - do you remember the dingle where we used to meet at the end of the park? where we used to charge against each other with the fury of a love defended Knight and an enraged Amazon? Emily's dreams of Knebworth are a constant theme of letters to her brother

CHAPTER 30

~ Knebworth - 1846-1847 ~

My dearest Emily, Many many thanks for your kind & most affectionate letter, which gave me great pleasure. I am very grateful to you for the remembrance – the only one I received.....dead or estranged, those who once welcomed that day – ainsi va le monde [so goes the world]***.....As we "recede from Spring, we lose the blossoms"...*** Edward Bulwer Lytton responds to his daughter Emily's birthday good wishes as he turns 43, on 25th May 1846.

* * * * *

In her final few weeks at Miss Ridout's - on 27th June 1846 - Emily turns 18. Her schooling is over. She is what our generation calls an adult; her generation, a spinster. If she's a Brontë, she's off to be governess; if a Bennett sister, off to find a husband; if Sarah Man (the future Madame de Weling) both.

But Emily Bulwer Lytton's father is already a baronet, with a generous legacy of land from his mother - so, in theory, there is less pressure on her. She is primed to take her place as chatelain of her family's country home, Knebworth House.

This is the dream that has lived with her throughout her exile. It has been her father's promise. But, as we've discussed, it is a thoughtless promise. Despite what Edward says about everyone who loves him being either ***dead or estranged***, there are at least two other woman in his life - two other women with an active claim to a place at his side.

But, to give Edward his due, for the next year and a half, this thoughtless promise, this childhood dream, does - sort of - become a reality.

The catch is, he won't be at her side.

* * * * *

There does however need to be someone at Emily's side. She is not, like her grandmother, the widow who can live respectably on her own at Knebworth House. The times require that she has a 'companion' - and it must be a respectible elder lady, a 'chaperone'.

Edward has been pushing for the only one he fully trusts, Miss Greene. But our confused teenager does not believe Miss Greene is respectable enough. Mrs Thomson has been pushing to take the role - she has children that are direct contemporaries of Emily and Teddy - but Edward does not trust this meddling (to use Madame Heine's expression) ***personne exaltée***. So, instead, Emily is to get Edward's second choice, who is considerably less respectable than any of them.

She is not the least respectable. The least respectable would have been his new 23-year-old girlfriend. But she is the second least respectable.

Edward is about to set his daughter up with the mother of her half-siblings, his mistress for the past decade - Laura Deacon.

* * * * *

Miss Greene quotes Emily, *"Papa has at last found a lady to live with us. She is a kind of a step-mother for me, as she is a person to whom he was very much attached before he married, and she to him. She is the widow of a French Viscount d'Azzimart, has four children, and was a Miss Foxcroft, a daughter of General Foxcroft."* No record of a General Foxcroft exists. I have looked.

I am initially confused by the pseudonym used by this 'chaperone' - Viscountess D'Azzimart. The Viscountess who accompanies Emily to Knebworth in the last week of July 1846 is described as a French woman - and Marion Waller, having been brought up in Nice, seems, at first, a closer fit for a 'French' woman.

But from Miss Greene's description we know that this woman is older than Marion. The Viscountess knows details of Bulwer Lytton family history that Marion is not going to be conversant with after just a few months with Edward on the Mediterranean. Particularly, Miss Greene mentions, the Viscountess knows Edward's brother Henry. Henry, if you recall, is once sweet on Laura's younger sister, Louisa, who becomes Louisa O'Shaughnessy, mother of Arthur 'the dreamer of dreams'.

There are other clues that I have missed. Edward writes to Emily from Paris the previous December, ***I had hoped to have found at Paris a lady whom I think might be induced to live with us as your companion etc. when you leave Miss R's – a thing that I consider henceforth quite indispensable to obtain preparatory to your return - but I could not find her, and suppose she must have left it. The search after the kind of person we should both like & trust isn't easy – but I hope to succeed.***

When I first read this, I thought it an oddly deceptive way to describe the woman he is actually travelling with. I assumed the Viscountess D'Azzimart was Marion, aka Angelo. Consider too, the name - Viscountess D'Azzimart - which is more Italian than French. Nice, in the Kingdom of Piedmont-Sardinia, where Marion grew up, is more Italian than French at this time. What is more, the Italian word 'Azzimare' means 'to dress up' - which is exactly what Marion is doing on this trip, as Edward's male valet.

'Azzimare' means 'to dress up' - but it means 'to dress up' in the sense of 'titivate'. I splutter my Evian reading this direct translation. The Viscountess of Titivation. That is a sophisticated joke. One that belongs in the canon of an older mistress than 23-year-old Marion Waller.

* * * * *

I recall that in the early days of Edward and Laura Deacon's relationship, he and his brother Henry had made a visit to Boulogne, on the French coast, where we suspect Laura spent her confinement with her first child Georgina. France, it appears, is the place de rigueur for any necessities regarding your illegitimate children, sufficiently far from the chatter of London. Having packed his legitimate daughter off to educational establishments in Germany, Edward packs his illegitimate children off to educational establishments in France. At first their mother is with them, but then they - like Emily - are expected to suffer the bruising influence of boarding school.

Whatever Edward's sexual relationship with Laura at this time - and it appears to have cooled - he remains on sufficiently good terms to consider her a trustworthy companion to ask to Knebworth as a companion for his eldest legitimate daughter.

He will, however, keep his London residence at Buckingham Gate, as a residence for his 'valet' - or as Marion/Angelo appears to become known, his 'secretary'.

Are you shocked? Miss Greene is. But she knows Edward Bulwer well. And her loyalty to his children has weathered worse. However it reflects her confused position that the next section of her *Recollections* - which begins as Emily leaves Miss Ridout's in July 1846 - is re-started three times, in November 1846, January 1847 and August 1847. All three entries cover similar ground, each time with a deeper realisation of the position Emily has been put in by her father - and of the position that she, Miss Greene, is being put in... as it becomes apparent - of course - that she is the better option.

* * * * *

Miss Greene's first version is written prior to Teddy's 15th birthday at the beginning of November 1846. She recalls how, towards the end of July, *when the holidays were within a few days of commencing, I received a letter from Emily asking me if I would receive her at* _______[indecipherable - Kensington?] *for a few days before she went to Knebworth, and that her Father had desired her to ask me. As Mrs Lyal* [Miss Greene's apparent spelling - and there are Lyals living in London in the 1851 Census, but not in Kensington (although a Mary Lyle does live in Bedford Gdns)] *had been kind enough to receive my sister for more than a month before she went to Ireland, I asked her if she would again oblige me by admitting a friend for a few days, which she consented to do.*

Luckily it was the holidays here also, and Emily and I had a delightful time here together, and I found her more herself than I had seen her since we first parted; and she told me a great deal under the seal of secrecy, so I shall not even write them here, during the short time she was here. She and the Wilkinsons [also in Kensington] *were together every day...*

* * * * *

On the sixth day of her being here her father sent _______[indecipherable - looks like T. or J. Green], *the manservant with a cab for her and her luggage, and desiring her first to go to Bigg's, the dentist, to have a tooth drawn, and then to drive to Mr Thomson's* [in Welbeck Street, Marylebone] *where he would call for her, at 12 o'clock to take her down to Knebworth.*

Before I parted from her, she told me that her Papa would see all the letters which she wrote or received and begged to me to be careful what I said; and that she must be the same. I found out by chance that her father did call for her at Mr Thomson's, and made it appear as if he went down to Hertford by the Railroad - but he did not go down for some days, but sent her alone. She never mentioned anything of that in her letters, and all I have ever heard from her since she went to Knebworth had been very unsatisfactory, nor should I know any particulars if I could not understand a hint which she sometimes let drop in her letters, with strict orders to burn that letter when read.

She told me a charming French lady was living with them, this lady she had told me of before. God knows who her father may choose to introduce her to, but he pays me the compliment of not inviting me to meet them. Though always promised the honour of being invited to Knebworth - and Emily seemed sure of it when she left - that great day has not yet arrived. I give Sir E. as great credit, as I should to 'Bodan' [name/reference not clear], *for the clever manner he has managed to shield and separate Emily and myself the last four years, and all the time appearing not to intend it. Time, power and craft have been his auxiliaries, and up to this day I cannot grasp how it is to end, but I will make it appear plainly before I have done.*

answers on a postcard please

* * * * *

In January 1847, Miss Greene rewrites her account of Emily's move to Knebworth. *On the 26th of July Emily left this house* [Miss Greene's lodgings in London] - *and as plainly as she dared say it, gave me to understand that I was to be invited to follow her to Knebworth soon. She even left a trunk here which I was to take down.*

One month passed, and two, and three, when I began to open my eyes and ears, and understanding, and to see there is something wrong at Knebworth. With all the accounts of the 'people staying with them' I never could see any mention made of company at Knebworth in the Court Journal (which I took for the purpose of seeing who was there). In fact, after a good deal of cautious enquiry in London, I am convinced that 'The Viscountess' is no other than the lady and her children who had been ruining the comfort, respectability and happiness of the entire family for so many years.

Mrs Thomson has not even been admitted into the coterie, and the last sad answer I heard of, from a gentleman who had been there, was "No ladies visit there." Mrs Garrod and her daughter, and Mrs Maberly, were there, but 'Birds of a feather' etc.

* * * * *

All the mystery is now explained, and I fear unfortunate Emily must know it - as her Father has talked to her already upon the most improper subjects. All the comfort I have is that I never refused going with, or taking her and myself anywhere she chose, if her Father wished it - though had I thought only of myself, instead of my dear Emily, I should certainly have refused having anything to do with a man who had in every possible way behaved to me with such treachery.

I now see with regard to my being invited to Knebworth, he has only paid me the proper compliment due to any lady of character. Poor Miss Ridout, in the innocence of her heart, and ignorance of the company she was in, went down there for some days, and was, I daresay, charmed, as everybody is, with the Viscountess.

My great apprehension now is that Emily will next be sent to Paris with her, where nothing can save her from contamination. One thing may prevent that, and I will trust in God that he will yet save my child.

* * * * *

I can scarcely say that I have corresponded with Emily since she has been at her Father's house, now six months, for the first time in her life - and a pretty house it has been!! Her last few letters have been longer and more affectionate, and one a few days ago to me, evidently written by her father and copied by her, mentions with regret that her Papa's many trips to London, business and money matters, prevented him asking me to go down for a time to share their elasticity [surely 'domesticity'? - unless used in some financial or scientific sense - oh for Miss Greene to have had a typewriter!] - *implied in a very clever manner, in a passage saying, the reason she did not speak more of the lady who was staying with her, was hoping I might, when I went down, see and know her, as I should be delighted with her - she was so charming, etc., and had done her so much good by her advice -*

But she regretted to say, she [the lady] *was on the eve of her departure for France. There, her 4 little children were educating in a* _________ [indecipherable - frustratingly - again I throw this one over to you] *convent, and that she (Emily) was coming to London for a short time. Where in London I am to learn - perhaps here, as I think she cannot go to her Father's town house where his 'Secretary' lived, whose precepts and example might not be quite so improving as the 'Viscountess'.*

* * * * *

Miss Greene finally receives her invitation on 30th of January, 1847.

After it being many months since I had had any intercourse whatever with Sir Edward, I received a most kind and polite note asking me to go down to Knebworth to visit on the 17th of February. The letter from Emily which told me 'The kind lady she had been living with there was going to France to see her 4 little children', notified to me that the coast was clear for me; and my love to dear Emily, and anxiety to see and hear how she is settled and going on, makes me accept the invitation - though were I only to think of her Father's treacherous conduct towards me, I should never enter his house.

I go tomorrow, the 17th of February, to Knebworth, and will take up my Memoirs when I return.

* * * * *

Miss Greene picks up her memoirs again in August 1847. She leaves Knebworth in July, having been Emily's sole companion and confidante for *nearly six months* - but for visitors such as Mrs Thomson and the D'Eyncourt

Stair-case - Knebworth. — Herts.

by Ellen D'Eyncourt

Courtesy of the Tennyson D'Eyncourt family

sisters - and she now understands a good deal more. *For many reasons I am glad I went there, as I had a power of judging of my dear Emily in such a lengthened visit and, being so much alone with her, better than I could possibly have done in a shorter time of less intimacy.*

Still it is difficult to understand her as, though I am certain she loves me, yet, the attempt to poison her mind against me by Madame de Weling and others - when it was thought necessary to separate her from me in order to keep her abroad and out of the way - sometimes shewed its effect. Yet whenever she was in distress or a dilemma, she always came to me and opened her heart and mind to me in the same manner she always used to do before we were separated, and in a way that I am certain she never does to any other human being.

I have not the slightest hesitation in saying that I have often, whilst with her, seen her manner and expression so odd that I would pronounce her a little like what I saw her at Cannstatt - but not nearly so bad. Her chronic mania seems Nathalie - and her attachment to her does not at all surprise me. When Emily saw her first, Nathalie was a most accomplished, agreeable, pretty and elegant child of 11 years old. She, Emily, was cut off entirely from anybody and everybody whom she had ever loved, particularly her brother and myself, and having become wild and enthusiastic does not at all surprise me - in Germany, and undergoing the troublesome and disagreeable discipline she was subject to alone at Dr Heine's. Besides this, having to reflect upon wretched family circumstances which her father had told her, and which she was, from his advice and her own feelings of wounded pride, obliged to keep penned up in her own breast.

* * * * *

All this, as I say, working upon her mind, it does not at all surprise me the effect it had upon her brain. There remains upon her mind the prejudice of me, that I might betray the truth of the position I have held towards her, which would betray the secret about her mother. As in every instance since we have met, she tries to divide me from everybody she knows; her pride, also, does not choose to recollect all I have been to her.

It may be that her father continues to make <u>his</u> act seem to himself and others as if it was <u>hers</u> - and that it is he, in fact, who wishes the world not to know how cheaply he had his daughter brought up and taken care of up to the age of

14. The report, which certainly came from him, that he paid me £500 a year for his children's care and education at Cheltenham makes me suspicious.

I dare not venture an explanation with him, as it might get dear Emily into a scrape. I am sure she was betrayed into saying some things which were not true - whilst at Madame de Weling's - of me, when I knew she was nearly distracted; and I dread the effects which a scene of éclaircissement [the revelation of something previously unexplained] *with her father might have upon her mind.*

She has told me she could have physical courage to throw herself under the feet of a mad bull, but not the moral courage to stand an explanation of any length with her father - as she says, "after one which once passed between us", and the consequence [of which] was she very nearly destroyed herself.

Hold this thought as we approach the closing chapters of this story.

* * * * *

I was rather disappointed in her, upon our meeting, with regard to her manners and the little forms of society - as they were not nearly so good as they had been upon her leaving Miss Ridout's. She seemed totally ignorant of all the little courtesies of life, particularly domestic life, except when brought forth by some great object - and then it is awkward, and over done.

The week she was with me [in London], before she went to Knebworth, all my family, as well as myself, were charmed with her engaging manners, and thought them like her mother's in her best days. I think the cause of the alteration was her having passed six months with the French Viscountess alluded to. She, I am sure, is a most artful person, and they spent their time when alone (which was very often) in her giving Emily instructions of what was politic for her to do with regard to her father, and every other person she knew.

She [the Viscountess] *must be a woman of acute understanding, which she has used for the last ten years in the entire control of Sir Edward's mind and actions - and I suspect one of the objects of her being introduced to his daughter was to find out for him whatever in her character he could not, in order that he might the better know how to work upon that character.* Miss Greene's paranoia is peaking here, reaching levels we more associate with her old friend Rosina.

* * * * *

All the time she was there, she [the Viscountess] *was a person standing between the father and daughter, instead of allowing nature to take its course at last, when time and a knowledge of each other might have established a strong affection between them. Instead of this, I think expediency has taken the place of this affection, on both sides, which I at one time saw dawning.*

Emily could not, nor did not, esteem the lady - but it was evident to her that it was for her advantage to seem to do so. Besides Mde d'Azzimart was given many opportunities of doing little kindnesses for her, and being the medium of giving presents - which I am sure came from her father - and asking favour for her, which did not rob herself.

She also wound herself so entirely in Emily's interests, and took her part apparently in everything, that they kept good friends. Though I could well gather from what Emily told me, that they were often on the verge of a quarrel - Madame from wishing to be first in the house, as well as with Sir Edward; and Emily determined to keep her place as mistress of the house, which she did not allow any forms of hospitality or politeness to restrain.

She [the Viscountess] *told her many circumstances about her father and Grandmamma which she could not in any other way learn, and seemed to be so entirely acquainted with everything concerning the family, that I have no doubt upon my mind that she* is *the Mrs Beaumont whom Emily told me of when first she returned from Germany - and from what I also learned of her conduct in walking out, and being closeted for hours, with Sir Edward whilst on her visits to Knebworth, as well as scenes which passed before company.*

He seemed aware that he had done, at the least, an unwise thing in bringing her there, and was not a little anxious that she [the Viscountess] *should leave, and indeed I believe she was also very glad to get away.*

* * * * *

From the moment I began to suspect who it was that was now with Emily, I knew I should not be invited till she left, and it proved that I was right, as directly she was gone I was invited.

She [the Viscountess] *told Emily that she did not like Edward [Teddy] at all; he was, she said, exactly like his Uncle, Henry, and that it was such a shame that he should be left so well off, and Emily a beggar - as she told her that her father (except for the Estate) was worse than penniless, as he was deeply in debt, and indeed that he had got all his 'money', which was something considerable, and spent it.*

In every instance she [the Viscountess] *seemed to be his counsellor, and she said if he did not get into Parliament* [which he does not until 1852], *he would be obliged to let Knebworth and go abroad.*

This disagreeable change hanging over poor Emily, both she and I talked over the business of her friend Nathalie's coming with her family to visit her this summer - whilst at Knebworth - rather than put it off till next, when it might be let. As, amongst her sufferings in Germany, one was people thinking she was either a natural [Miss Greene's polite word for 'illegitimate'] *daughter, or else the daughter of some petty poet, and not what she represented herself to be, and was.*

All this was brought on by her being left, as she was, so totally alone in a foreign country, which thing I over and over again remonstrated with him not to do.

* * * * *

Poor thing! she little knew how bitterly she grieved me whilst relating the insults which she suffered, and the many disappointments she met with, from her father - all of which made me make great allowance for many extraordinary precis [abstractions] *of polite attention to myself whilst with her; and, upon the whole, she and I were as happy together as we could have been under the circumstances.*

However, directly I heard that Madame de Ritter and her daughter were expected, I wished to go away before they came. I guessed that Emily would be so engrossed with them, that she would not have time to be commonly civil to me.

Upon my proposing to leave, Sir E. begged of me to remain till Madame de Ritter had been come some days. Sir Edward and I spent a most anxious three weeks watching for her arrival, during which time I had a most alarming cough, and hoped that a change of air would remove it, which, along with a wish to see some of my family who had been ill, made me anxious to come to London.

In making your excuses, saying you wish - in the summer - to go from the country to London to improve a cough is not especially subtle.

Poor Emily anticipated the pleasure of her friends' coming so much, that I quite pitied her from the delay, and was nearly as glad as herself when Madame arrived.

Courtesy of the Fondazione Palazzo Coronini Cronberg

Madame de Ritter - née Amalie Hofmann - Natalie's mother

* * * * *

I was much pleased with Madame de Ritter, and delighted to think that I could leave her with so respectable, agreeable and amiable a person whom she loved so much; and determined to go away immediately - particularly as, upon the second day of her [Madame de Ritter's] arrival, Emily's manner towards me was quite changed, and I did not know what sort of a mean dependent Madame de Ritter might take me for when she saw the marked rudeness and inattention with which Emily treated me.

Besides, Madame de Ritter had told me that all her friends had tried to dissuade her from coming to Knebworth, as they told her that the cause of Sir Edward being separated from his wife was that he had "made his children's Governess his mistress, and that she was living now at Knebworth."

Therefore, the day before I left, I said to Madame de Ritter before Emily, that I was not, nor ever had been, a Governess to Emily - whatever conclusion she might come to from the manner in which she had seen me treated by her (and which was not the case when she was not present, as only a few days before had she begged of me to remain, even after her Father's return.)

I had written to him directly after Madame de Ritter had arrived, saying that now she could remain with Emily, I should wish to leave - which I did at the end of a week, before Nathalie and her Governess had time to come from Paris. As I calculated, if one of the party made such an attraction, what would three do. Besides, poor Sir Edward lost his election at Lincoln, and I was glad that I should not be at his house on his return there to witness his disappointment.

I have heard twice from Emily since my return, and her father has not yet come, but she has Edward [Teddy], *Madame de Ritter, Nathalie and her Governess, and I trust she is happy. God bless and protect her and dear Edward.*

* * * * *

While Miss Greene is at Knebworth - between February and July 1847 - the occasional letter from Edward survives, mainly from Malvern, and usually containing household instructions. The layout of the Gardens is a common theme - for instance, to tell Connan [transcribed also as Connon and Cannon] the Gardener to plant ***shrubs on the banks of the moat***, and - as though entwining Emily in some Sleeping Beauty castle - to use ***quick growing ivy*** and, especially, ***before all things***, put ***creeper on the House***.

After all the sweet Cannstatt correspondence between father and daughter about the dogs, it is distressing to read - dated April 24th - ***Allow me to say it is entirely your fault if the poor dog*** [Beau] ***got into bad habits. In London he was the cleanest & best dog I ever knew, & he would be at Knebworth, if you remembered & took care that he was constantly put out every two or three hours & well beat if he dirtied – which I am sure he never would do, with the least care & forethought.***

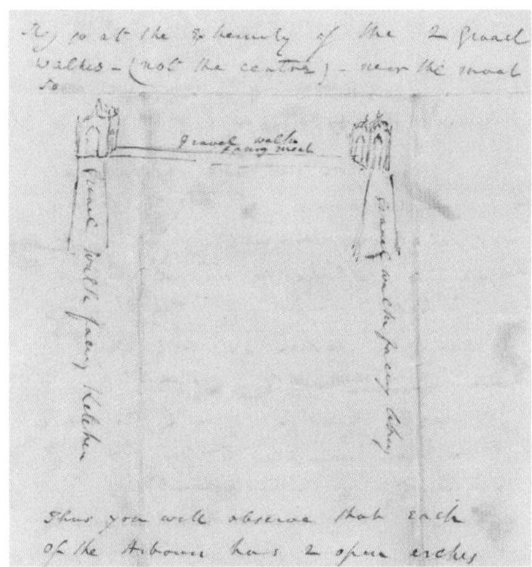

Instructions on Garden layout

But in a following letter - on 28th - he does ***beg pardon for hurting your poor affectionate feelings as to Beau. I meant my letter as a sort of lugubrious joke, but I dare say I was in too ill a vein for joking to give it that appearance. I know you meant & probably did for the best. By taking care that he is constantly out, I have all hope that he will become a Chesterfield – the pattern for all Beaux*** [Philip Dormer Stanhope, 4th Earl of Chesterfield's (1694–1773) *Letters to His Son on the Art of Becoming a Man of the World and a Gentleman* (1774) and *The Art of Pleasing* (1783) are widely read and make the author a synonym for the same]. I do sympathise with Emily. I have received similar admonishment over dogs that can do no wrong.

Also written in this same week, is the very first letter I found in Box 118, seventeen years ago, which is mentioned in Chapter One. This is the touching response from Malvern of Thursday April 29th - a year to the day from Emily's death - thanking her for the strawberries she has sent him from the greenhouse ***& tho' I did not dare eat them, further than taste two, I was very glad indeed to feel so much obliged to your rememberance.*** Knowing now, that this may have been a peace offering for not minding his dogs, or possibly a gesture prompted by Miss Greene, then her companion, takes a little of the shine away from this touching gesture. But I prefer to believe that Emily sent this gift at her own volition.

It remains Emily's lifelong desire to do right by her father. I believe that - however troubled this 17-year-old - there remains in her the sweet child that wants to send her papa strawberries, especially when he is unwell.

* * * * *

Not one single letter, however, survives from the time when the Viscountess D'Azzimart is at Knebworth. All correspondence from the previous six months - from August 1846 to January 1847 - has been destroyed. This period of Emily's single year at Knebworth is left our imagination.

This is not because Edward is there too and there is no need for letters. He appears to have kept away. It is because, in retrospect, he does not want a record of this time.

He does makes an occasional appearance. We know he is there at the end of October 1846, because Teddy tells Miss Greene that Emily is taken to a Royal Ball at neighbouring Hatfield House. The newspapers confirm Edward's presence at this ***substantial entertainment*** on Thursday, 29th October - but not Emily's. Although Emily will have been a useful interpreter as German songs are sung for the German-mothered Queen and her even more German husband.

You will not be surprised to hear that the Viscountess is also not listed by the newspapers as attending the Royal Ball. Whether or not Cinderella went, we can be certain the Wicked Stepmother didn't.

Under normal circumstance the Lytton family would be certain to leave family letters describing this exciting local event. Not, however, when a news blackout is in place.

So it is, that we need newspapers to confirm Edward's presence at home with his daughter during this period. ***Her Papa's many trips to London*** were the rule, not the exception.

* * * * *

Marion tells us that, in July 1846, she is with him in Buckingham Gate. ***He was then writing*** *The New Timon,* a longform poem of philosophical musings that - reflecting his bitter mood - criticises a ***School-Miss*** poet like Alfred Tennyson (1809–1892), ***in the prime of life***, and ***belonging to a wealthy family***, and - most significant to Edward - with no dependents... for receiving a public pension, unlike other more worthy recipients. A bit like today complaining that the film company Working Title receives lottery money to make Richard Curtis films.

Tennyson hits back in *Punch,* with an equally cutting satirical poem about Bulwer Lytton's day being long past. However, the feud does not prevent the future Poet Laureate later conceding that - in his day, no one ***did more towards intellectually raising the public, piquing its interest in better things, and enabling it to separate the wheat from the chaff*** than Edward Bulwer Lytton, and that Edward's soon-to-be-begun twelve books of *King Arthur (1848–9)*, helped to create the public taste for his own masterpiece *Idylls of The King*, published ten years later.

I.

Our land's first legends, love and knightly deeds,
And wondrous Merlin, and his wandering King,
The triple labour, and the glorious meeds
Won from the world of Fable-land, I sing.
Go forth, O Song, amidst the banks of old,
And glide translucent o'er their sands of gold.

*Edward's **King Arthur** (1848)*

* * * * *

Marion next tells us that Edward, ***during that year, went to Malvern*** - although she may mean the beginning of the following year, 1847, when he was definitely at Malvern. ***He complained of numbness in one arm. But all that time he complained, more or less, of that oppression on the head & giddiness - and was very low spirited at times. He also began to call on 'mesmerisers' & had a French man to mesmerise him - but it never did him any good. I think we must have spent the winter in London - yes, I am sure now we did, for I distinctly remember Tate*** [his trusted housekeeper, Sophy Tate (1800-1887)] ***scolding me for keeping so small a fire.***

Clearly during this period he prefers the responsibility-free company of his new young muse - the nurse nymph - than the responsibility-laden company of his previous mistress and his unmarried daughter. Clearly also, this period of extended illness, money worries, and relationship upheaval, causes in him what we, today, would call clinical depression.

Emily receives the following undated letter from him while she is at Knebworth - we may guess, after he has rowed with Laura, and her departure. Reading this letter, and remembering Emily's previous letters of similar misery - Miss Greene transcribes the beginning pararagraph of Emily's Christmas 1844 letter about ***indescribable feeling of melancholy*** in her *Recollections* at this point to illustrate how Emily can be *out of her mind from sadness* - it doesn't help to say it, but Emily is her father's child.

* * * * *

My dearest Emily, I am sensible, believe me, of your kind & genuine frankness – which you may be assured you will never regret & which will not fail to join my own confidence. With regard to my health, it is certainly much better than it was at Knebworth.....but Darkness surrounds & covers me.

Often in this struggle for Health – which is something like a daily War, with a living foe – when I suffer myself to contemplate the failure that is beyond: youth gone – with all that could cheer it - & thereafter of suffering & sickness probably to enclose me, as life now must tend to decline; a desolate hearth – widowed & yet shackled; those with whom I "took sweet counsel" in the past, gone from me, or departing; no love, no companionship – except, my children, in you both, & you are with me but for a while. Our years themselves divide us.

Before you, lies the Future, of new ties; before me, but the grave of the old. My career over. My frame no longer able to bear on what ambition may be yet left to excite & absorb me from regrets. My heart almost hopeless. When all these shadows rise before me, often I am tempted to give the strife & lie down & die.

But then, happily, comes a better courage, & a sense of the duties yet left to me; gratitude to Heaven for all that promise so fair in you & your brother; a belief in God's justice, & the soul within me, which must endure here, to be worthy of new spheres hereafter.....& so I march on thro' the Valley of the Shadow. If one great & terrible Affliction which now dogs me as a ghost, & makes every hour a ______________[indecipherable] ***& fear, be spared to me, I think the world will grow bright again. But eno' of my egotisms....***

I wonder how Marion dealt with these dark moods? In her words, ***He was also very fond of speculating on the future state, and when I used to see him so melancholy & despondent, I used to get so frightened that I have hidden his razors & slept nights at his door.***

Whenever in 1846 or 1847 the above letter is written, Edward sees himself with ***no companionship – except, my children.*** Is this disavowing Marion, or has she also left at this moment? Marion reveals in her 1870s letters, ***I left your dear father three times - but every time he got me back again, & what could I do, but return to him - I suffered away from him, & suffered torture near him!***

Picture 23-year-old Marion - back from their romantic Mediterranean travels - facing the prospect of living in England with this 44-year-old invalid and manic depressive. Installing herself at Buckingham Gate, or Malvern, or even Knebworth, is a very different thing for a 23-year-old to contemplate than a road trip through the orange groves of Provence, or evening passeggiati in the hills of Sorrento and Rome.

Even if she becomes dependent on Edward, I suspect there are plenty of periods of 'darkness surrounding', when Marion, also, is inclined to walk away. Or - as Emily will come to contemplate - escape to Italy.

* * * * *

Teddy, we have heard from Miss Greene, is finding his father difficult to deal with. Joining Harrow School in the autumn of 1846 must be a relief from being packed off to Water Cures. Miss Greene is discouraged, again, from interrupting his studies, but she does manage to visit him, soon after his 15th birthday in November - *and was delighted I did so, as I found my dear boy at last where he ought to be and very much improved. Softened down into being what he is, a school boy, not aping the man, as he had been the last few times I saw him.*

He seemed happy and content instead of sour and discontented. His sentiments upon certain subjects I thought improved - but was sorry to trace his father's influence over his mind, in matters certainly wrong. He seemed quite to have altered his tone of speaking of his father since I had seen him, and was very <u>bold</u> when he talked of the great blood from which he was descended and "hoped *he had not got any from the other side which might disgrace it.*"

He also talked of the fine natural religion of his father - his charity to Authors, etc. None of this did I let go with him, and we had some private conversation which I must not even write. I fear he and Emily were not as happy in each other as they used to be with me, before their affection was torn asunder. He seemed not to suffer so much as when he first began to think [that] his [father] did not love him either.

Upon the whole I have reason to hope that he is in a much better way than he has been, and God can change his heart and guide him to the right. What his father implants into [she has crossed out 'teaches'] *both of these children is calculated to teach them selfishness and hard heartness! and all appearance of kindness to others is only to be used to bring back some gratification or advantage for themselves.*

* * * * *

Miss Greene's third version of the events of this period includes a recap that extends all the way back to *the unfortunate entrusting of his daughter for a few months to Madame de Weling.*

Courtesy of the Tennyson D'Eyncourt family

Knebworth House at this time...

It is pleasing to see her acknowledge that - until that point - his house had been a place where *I had so often been before, and uniformly treated by him with such friendship and respect,* and where their *long and intimate acquaintance had never been interrupted by an unkind deed or word.*

However, Emily's time at Madame de Weling had been an *éclaircissement* of things *I had always carefully guarded poor Emily from hearing* and *this artful person* had *enraged his mind against me in such a manner that for the first time in his life he seemed to withdraw all confidence about his daughter...*

But four years later Miss Greene is back in favour and back beneath his roof. Emily reveals that he has *often quarrelled* with Madame d'Azzimart - *as much as either of them dared - as it was evidently for both their interests to seem at least to be on good terms...* but *Sir Edward at last saw that he had made a false move in bringing Madame to Knebworth, and often in bursts of temper shewed it; and at the end of six months, when the time for his going to London* [more permanently] *arrived, she left, and I was then invited - one of the points which convinced me who and what she was, as I knew he dared not ask me there whilst she was.*

He was at Knebworth, as I said, three times while I was there - for a week at a time - and was as frank, polite and well-bred as ever to me, and was not once out of temper, which, Emily told me, was a remarkable circumstance. His

Courtesy of the Tenny.on D'Eyncourt family

...by Ellen D'Eyncourt

health was wretchedly broken, and I should fear much for his mind, which he must have quite lost in some of the paroxysms of temper described to me, and indeed which he described to me of himself.

For a long time I have thought his conduct about his children that of a mad man, and indeed - independent of conscience - he must have enough upon his mind to drive him so. As, besides all his other torments, he is deeply in debt - and Lady Lytton has come to England to demand a larger separate allowance.

He says, if she persists in refusing an allowance as a compromise, he will sue for a divorce - and asked me if I would stand by him in giving evidence as to her conduct whilst she was in Ireland. To this I answered that whatever letter or promise I had ever made him on that subject I should always stand to, but that now he had for so many years taken the children so entirely out of my care - and had them so completely in his own - I did not see what use it could be, as I never could prove anything against her character farther than what I had said, "That I thought her an unfit person to have the charge of her children, from her want of natural affection, and from her drinking."

Rosina's return from the Continent in the summer of 1847 - along with a possible return to court proceedings - is the probable reason for Miss Greene's recap in her *Recollections*. Her account is once more potential testimony, or notes for testimony. Thus the restating of Edward's original courtesies to her, and an attempt to rationalising his bizarre parenting despite her strong disapproval of his current behaviour. Miss Greene is reminding herself why Edward is the lesser of two evils for the children.

Rosina's return also gives reason for Edward's second foreign escape with Marion - and an increased need to settle on an appropriate guardian for Emily.

* * * * *

Thus matters stood when I last saw him, and as he left Knebworth to attend his election at Lincoln - which election he lost - and he will, I am led to think, be obliged to let Knebworth and go abroad, which, after all, he may find suits him better than England.

But what is to be done with Emily? Poor girl! upon her foreseeing the possibility of Knebworth being let, she urged the girl about whom she has a 'momie mania' [French expression - 'mummy mania' - from the Egyptology craze of the late 18th Century, meaning a fascination for bringing home something exotic], *to come and visit her this summer instead of next; and I was delighted to find that her mother, Madame de Ritter, consented to come herself also.*

Here Miss Greene's recap adds more detail to the account of Madame de Ritter's arrival. This offers more clues to Emily's state of mind and situation, and is therefore worth slightly retracing our steps for.

I had the pleasure of spending one week with her, after her arrival, and found her a most kind, agreeable, motherly, good German lady, who is very fond of Emily and she of her. I should have wished to leave the day after her arrival; and wanted to go when she was expected. But Sir Edward requested of me to remain, as "Emily could not be found alone when that German lady arrived."

I consented to remain, though I knew how Emily would behave to me when she arrived, and - but for the appearance, and that I did not choose to quarrel - I should have gone away suddenly one day after Emily had been particularly rude to me and I asked her, did she wish to quarrel with me? And she said, she did.

At all events I was determined not to remain when the great favourite, Nathalie, and her Governess, came; though Emily, after all, came to me to beg I would remain, and be with them when her father returned, to talk to him, and keep him in humour.

It seems strange to think that I yielded to Emily - but seeing her, as I did, so often on the very borders of insanity, it was not wonderful that I tried to soothe her whenever it was in my power.

* * * * *

The second night after Madame de Ritter came, after she left her and went to her own room, I followed her [Emily] *and found her in a most excited state, fearing that Madame de Ritter would "not like her" and what would become of her then? Next, if Nathalie came (which she wished she would not), she would be too happy, and it would not last - and then what would become of her?*

She continued, for some time, like a person in despair - deadly pale and tears seeming to roll unconsciously down her cheeks. I remained with her a considerable time till she got to bed and was composed, and she seemed quite to throw herself upon me as she used to do as a child.

One circumstance about her which I can't at all understand is that she seemed always ashamed if a servant or anybody came into the room when she seemed affectionate or as if she wished to be with me. Several times she has stolen into my room and bed at night when she felt lonely or could not sleep and I used to talk her into composure - but if any of the maids came and caught her there, she would jump out of bed and make it appear that she had only just come into my room to look for something.

The same if she and I were sitting beside each other and laughing, or seeming companionable in the drawing room, and the Footman came into the room - she would start up and walk about the room as if looking for something. And she could not bear me to be with her when people called. I think she wished to be thought all alone and to be pitied for it.

* * * * *

Again, I think Sir Edward and Madame d'Azzimart roused her pride in a manner to resist any obligation she might feel for the love and affection I had shewn her for so many years. Or that none of them wished it to be known how little any of the family had to say to either herself or dear Edward [Teddy], *whilst I was so happy in the enjoyment of their affection and society.*

In short, her manner to me - a point I can in no way explain except by calling it madness - [was] brought to this point by her throwing all her love into Nathalie. [And because of this obsession for Nathalie] she seems still more estranged from Edward, who, poor fellow, suffered dreadfully from the very idea. Perhaps God may direct that kind and amiable Madame de Ritter in bringing about a better feeling between them during their holidays, whilst they have been together with her and Nathalie.

I said all I could to both of them, but never could gain a kind word or look from her for him. D'Azzimart slyly worked against him by saying what a shame it was that Edward should be heir to so much money and she so little; and said he was exactly the same character as his uncle, Henry, and made her jealous of him with his father, who certainly once liked Emily the best.

* * * * *

She, Emily, seemed also to wish to divide me from Edward, and once [whilst at Miss Ridout's] made an attempt at it about some letters of his, which was very shabby to say the least of it. I could learn all from Edward, but do not wish to let him see that I distrust her or have reason to do so.

There was certainly something wrong going on at Cannstatt, which she wished me not to learn, and prevented my going for her there from Brussells lest I should learn it. Mrs Parsons [of the friendly English family in Cannstatt, wife of the Minister of the English Church] *told me it was the most improper place she could possibly be in, unprotected as she was; and that she was sure Sir Edward would not have her long at home, till he would regret her being left.*

Upon the whole, whilst I was with her, I pitied her; and even admired her to see the manner in which she employed herself in the house and about her work, music and writing; reading, I am sorry to say, she had no taste for; and religion she seems to put quite aside for 'a more convenient season' [*Acts 24:25, King James Bible:* ***And as he reasoned of righteousness, temperance, and judgment to come, Felix trembled, and answered, Go thy way for this time; when I have a convenient season, I will call for thee.***] *God grant it may ever come, but <u>that</u> change has, and does, give me more pain than all the rest.*

If God is pleased to soften her heart in that way, all will yet be well. If not, God forgive her father for so completely lifting her out of the good path when both she and Edward [Teddy] *were in it to my certain knowledge, and shewed it, young as they were, by their conduct and conversation.*

A consequence of Emily seeming *in every way to try and wish to separate me and Edward* [Teddy], is that *he has been with her and her friends all the holidays* [the summer holidays of 1847] *and I have never heard from him, and she never mentions him when she writes.*

I hear Sir Edward spent three days at Knebworth since he lost the election with Emily and her friends and then went to Germany to drink the Waters!

Emily and Madame de Ritter and Edward were to come to London to my niece Bonnie's wedding in about a month, but it has been put off by severe illness of my brother's. And so matters stand this 30th day of August, 1847.

* * * * *

The way Marion tells it, ***In August 1847, he*** *[Sir Edward]* ***was ordered to***

Gastein [for the Water Cure] - ***we travelled post*** [as the post does], ***in his carriage*** [swopping horses at each stop], ***saw the Rhine for the first time, visited Dresden, Prague, Salzburg, Vienna & we were in Gastein in Sept 1847.***

I think [it was], in that year, that we went to Leipzig & that the Messrs Tauchnitz [the second generation of the popular German publishers who were respectful of the copyrights of English authors such as Bulwer Lytton and Dickens] ***gave a banquet in his honour. If I remember right, there were then no nice hotels or houses at Gastein [so] the Prefect placed his house at his disposal - it was away from the village or town & near the waterfall which prevented his sleeping for a long time. We had our own meals sent us from the hotel & his courier acted as valet.***

There he must have been writing *King Arthur* ***his beloved book. We took very long walks round about there, and if I had any memory & talent I ought to be able to write the most amusing book - for his conversation was most interesting and I never tired of listening to him.*** And more... for it is here that we can presume that - while the waterfall is keeping them awake - Marion and Sir Edward conceive their first child.

* * * * *

Back in England, *the time for Bonnie's marriage drew near.* It is not clear which of Mary's brothers is delaying it, as one brother belongs on each side of the aisle. Bonnie Wilkinson is about to become a Greene again, marrying her mother's first cousin William Greene (1819-1915), the child of Major William Greene. [If Volume One is at hand, see the convoluted Greene Family Tree on p.62.] Bonnie is 16 (17 in November), William is 28 - and they will be married for 60 years, with William outliving Bonnie 7 years, to the age of 96.

I gave Emily and Madame de Ritter warning, as Emily had begged me to do so, in order that she might make preparations about her dress. I also told Edward, who was at Knebworth for his holidays, but I guessed that she would manage that he should not come.

The 21st of September was the day fixed for the wedding, and they came to town to the Thomsons two days before; though she did not let me know she was in town, so that I did not see her, or Madame, till at Albert Place [in Kensington, where the Wilkinsons are living, near Hyde Park Barracks] *the morning of the wedding - and then she was a perfect disgrace to herself, and everybody about her, from the dirt of her dress and all being so ill put on and crushed.*

The only new thing she had got was a fiery red satin bonnet which misbecame her very much. Madame de Ritter was particularly well dressed and we were all surprised that she had not interested herself more about Emily's dress.

I had very little opportunity of speaking privately to Emily, but the little I had, she made use of in telling me that Natalie had written her a proposal of marriage from Carl [Natalie's 17-year-old brother] *- and when I asked her what answer did you give, she said, "I said yes!"*

She also told me how cross and disagreeable her father was, when at Knebworth, to the de Ritters, and that she dreaded his coming home - but still had a hope that she would go to Paris and Vienna with Madame de Ritter.

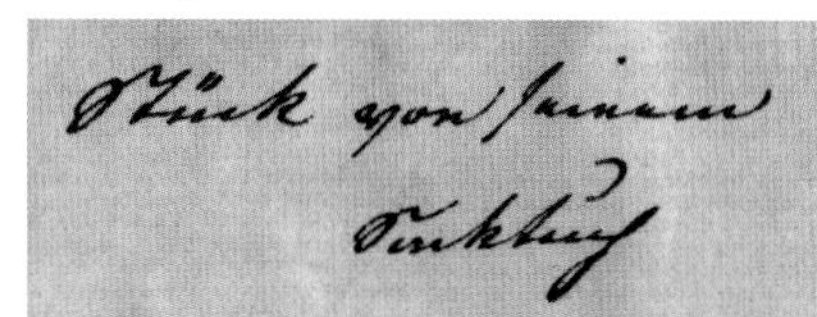

One of the last things I discover tucked away at the bottom of Box 88 is a white cotton handkerchief wrapped in brown paper with these words, 'Stück von seinem Sacktuch' - which Joachim tells me is Austrian German for 'piece of his handkerchief', or 'something of his trouser pocket' - a fetishistic memento I imagine procured by Natalie from her elder brother Carl de Ritter as part of this dubious match-making

All the day of the wedding, I saw Emily talking unlike herself - and I did not see her after, though she remained another day at the Thomsons, when I was determined to leave her to herself.

After she returned to Knebworth, I got almost daily letters from her, more frank and more soft and like herself, as she felt more happy and had something to look forward with hope.

Courtesy of the Tennyson D'Eyncourt family

Bayons Manor, Lincolnshire, by Ellen D'Eyncourt

CHAPTER 31

~ Bayons - 1847-1848 ~

To The Right Hon. C. T. D'Eyncourt, M.P. I dedicate to you, my dear friend, a work [*Harold, Last of The Saxon Kings* (1848)], ***principally composed under your hospitable roof; and to the materials of which your library, rich in the authorities I most needed, largely contributed...***

...pausing from my labour, I look through that castle casement, and beyond that feudal moat, over the broad landscapes which, if I err not, took their name from the proud brother of the Conqueror himself; in those winter nights, the grim old tapestry waved in the dim recesses, I hear again the Saxon thegn winding his horn at the turret door, and demanding admittance to the halls from which the prelate of Bayeux had so unrighteously expelled him.

-- what marvel, that I lived in the times of which I wrote... that I entered into no gossip less venerable than that current at the Court of the Confessor, or startled my fellow-guests (when I deigned to meet them) with the last news which Harold's spies had brought over from the Camp at St. Valery?

-- with all those folios, giants of the gone world, rising around me daily, more and more, higher and higher--Ossa upon Pelion [in Greek mythology the giants Otus and Ephialtes attempt to scale heaven by piling Mount Ossa upon Mount Pelion]--***on chair and table, hearth and floor; invasive as Normans, indomitable as Saxons, and tall as the tallest Danes (ruthless host, I behold them still!); with all those disburied spectres rampant in the chamber, all the armour rusting in thy galleries, all those mutilated statues of early English kings (including St. Edward himself) niched into thy grey, ivied walls***

-- say in thy conscience, O host, (if indeed that conscience be not wholly callous!) shall I ever return to the nineteenth century again?

Edward Bulwer Lytton, dedication, *Harold, Last of The Saxon Kings*

* * * * *

After a long year on her own at Knebworth House, effectively playing her absent father's country secretary (in the literal sense of the word), the shine is beginning to come off Emily's châtelaine dreams. The letters she now receives from him - consistently harrassed, unwell, and forever on-the-move - are no longer about her. They are no longer the loving expressions of fatherly advice and hopes for the future. When they are not fretting about the garden or the dogs, they are now, almost exclusively, about him.

...look out & send me by coach:

1st – some small knee buckles – in chased steel – there is either one or two pair on my toilet table I believe in a little basket or box with other odds & ends – or in one of the gilt toilet boxes.

2nd – a pair of black silk knee breeches, not cloth.

3rd – a pair of very short calico or linen drawers, to wear under.

4th – a pair of gauze long under stockings to wear under silk, & a long pair of ribbed silk – Dawson says there are 2 or 3 pair- but what I want is the best, long pair with rather broad stripes or ribs – all white silk.

5th there are some white stiff ________[indecipherable] ***for neckcloths, with a stock buckle to fasten them*** _____[with? - obscured by an ink blot]. ***Look out all these carefully & send them as the Duchess of Sutherland has just asked me to meet the Queen & I must go in court dress.***

Somebody is having all the fun, and it is not her. The only party Emily appears to be invited to in the year she turns nineteen is her childhood friend Bonnie Wilkinson's wedding. Even more dispiriting, the bride is two and a half years younger than her.

* * * * *

When her father does speak of her in his letters, it is usually only concern that she has a suitable chaperone. He is pleased that her childhood guardian is with her, Miss Greene, and happy that his friend Charles Tennyson D'Eyncourt (1784-1861)'s daughters, Clara (1812-1863) and Ellen (1817-1900) - both in their 30s and not yet married, visit in the spring for an extended stay.

The eldest daughter, Julia D'Eyncourt (1811-1879), Marion Waller tells us,

had fallen in love with him (long before then I think), refused several offers of marriage, turned roman catholic & entered a convent. We will discuss the D'Eyncourts later, but in many ways Julia D'Eyncourt's response to Edward Bulwer Lytton is a portent of Emily's - we are already familiar with Emily's predisposition to wallow in self-sacrifice in her letters during, and since, her time in Germany.

When her father does come across a possible friend for her, the best he can find is the married-with-children, and also in her 30s, Ada Lovelace (1815–1852). ***She is Byron's daughter you know*** [his only legitimate one - she and Emily at least have that in common] ***& thought very clever*** [and still so today, for having been the first to see the potential of computer programming]. ***She is very friendly to me & I think may visit us in the Summer. She is handsome to my eyes, more from a rude likeness to her father, & my associations of sorrowful love for that great creature, than in herself. Her manner is not good – but she has 'the womanly charm' nonetheless...***

Ada Lovelace

[Later:] ***I have seen more of Lady Lovelace. She is a very remarkable person, extremely original – but too prononcée*** [I read 'conspicuous'] ***for my taste, womanly in mienne*** [bearing] ***but masculine in mind...***

[Later:] ***Neither need you fear for Lady Lovelace's disastrous influences - she interests me as a mind, not as a woman, & indeed I am even thinking she might be a good friend for you... For the rest, she is not dark – we communicate on the most abstract of metaphysical questions, the source of ideas, the destinies of life, the nature of the soul. And in all these we fight gallantly against each other.***

It will be another two generations before the link between the Bulwers and the Byrons is made, when Ada's granddaughter Judith Blunt (1873–1957) marries Edward's grandson Neville Lytton (1879–1951) in 1899.

* * * * *

Then there are the Thomsons. Edward, we have seen, is mercurial about this association. There is clearly respect for Dr Anthony Todd Thomson (1778–1849), a prominent American-Scottish skin specialist; and there has been motherly kindness to Teddy from Katherine, Mrs Thomson (1797–1862), whose father was a partner and relative of the Wedgwood pottery family. Their daughter Elizabeth Anne (1828-1915) is the same age as Emily and their youngest son John Cockburn (1834-1860), although a couple of years younger than Teddy, has become his regular companion.

Dr Anthony Todd Thomson

Mrs Thomson is author to a string of romantic novels - described by the *Oxford Dictionary of National Biography* as ***vacuous*** - and, in later life, society biographies, with her son Cockburn - writing under the pseudonyn Grace and Philip Wharton - titles such as *The Queens of Society* and *The Wits and Beaux of Society*. The clues to Edward's suspicions about Mrs Thomson are all here.

Mrs Thomson spends time that spring at Knebworth with Emily - I have mentioned in Chapter Two the inscribed gift of her romance, *Tracey; or the Apparition* (1847), to ***Emily Bulwer, Knebworth Park*** in May 1847.

* * * * *

Before he becomes ***the odious Cockburn*** (13th August 1847), Emily is friendly to her brother's companion. Cockburn (pronounced "Co-burn" for those of you at the back) is the only young man Emily is ever in company with, aside from her brother. She is 18 years old that May (19 in June), and he is 13 or 14 years old (depending when his birthday falls - a detail I am yet to discover).

Cockburn is specifically mentioned in her company in a passage in Bonnie Wilkinson's journal of this month, May 1847, which is intriguing on more than one level.

Today, according to a yesterday-made-appointment, Mamma [Mrs Wilkinson] *& I met Aunt Mary* [Miss Greene] *at the Duke of York's Pillar & walked across St James Park, which looked beautiful, to James St, to Sir Edward Lytton's house, to see Emily. She came up to the door almost at the moment we did & we went into a most gorgeous drawing room, painted and decorated like an antique missal* [illuminated, i.e. illustrated, book of worship] *in blue & gold with the heads & figures of ancient English kings & all sorts of magnificent blazonry & colouring.*

At first Emily's manner appeared constrained & strange, but this soon went off & then I liked her again. It is very strange how people change in growing older - though indeed, to do us both justice, not at all in the style of the Petit Diner [as a hostess] *for she was very anxious that I should go down to Knebworth then, or soon, or any time. I think Emily much to be pitied in her present position. It is such a false one - & she I am sure feels that it is so. Cockburn Thomson came in & we left them together.*

This is the only description we have of this London home of Edward's - his and Marion's love nest - 19 James Street, Buckingham Gate. He may have moved out of Mayfair, but he is not slumming it. The painted walls sound similar to what is, today, still to be seen in the interiors of Ludwig of Bavaria's castles. Emily's presence suggests that Marion is not in residence, therefore we may guess Marion has accompanied Edward to Malvern. But most intriguing is the final comment. I repeat it. *...we left them together.*

If they are literally 'left together' by Miss Greene and Mrs Wilkinson, it can only be because these ladies consider Cockburn at 13/14 still a child. Can such a pairing ever be considered a romantic attachment? We have heard Emily's fixation over 11 to 16-year-old Natalie called such. However we have also heard Miss Greene explain it as Emily seeking a replacement for her brother, the companion of her childhood. Both, I think, can apply.

* * * * *

I remember at 15 receiving the attentions of an 18-year-old girl - and I recall my brother widening that age gap still more, at both ends. When you are a pubescent teenager locked away for most of the year, and the options are few, needs must. The emotional risk is greater at that age. What we know, is that Cockburn develops a serious crush on Emily. This will have painful and serious consequences the following year.

Emily strongly denies that she does anything to lead Cockburn on - she cites the age difference, and says she was just being nice to her brother's friend. The latter is the better excuse, based on her previous history with Natalie. But clearly Emily is in need of companionship beyond 30-something spinsters (the D'Eyncourt sisters) and her now 61-year-old childhood guardian, Miss Greene.

So, what happens, is that she starts to fixate on her first love. The prospect of Natalie coming to visit becomes: first, a promise of the reawakening of her first intense - if we don't say love affair - 'personal relationship with a contemporary'; and second - now become more important - a promise of escape.

* * * * *

The things arrived safely, but you did not send a stock buckle - only three old knee buckles. However I can do...

I take the liberty of stopping your choice of [wall] ***papers as all I saw were ugly and dear...*** oh dear. Put yourself, for a moment, in Emily's shoes. Imagine receiving irritated and condescending remarks like this from your father. Is he trying to make this long-promised position so unpleasant that she will seek independence?

I have just heard from Mr Hall [presumably Samuel Carter Hall (1800–1889), editor of the *Art Union Monthly Journal*] ***that his artist*** [Frederick William Hulme (1816–1884)] ***will be down this evening to draw the House on Tuesday*** [6th July]. ***You will get this too late to be aware of his visit, but no doubt, you will have received him!***

I wish you would take him to that part of the Park where there is an old row of oaks (Mr Webb knows it) & where he can see the gardens front & the north front together. It is perhaps the best point of view for a drawing.

This execution of this last instruction - which we assume Emily performed whether or not the letter arrived in time - is possibly the most long-lasting and significant influence that the heroine of this book has on the famous house of which she is active châtelaine for a year and a half.

The illustration that F. W. Hulme makes is to become the most recognisable image of Knebworth House to this very day. If Emily took Mr Hulme to that spot in Knebworth Park, we have her to thank for the angle of this classic image of the home of the Lytton family that, today, is the root of the logo on all our stationery, adorns countless items in our Gift Shop - postcards, mugs, erasers, pencil sharpeners, etc. - is even the cover of both the CD and DVD of *The Beach Boys Live at Knebworth 1980.*

Knebworth House on 6th July 1847

* * * * *

After Malvern for the Water Cure, then Lincoln for the election - having barely been in Emily's company all year - Edward arrives at Umberslade Hall in Warwickshire at the end of July 1847 to attend Dr Edward Johnson (1785-1862). Dr Johnson is another disciple of Vincent Priessnitz, and author of *Life, Health and Disease* (1837) and *Results of hydropathy; or, Constipation not a disease of the bowels; indigestion not a disease of the stomach* (1846) [good one for the coffee table]. He has recently moved his practice from Hertfordshire - Stanstead Bury, 15 miles from Knebworth - to be closer to Malvern, and will move again in a few years into Malvern itself. ***I only propose to stay*** *a few days just to get into trim. The election has done me no harm in point of health.....but I am anxious to try if I could get off the German Baths by a slight course of quinine here, backed by the habits of the W[ater] C[ure]...*

1st then, have you any idea how long Mad^e de R & Natalie will stay with you. I hope very long, till Autumn. If not, perhaps, if Mad^e de R goes back thro' Germany, she may bring you to me or on my way? - northward, should I be detained longer than I expect, but this is not likely as the season is so soon over.

2nd, Can you get me any information about the different German springs from Mad^e de R? For I have no idea which is the best.

My complaints are these.

1. Languid circulation

2. Deficient vital energy & nervous exhaustion

3. Weakness in the spinal cord which produces depression in the brain & threatens symptoms of paralysis.

[Sounds like back strain to me - a common writer's (and traveller's) complaint - and, having some knowledge of it, significantly more debilitating that its matter-of-fact title suggests.]

She may know of cases similar, or what are the best baths for each complaint, & whether the season is over for them. I am recommended Gastein, but that is so far, and the time now is late. The nearest Baths are the best for me - I could not get to the Austrian.

* * * * *

Austria, however, is clearly where Emily needs to set her sights. Thus the comment at Bonnie's wedding - about how she, too, has received a marriage proposal (from a 17-year-old Austro-Hungarian there is no evidence she has ever met). But two catastrophic world events are about to intervene. Two revolutions that, tragically, blight the remaining six months of Emily's story.

The first is waiting for her father on his return from the Germany at the end of October. Two decades of 'Railway Mania' is replaced, that autumn, by the 'Panic of 1847'. Both headlines have their own Wikipedia entries. Explore the details if you will. Or picture 'Mortgage Mania' and the 'Panic of 2008'.

Basically, the Railway investment bubble of the 1830s and 1840s bursts, and a lot of people lose a lot of money. Including Sir Edward Bulwer Lytton.

Alongside the crash of his Railways shares, Edward's return is met by ***a note of Madame de R. to invite you*** [Emily] ***to go to Paris with her if she goes. She touched on her proposal to you - [and] that you had written to me on it with your own views & wishes*** [Emily has not yet written]. ***However (passing by that) I come to the point. I shall be very happy to give you the pleasure of seeing Natalie, & having the gaiety natural at your age at Paris, under the care of Mme de Ritter, provided (as I have written to Mme de R) the invitation is meant for more than a few weeks – that is for the Winter.***

If for a less time than that, I shall be left alone with an establishment at Knebworth without the power of reforming plans _____ ________[indecipherable]***............But go for that time, I should give up Knebworth for the Winter, & be at liberty to go to some cheap climate in the South of England or Wales - economize.***

There is another point on which I feel embarrassed. I do not know Mme de R's circumstances. It may be a charge upon her to receive you for the longer time - while on the other hand, I could not afford paying separately for you & myself, while to a certain extent Kneb. wd go on all the same.

With an English lady, there could be no doubt as to the nature of the invitation - but the circumstance of the maid [Madame de Ritter has bought a Germain ladies' maid with her, whom Emily it appears has been making use of, and the question of whether Edward should be contributing to her wages, we can guess, has arisen] ***makes me doubt what Mad. de R may really intend & it would be awkward to both if she thought I ought to pay her, & I, on the other hand, thought such a notion an affront to her & as a meanness in her. It will be well, my dear, to be open & frank with me in these matters. You perceive how the case is - & you will inform me both of your wishes, & the true plans & wishes of Mad. de R.***

This note, meanwhile, has again confused all my projects. I have delayed taking a servant accordingly & shall, if you go, to put off Miss G & some others.... yrs aff E.B.L.

* * * * *

This letter hits Emily hard. He has spelt it out. She is a burden on him financially. He does not have a home for her. She is upsetting his plans.

From her father's perspective, it is an offer to sanction her spending the holidays in Paris.

I believe Emily wants to go. But the bigger picture is more important.

Does he want her? Does he love her?

My dear Father, I am quite in despair to find by yours just received that, after all my entreaties to the contrary, Madame de Ritter wrote to you about my accompanying her to Paris.

When she mentioned this plan to me, I requested her not to communicate it to you; I know and must daily feel that I am of hardly any use or comfort to you, and my constant mistakes and many faults often make me despair of myself and wonder at your forbearance. Still as you kindly say you wish to consult my own wishes, I can only with sincerity reply "my own wishes ever chain me to your side", and – more especially as I have so lately had the great pleasure of Natalie's society – I particularly wished for Madame de Ritter not to mention this plan to you.

However, as it seems she has done, so I have endeavoured to put myself in possession of all facts relating to the nature of her invitation and with which you desire to be acquainted. I deliberately hinted that it would be hard to wish you to keep up your establishment here for no one, another for yourself elsewhere, and a third for me in Paris. This nerf de guerre [war of nerves] *of mine elicited her desired reply. She was evidently much hurt, almost offended, at such a supposition - and replied somewhat haughtily that tho' she "could not offer me 'vie de Prince'"* [the life of a Prince], *what she could offer was "proffered as a friend and not as a lodging house keeper!" And that "the longer you could spare me, the better she would like it." "Her invitation," she said, "was always meant as one for the whole winter." This was her answer, word for word.*

* * * * *

But, as in addition to her views, you, with your accustomed kindness also desired to be informed of my own wishes on the subject. I can only repeat what I have said before, and what I shall always feel; that, I could never be happy away from you and feeling that my presence could in the slightest degree add to your comfort; that would be a thought sufficient to poison my pleasure.

You wish me to be sincere and open with you, my dearest Father, and I know my innate reserve - against which I indeed struggle but, wh too often gets the better of me - must often annoy you.....but will you forgive me the perhaps too candid [remark] that you yourself often make me retreat into myself!

I have so often, and with so much sorrow, observed that you never really - and from your heart - believe in my affection. E.g., expressions of attachment, I have long noticed, you regard as polite '_______'[indecipherable - it looks like 'miseries' - 'ministries'?], *which are well meant but still mean nothing. Faults of carelessness, forgetfulness – 'étounderie'* [thoughtlessness] *– you immediately attribute to want of regard and affection.*

Long and close observation has made me feel this want of trust in my affection acutely – and the result is, that I have become more reserved, more cold, less frank, even than I am by nature. I always fear either to weary or disgust you.

* * * * *

I entreat you to forgive me for the very great liberty I take in thus addressing you, but I am very unhappy, and perhaps when this letter is gone I may not be able to forgive myself for having written it. I trust, however, to the generosity of your noble soul, as great in its justice, as in its truth, and I hope that - amid the morbid murmurings of a child's wayward heart - you will not shut your ears to the voice of your child's love!

Believe then, for once, the sincerity of my desire to remain with you - should such be your own real desire. To feel you like me to be with you is my greatest happiness - but if you think you would be happier free, and that it would be much to your advantage to economize during the winter, and to be rid of me and any expenses you may be at on my account, then give me to Mad[e] de R.

I have said shortly, perhaps abruptly, ce qu j'avais sur le coeur [that which I have had on my heart], *and I have told you sincerely and without reserve my wishes; it rests with you to believe or disbelieve them. Forgive me if I have made use of improper expressions - at least I have spoken from my heart, from the heart upon whose affection you may ever rely, Emily Lytton*

* * * * *

There are two ways to read this letter. With exasperation, and suspicion that there is art to the manner in which the teenage girl has written it. Or with sensitivity, and concern at the trauma the teenage girl is expressing. Emily's father chooses the former. He replies with another lecture, again laced with melancholy and self-pity for his own problems. I don't belittle the problems - but you can hear Miss Greene's disapproval and warnings, were she to read it.

My dear Emily, I should have answered your letter by today's post [Monday 22nd November 1847], *but I have been incessantly occupied about the railway, & so unsatisfactorily that I have now the most gloomy anticipations as to the result, which if verified will leave me no option but to leave Kneb. as soon as possible - & even then – but I will not pursue this subject –*

Far from being offended at the way you excuse yourself, I can only be grateful for your assurance of affection - & for telling me so frankly how far you think me the cause of any want of candour on your part. First, however, let me tell you expressly, that you are wrong in thinking me insensible to your affection, or of the many & evident acts on your part designed to please me – on the contrary – it is these that have disarmed me when I have seen cause to complain of that want of openness which did not, therefor, imply want of affection.

You have, my dear Emily, I firmly believe, many most admirable & rare qualities, which I trust will one day, with some one of whom you will not be in fear, ensure the development of all that is good. But for my part, I have suffered so much from want of truth in others, that the suspicion of being again deceived chills me, as much as the coldness so occasioned, chills you.

* * * * *

In points small & trifling in themselves, you have not seemed to me to speak the truth, plainly & simply (& there is a difference between speaking the truth, & giving me your confidence). Now if you would but understand this all would be well. Reflect – that if something is done, which may make me angry – if it is told me at once, the pleasure of being told cancels the anger. And grant even that I put myself out of temper & scold – it is but a moment, & the anger is forgot instantly. But on the contrary, if I find an untruth – the smallest matter to which it refers swells into perhaps morbid importance in my mind & alienates me, while it rankles within. It then becomes hard to convince me of truth in other & more important matters & where it exists.

It has been my fate to sit by a hearth full of snares & pitfalls – with Deceit smiling at me, & vowing devotion - & one who as that memory scorched into his heart will always think truth the greatest virtue, as affects himself.....& behind the smallest lie, will see the face of a Poisoner.

If I have been cold (I own it) then 1st, my habitual manner to all is so - & rendered more so, by cares & illness & the self absorption they produce. 2nd, I have believed that something like untruth was near me.....I have said all now – judge how far I am right or wrong.

* * * * *

In either case the evil is yet to be cured. I have made the distinction between truth & confidence - the first is my right; the second is not to be extorted, tho' better for both that it should exist.

And remember , my dear Emily, that there are few things indeed, which a child cannot confide. A happy privilege it is! we lose it as we advance in life... we can confide to those older than ourselves; never, (at least a man) to those younger. A man who has gone thro' what I have, of experience & emotion, has not furrows in his heart – he has abysses! The sole confidant I ever had is in the coffin! ... confide while you can!

I will consider about the plan of Mad[e] de R's against my return. I accept your affectionate wish to be with me – fully & implicitly – but I don't wish you to sacrifice too much to that. [Not, I don't want to sacrifice too much to that. You can hear Miss Greene howl.] *My present idea is that perhaps later in the Winter, or early in the Spring, if Mad[e] de R is at Paris, we may arrange it better. But of this, when I come.....which now will be as soon as I can, for the railway difficulties are now gigantic & a matter not of days to settle – if ever; while Difficulties crowd around me thick & dark, leaving little option but borrowing at a rate of usury, that will reduce my income (to pay the interest) to something very like beggary. Yrs ever E.B.L.*

* * * * *

This is followed two days later by, ***Alas! I cannot come as I expected. I am wanted from day to day. I had hoped by certain arrangements with publishers & the ______***{indecipherable] ***action of the railway business, to clear myself of the difficulties that beset me. But all fail - & I see, at the moment, no escape & no choice.***

At all events, I am detained here - perhaps for many days.....tho' not perhaps of use, I could not sleep in my bed if absent. Don't tell Pearson [Charles Buchanan Pearson (1807-1881) the Knebworth Rector from 1838] ***or any one that I am in trouble about the railway, or that that detains me. I don't want gossip on the subject. You may judge what I think of things when I add that I am going to a house agent about Kneb. today.....& that I am meditating asking Lord John R.*** [Russell (1792–1878), the Prime Minister] ***for some appointment in India – my difficulties at this moment are beyond meeting by Literature.***

A house agent? India? Where he will have escaped half the world away from her, and is certain to die of cholera like Miss Greene's relations. I wonder if he recalls her childhood poem, ***Roam not to India's sunny strand...***

Now Emily not only faces the potential ignominy of her celebrity father, but, once more, he places the burden of a terrible secret on her. We don't have her reply, but perhaps remarkably, it is tender and supporting. But perhaps not. As here he is feeding her the role she craves - his confidante and emotional support.

* * * * *

My dearest Emily, I cannot say how I thank you for your affect. letter & what comfort it gives me. I have only leisure to write you one line now. The

plan you form, however bold, doesn't meet the present evil, which is an instant demand for £5000. I must get that first & to pay the interest of it – must save & pinch afterwards. I hope to have formed a plan by a week. The Agents give me small hope of letting Kneb well, because they say it wants sleeping room & offices for a nobleman's establishment. [We have the same problem today - although no bathrooms and no radiators is more the issue.]

Say nothing of all this yet. I am going to meet Lawyers & Booksellers & all sorts of people. Adieu yr. Most affectionate father E.B.L.

£5000 would be a lot of money even if he wasn't supporting an estranged wife, her two children, an estranged mistress, her four children, a new mistress, her unborn child, a large trophy house in the country and renting a fine trophy house in St James.

The latter is the first to go, replaced by an address in Pimlico for his pregnant girlfriend, 22 Upper Eaton Street.

* * * * *

Three days later - 27th November - a plan has been made. *My dearest Emily, Will you kindly tell Mr Pearson that I hope he will excuse my writing in reply to his, as I am so busy – but that he will accept an answer thro' you, to the effect that I don't want my coachman at present, as we think of going on some visits at Xmas. I have accepted, indeed, an invitation from the D'Eyncourts for us three to spend the Xmas holidays there - &, as I know many people in Lincolnshire, we may be delayed some considerable time.*

Now, therefore, as regards Mad[e] de R., can you just break to her that my friend has returned to England & presses us so urgently to spend the winter there that I have fixed the 20th of Dec. If she stays in Paris, & will kindly accept your visit later, I shall be happy, I hope, to bring you over.

I have only the same bad news – the worst is, that it won't come quite to a head - but I am kept in all the worry of suspense. Tho' I see that there is but one termination to it.... I have some large offers for Books if I can but get time to write them. My hand is my only friend - & only wealth. As long as I trusted only to that, all went well in the money way.

* * * * *

So it is determined. Knebworth House will be mothballed for the winter of 1847 and Sir Edward Bulwer Lytton and his two (official) children will spend the time at Bayons Manor at Tealby in Lincolnshire, the home of the Tennyson D'Eyncourt family, cousins to Alfred, the future Lord Tennyson.

Charles Tennyson D'Eyncourt

Bayons is a fabulous 19th Century castle, perched on the rise of the Lincolnshire wolds, looking to the west, and Lincoln Cathedral in the distance. It is the vision of Edward's parliamentary colleague and mentor in the medieval, Charles Tennyson D'Eyncourt (1784-1861), who reworks the small 17th Century manor house he inherits in 1835 (over, contentiously, his elder brother George, Alfred's father) into a splendid sprawling masterpiece of medieval make-believe, worthy of a Tennyson imagination.

Here is to be found much of Edward's inspiration for his reworking of Knebworth House, which he inherits eight years later - but with less cash. Comparing images of the 19th Century rooms, their shared tastes are everywhere in evidence. I notice, in particular, the distinctive octagonal table that both

Bayons

Knebworth

Knebworth

Bayons

Courtesy of the Tennyson D'Eyncourt family

Bayons Manor by Ellen D'Eyncourt

houses possess and is, surely, some symbolic Pentecostal Round Table for a reunion of medieval knights... over a smoke and an illuminated manuscript.

* * * * *

At Bayons, Edward will write his way out of debt with the novel *Harold, The Last of the Saxon Kings* (1848), and Emily will catch cold.

In fact everyone will catch cold. I confirm this by mothballing Knebworth House myself for a few weeks of the winter of 2014 and driving to California, where - in the archives of the Huntingdon Library - I discover a letter written by Edward from Bayons Manor on 29th December 1847 confirming that he too has been ***very unwell.*** [The letter, to the sericulturist (silk farmer) Mary Anne Whitby (1784–1850) discusses introducing mulberry trees - and therefore silkworm - into his garden at Knebworth. More handkerchiefs needed?] The bitter course of this rare and final Christmas reunion of father, daughter and son is that the father either has his nose in a manuscript or a mouchoir.

Emily never fully recovers from this cold - and it becomes the root of the physical illness that - at least at some level (to be discussed) - is the cause of her death.

Beautiful Bayons Manor I do not hold responsible. I mourn, too that its day is dead - as Alfred would say - and will never come back to us. A victim of the slings, arrows and outragous taxes of the 20th Century, the remains of this magnificent Tennyson dream are dynamited in the 1960s. The castle's distinctive yellow stone is used to make a road across the farmland, from which a new beautiful legend grows, that it becomes one of local lad Bernie Taupin's inspirations for his and Elton John's *Goodbye Yellow Brick Road.*

Bayons Manor in 2017 - a hillock of brambles

* * * * *

But before the Bulwer Lyttons convene at Bayons, there is one more quarrel for the frayed nerves of father and daughter. This is the last of their quarrels - indeed the last significant exchange we have between Edward and Emily. Its themes are familar - money and the out-martyring of each other - but what haunts me, and very possibly haunted its protagonists, is that it is starting to read very much like the correspondence between Edward and Rosina, when she was not so very much older than Emily. Once again, the same old family flaws and frailties - recognised, but resolutely irresistible - come full-circle.

Had Emily lived, like her mother, the longer she was dependent on her father, the longer these quarrels would have persisted. How easy it is to imagine what might have been, and how difficult for the players to change the course of their drama.

Note, however, that in the predictably silly catalyst of this last quarrel, unpredictably, Emily wins. Miss Greene has already mentioned it. The German ladies maid that Madame de Ritter has bought with her to England is clearly for appearances at the grand English home of the celebrity author she believes she is visiting, not because the proud widow can afford it. If Emily is now to join a grand house party for the winter - and this same widow is her counsellor - does it not makes sense for her to adopt this same accoutrement, and save Madame the expense?

My dear Emily [writes Edward, undated]***... You somewhat disappointed my expectations with respect to the Maid. I should have guessed it likely that, under existing circumstances, you would have proposed to dispense with one – especially in going to a friendly house where you could have no want of attendance.***

...I have begun privations with myself. I have no servant, tho' almost a necessity rather than a luxury in Town - & I live in a ________[indecipherable] ***Lodging at a few shillings a week – of which I can give the address to no one*** [another reminder that she should not mention it while they are in company].

In regard to your Toilet I had hoped that you were not deficient in the ordinary articles required for country visits. But if there is anything you would like to have pray say so without scruple & openly. Yrs very aff E

* * * * *

My dear Father, [also undated, endorsed in Edward's handwriting, '***an ungrateful letter from poor Emily - almost the sole one, & soon repented and atoned for***'] ***I feel much wounded at finding by your letter received thro' Mr Webb that you imagine me endeavouring to grapple at luxuries and comforts for myself at a time when your circumstances do not allow you the necessary***

comforts to which you are accustomed.

I confess I was rather astonished after your last communications, to find you had accepted an invitation [to Bayons] *which, at the least, will cost you I should think £20. Before you told me this I had been making all sorts of little plans, trifling in themselves, perhaps, as far as you were concerned, but which at least would have saved me the pain and mortification of finding myself a burden upon you.*

I want no luxuries, I expect not, (what the world calls) 'pleasure' and when I proposed to you exile – and penury – I looked forward to such a life with more real happiness than the most dazzling prospects could have afforded me. But if you wish me to make this round of visits... It is harder to save, manage, and economize in other people's houses than at home where one can be alone and need not be accountable to any one for one's appearance.

I am grieved I should appear to your mind so loaded with selfishness & egotism - my only comfort is conscience, which tells how unjust is the accusation. It costs me no pang (as you suppose) to relinquish a maid. It costs me no pang to make this visit in any way you wish. I could have only have wished that my plans for economizing might have been carried out on retirement, and not 'en évidence' [for all to see]. *You seem however to think that there is no 'évidence' in the matter - and I am content. Only I should not advise taking the under housemaid, who will be of no use & who will cost exactly the same as the ladies maid .*

As for my toilet, of course I have necessary things – a respectable morning dress & a respectable evening dress – and if you do not mind my being always the same, I am sure I do not care. I am very badly off for shoes & gloves, but one can do with everything – if it comes to that - and I will patch up & wash what I have got.

* * * * *

And now allow me earnestly & seriously to tell you how painfully it weighs upon me - the sense of my utter dependence. Why should my existence be so useless – so idle? I can embroider (some are kind eno' to say) pretty well, I feel confident in my knowledge of German, & my most ardent wish is not to cost you a farthing more. My greatest delight on Earth would be to add to your means, rather than take from them. There is no use promising what one cannot perform [but] I can, for the present, hope to support myself.

Poverty is no shame – Independence, our best cause for pride. I am now nearly 20 years old, at this age one no longer feels oneself a child – why should you struggle & I not? Why in the midst of misfortune not retain at the least the happiness of thinking that I have proved to you how unjust were your reproaches. Retain, I entreat you for the future – the £20 – perhaps some day I shall be able to repay you what you have already expended on me.

I will see that the house is packed up in due order. Yours affectionately, Emily Lytton

* * * * *

My dear Emily [dated Sunday 5th December 1847], *I am sorry that you have written me a letter which is neither proper nor considerate, & which is calculated to make no* _______{indecipherable] *impression on my mind. In vindicating yourself from selfishness, allow me to observe that there is no selfishness more striking than that allusion of sensitiveness when self seems touched; which forgets all consideration of time & season; & the large calamities of others.*

In the first place I made you no reproaches. I merely said that I was sorry that suggestions to dispense with your maid had not, under existing circumstances, come from yourself. I am so still. Propositions of extreme sacrifices - not likely to be called for, or accepted - is a bad way of meeting a very slight one. And the way in which the last is met, is not harmonious with the sincerity of the first.

I attribute to want of consideration your astonishment that I should accept an a invitation for myself, you & Edward - and your idea that it is at variance with my present necessities. Some small thought would have shewn you that six weeks or so spent under another roof must effect large savings in housekeeping at Knebworth, not only in ordinary bills perceptible at first glance, but in fires, light, etc at the heaviest time of the winter...

In regard to clothes – what you say, might have been put more kindly & more frankly. I argue with you that shoes & gloves are necessary; & if your allowance was ________[indecipherable] *in linen... this could be seen to.*

I regret that your dependence on me should be so painful - it is however necessary - I have sought to make it as little so as I could. You will find few girls who have had the same trust, & household authority. Your friends have been mine & my roof at your disposal.

Whatever my plans may be, in my present terrible embarrassments you need not fear (& therefore need not talk) of "penury & exile" for yourself, nor contemplate the necessity of supporting yourself........ As to the matter of the maid - which I suggested - there would have been no 'évidence' of poverty had you gone without one.

In the first place it is not every young lady who has a maid – nor do I know one (except yourself) who does not dress her own hair... Granting that one was habitual to you, the going without one to a House where there were two Ladys (sic) Maids kept would not have seemed strange, & would have been interpreted into a delicacy on your part – when three of us were already making a large demand in hospitality, & when I could have made my health an excuse for taking a man servant. And this is the first time I have done so – nor do I Know now if I shall – tho' I might well be supposed to be as accustomed to a valet as most ladies are to a maid. All these things, when you have my experience of the world, you will see in a different light.

* * * * *

Be kind eno' to tell me what money you like for the necessaries you require.

Having stated economical reasons for my visit to Bayons, I didn't wish to purchase credit for any more _____[indecipherable] *motives – apparently not guessed – but I had an idea also that it would afford you some pleasure...& it was the only gaiety (such as it is) that I could offer you. Yrs aff. E.B.L.*

P.S. The talk of repaying me for your allowance hereafter etc. is an insult not meant, no doubt, but which no mind – comprehending the right relationship between us – or _________[indecipherable] *with true generosity could have blundered upon. If you had the wealth of the Indies you could not repay me.. for some things which I would disdain to repeat & for others which remain with myself. They are not obligations upon you, for I obeyed my duty – but they cost me more than can be paid thro' the Bankers.*

* * * * *

My dear Father, [dated *Thursday evening*, presumably 9th December] *Will you, can you, forgive me? You have shewn me myself in a new light, and I can only now bitterly repent - what I would give, worlds were they mine, to retract. Yes I was selfish – inconsiderate, indelicate, & I am afraid, impertinent. I forgot myself in the most strange and unpardonable way; and at this time too! Oh, can you forgive? – can you forget, that for which I can offer no excuse and which I will neither forgive nor forget?*

I will not dwell on my own sorrow, I will not attempt to picture my own remorse, you might think perhaps both were professions. It is right & just that you should feel offended & that my own heart shd be my worst tormentor... [etc. - more painting a picture of her own remorse]

Do not banish me quite from your affection, do not, my dear dear Father, much as I have erred, weary as you must be of forgiving me. Listen this once again to the voice of my sincere repentance & remorse, & trust me if you cannot love. My own faults drive me daily further from you, and I myself am my greatest enemy. It becomes now hard, almost impossible for me to assure you, or make you feel- but this is again selfish. Could you but know how unhappy I feel at having so hurt you, you would have I think pity for, & patience with me.

* * * * *

There are two or three things which you have taken in a harder interpretation than they were meant - but I have no need to vindicate myself and deserve all & more. I indeed did not mean that you should give me money for more clothes, dearest Father, & do me the great favour not to force any upon me indeed (I speak from all truth & sincerity & not from any feeling of delicacy). I can do without.

You will be shewing me a great kindness, also, if you will allow this hated subject of the maid to be dropped between us. I, of course, should not think of accepting your proposition of taking her. Between this & then, I shall learn no doubt to do my own hair and pray do no give this (for me) so very painful subject another thought.

It would have been worse than "ungenerous", it would have been, hard hearted, unjust, unfeeling – wrong (to say nothing of the coarseness of such an idea) in me to suppose I could ever repay you for what you have done, & are ever doing for me. Do not think I am insensible, or callous to so much uncalled for & undeserved kindness. I did not (God knows) mean that; nothing could repay you for the self denials, the self mortifications, the wounded pride, the sacrificed hopes & happiness of which Edward & I have been the cause. Those are the debts which your own heart can best repay. Your children, Never. But I felt, & feel still, that it would be a sentiment replete with delight if ever I could add - instead of taking from - your means (I only speak in a pecuniary point of view).

The gentle tone of your letter - its sad & mournful, & hopeless cast – has touched me to the soul. But I can only timidly ask you to forget. Forget, if it is possible, what I never can. Your sorrowful, & gratefully attached child, Emily Lytton

* * * * *

My dear Emily, [not dated] *Let the past rest. The best way to forget it is not to disturb it. I am willing to ascribe all to mere inconsiderateness.*

With respect to your maid……you have arranged such good terms, you will take her. Let that be so – without further discussion - on the understanding that, if necessary, after our visits, she be discharged.

But have you been quite ingenuous & candid as to the said terms. Is it really only £8 she has – without any reserve or equivoque [possibility of more than one meaning]*? If there is anything in these terms not plainly spoken out, say it my dear, & have done with it.*

Gloves. You are not likely to have any visiting out of the D'E's - or any other house we go to - & therefore no great choice of clothes is required, especially as blame for monotony can always be laid on men who don't like to be encumbered with boxes etc. when they travel with ladies. Gloves are necessaries & shoes too – can you get them well at Hitchin [a market town neighbouring Knebworth] *or shall I see to them if I have the measures? If the former, as they are not very expensive, you may have eno' in hand from Mrs Balderoe's money* [in the 1851 Census, *Mary Anne Baldero* (sic) is the 63-year-old *Servant* - profession *Dairy Maid* - living alone (the day the Census is taken) with her daughter and granddaughter at (Manor) *Farm House*].

Miss Greene writes she is going down to you. Edward will stay in town till you come up.

Will you have the goodness to look in the Library - the Poetic Division near the door - & you will see several editions of Pope's works [thence follows detailed instructions of where and what she should look for] *...in opening the pages you will observe that it differs from modern editions, not only in the old print, but in having a great many more capital letters to the substantive words...*

I don't know how to get down all the flues & candles which I bought. I wonder you disliked those patent ones at 1s a lb – I burn them & think them the best I ever knew – much better than sperm [before you ask, wax from the sperm whale].

Adieu yr aff E.B.L.

My poor June [his dog]. *What is to become of him. I can't leave him, & can't well take him. Have you seen that he sleeps with John – or has he again fallen into discreditable practices? This I should know – I forgot to recommend special attention to his always sleeping with John & being put out last thing. Poor Dog – he is old – Beau, young & gentle, can console him for worse woes than being left behind.*

By the way – talking of hair drapery, I ought to have told you that wreaths are never worn except at Balls & large parties......&, tho' it mattered little at Knebworth, it may be as well to remember that – elsewhere – the hair (when unmarried) is worn perfectly plain & even one flower is rare, & requires judgement – always excepting Balls.

I am just in the same state – and so shall be – I suppose - & get the _______ [indecipherable - nerves?] *if I once leave town.*

You understand I don't want the books merely the dates.

* * * * *

My dearest Father [not dated] *Your letter has filled me with indescribable sorrow & remorse! How can I sufficiently paint my sympathy in this your new and unforeseen misfortune, how sufficiently upbraid myself, for inflicting upon you my own selfish sorrows at such a time!!*

Oh thank you, my dear kind Father, for your trust, thank you again and again for your touching and beautiful admonitions, full of faults as I am [etc..]

Frankly then & without reserve I own to you - it is very difficult for me to be what you call "open", but I will try, I have tried – but if you will continue to have patience with me... I may at last succeed in conquering that which nature, education & circumstances have combined to strengthen.

I only ask you to have patience, and remember the difficulties I have in confiding, and you in believing. It is with an anguish long felt & artfully concealed, that I have been sensible how inseparably I am & must be connected in your memory, with the source of all your misery. Oh, but how well I understand now, at the side of any want of openness in the child, the ghost of the mother's perjuries rises – from the abysses of the past . I understand this and more, I understand all you feel – [section missing]

* * * * *

Thank you very much for what you so kindly say respecting the gloves and shoes. I think it would be too much trouble for you to see about them, and I could get them at Hitchin if you would allow the carriage to drive there. Of Mrs Balderoe's money there are £14 in hand. You surprise me about Miss G. She does not mention her intentions to me.

I enclose the copies of the dates, & publishers you wish. I hope they may be right. I thank you also very much for your very kind hints as to dress, etc. I will attend to them. It is indeed a pity about the flues, and as E is not coming down I do not know of any opportunity except perhaps Miss G if she really comes.

I have so often thought of poor June. Cannot you really take him? Miss d'E was so fond of him when she was here. If you must leave him, would not Mrs Balderoe be the best person to entrust him to – she is very good natured to animals and would strictly attend to any orders you might leave respecting him. He does sleep with John & has done so since you… [incomplete]

* * * * *

The big concern that Emily does not express to her father is what Madame de Ritter will do while they are all at Bayons. If she leaves and goes to join Natalie in Paris, she may not come back.

Miss Greene is to be the saviour once more.

At last came a letter from her Papa, which was very shocking, that he had accepted an invitation for them all to Bayons. What was to become of Madame de Ritter? If she left England for Paris before Easter, it would be most inconvenient to Madame and ruinous to her.

She [Emily] then asked me would Madame Lyal accommodate her - and would I go again to Madame Lyal and live with her till after the visit to Bayons was over? Upon my telling her that Madame Lyal no longer had a house, she proposed to me going into lodgings with Madame de Ritter - and, if I ever loved her, to try and keep her in England till Easter.

This I promised, and performed - and took a lodging at Brompton for Madame and myself where she came on the 23rd of December; and Emily came on the 24th to the Thomsons, where we met her.

She was looking, I thought, in good health and was plainly but neatly dressed by Madame de Ritter's maid - as her father had told her he could not afford her a maid to go with her unless it was one of the under housemaids of Knebworth who could be got for the same wages she was to give the German.

At the Thomsons I had again but a minute's conversation with her, but from what I had heard of Cockburn Thomson, I, in that moment, warned her to be neither distant or too friendly with him - and her answer was, oh, never fear, I have a good safe guard in Carl! [Natalie's brother]

* * * * *

Madame de Ritter and I returned to Brompton and both of us did the utmost in our power to content ourselves with each other, striving to do what we thought most beneficial for poor Emily - from whom Nathalie got constant long German letters.

When Emily did write to me, she used to direct to Kensington [the Wilkinsons' new lodgings in Albert Place] *and beg of me not to tell Madame de Ritter that she had written to me, which shewed me - what I discovered, after a long acquaintance with Madame - that [Madame] was rather of a monopolising and jealous disposition. This I did not mind, as the more she loved Emily, the better pleased I was.*

I, according to my promise to Emily, introduced her [Madame] *to as many of my friends as were near us, and we went on very comfortably together. But in our conversations about Emily, she seemed much surprised at some facts which she had heard in a very different manner from Emily. And from things she had told me of Emily's conduct to her whilst a Knebworth, I continued in the idea that I had formed since the time she was first left alone in Germany - namely, that she was often out of her mind, and that etc. etc.*

Notwithstanding all this, I found by Emily's letters that her mind was gradually coming to its old tone whilst she had the good natured motherly kindness of Madame and tho' the "shocking letters" - as Madame used to call them - from her Father, and his still more shocking visits, interrupted their quiet, they went on very well. [This is because] poor Emily was living upon the coming summer, when she was to go to Paris, and from there to Vienna, and from that to Gorizia to be made one of the de Ritter family. All this was fostered and kept up by constant conversation with Madame de Ritter, letters from Natalie and her brother Carl, to whom it was settled amongst them she was to be married.

How much of all this conversation Sir Edward was acquainted with, I cannot grasp, but as he visited Vienna when on the Continent in the summer, I think he made himself master of all particulars, and consented to Emily's going with Madame after Easter.

In the intermediate time, however, he began to think from Xmas to Easter rather too long a time for Madame to remain at Knebworth. He therefore accepted an invitation to Bayon Manor for himself and his children and let the poor Baroness see and feel that she had better be off. Then came poor Emily's time for throwing herself and her friend upon me.

* * * * *

The next great point upon which my dear child's fate seemed to turn upon was the French Revolution, which was the means of driving Nathalie from Paris to London to her Mother - and thus finding herself with a person so totally unacquainted with her history, she found a ready pen for any romance her morbid and very vivid imagination chose to invent.

Her wish to excite pity or compassion made her not satisfied with telling the truth - which was bad enough - of how miserable she had been for the last four years, but she declared she had never in all her life had any peace or happiness, and that her Mother used to beat her most unmercifully. This I knew to be perfectly untrue - as I am certain her mother never did beat her, indeed she never allowed her to be with her long enough to give her an opportunity, and never was she in her home except when I was with her also.

I used, in conversation with Madame de Ritter, to express my ardent love for Emily and say I had the comfort of knowing that, for all the years she was with me, she was happy; as well as Edward, when they were both so fond of each other and myself. At this Madame de Ritter seemed much surprised, and wondered at Emily's ungrateful conduct to me the last days I had spent with her at Knebworth. When I made the excuse that I did not think she was herself, her answer was that I was more forgiving to her than she would be to her own child.

At the same time Madame de Ritter said that her conduct to herself whilst at Knebworth was often very extraordinary, and like a person out of her mind. She declared that, but for her love and her pity towards her, and some pecuniary reasons of her own, she would have left Knebworth and gone to Paris. Madame said that whilst out one day she missed 5 sovereigns out of a purse which contained 50 and that nobody could have taken them but Emily whom she used to send to bring her the purse. Such covetous habits I sometimes saw in her, which alone all convinced me of her madness. She was so entirely different at other times.

* * * * *

Here Miss Greene breaks off, not writing another word for two years.

But for Edward's colourful dedicatory note in *Harold* and his two words to Mrs Whitby - ***very unwell*** - I can find no description of his six week winter stay at Bayons Manor. But if the relationship between father and daughter warms once they are in each other's company, it would be against the winds.

I hope they have a happy Christmas.

It is not going to be a happy New Year.

Drawing by Amalia de Ritter - thought to be Natalie and her younger brother Adolf

CHAPTER 32

~ Natalie Ritter de Záhony ~

Her works weave a thorough understanding of the human heart with beautiful story-telling ~ entry for Jánosné Ciotta (Natália Ritter Záhony) in *Magyar Írók* [*Hungarian Writers*] by József Szinnyei, 1981

* * * * *

There is an image of Bayons Manor pasted into an album in a map drawer in a room of map drawers at the back of a house museum in a town in Italy. It is the only image of England in a souvenir album full of images of towns and landscapes in Europe in the first half of the 19th Century.

Why an image of a Victorian castle in Lincolnshire in a book of pictures of Neapolitan ruins, Hungarian palaces and German river towns?

Nobody in Italy knows.

There are empty pages in the completed album, where images have been removed - maybe to frame and brighten up a passage or bathroom wall. It's understandable. Many of the images are beautiful prints of beautiful places. It is a family album. More fun to enjoy the images on the wall every day than keep them closed away in a book in a drawer.

But it means the album does not, now, tell the full story it once told. Because, certainly - on a blank page before Bayons Manor - this album once also contained an image of Knebworth House.

An image of the home of the Bulwer Lytton family would have given the only certain clue to a passing Italian historian as to why there is an image of Bayons Manor, alone, amongst the Continental views. But that image of Knebworth House - extracted from the album and no doubt faded in its frame by daily sunlight, its relevance forgotten to subsequent generations - is

Courtesy of the Fondazione Palazzo Coronini Cronberg

Bayons Manor by Ellen D'Eyncourt - found in a drawer in Italy

presumably long lost to the ashes of a fire grate or a town incinerator.

And so the story is lost.

Almost.

* * * * *

The album belonged to Amalia Ritter de Záhony (1797-1870) the Swiss second wife of the Austro-Hungarian sugar baron, Johann-Christoph Ritter de Záhony (1782-1838). It is a record of her travels, beginning as a teen-ager, in the 18-teens, when she was growing up in Naples where her father, the pioneering German-born educator Georg Franz Hofmann (1765-1838), was running a popular Pestalozzian international school. [Here I would love to write you an essay on both the fascinating Hofmann and his mentor and colleague Johann-Heinrich Pestalozzi (1746-1827), the Swiss father of an en-lightened and rounded education, but I can't - not in this book - I am 32 chapters into another story.]

Amalia's album contains beautiful watercolours of the ruins of Pompeii and Herculaneum, illustrations of the majestic views surrounding the city of Pest in Hungary where Hofmann moved his family in 1819 to set up a teaching institute, and drawings of picturesque Alpine cattlesheds reflecting her father's later retirement to a dairy farm south-west of Vienna. [There's a beautiful digression to be made here, too, of how I discover the location of "Wällischhof" - a farm and building that went on to become, would you believe it, a Prießnitzian Water Cure Sanitarium - which I know only because my second cousin's wife, the current Countess of Lytton, is Viennese... oh, for more of your time!]

Courtesy of the Fondazione Palazzo Coronini Cronberg

Amalia's album...

Courtesy of the Fondazione Palazzo Coronini Cronberg

...examples of her own artwork in the album

Courtesy of the Fondazione Palazzo Coronini Cronberg

Then there are images of Amalia's own travels, after her father and husband's death, a month apart in 1838, when Amalia is only 40 years old. Bavarian cities, Parisian monuments, hilltop castles on the Rhine... and two views of the town of Cannstatt-bie-Stuttgart, where her only daughter Natalie is enrolled, in 1843, at the Orthopaedic Institute of Dr Jacob von Heine.

And the album contains a single image of England, where Amalia spends almost a year from the summer of 1847. Bayons Manor in Lincolnshire. A place that a passing historian browsing through this album may reasonably presume

Amalia visited during this year in England. But which she did not.

* * * * *

Look deeper into these Italian map drawers - through prints and maps of Trieste and forgotten generations of Friuli Venezia Giulia families - and you will no other images of England.

But you will find a lone image of an English girl.

Here, tucked away in an archive room of a house museum in Italy is a watercolour copy of the now familiar image of Emily that we know from her Grandmother's bedroom wall. Written at the bottom, in German, is ***For my daughter Natalie*** - but the image is also signed on the front in Emily's hand, ***Emily Bulwer Lytton...*** and on the back, also in Emily's hand, ***Ai Natalie*** - Italian for ***To Natalie*** - ***Te E....,*** which may be Italian (do tell me if it is), but reads to me as an abbreviation of the Latin ***Te Amo, E....*** or, ***I love you, Emily***.

Am I over romanticising? I don't think so.

Was this watercolour made by Amalia or Emily? I am guessing Amalia, whose Pestalozzian education ('Learning by head, hand and heart') recognised and nurtured painting skills that are evident elsewhere in this collection and in her album. I guess it is made by Amalia, from the original, when she is staying at Knebworth with Emily - and Emily signs it as a gift to Natalie. If Emily makes it, I apologise to my great-great-great-aunt and wish that she had made more watercolours, as the amateur that made this is a fine artist.

Most intriguing, however, is that, also written on the back, is another couple of lines of inscription, also apparently in Emily's hand. But this inscription has been scratched out so that it is illegible. Properly scratched out. It looks like an unsuccesful attempt was made with an eraser, followed by careful intent with a pen to obscure every word.

There may be some x-ray technique that allows us to read this. But we don't need it. Because the position of the dotted "i"s, and the tails of the "j" of ***je*** and the "z" of ***pensez*** tells us that this is the same ***Quand je ne serai plus, Pensez a moi!*** - that I discovered on the back of the original print at Knebworth. ***When I am no more*** [or ***no longer there***], ***Think of me!***

Did Emily scratch this out, or did Natalie? If Natalie scratched it out, it

The image of Emily in a map drawer in Italy

Courtesy of the Fondazione Palazzo Coronini Cronberg

presents all manner of possible meanings - reproval of Emily's gloom before her death, or anger and upset after her death...

But the pen looks like Emily's. It looks like it was scratched out just after it was written. It looks as though Emily has a second thought after writing this on Natalie's copy. This may be Amalia's reproval, but I don't think I am wrong to choose a more romantic theory. I think Emily writes it instinctively, then scratches it out because she does not forsee a time she is ***no longer there*** for Natalie. Because Natalie is her future.

* * * * *

When I first read Miss Greene's Recollections - the typed transcription in the yellow folder - one sentence stands out as particularly teasing *...poor Emily was living upon the coming summer, when she was to go to Paris, and from there to Vienna, and from that to* [blank] *to be made one of the de Ritter family.*

To [blank]?! Here is the place where de Ritter family comes from. The secretary transcribing the manuscript in the 1880s has, understandably, not paused to pick apart Miss Greene's scrawl, and guess a town name that Robert is likely to remember.

And so, at the beginning of this century, I spend a year staring at the actual handwritten word in Miss Greene's manuscript. A whole year. [I am doing other things at the same time.]

The word seems to start with a 'G'. I scour maps of Austro-Hungary for towns beginning with G. There are hundreds of them.

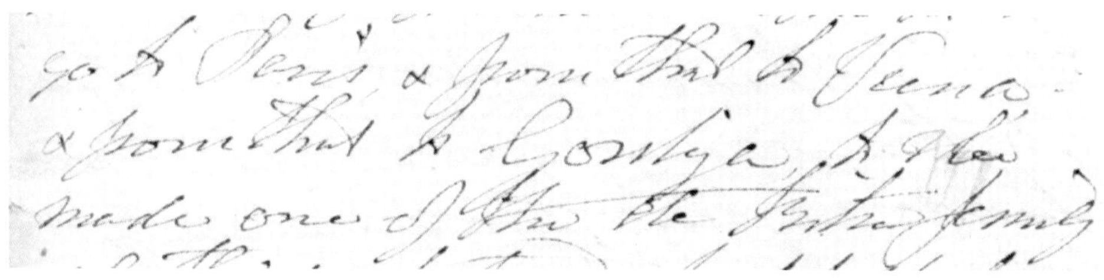

The mystery town beginning with "G" in Miss Greene's manuscript

It looks like 'Gosilya'. There's a Gosfa... And a Gosztola...

Maybe that 'l' is an uncrossed 't'? Still none of the possible candidates seem likely...

Finally, it clicks that Miss Greene, fine educator that she is - and perfectly proficient at spelling words that she's seen in print in *The Vicar of Wakefield,* and the rest of her wide and varied reading list - is not infallible at spelling proper names. Particularly proper names that do not crop up regularly in the works of Goldsmith, or Miss Burney or Miss Edgeworth... or even Bulwer Lytton.

As we all do when we are not familiar with a written word, Miss Greene scribbles it phonetically. I try to read the work phonetically... Soon I am pronouncing 'Goritya'.

Miss Greene means Gorizia. The town of Gorizia is not in Austria. Nor is it in Hungary. But it was then.

I type 'Gorizia + de Ritter' into Google.

Google doesn't ping like a mailbox, but my brain pings - as every entry shows me I've had my little Turing moment. Someone called ***Elvine Ritter von Záhony*** is ***a noble woman from Gorizia.*** The Italian Wikipedia entry for Gorizia talks of a ***famiglia*** with a ***spirito imprenditoriale*** (an entrepreneurial spirit) the ***Ritter de...*** I don't even need to open the web page - I've already seen in the next entry - the English Wikipedia entry - that, in the town of the Gorizia, there is a ***Villa Ritter de Záhony.***

Emily is headed to Italy. To Gorizia. A town that, in the 20th Century, is to become a hook in the rail of the Iron Curtain. A town that, today, is half in Italy and half in Slovenia - but in the 1840s was part of the Austro-Hungarian Empire. A town where the Ritter de Záhonys have a villa that still carries the family name, a town where there is even a large square called the Piazzale Enrico Ritter.

* * * * *

Town Hall, Gorizia

There are no Ritter de Záhonys living in the Villa Ritter de Záhony today. It is a language school. And indeed it is not where our generation of the Ritter de Záhonys lived. The family house in Gorizia that Emily would have returned to with Amalia and Natalie is even more in the centre of town. It is now the Town Hall. And even this lovely palazzo is not the finest Ritter de Záhony house in Gorizia - but we will come to the beautiful Palazzo Coronini Cronberg in a moment.

Having found the home town of the Ritter

de Záhony family - and it being clear that this family were not just passing though - I tell myself there must be Ritter de Záhonys still living in the area today. The internet (back when I am telling myself this) is not as sophisticated as it is today - so, the next time I am on a family holiday in Italy, I find a Friuli Venezia Giulia phone book. A phone book, for those born since the 1980s, is a book of printed telephone numbers.

There is indeed a "Ritter de Záhony" listed. Someone called ***Manfredo Ritter de Záhony*** is then contactable at ***Camping Aquileia, Via Gemina 10, 33051 Aquileia.*** Aquileia is the lagoon town on the coast south-east of Gorizia. Ritter de Záhony is not a surname like Rossi or Russo or Ricci, or even Ritter. This has to be the same family. Are they now living in a camp site?

* * * * *

Dear Signor Ritter De Záhony, In searching for the Ritter De Záhony family, I found your name. I wonder if you can help me, or perhaps direct me to another member of your family who can help me.

I am trying to find information on Carl and Natalie Ritter De Záhony, children of Giancristoforo and Amalia Ritter De Záhony (images enclosed). I am writing a book about my great-great-aunt, Emily Bulwer Lytton (see the marked page of the enclosed book, 'Knebworth House'), who was best friend to Natalie at Jacob Heine's Orthopaedic Institute in Stuttgart in Germany in 1843–1845 and subsequently when the Ritter De Záhony family visited England. Emily hoped to be wed to Natalie's brother Carl and move to Gorizia, however tragically she died, aged 19, in 1848.

I am hoping that you may be a descendant of Carl's and that you may have images of Carl and Natalie and perhaps further information about them, or Natalie's subsequent family, the 'Scarpa' family. If not, I am hoping you may know someone else who does. I am very much obliged, Henry Lytton Cobbold.

I receive no answer to this letter.

* * * * *

Meanwhile in Germany... my friend Joachim Mathieu has more success. Ritter is a difficult name to search in Germany as it is the word for a baronet, or knight - there are a number of these - and 'Ritter' is used as the title 'Sir'.

Also, sweetening feelings for the aristocracy in Germany, 'Ritter' is a word the Germans associate with chocolate. A Ritter chocolate bar is the square one you see at petrol stations tills all over Europe. To truly throw us off the scent - would you believe it - the Ritter chocolate bar comes from Cannstatt.

Alfred and Clara Ritter found the Ritter chocolate factory in Cannstatt in 1912. Production has since moved the other side of Stuttgart, to Waldenbuch, but this Cannstatt coincidence - and the fact that the Italian Ritters are in sugar and the German Ritters in chocolate - does cry out for a link.

I haven't found one yet. But Joachim has discovered, he tells me, in a German genealogical handbook published in 2000, a 'Ritter' family that descends from a monk in Frankfurt am Main in the early 16th Century. A family descended from a monk? Yes, but a monk who travelled to Rome with Martin Luther and came back a propagating Protestant.

By 1807 a branch of this family has migrated to Austria - and on May 10th, 1830, a Johann Christoph Ritter is given the Hungarian aristocratic title 'de Záhony' in Vienna. An Austrian barony (Freiherr) follows on April 14th 1855 for Johann Christoph's son Hektor Ritter von Záhony, who is a factory owner in Gorizia.

Courtesy of the Fondazione Palazzo Coronini Cronberg

Giancristoforo (or in the German) Johann Christoph Ritter de Záhony, Natalie's father

* * * * *

Joachim has also been busy with German and Austrian phone books. He has found a Peter von Ritter-Záhony living in Gröbenzell, a town on the north-western edge of Munich, and a Christiane Ritter-Záhony living in Graz Austria. Eichstatt, where Joachim lives, is only 100 kilometres up the road from Gröbenzell - and his letter to Peter von Ritter-Záhony does receive a response.

Knebworth is a bit further up the road from Gröbenzell, but this is an opportunity to meet a relation of the one ***I think I shall really in time be forced to love - and if I once love her, I shall love her the best of all.*** It is time for a 21st Century Bulwer Lytton to go to Germany to meet a 21st Century Ritter de Záhony.

The meeting takes place on a dark winter's evening - Friday 9th December 2005 - in a bar in Gröbenzell. Peter von Ritter-Záhony, a grey-suited 53-year-old accountant, is friendly, politely interested, but clearly his main emotion is bemusement at the over-excited Englishman sitting opposite him across the beer mats. Peter orders a well-deserved weekend pint - the Englishman, a mineral water.

First meeting of de Ritter and Lytton in 157 years with Peter von Ritter-Záhony in Gröbenzell

Joachim of Eichstatt - who's 8th Century bishop and local saint was an Englishman, Willibald (clear why he had to leave England) - is on hand to translate, as neither Ritter de Záhony or Bulwer Lytton is as well educated in languages as his teenage forebears.

* * * * *

Peter has a bombshell for us before we even start talking of the past. One of his children - if I remember correctly, as I am knocked off my history high by this, and my brain cells thrown into confusion - has recently been killed in a car accident, and his brother has just died of cancer, so he apologises if he seems subdued talking about his family.

Peter wishes we could have met his brother Michael, since he was the member of the family interested in genealogy. But he does have a document to show us, a *Stammbaun der Familie Ritter aus Frankurt a. M.* - a *Family Tree of the Ritter Family of Frankfurt am Main.*

Time to skip forward, Genealergics - to the end of the chapter if you want to get on with Emily's story; alternatively, go get a cool German beer - or Italian mineral water - from the fridge and glance over what could be another book in itself... Natalie and Carl's backstory.

The document is large, A2 size. Spread out across the bar table, it shows the 16th Century Ritters of Frankfurt - two generations named Mattias - then the 17th Century Ritters - all called Johann. The fourth Johann, Johann Balthasar Ritter IV (1738-1793) has nine children, all born in Frankfurt, three of whom are also called Johann. The fifth child, and third Johann, Johann-Christoph [are you with me?], and his youngest sibling Hektor Wilhelm, are the two members of the family who end up in Austria.

Hektor Wilhelm's only son, Karl Johann dies aged 13 [will children please stop dying - I am writing this the morning after a fund-raiser for the Keech Hospice for dying children, on the 20th anniversary of the Dunblane Primary School massacre... and the next chapter is Emily's last. I am miserable. Maybe I will have a beer.] Hektor Wilhelm's elder brother, Johann-Christoph, however, has children in numbers surpassing even Edward Bulwer Lytton.

* * * * *

Johann-Christoph Ritter de Záhony (1782-1838) has fourteen children, eight by his first wife, the Hungarian Maria Bressiac (1787-1820), and six to his second wife, the German-Swiss Amalia Hofmann (1797-1870).

Natalie Ritter de Záhony is child number 13.

The tree tells who the girls married, but the whole right hand half of the A2 sheet is taken up with the descendants of the nine Ritter von Záhony boys ['von' when stressing their German heritage - 'de' their Italian or Hungarian].

Peter shows how he and his elder brother Michael are great-grandchildren of child number 14, Adolf Ritter von Záhony (1833-1907). Reasonably enough, he cannot help us on the descendants of the other 13 children - from whom he is a cousin distantly removed.

But there, on the A2 sheet, is Emily's friend Natalie - and the name of her future husband, "von Scarpa". And there above her, born on 21st April 1830, is the brother Carl - spelt Karl with a "k" - whom Emily might have married.

The children of the next generation are almost all born either in Gorizia or nearby Trieste. And a further three generations are listed - but no one born after 1910. So there is no Manfredo Ritter de Záhony listed on this tree.

But Carl's grandchildren are still being born in Trieste. So it is very possible there is a descendant of Carl's still living in the area. Maybe, just maybe, Manfredo Ritter de Záhony is that descendant, and he can tell us what happened to Emily's would-be husband - his great- or great-great- grandfather.

When we find him.

And here is the third of the four great serendipidous moments of this book.

* * * * *

A year after writing to Manfredo Ritter de Záhony, I have had no response. It was a telephone directory I found him in. So, why don't I phone him? Because I don't speak Italian - and I am brought up to believe it is rude to presume that someone from a non-pink part of the Victorian world map speaks English.

Do I have any friends who speak Italian? Do I have any friends? Who aren't Victorians? My wife does. Martha is a History of Art major (and I am only a History of Art minor, but I can beat her at 'spot-the-Titian') and came away from the course at New York University with three lifetime friends, one lovely Ecuadorian boy and two lovely Italians girls. One of the Italians, Anna Puissi, returns to her native Florence having progressed to a doctorate at Oxford University that makes her forever Dr Pussy to her [English] friends. Might Dr Pussy make the call to Aquileia for me?

Dr Pussy does. And this is the honest truth. Manfredo Ritter de Záhony grew up with her father, who is from Udine, just north of Aquileia.

Not only that. They are related.

* * * * *

Manfredo Ritter de Záhony is pleased to speak to Anna. Her father used to spend summer holidays with him in Grado (on the Aquileia penninsula) because they were both part of the Austrian 'Wirt' family. Manfred's mother was a Wirt and Anna's father's grandmother re-married a Wirt, who was also in some way a blood relation. The families would have Rooms One and Two in the main hotel. Anna's father was particularly close to Manfredo's elder brother Gianni, who died young [another one!].

Yes, he did receive the letter, but he didn't answer it because he had no further information to add. He is sceptical of genealogists and their motives, but Anna is able to persuade him that ***her school-friend's weird husband*** is only interested in the distant past. As Anna reminds me, the wounds of civil war still linger in a part of Italy was that 'annexed' rather than 'occupied' by Fascist Germany.

Manfredo recommends that I speak to experts on local nobility, Giorgio Geromet and Renata Alberti, authors of the giant two-volume compendium, *Nobilita Della Contea*, of *Palazzi, Castelli e Ville, a Gorizia, in Friuli, in Slovenia.* This splendid pair of huge bright blue and red books now sits prominnently on my study shelves next to *British Envoys To Germany, 1816-1866: Volume II 1830-1847,* impressing all who enter.

The two volume set is packed with distinguished Ritter de Záhony history, and images of the fine palazzos that the family have built in the area over the years. It is clear that Edward Bulwer Lytton can be quite content that this is a very respectable family to whom he is consigning his eldest daughter.

* * * * *

Not only are Natalie and Carl the scions of sugar, but their father Johann-Christoph Ritter von Záhony, has been riding the prosperity wave of Austro-Hungary's industrial revolution in a number of ways. Earning his initial fortune by trading saltpeter (potassium nitrate, a crucial element of gun powder) behind enemy lines during the Napoleonic Wars, he tops a highly successful mercantile career by becoming the first president of the Generali insurance company, which is founded in Trieste in December 1831. Generali is still today one of Europe's biggest insurance companies, and even I pay them an annual cheque to cover the few bits of IKEA furniture that fit into my holiday studio in France. That is a connection to Emily's friend Natalie that I do not see coming.

The family's success in trade and commerce continues into the next generation, but family histories tell primarily of the sons, and the nobility books primarily of the elder sons. Manfredo is a descendant not of the eighth son, Carl, but of the second son, the Austrian Baron/Freiherr, Hektor (1816-1878).

When Amalia, Johann-Christoph's second wife, is widowed, aged 40 with six of her own young children, her home becomes the home of her elder step sons. I will discover later that she remains an important and respected matriach to the whole family, but in 1838 the Ritter de Záhony businesses - and the greater part of the family income - pass into the hands of eldest Ritter de Záhony brothers, to whom Amalia therefore becomes a dependant.

Courtesy of the Fondazione Palazzo Coronini Cronberg

The Ritter de Záhony boys

From then on Amalia's homes will be the homes of her children - or rented boarding houses in far away towns. When she returns 'home' from England in April 1847, she goes first to Vienna, fearing for the safety of her son Carl, a dashingly-revolting student flying the Schwarz-Rot-Gold Reichsbanner [Black-Red-Gold Banner of the Reich] for a united Germany in a city in flames. Her letters from Vienna use the address Spiegelgasse No. 1,098. I write to this address in 2001, but my letter is returned. The high number suggest to me it is a mailbox - or an apartment. Amalia is 'homeless' until her own children are married - or she is at the homes of her step-children in Gorizia.

* * * * *

I travel to Aquileia in May 2007, and am kindly welcomed by Manfredo at his family's villa. Manfredo lives in a modernised annexe and I am fortunate that his sister Rachele (known at Pupa) is at home and I am given the special treat of a tour of the main part of the villa where she lives. Its interior is dark, shielded from the Italian sun, but very beautiful. Everywhere are lovely family heirlooms which I scan for any possible images of Natalie or Carl.

But of course Natalie and Carl are distant cousins, and there are plenty of other closer-related Ritter de Záhonys to display on these walls. This is why Manfredo did not feel he had further information he could add to my letter.

But he does. Crucial information. For during this happy visit, Manfredo suggests that I contact his cousin Ivo Lazzari in Germany, who has researched the family's history and has a fascination for it; and also that I visit the Palazzo Coronini Cronberg in Gorizia, which is home to the legacy of the eldest of Johann-Christoph's sons, Heinrich [Heinrich Freiherr Ritter von Záhony] (1815-1903) through his daughter Caroline (1850-1928) who, in 1870, marries into the ancient local family that gives its name to the palazzo. The Coronini Cronbergs have been in Gorizia since the 16th Century.

It is these two recommendations that open up the world of the Ritter de Záhonys to me.

* * * * *

I hope, one day, you will visit the Palazzo Coronini Cronberg in Gorizia. It is open to the public April to October, and - like Knebworth House - is not only a very beautiful house and gardens, full of lovely art, but also a treasure house of wonderful family and local stories. I turn up that May 2007, unannounced, and receive the warmest of all the lovely welcomes I receive on my Emily adventures from three of the very nicest Italian ladies. Serenella and Cristina - who work for the Foundation that looks after the Palazzo - tell me I have to meet

Courtesy of the Fondazione Palazzo Coronini Cronberg

Palazzo Coronini Cronberg in Gorizia

local historian and teacher Maddalena. Together the three ladies show me beautiful portraits of Johann-Christoph (in Italy called Giovanni Cristoforo) and Amalie (in Italy called Amalia) - Natalie's parents - hanging in pride of place amongst the many beautiful paintings at the Palazzo.

The paintings are by Guiseppe Tominz (1790–1866), a prominent local portraitist of his day, and are breathtakingly lifelike (p.757 & p.811). The image of Amalia - the Madame de Ritter of our story - is almost a photograph. If only I had an image of Emily, or Miss Greene, or Rosina, as close to the reality of this image.

I am then taken to the Palazzo Coronini Cronberg Archive - the back room, with the map drawers - and here is Amalia's album. I am able to tell Serenella and Cristina and Maddalena why there is an image of Bayons Manor in their Archive, and two images of Cannstatt in Germany.

with Maddalena Malni at the Palazzo, discovering Madame de Ritter's album

And then - the pièce de résistance - they pull out the image of Emily. They have been wondering who this is.

* * * * *

After all the excitement I am treated to a local restaurant that has probably never heard a Milanese or Roman accent, let alone an English one - and presented with a bowl of the local speciality, sliced octopus legs. Hertfordshire provincial that I am - pescatarian at best - I have never eaten anything that looks as alien as this before - and wouldn't, but for the completely irresistible company and my, now cloud nine, history high. Those who know me would not believe the sight of me biting into the suckers of sliced octopus tentacles - but I have just been shown a watercolour of my great-great-great-aunt in a house map drawer in Italy!

* * * * *

At his father's death, eldest son Heinrich becomes the pater familias, and outlives his step-mother Amalia by thirty-three years. In all but one respect it makes sense that her personal belongings would end up in his family's possession.

But that one remaining respect is puzzling. Why do these personal items of Amalia's - in particular a picture of Emily Bulwer Lytton marked with her words ***For my daughter Natalie*** - not end up with Natalie, or indeed Carl?

I still do not have the continuing stories of Natalie and Carl. For the former I need to go to Croatia. And for the latter I need to go back to Germany, to visit Manfredo's cousin Ivo Lazzari.

* * * * *

Ivo Lazzari lives in Bad Wörishofen, another German Water Cure town - this one in Bavaria, an hour west of Munich. Like Manfredo, Ivo is a great-great-grandchild of Johann-Christoph's second son, Hektor. He is the son of Manfredo's eldest aunt Hertha. My correspondence with Ivo has been the most productive of my Ritter de Záhony quest, and the highlight of our collaboration and friendship is a trip to Graz that we make together in May 2009 in search of Carl's son, Carl Freiherr Ritter von Záhony (1861-1945) and a granddaughter (of Carl Jr's) still living, Christiane, whom my friend Joachim had found in the phone book some years before.

Ivo has in his possession *Geschichte der Familie Ritter von 1525-1940* [Story of the Ritter Family from 1525 to 1940] written by Carl Jr - who uses 'C' for his name, but 'K' for his father to stress his German roots - in 1939, a time when stressing one's German roots was an important exercise for a nationalist in this part of the world. This document brings all the strands together.

The copy comes from the Biblioteca of the Fondazione Palazzo Coronini Cronberg - and seems also to be the source of the A2 family tree that Peter Ritter-Záhony had in his possession back in 2005.

After years of searching for descendants of the 14 children of Johann-Christoph Ritter von Záhony, in the end, it is the 12th child - Emily's 'prospective husband' Carl/Karl - whose son has written the family history. It is thanks to Carl Jr. that the 19th Century Ritter de Záhonys are revealed to me.

* * * * *

So what would have been Emily's future had she married this boy she had never met, Carl Ritter von Záhony? Carl was, according to his son, ***extremely modest and self-effacing, few recognized and understood him. He was also very religious and his repeatedly pronounced motto was: "With God".*** The history tells us he travelled to London in 1851 to work as an apprentice to this elder brother, Julius Hektor (Manfredo and Ivo's great-great-grandfather), then spent time volunteering at French sugar refineries refining his refining skills. After this two year walkabout, Carl returns to Gorizia to become a successful mill manager, earning financial success for himself and his brothers.

Carl by Guiseppe Tominz

In 1855 Carl marries the daughter of a Privy Councillor from Fiume, the industrial port of the Austro-Hungarian Empire - now Rijeka in Croatia - where his sister Natalie has married and is living. Their son describes his mother, Karoline von Rauchmüller, as a ***fun-loving, temperamental and spirited woman***, and I wish the same might, one day, have been said of Emily had she followed the unlikely course of falling into that same role.

Carl later in life

My father was kind-hearted, especially noble, petty in nothing, and in particular insurpassable in duty and loyalty. True to the purpose of his 1939 biography Carl Jr calls his father ***through and through a German, not only in his mind, but also in everything that he supported and promoted.*** This includes the first German school in Gorizia, the first Gorizian newspaper, the construction of a Protestant church in Gorizia, and the German Men Singing Association - ***where all the Gorizian Germans gathered late into the night to preserve the tradition of German song.***

* * * * *

There resteth to Serbia a glory,
A glory that shall not grow old;
Their remaineth to Serbia a story,
A tale to be chanted and told!

This is not a German song. This is from *The National Songs of Serbia* - an Heroic Pesma [song] entitled *The Battle of Kossovo*, translated by Owen Meredith in 1861. It is a Serbian assassin who splits Europe and sends the German-speaking nations to war with the English-speaking nations for much of the 20th Century.

Owen Meredith is the pen name of Emily's brother, Edward Robert Bulwer Lytton. Teddy - though at heart a poet and writer - is to make his career in the Foreign Service promoting English-speaking interests around the world. His younger son will face the trenches of the First World War and his elder son will lose a son and a son-in-law in the Second.

I cannot help my imagination spinning a scenario where my great-great-great-aunt lives to travel - in Miss Greene's words - *to Goritya to be made one of...* a proudly nationalistic German family. I see Emily's son growing up as 'Carl' (maybe middle name Edward) Frieherr Ritter von Záhony and writing this family history in 1939. In his concluding lines, Carl Jr declares how proud he is of his 400-year-old pure German-Aryan blood - ***stolz sein und mit Recht*** [be proud and rightly so]. My family would have added some wild Irish in there - and blood from all the races that make up the beautiful melting pot of 3000 years of the British Isles...

...but still, cousin Carl Jr would have been on the other side.

I imagine my family split by the battlelines of the 20th Century. Nothing, I suppose, to a German royal family living in Buckingham Palace. But, all the same, thought-provoking.

I notice the date of Carl Jr's death. 1945.

What happened to my would-be Austrian cousin?

* * * * *

In May 2009 I have the great pleasure of travelling to Graz in Austria with Ivo Lazzari. This beautiful red-roofed river-and-cliff-edge city, two hours

Graz in 2009

south of Vienna, is where the younger Carl Frieherr Ritter von Záhony and his descendants make their home. Before the pleasure of the ride in my Toyota Aygo from Bad Wörishofen - and the free glass of wine that my Accor 'A' Club card secures him at the Graz Mercure (two, because he can have mine too) - Ivo has been in touch with City Archives at Graz and his distant cousin Christiane Ritter-Záhony, the granddaughter of Carl Jr.

Christiane is very suspicious of us. She may see us, she may not. She does have a painting of her great-grandfather, Carl the elder, but she doesn't have the means of making a copy of it for us. We can call her when we are in Graz.

Dr Elke Hammer-Luza of the Stadtarchiv is more helpful. There is a small folder on Carl Jr amongst the 26 boxes of Ritter Záhony material. 26 boxes! Is there anything that might help us find his aunt Natalie? No - there is nothing on Natalie.

As I remember it, Ivo and I, in our enthusiasm, are significantly early for the appointment at the Stadtarchiv - so we head first for the St. Leonhard cemetery. After a large fortifying plate of kaiserschmarrn [one of my father's specialist subjects is Austrian puddings - you don't want to get him started on a Saltzberger Nockerl] we visit the impressive doric temple that is the mausoleum of this branch of the Familie Ritter-Záhony. It is a thrill to see this exotic name that has teased me from the thin tissue of family letters for so many years carved in stone above the iron door.

The Ritter Zahony Tomb in the St Leonhard cemetery in Graz

It is Carl Jr that has built this fine home for the family dust, first for his wife Marie Therese, who dies 14 years before him in 1931, and then his son Johann Christoph, who dies in 1937, aged 38. Carl Jr himself is the earliest-born resident. We will not find his father or Natalie here.

Set in the centre is a beautiful stone Christ on a Crucifix. It distresses me to call an image of man being tortured to death 'beautiful', but Carl sets me right with a quote from Goethe's poem *Urania* carved in gold letters above it, ***Des Todes rührendes Bild steht nicht als Schrecken dem Weisen und nicht als Ende dem Frommen*** [Death's touching image is not frightful to the wise, nor an end to those who believe].

As I wind my way out of this suburb of Utopia, I pass the earthly remains of Dr Richard Freiherr von Krafft-Ebing (1840-1902), author of *Psychopathia Sexualis* (1886). Krafft-Ebing tells us that martyrdom has its roots in hysteria and masochism. So from my visit to the St. Leonhard cemetery I have learnt that death is both liberating and sexy. It's a wonder we're not all doing it.

Christiane still will not see us. Ivo keeps trying throughout the visit, and through subsequent years. But, to this day, I still have not seen the image of Emily's Carl that his great-granddaughter has in her possession in Graz.

I mind less now that I have a seen a photograph of Carl. I cannot remember who first found this photograph (p.820) - whether it was Ivo, or Maddellena or Serenella at the Cronini Cronberg - but I am most grateful for a sole glimpse of Carl in mid-life, the man who might have been Emily's future.

His son Carl's folder amongst the 26 boxes at the Stadtarchiv in Graz is, as we have been warned, small - and mainly a collection of school certificates - however it does contain one image that, whilst not reproduced in this book, does stick in my mind to this day. Randomly, amongst his preserved papers, is an invoice for linoleum for his kitchen ordered in 1937. At the bottom is handwritten, ***Heil Hitler!***

I ask how the younger Carl died. When the Russians entered Graz in 1945, he blew his brains out.

Not ***an end to those who believe.***

* * * * *

Putting aside its aberrant intent, Carl Jr's family history remains a rich and rare resource for the characters in Emily's story. It tells us more about the Madame de Ritter with whom Miss Greene is *much pleased... and delighted to think that I could leave (Emily) with so respectable, agreeable and amiable a person, whom she loved so much.*

Carl Jr writes of Amalia Ritter de Záhony, ***Grandmama was extremely orderly, and very knowledgeable in financial matters. She was not beautiful, but quite severe - with some masculine features*** [age clearly wearied the young belle that Tominz captured - but the grandchildren of "radiantly beautiful" young Rosina Wheeler could well have said the same had they met their grandmother]. ***She was very musical, very talented and educated, but did not flaunt it. She was a splendid housewife, a great connoisseur of good food, cheerful and chatty and showed much outward good character.***

She had an extraordinary musical talent and accomplished technique, reflected by her ordered mind. She knew about 60 classic piano pieces by heart, the titles of which were written, in her beautiful clear handwriting, on boxes.

Sometimes she would let guests pluck a sheet from a box and she would play the piece by heart, flawlessly.

Amalie Hofmann kept a tight ship, kept the [de Ritter] ***children considerably more in order, and in cleanliness, and gave them a fine education. When a girl, she had spent time in Rome*** [sounds less decadent than Naples], ***where she had developed her high educational standards*** [better not to mention her radical father]. ***She was also friends with the two daughters*** [children] ***of the famous English author Litton-Bulwer*** [Bulwer Lytton]. ***She lived for a long time*** [less than a month] ***with his daughters*** [children] ***in a suburb of London*** [Brompton - unless Carl means Knebworth, where she did spend six months, which isn't yet a suburb of London... but may be by the time you read this].

I have an album inherited from my father, in which - along with a number of wonderful etchings engraved by his mother - is a pencil drawing with the caption *View of Knebworth Castle, Residence of Sir Edward Bulwer-Litton. Amalie fecit* [latin - made by Amalie], *from nature.* ***Unfortunately no date.***

So there it is. I am right. There was once an illustration of Knebworth House in Amalia's album. And we can add here that it was *fecit* in the latter half of 1847. And strangely - but wonderfully, for its survival - the album was bequeathed by either Carl Jr or his descendants to their cousins' archive at the Palazzo Coronini Cronberg in Gorizia.

Overall, it is clear from this short resume that our grandmother was a grand mother, and should be remembered with pride by her grandchildren and great grandchildren. I give honour and thanks to her memory.

* * * * *

And what of Aunt Natalie? There is only a short paragraph on Natalie in Carl Jr's account, but it is precious information - and telling, both for what it knows and what it does not know.

NATALIE. born Trieste, 25.Dez.1831. died . . . . . . First off, Carl Jr does not know when his aunt died, although he was 33 when it happened in 1895. He has spoken of his father as quiet and unassuming (but for the singing) and if that generation retained the close bonds of childhood, clearly that closeness does not extend to the next generation. This may not be simply family-led - it may have something to do with the national borders that form between the communities of Austro-Hungary's two ports, Trieste and Fiume.

Natalie was a sensitive lady of great education and made a name for herself as a novelist in German. Her novel *Aus dem Geleise* [Off The Rails] ***was widely read.***

Natalie's first husband Pietro R. v. Scarpa came from a Fiume patrician family that thanks to their great wealth led an active, social life, especially at the still surviving, and well-known, Villa Angiolina.

After v. Scarpa's death, Natalie married Johann von Ciotta, at the time pursuing a military career as an adjutant commander for General Gf. Nugent [Irish-born Austrian hero, Laval Graf Nugent von Westmeath (1777-1862)], ***in the war against Italy. After the war, Ciotta devoted himself to a political career and was elected deputy for his native city Fiume in the Hungarian Parliament. Later he was elected mayor of Fiume and held this post for an impressive 30 years. For his services he was awarded the highest Hungarian orders and after his death particularly honoured by the dedication of a memorial. (Unfortunately I can record nothing about the children of this marriage because my written requests have remained unanswered.)***

And so there we have it. The families do not remain close, despite each remaining high profile within their respective communities. Divided national loyalties presumably is the cause of this family split, which will only have been exaggerated by the conflicts of the 20th Century. Few places have seen as much internecine strife in the last hundred years as Croatia.

* * * * *

Go to this part of Croatia today, however, and you visit what the French Riviera must have been like a couple of generations ago - a simple Mediterranean paradise - with the bonus that you don't have to speak French. The more Croatian the Croatian, in these tourist towns, the more likely to speak perfect English.

So, armed with Carl's few facts, off I head - in May 2008 - to what is now called Rijeka (then Fiume) and its neighbouring resort Opatija, where still - seventy years on - the Scarpa family's Villa Angiolina stands overlooking a beautiful blue Mediterranean bay. Now a public museum and exhibition space, it is named after Natalie's mother-in-law - so when I see that the villa

Villas Angiolina (pink) and Amalia (yellow) in Opatija

next door is called Villa Amalia, I eagerly assume that it is named after Natalie's mother, Madame de Ritter.

It isn't. It is built 20 years after Amalia's death, when Natalie has been long married into a different family. But it is built as the annex to a very lovely sea-front hotel - Hotel Kvarner - so where better to book a birthday break with my long-suffering genealo-tourist spouse?

Deserting Martha on our - honestly - very lovely and peaceful stone balcony overlooking the sea, I disappear with brilliant local guide Josipa to find what is left of fin-de-siècle Rikija, the dominant industrial port of the Adriatic - where Emily's little 11-year-old friend from the 'Palace of Hunchbacks' grew up to be Mayoress - or Mayor's consort - for three of the most prosperous decades of the city's history.

Rijeka in 2012

And, to be frank, there is not a great deal of it left. Industrial ports being the first thing to be pounded in conflict, not much of 19th Century Rijeka survives. And even less survives of the memory of Natalie von Ciotta - despite her being the most famous woman in town for the latter quarter of that century.

However, somehow, Josipa finds for me the one person in Croatia who does know all there is, currently, to know about Natalie von Ciotta - engaging and friendly local author and historian, Irvin Lukežić. Pleasingly I am able to give Irvin one or two details of the de Ritter family and Natalie's early life that he does not know, and he has subsequently pulled together all of his research into a long article on Natalie, *Natalia de Ciotta – ugledna riječka dobrotvorka i njemačka spisateljica* [eminent Rijeka benefactor and German writer], in the Croatian review *Novi Kamov* (nr. 4/2011., vol. 41, year XI, pages 49-73) with which we can now fill in the details that, in 1939, were beyond Carl's reach.

Irvin's first happy fact is that she was named Natalie because she was born

Courtesy of the Fondazione Palazzo Coronini Cronberg

The only identified image of Natalie as a child is this watercolour made by Amalia of her three youngest playing at the back of the Palazzo Ritter, now Gorizia Town Hall - I could enlarge it more, but need to accept it is only ever going to be a splodge of colour

on Christmas Day - 25th December 1831 - a month and a half after Teddy/ Robert Lytton Bulwer. The first new eye-catching fact is how quickly she gets married on her and her mother's return from England. Natalie is 16 when she leaves London, in April 1848, and within two years she is married to the second son of Rijeka's richest trader. So much for the teenage love affair with Teddy - there is no going back to London, clearly, after Emily's death, but one gets the impression that the Bulwer Lytton family would not have offered sufficient financial security to the fatherless 13th Ritter de Záhony child.

I have already mentioned the aphorism from Georgette Heyer's *The Convenient Marriage* that one's choice of husband is best determined by how many lodge entrances his estate has. Amongst the merchants of Trieste and Fiume it's all about how much tonnage his boats have. And Pietro has plenty.

Pietro Scarpa (1823-1860), owned a part share of three family sailing boats: the Iginia, with a carrying capacity of 325 tonnes; the Paolo, capacity 389 tonnes, and the Paolo Maria, built in Rijeka in 1853, with capacity of 162 tonnes, owned by Pietro (4 carats), his father Iginio (8 carats) and Natalie's brother Enrico Ritter de Zahony from Trieste (12 carats). Clearly business was flourishing in the early years of Pietro and Natalie's marriage.

Villa Scarpa in Rijeka

* * * * *

Equally bountiful was their conjugal union. Together they produced five Scarpa babies, Iginia, Enrico, Carl (which suggests good relations with her brother at least through the 1850s), Natalie and Pietro Junior. Pietro Junior is born a year before his father's death aged only 37 in 1860 - but clearly Pietro Senior has made the most of his young years.

Her mother Amalia having been widowed at 40 with six children, Natalie is now widowed at 29 with five. She moves quickly to find the security of a second husband, marrying a contemporary of her husband's, the similarly dynamic and enterprising, ex-military man Giovanni [which Carl Jr prefers in its German, 'Johann') de (which Carl Jr prefers in its German 'von') Ciotta (1824-1903), who goes on to become Rijeka's greatest Mayor.

Under his jurisdiction all traffic and street regulations were made, a new water supply and sewage system (acquedotto Ciotta) organised, a luxurious town theatre built (1885), the town market put in order, the public parks laid out, etc. He believed that "only good schooling creates good citizens" and due to his efforts many public schools were opened. He also supported the Whitehead family's Torpedo factory [Englishman Robert Whitehead (1823–1905) gives Rejika one of its most enduring legacies - and purpose to a submarine - by developing the torpedo in the town in 1866], ***as well as many other educational and humanitarian*** [more humanitatian than the torpedo] ***institutions. He was the father of the new town planning of Rijeka.***

Courtesy of the Art Collections of the Maritime and History Museum of the Croatian Littoral Rijeka

Giovanni Ciotta

Quite a legacy. And his wife - who as a teenager is chasing to see the Chartists revolutionaries in London and climbing the barricades of Paris and Vienna - is no shrinking violet either.

* * * * *

Irvin describes how ***Among the wealthy and noble ladies in Rijeka, Natalie de Ciotta was always the first in charitable and philanthropic work, distinguishing herself for her generosity and willingness to help those who were in need. Because of this, she and her husband were highly thought of. They both had 'cuore nobile aperto' ('an open and noble heart'). There was no***

charitable institution in the town that was not helped and sponsored by the Ciottas. There was no charitable occasion at which the Ciottas were not helping, advising and supporting the helpless, and setting an example to others.

Whilst her brother is building a Protestant church and a German school in Gorizia, Natalie's energies and financial support are more broadly spread - as befits the Mayor's consort - across ecumenical and racial allegiances. She is a ***benefactress and supporter*** of - to name a few - Rijeka's ***Asilo Infantile***, its charitable nursery school, the ***Associazione di beneficenza Maria, a caritative institution of the Catholic church in Rijeka,*** and ***Presidentessa of Rijeka's branch of the Hungarian Red Cross.***

She read a lot and with pleasure, and was involved in creative writing whenever she found spare time. She owned a rich and valuable private library. In 1880 she donated seventy-six volumes of different books printed in various languages to the Town Hospital in Rijeka. This was intended to be the core of the future hospital library. Her example was followed by other citizens...

Amongst the long list of inaugurations and public events she either presided over or contributed to, Irvin mentions that ***in December 1880, [she] donated 20 fiorins... to help people affected by the catastrophic earthquake in Zagreb. Her*** [two further] ***daughters*** [with Giovanni Ciotta] ***Alice and Edmea performed in 'living pictures'*** - now clearly a more respectable thing for your daughter to do than it was at the Palace of Wied in 1842.

Giovanni Ciotta and his wife Natalie were happily married for more than thirty years, respecting each other, working successfully with each other, and representing a model of marital harmony. The grounds for their understanding was based on mutual freedom and tolerance. They were both very disciplined, decisive and hardworking people, and complemented each other excellently every step of the way.

Giovanni

Natalie

* * * * *

Both Carl and Natalie's legacies spin me a seductive sentient dream of what Emily's life might have been had she been absorbed into Austro-Hungarian society and lived out the latter part of the 19th Century. For certain, I believe Emily - wherever a longer life might have taken her - would have become, as Natalie did in later life, a successful author.

Natalie ***published a series of novels in the German language, which would earn her an important place among the writers of that time.*** Due to the high profile of others sharing her many names, de Ritter, Scarpa and Ciotta, ***in Rijeka she published her work under the name R. Enze.***

The first appears to be *Lotta senza Gloria* [Fight Without Glory], which is ***translated into the Italian language*** and ***published as a feuilleton*** [a non-news or non-political newspaper supplement] ***in the main local journal*** *La Bilancia* ***from August of 1872 to February of 1873.***

Also appearing in 1873, is R. Enze's *Ausser dem Geleise* [Off The Rails] that, according to *La Bilancia,* ***meets favourable and flattering judgement from the field of criticism, that eshews ordinary things.***

In 1879, in Budapest, a two volume novel entitled *Metamorphosen* [Metamorphosis] appears under the name Natalie v. Ciotta, having been ***published at first as a feuilleton in*** *Pester Lloyd* [Hungary's leading German language publication].

The next, *Vom Markte des Lebens* (1887) [Of The Market of Life] is published in Vienna in 1887, also under the name Natalie v. Ciotta. These are not local novels by the Mayoress of Rikeja - their reach extends through the German-speaking world. Before appearing as bound volumes, they are likely also appearing ***as newspaper feuilletons in Berlin and Vienna.***

Somewhere amongst this oeuvre is also the less-romantically named *Geschichte eines Regenmantels* [History of a Raincoat], which I have not been able to date - unless that's the German title of *Lotta senza Gloria* [Fight Without Glory], in which case the German

Außer dem Geleise.

Von

R. Enze

(Natalie von Ciotta).

Wien.

Verlag von Friedrich Beck

Augustinerstraße 8, Albrechtsplatz 1

Ausser dem Geleise (1873)

publishers are pleasingly more confident of the appeal of its author's name. Although I, personally, would prefer to read a book called *History of a Raincoat* than one called *Fight Without Glory.*

But I can't. Because these books are now very hard to find. I have managed to acquire a treasured copy of R. Enze's *Ausser dem Geleise* on www.abebooks.com, and have photographed every page of copies of *Metamorphosen* and *Vom Markte des Lebens* at the Gorizia Bibliotec, but *Lotta senza Gloria* and *Geschichte eines Regenmantels*, so far, remain lost to me and the world.

* * * * *

I am most intrigued to see if Natalie anywhere fictionalises her experiences in Dr Heine's Institute, or her relationship with Emily. Raising hopes of this, is the fact that all of these books post-date the death of her mother in 1870 - mothers, in my experience, are the greatest cause of self-expurgated autobiography. [Not for me, however - when my moment of memoir-therapy comes, I can assure you I shall be relying on my mother for all the most inappropriate tales of my youth.]

Quite surprising to me, is that in none of the text that I've as yet glanced over does there appear to be any reference to - or borrowing from - these intense moments of Natalie's childhood and teenage years. But, to my eye, the German Gothic typeface is hard enough to read, let alone its meaning - so there is clearly more research to be done here. I do look forward to studying all of Natalie's novels in detail one day. Ivo Lazzari assures me that in *Ausser dem Geleise,* there is nothing to suggest Natalie's past with Emily. Irvin, like me, has the disadvantage of German not being his first or second language, but his research gives the sum of Natalie's oeuvre as follows:

She was skilled story-teller whose life-view was somewhat idealised, in the best sense of the word. In her novels and stories Natalie did not like describing life's misfortunes and rougher side, which distinguished her from popular and widespread writing styles of the time.

Which is probably why she doesn't write about Emily.

* * * * *

Natalie dies on May 19th 1895, aged 63. The town of Rijeka is plunged into mourning at the death of a popular consort of a popular Mayor, with ***black flags flying at half-mast on the consular and municipal buildings, and on a number of the steamships and sailing boats of Rijeka...***

According to an article in *La Bilancia,* ***the funeral of Natalie Ciotta started at 11 o'clock in the morning on May 21st, 1895. It was a striking and dignified ceremony in which participated many formally-dressed dignitaries and a large number of citizens. The procession started from her family home in Corsia Deak No. 30, continuing through the streets Alessandrina, Governo, Municipio and Belvedere and stopped at the municipal cemetery in Kozala.***

The funeral procession was arranged in the following order: Horseman in front of the coffin carriage which is pulled by six black horses, the cross, the boys and girls of Children Orphanage, protégés of the Foundation for Poor, nurses, the students of the Female convent, the students of the Civic Female School, the students of the Civic Male School, the students of the Imperial Croatian Gymnasium...[etc. etc.]

It is not a quiet family affair.

* * * * *

How odd then, that Natalie is all but forgotten today. It is symptomatic of the troubles that Croatia, and the town of Rijeka, have seen since.

Irvin has successfully researched the spouses of Natalie's seven children, but has had no joy finding any subsequent generations. There is no www.ancestry.hr yet - and, as with German Italy, there seems no great desire yet to go exploring the family histories and allegiances of a war-ravaged 20th Century. So there will be no happy 21st Century reunion of a descendant of Emily's with a descendant of Natalie's in time for this book. But I'm sure there will be one day.

I do not recall whether it is Josipa or Irvin that takes me, that May, to the Rijeka town museum to see the two fine portraits of Giovanni de Ciotta, and where the walls are covered with town dignitaries dating back to the 18th Century. What I do remember is that, although there a number of paintings marked ***Riječka patricijka*** (patrician lady of Rijeka) on display, there are none marked ***Natalie de Ciotta***.

Courtesy of the Art Collections of the Maritime and History Museum of the Croatian Littoral Rijeka

Nepoznata Gospoda

There is one 18 by 25 inch oil portrait of an elderly woman that is marked ***Nepoznata Gospoda*** [Unknown Lady], dated ***oko*** [about] ***1899***. In the museum catalogue ***Portreti Iz Fundusa Muzeja*** [Portraits from the Museum] a parenthesis is added to this title with a question mark: ***(Amalija Ciotta?)***.

Amalia? None of Natalie's seven children, that we know, was known by their grandmother's name. No, comparing this portrait to the one photograph we have of Natalie from an Hungarian encyclopedia (p.831), I think this portrait was painted a few years earlier than 1899, and the Nepoznata Gospoda is, indeed, Emily's Natalie.

The small stretch of Pelham Terrace that remains today, in Pelham Street off the Brompton Road

CHAPTER 33

~ *Brompton - 1848* ~

My dear Clara [D'Eyncourt] ***I thank you gratefully for your kind sympathy. Hereafter I shall feel more all the consolation it conveys –***

I believe that you have written to Miss Greene for an interview to hear the last mournful particulars - it is natural. But Miss G is excited & excitable without competence in how much- [he begins again] ***in the peculiarly painful circumstances as concluded with Lady B, who must I fear be considered the immediate cause of my daughter's death. As all discussion revolts me & Edward – with great pains, I fancy that she is now somewhat bridled. But to talk over with you, a new person, will set her afresh - all you say & do not [say] may be repeated God knows where –***

Now you have made the appointment, I think you must keep it – it will never do for her to fancy I want to prevent it - & she would so I think – But pray be as brief & guarded as you can & I should care much less if you would see her at Mrs Wilkinson's, her sister [niece], ***who is a very superior woman, & who saw more of Emily at the last & heard E's last conscious words. She lives 12 Albert Place, Victoria Road, if you could think of any plea to see both at the same time - I write this more at poor Edward's wish than mine – At his age sores are not callous. Don't let Miss Greene think I have written this somehow or another. I ask all for the whole sacred story. Yrs ever E.B.L.***

I cannot say how kind more than kind your father has been - & he goes with me tomorrow [to the funeral, we may presume]. ***He has stamped upon a heart crushed & torn – more than words can say – a grateful memory – sweet amidst all grief & desolation.***

Edward Bulwer Lytton - May 1848

* * * * *

The final section of Miss Greene's *Recollections* is the heartbreaking account of Emily's death.

In picking up this book you have made an appointment with Miss Greene. And I think you must keep it.

My great-great-great-grandfather would rather there is someone else in the room when you hear this part of the story. Miss Greene is ***excited and excitable***.

The fuller story will come. In the chapters that follow you will hear the perspective of others - most of which is decidedly more excited and excitable - but Miss Greene's account is, in itself, so devastating and affecting that I will not interrupt it.

Miss Greene deserves that you should hear it from her.

* * * * *

First, historic context.

Miss Greene is writing of the late Winter and Spring of 1848 when the whole of Europe is unsettled, not just Emily. The path Emily is planning - to

Revolution in Paris as depicted in the London Illustrated News

leave her problems behind - leads right into the thick of this collapsing world.

To give you just a flavour, a recent article by Dan Snow - *1848: The Year of Revolutions* - compares our decade's 'Arab Spring' with the European unrest of 1848. ***In January the first crowds gathered to demand reform – barricades went up, and within hours the news was transmitted to millions. Like a virus, the unrest leapt from host to host. Encouraged by what they saw and heard, crowds turned out in cities thousands of miles apart to demand votes, jobs, constitutions and their human rights.*** London itself, by April 1848, is teetering on the brink of social upheaval, with the Chartists - a group of radical reformers - planning mass demonstrations, which all fear could erupt into revolution.

What if Emily had faced this crossroads in her life in a different year? Any other year. It would have been different...

But I've already said that about the 'Panic of 1847' the autumn before.

One can say that about every flutter of butterfly wings that came together to create Fate in April 1848...

* * * * *

Resumed January 8th, 1850, not having had health or nerves to write upon the subject since - which was about the end of January [1848], or the time when the French Revolution drove Nathalie from Paris to Brompton to her mother [after the summer of 1847 Natalie has returned to France with her governess to continue her schooling], *and where I experienced great pleasure in witnessing their meeting, after the poor girl's escape from such horrid scenes as she described having been witness to in Paris.*

Both mother and daughter seemed to be very fond of each other, and we went on extremely well, Nathalie joining our little musical parties and thé a chambre [Tea parties] *and I thought her very clever but most 'précoce'* [precocious] *in everything, as she was three years younger than Emily. One thing I was disappointed in her, which was that I did not think she loved Emily as she ought, and talked with much more pleasure of Edward* [Teddy] *than of her.*

During this time the 3 *Lyttons were at Bayons, and Madame de Ritter and Nathalie in constant correspondence with Emily - and I was beginning to discover an improvement in the tone of Emily's letters and thought that the kindness of the d'Eyncourt family and her being in her proper sphere would restore her mind to its proper tone. However, even then, she was excited by a Mr Vane* [one of two brothers, neighours of the d'Eyncourt's, Henry Morgan Vane (1808-1886) or Frederick Nicholson Vane (1809-1878)] *falling in love with her and making her an offer, as well as being in the house with Mr G. d'Eyncourt* [Charles's eldest son, George (1809-1871), unmarried, however like the Vane brothers almost 20 years older than Emily] *about whom, and with whom, Mrs Thomson had made so much mischief; and she got ill and was confined to her bedroom. I think her conversations with Miss Clara d'Eyncourt were of use to her mind, but she gave me some accounts of intercourse with her father which she said terrified her - sometimes too kind and affectionate, and at other times quite the reverse.*

* * * * *

She and Nathalie at last determined that they must meet. But Sir Edward - I thought very properly - said she had better remain a little longer at Bayons, even though he and Edward were obliged to leave. This she did - however, still complaining that she was ill, but I never could hear more than that it was neuralgia; and when she wrote me word that she had lost the use of one of her legs I did not believe her, but thought it one of the many fancies she was apt to have and that she said it only to get to London, as it were for advice, when in fact it was to be with Nathalie.

She gained her point, got out of bed at Bayons on the 17th of March, and travelled up to London all the way with Madame de Ritter's German maid and surprised us at 29 Pelham Terrace, Brompton, at 9 o'clock in the evening by running upstairs and rushing into the drawing room and throwing herself into Nathalie's arms.

She looked delicate but not ill, seemed much herself, agreeable, unaffected and charming to me and, as I thought natural, proposed that she should sleep with me as Madame de Ritter had but one bed upstairs where she and her daughter slept together - but Madame opposed this with all her might, and poor Emily, at the end of her long journey, was given the third of a small bed with her German friends.

* * * * *

Early the next morning Emily stole into my room and told me some of her little secrets, and said she would tell me more after breakfast but must go to Madame now. Directly after breakfast, Emily and I went into my bedroom and she began telling me her news - when Madame de Ritter entered in a jealous German rage and said that Emily was under her care and she would not allow her to sit pratling with me in a cold room.

After this, I found Emily quite on her guard with me before Madame, seeming not to care about me, but doting upon her - and her love to Nathalie seemed perfect madness. In order to make room for Emily and give her a comfortable bed, I gave up my room and took a lodging for myself [at No. 20 Pelham Terrace] *within a few doors* [of No. 29]. *But to my great astonishment I found that Madame was to take it, and the two girls to sleep together.*

This after a few days I saw did not please her, as she became jealous that they seemed to think so little of her and lived only for each other. When I saw them together, I recollected what Emily had said to me when Nathalie was expected at Knebworth, "I shall be ill again when Nathalie comes - do you recollect the state you found me in about her when you came to Cannstadt?"

I should have mentioned before that while Emily was planning with Madame de Ritter her returning with her to Vienna, and coming to London, she wrote to me saying, "when Papa goes to London and calls at Brompton take care and stay in the room, do not leave him alone with Madame."

When he did call, what was my astonishment to see him go up and kiss her - and his last act towards her was turning her out of Knebworth. He and she had a great deal of talk about the bargain of Emily's remaining with her when she came to London, each trying to make the best bargain they could for themselves, neither thinking of poor dear Emily.

He certainly was very odd that day, dressed most shabbily and had even torn, worn and mended trousers. The most natural act was his last - when we all stood up when he was going away, and he leaned himself against the wall and said to me in the kindest manners, "Miss Greene, have you nothing to say to me?"

After he went away, Madame went about the lodging house boasting how he had kissed her! and I said to her "I have known him rather longer than you have, yet cannot say he ever took such a liberty with me." From what I saw, and learnt, of his intention of giving up Emily so much to her, I concluded that he had been pleased with whatever information he had gathered about the family whilst at Vienna.

* * * * *

But to return to Emily. Instead of living with them, as was at first arranged, I went and stayed constantly at Kensington with the Wilkinsons, only going to drink tea with them occasionally.

It was not long till I saw matters were not going on well - as, directly after tea, the girls retired to bed and left Madame and myself tete-a-tete.

She began to rail against Emily and her father; him, for his beggarly meanness about money, and having put his daughter upon her; and her, for her extravagant airs and teaching them to her daughter, whose affection she had completely estranged from her.

Whenever I met them all together, I saw that the two girls were quite afraid of her temper, and kept coaxing and flattering her, and kept as much as possible out of her way. She even allowed them to walk out alone.

I saw that one point in particular which Emily tried to please her by, was abusing other people - in particular the Thomsons and Mr George d'Eyncourt [eldest son of the D'Eyncourt family].

* * * * *

At length Edward [Teddy] *came to town, and the mystery and separation from me increased. They seemed anxious to keep him amongst them - yet did not dare to say it openly.*

One day the three ladies came to visit me, and Sir Edward called at No. 29 and heard they were gone down to Miss Greene's lodgings. After inquiring where the lodgings were, he followed them down.

Directly he came into the room, he came over and shook hands with me, saying he was surprised, as he did not know I was in town; said what nice rooms I had got, and could I get one in the same house with me for Edward who was come up to town for his holidays.

I said I should be most happy to do so, and it was soon arranged - to the astonishment and annoyance, I could see, of the ladies - and I could not then understand what they were all about. Sir Edward had lodgings for himself at Fulham [this is either at Charles D'Eyncourt's London residence, which he claimed to be using at the time, or it is not Fulham, but Pimlico, where Marion is], *where he did not choose to take either of his children. So the family were divided into three separate lodgings - and I was too happy to get dear Edward whenever I could.*

However, I soon found that the de Ritters chose to have him to themselves, and it was settled he should only sleep at my lodging.

After a few visits I saw the whole plan about Edward - which was a love affair with Nathalie, which indeed Emily had told me had begun in summer when Nathalie and he were so much together at Knebworth.

* * * * *

There had been some quarrel between Emily and Madame and, one day, I came and found my dear girl ill, and seeming very unhappy, and removed down to my bed which Madame de Ritter had been sleeping in. All was confusion to me, till my dear Emily whispered to me when I came to her bedside to "stay with her", which I did as long as I could, but never was left alone with her long enough to speak with her.

I was obliged to go away to dinner and when I came back early in the evening to see Emily, I found Edward had got a sore throat, and that Madame instead of sending him home to me to his bed, made up one on a sofa in his sister's room, to her great discomfort. When both she and I begged that he might be removed, Madame said she must keep him there to take care of him.

When I came again to see them, at about half past ten, I found those two poor children shut up in the small room for the night, both ill, and not even one drop of drink or anything left for them; and on going up to Madame's room, I found herself, her daughter and the German maid laughing and talking. I told her I thought both Emily and Edward were very uncomfortable, got no redress and was obliged to leave them!

* * * * *

Cheltenham, August 1st, 1850. The effects of the sad scene and their tormentors so entirely shook my nerves that I have been obliged to leave off - and now, seven months later, and two full years from the events, again resume the subject.

The last thing I find that I attempted to describe was the wretched and even dangerous state both my dear children were in when Madame de Ritter chose to take the charge and command of them and me. But I felt that I had no power - and that they might all fall from under me, and that Sir Edward would throw me over, as he did in the case of Madame de Weling; and that perhaps, if I submitted, I might have the power, by seeing them, of perhaps being of use.

This - or a fault I had discovered in my character, of my having too great a dread of a quarrel - kept me quiet, and I was satisfied to come the next morning to see may two dear ones. I found that Nathalie had gone that night of the 10th of April and walked to Piccadilly from Brompton in expectation of a London Revolution to compare if it was like the one she had seen in Paris a short time before.

I found my dear Emily in my bed more miserable than I can express or describe, begging of me to stay with her, for she wished to speak to me. Poor Ed-

Chartists marching in London in April 1848 - from the London Illustrated News

ward had got up and was in the drawing room, still with a sore throat but able to submit to the overtures of love made him [by the de Ritters].

* * * * *

I soon left them, and heard all from my dear Emily of how Madame de Ritter had insulted her, and declared she would not take such a beggar with her to Vienna and that her mean father would not pay even the expense of her dress. I cannot bear to go into more of the wretched particulars.....but I saw and found that this battle had been the means of opening my darling's eyes to the whole conduct and scheme of Madame de Ritter - and she declared that nothing could tempt her now to go to Vienna with them, even if they wished it. She said "I see that my pride is even stronger than my affection, and that my prayers have been heard, that my affection for Nathalie is cured!!"

From this time she never could bear any of them in her room, or me out of it - and as the day was fixed for their going, she wished it was come, and that they were gone. She begged of me when they were gone - if she lived - to take her down to my Lodgings, where I had Edward, and "When you get me, keep me, as I have found I cannot live with Papa: I have tried it - nobody can; even his friend, Madame d'Azzimart, told me she could not live always with him, he was so odd, and so had his mother been."

* * * * *

At last there was a Physician sent for, a plain good kind of a man from Fulham [Robert Rouse of Welham Green, Fulham], *brought by her father, and her* [Emily's] *remark was that she was sure he had a Gig, and would often take her Papa into Town free of cost, and that was the reason, amongst others, that he was employed.*

He said that he did not see much the matter, except that she was evidently very unhappy (which, as usual, Sir Edward did not desire either to hear or believe) and ordered her some medicine and desired her to be soothed and kept quiet.

Whilst in this state, a fresh commotion broke out in the shape of a Thomson brat of a boy of 16 [14], *who was in love with Emily and had written some frantic letters about her, and stolen some more from Edward about Carl. The first I heard of this business was being awoke out of my sleep at 6 o'clock in the morning by Mrs Thomson's coachman thundering at my hall door to enquire from Edward to hear from him what had become of her son, Cockburn.*

When I went down in my dressing gown, I found Mrs Thomson beside Edward's bed entreating him to tell her what had become of Cockburn, as he was gone off, distracted about Emily. He could tell her but little about him, and after she was gone I went to Edward's writing desk and took all his letters - which he had shewn me some of the night before - on the subject of Cockburn Thomson's love and Carl's for my poor Emily, and his own and Nathalie's, and burnt them. So that when one of the Miss Thomsons came the next day to demand them, I told her I had burnt them.

Before this silly, mad woman came to my Lodgings, she went and disturbed my poor dear child in the weak and nervous state I described her, and when I saw her, found her wretchedly altered and, if possible, more miserable. She then explained to me that she dreaded her Father hearing of this folly about Cockburn Thomson, as she knew he would blame her.

* * * * *

Being at Knebworth at the beginning of this new nonsense about this boy Thomson, I thought little about it, made no enquiries. I was indeed surprised when Madame de Ritter told me that Emily had said to her one day when she heard that her Father was going to call upon me at Kensington, "I hope Miss Greene will not tell him all about Cockburn Thomson"; however, this new scene and things which I then learnt for the first time, the folly of him, and the cunning of his mother made it more serious.

As usual my poor dear child was put into a false position which she had never dreamt of. And this fellow, going off as he did, half mad, made a most disagreeable uproar, and the éclaircissement [revelation] *etc. with Sir Edward drove poor Emily (in the state of mind she was already in) into a still more excited state.*

One evening I sent off for the 'Dr Rouse', the man I liked best, and when he came, he applied remedies which calmed her, and again said it was unhappiness and hysterics. Always after these excitements were over and I got her to myself, prayer, the Bible and religion soon calmed her; and she did not like any other subject but that and her death, which she still continued to look forward to as likely to be soon.

One of her expressions, I recollect, amongst others, was "My idea of happiness in this world was being with those I loved. Oh! what will be the happiness of being with God and loved by Him?" She asked her Father's permission to see a clergyman, and Dr Rouse sent one, and she and I spent a most comforting and happy half hour with him.

My sister and nieces used to come and sit with her, and her conversation with them was the same, and she scarcely ever saw anything of the de Ritters or Edward (who were in the next room, singing, and diverting themselves) and I always gave offence if I begged that they would not make a noise; and poor Edward, who was quite unconscious how ill his sister was, was carried away by the licence they allowed him in everything.

* * * * *

At last Sir Edward began to believe that she was ill, and, as usual, thought that some of his pet doctors should be called in, and Dr Marshal Hall was sent for. And of course he altered all that good Rouse had been doing in keeping up her strength by a little jelly and very little wine. He ordered that she should not touch any of them, but live upon rice puddings - which she would not taste - and not see anybody that she cared for - myself in particular.

The end of this was that she was shut up with a strange old nurse [Mrs Charlotte Bruce] *for some days, and only when the Doctor came did she see anybody else - and her Father, who used to go into the room along with them.*

I stole in one day and found her much altered; she said, "They say I am better, but I am worse." "Would you like me to be with you?" She said, "Much." I was obliged to leave her, and then went to her father and begged that he would let Sophy [Tate], *a faithful old servant of his mother's, to be with her; but he would not, giving the plausible* [persuasive but untrue] *answer that it would be bad for her.*

* * * * *

Leckhampton [a district in south Cheltenham], *July 9th, 1851. Again at the end of another year and half since I last wrote upon this painful subject, I again take it up, intending to finish the story, though even now I feel myself nervous and scarcely equal to the task.*

My attempt at having Sophy, the faithful woman servant, shut up with my darling instead of a strange old hospital nurse, was strongly opposed by her father. Still, the good woman (like myself) kept hovering about Brompton to hear how she was going on, and when I said to Edward "What a pity your Father will not allow Sophy to be with Emily", He answered in his usual grand manner (when proud of the confidence between them) "My father is quite right, a stranger is the best. Emily might say something which Sophy might <u>understand</u> and retell in Hertfordshire - perhaps in Mr Pearson's [the Rector's] *Kitchen."*

Before this all occurred I must tell that one evening when everybody but myself had gone out and I alone was with Emily, Dr Rouse came and brought a Dr Cope, a nephew I believe of Dr Locock's [Sir Charles Locock (1799–1875), 'the Great Deliverer of His Country', catches all of Queen Victoria's babies; Dr Cope is more obscure, but there is a Dr Cope on the board of the Royal Infirmary For Children in 1841 and a Dr Cope does attend the Duchess of Malborough with Dr Locock in 1850]; *they both came in to see Emily and I greatly liked their manner and so did she. She seemed more cheerful, and like herself. She talked German with Dr Cope and when the two Doctors talked in the next room together they seemed quite to understand the state she was in, particularly when they heard her moan, or rather scream, from the next room and I think called it a species of hysterics.*

Had these two men been allowed to act, I think, under God, all might have ended differently, but they were not - and Marshal Hall was called in and took the business entirely upon himself, with what I thought a very high hand; and Rouse told me that, but for the interest which he felt in the young lady, he would decline coming again, but that he would not; and also that Marshall Hall had told Sir Edward some falsehood about the state of her pulse when he felt it after him.

All this I was obliged to look on at, and saw all the rest of the party engaged about their own business - Madame de Ritter about her journey, which was to commence in three days; Edward and Nathalie with their love.

Sir Edward generally came about the time the Dr did, and I saw that Hall was a vain man and talked literature with Sir Edward, and German with Madame, when I thought he should only think of his patient; and he even one day brought a diploma which he had got in Germany, which he, in a pet, pointed to when I rather anxiously enquired the state of Emily's pulse. Both he and Sir Edward most particularly requested of me not to go into her room for fear of exciting her - and so I submitted, hearing that she was going on well.

* * * * *

At last came the night for the de Ritters to go away, and the noise of carrying boxes down the stairs past my dear child's door disturbed her so much that the nurse came out of her room saying it did so and begged it might be stopped. I accordingly went to Madame and told her so, which offended her very much.

I remained there till a late hour when I asked Edward to come home to his bed. Madame and Nathalie said he must remain and that he could sleep in their bed when they left. I accordingly took leave of them and went home to my bed.

The next morning I heard that Emily was as usual - and when Sir Edward came, he asked me to arrange to take all the rooms for him in order that strangers might not come into the house whilst Emily was so ill. I saw that he rather wished I should take them and pay for them, but I had learned too much of him to do so; therefore, preferred keeping my own lodgings.

I did arrange with the woman of the house to take all the lodgings for Sir Edward, as he desired - as he knew I could and would get them cheaper living there [in Brompton].

I remained all that day in the room next to dear Emily and rejoicing at the quiet day she was passing, and hearing at her door that she was going on well.

Edward and I went down in the evening to dinner at Kensington to my niece's, and in the evening on my return to Brompton, after hearing again that Emily was going on well, went up to the room that Madame de Ritter had left and got Emily's writing desk and papers which she had (early in her illness) desired me to take, and carried them down to my lodgings.

The next day, upon coming to hear how she was, [I} got a good account and drove into London with Mrs Wilkinson; and at five o'clock when we again called heard that the Dr had seen her and pronounced her much better, when Edward and I went to Kensington again to dinner.

Edward and I returned to Brompton about half past nine o'clock and as usual went to hear how our dear Emily was, passing our own lodgings where we were to sleep -

I forgot to mention that, in the morning of this day, when I called, I went in and when I got up to the door of the room which Madame de Ritter had occupied, I found it locked, and the woman of the house followed me and told me she had let it; upon which I said "surely I took it yesterday for Sir Edward." However, I took no further notice, nor did I in the least suspect anything but that the woman chose to make the most she could of her lodgings.

- but to return. When Edward and I came to the house to enquire how she was, we heard that she was much better, and I then walked on to go upstairs to enquire more particularly from the nurse - but was met by the woman of the house who told me Miss Lytton was asleep, and that I had better not go up for fear of disturbing her. I, still, went on, till Edward followed me with his strong heavy boots, and I, in vain, tried to make him not follow, or make a noise - I alas! gave it up, and returned with him to our lodgings which were within a few doors of us, thankful that she was better, and satisfied that Sophy would call as usual, early, and bring me word how my child was, and that I could go myself a little later.

However, when Sophy did come, her account was that Miss Lytton was much worse, and had been delirious since twelve o'clock last night.

I instantly went off to the house and went up directly to her door and called to the nurse, and upon my hearing that she had become so suddenly worse I said to the woman, how do you account for this, has anyone seen her? Upon which she became saucy and said, "No, Ma'am, I know my business better."

As I heard that she was quieter I went with Edward into the sitting room to wait for the Doctor who was expected every moment. Emily had been so well the day before, that Marshall Hall had not been to see her - only Rouse.

* * * * *

We had not been long in this room till the woman of the house came in and told Edward that his Papa was down at Miss Greene's lodgings and wished to see him. He went immediately - but soon returned with the news that Lady Lytton was in the house; that Dr Rouse had seen her there the day before, and had been driving about London all the day and could not find Sir Edward to inform him till this morning.

I immediately went to the woman of the house and asked her to explain, and she told me a pack of lies that she thought the lady was a Mrs Johnson. Next came Marshall Hall and Rouse, who pronounced Emily very much worse than she had ever been, and that her life was in danger, and that they could not in any way account for the alteration unless something very extraordinary had occurred.

I went to my lodgings where Sir Edward and his Lawyer (Mr Loaden) were, and I will try and describe the scene which I witnessed there, when the Doctors came from the other house. When, from some point of law [that] Sir Edward must not go and be under the same roof with his wife, it appeared to me as if the two physicians had been employed to request of her ladyship to leave the house.

The doctors represented to her that the life of her child depended upon her not being disturbed or excited. At the same time they gave her to understand that they thought she had gone into her room in the night - [and that this] had been the cause of the dangerous state in which they now found [Emily], after leaving her so much amended the day before. This both she [Rosina] *and the nurse denied, and poor Emily continued in a state of delirium or insensibility.*

Every person in the room seemed in a state of wretched excitement - Mar-

shall Hall the most hurt and angry from what had passed between him and Lady Bulwer; and upon Sir Edward asking him what should be done, his answer was: "As a Physician I tell you that the removal of your daughter, even to this house, may cost her her life; but as a man and a Father, I should prefer doing so to leaving her where she is, if her mother will not leave it."

Poor Edward was, during this scene, put into his bedroom, which was off the room we were all in, and each person not knowing what either to think or advise.

* * * * *

At last a lady entered [Katherine Planché (1823-1901), daughter of Brompton-resident playwright, James Robinson Planché (1796-1880)] *who seemed to be the companion of Lady Bulwer, and came forward in a most grand and theatrical manner and walked up to the table and said: "Lady Lytton sees the plot, and therefore consents to leave the house"; and then particularly addressing Sir Edward, said: "I presume you are Sir Edward Lytton, and think you ought to have had the politeness to stand up", to which he made a quiet bow.*

My first wish and proposal was to send for good Sophy to be about the darling invalid, which Sir Edward then grasped at - as he now saw she and I had been got out of the way on purpose to bring this scene about. I immediately went to the house and sent for her, after Lady Lytton had left it; and Sir Edward, after requesting of us to keep guard, went off for more and more medical advice - but all was too late!

* * * * *

My darling never knew me after, but continued dying all that day, and expired at 9 o'clock that evening, with Sophy at one side of her bed and myself at the other - and even at that moment God enabled me to say "Thank God" though she was the idol of my life then, and for years before. And, but for my persevering love to her, she would have been, during her last illness and at her death, surrounded by a hired nurse who had seen her but one week, and a strange lodging-house keeper! Edward and his Father were in the next room when she died.

She died as I at first found her - neglected by all who should have cherished and taken care of her.

* * * * *

Her father and Edward soon came into the room, and Sir Edward made signs to us to leave it, and he remained a short time there. When he returned, there passed a most frightful scene of anguish on the part of poor Edward and his father. After becoming a little composed, Sir Edward came over to me and stood quite erect, folded his arms and said: "Miss Greene, what have you against me?" "Nothing," said I, "except having left Emily so long alone in Germany."

Poor faithful Sophy remained with the remains of my darling and did whatever was right; and, at about the end of an hour, Sir Edward left the house after giving some directions to Sophy and Edward, and I went down to my lodgings where we remained several hours talking before we went to bed - and the poor boy wanted to sleep in my room, or even at the door, neither of which requests dared I agree to in a public lodging as I did not know what might be said.

* * * * *

The next day I found him pretty calm, and I read to him some letters of his dear sister's and we talked much about her, and I tried to impress upon him my own feelings about her death being such a happy release from this world of sin and sorrow to one of peace and happiness. I repeated to him much that she had said to me upon the subject of religion, and her hopes and assurance of Heaven through the merits of our Saviour. His Father came and took him away for some hours and my friends from Kensington came to me.

I knew little of what was doing at the other house, but got Sophy to bring me all her hair [locks of hair cut as 'Memento Mori' - Latin: 'a reminder of death'], *and let me know when Edward and I could go and take a last look, which we did together.*

* * * * *

Sir Edward wished me to go down to Knebworth to the funeral which I declined, and sent Mr Forster [John Forster, his best friend] *to me (as he knew I rather liked him) to soften me down and discover my opinions and intentions. As Edward had begged of me to shew his Father some of Emily's letters - which told me all her sad feelings, which he thought I knew nothing of under his schooling of 'divide and govern' - I told Mr Forster much which I knew from her, and more which I had learnt and suspected myself, and all of which I hope he told Sir Edward.*

After reading the letters to his Father, which Edward desired me, Mr Forster and Sir Edward both left my Lodgings, and I asked Edward "How did your Father seem after hearing those letters?" His answer was "Much better: I wish he had seen them long ago."

Mr Forster seemed much affected whilst I was speaking to him about Emily, my vain endeavours at getting her home from Germany and other facts which had occurred at Knebworth; upon which he observed, "we must hope the suspicions about Madame d'Azzimart and Mrs Beaumont (the same person) were not true." [Forster must know the truth, but wishes for Miss Greene not to believe it. A interesting position for the future biographer of Charles Dickens.]

I, at the same time, told him that my great interest in the family was now buried in my dear Emily's grave. Much as I love Edward, I knew he would be quite separated from me and so entirely influenced by his father that I must give him up.

* * * * *

During the time before the funeral all remained as usual; the faithful Sophy remained at her post packing up the clothes which were left. One day she came to me and, in the most delicate manner, hinted that there were some handsome pocket handkerchiefs and should she pack them up? I desired her to do so.

During this time Edward remained mostly with me and we had many conversations together, and I told him I had his sister's private journal which she had given me to keep and a manuscript kind of novel that she was writing - one of the characters in which was Madame d'Azzimart. Both these manuscripts, directly Sir Edward heard of, he determined to get possession of from me and I, in the state of affliction I was in, did not much care for anything and so far yielded as to consent to the Journals being burnt, which was done one morning that he and Edward came to Kensington to me.

He also got the novel, promising to return it - which he did not, saying "it was better destroyed as it did no credit to the writer." He also wished to get possession of the letters which I read to him, and others which he had not seen, but I steadily refused. Upon his seeing me in the morning he generously offered to pay for it which I refused, I hope, with contempt.

* * * * *

The last time I saw Sir Edward was soon after his return from Knebworth when he told me there was no doubt but that Lady Lytton had gone into her child's room that night and consequently, as he said, was the cause of her death.

We parted good friends, but I determined that I would give up all intercourse or writing to him, and once more went down to see Edward before I went to Ireland. Poor fellow, he seemed as affectionate and frank as ever and we agreed to write to each other, as I was going to Ireland to my friends.

I did receive several letters from him, one written whilst he was ill and in wretched low spirits; another gave an account of his mother's having made an attempt to see him at Harrow, and saying he had steadily refused seeing her, and that the whole was a most disgraceful scene.

After that I did not hear from him again - but found out that he was at Bonn in Germany; and upon a friend of mine going there to enquire for him, heard he had been there for some time, was in bad health, and subject to the most frightful depression of spirits; but that he had left, and was in England, at Stowe in Gloucestershire, with a Clergyman of the name of Dean[e].....so that my dear boy was within twenty miles of Cheltenham, where I was for some months, and I never knew it.

Upon enquiring, I learned that he was gone to America as Attaché to his Uncle, Sir Henry Bulwer - and at the end of some months Mr Forster forwarded me a letter from him to myself from Washington, begging of me to write to him, which I did, but have never had any answer, and so end these Memoirs up to July 20th, 1851.

M. L. GREENE

Part Six

~ Conclusion ~

Frontispiece of Charles Dickens' ***Dombey and Son****, published over 18 months to April 1848, about a father who neglects his elder daughter in favour of his son*

CHAPTER 34

~ *Typhus* ~

The death of the teenager May Egerton - from the novel *Very Successful* by Rosina Bulwer Lytton, 1856:

"You are cruel to mourn," said she faintly, trying to look round on them all, but finally resting her eyes, with their fast fading light, on her grandfather's pale, heart-stricken face; "very cruel, when I am so happy."

"My child! my darling!" faltered the old man, "I mourn that I am such a loiterer. I should have gone before."

"Does not God know best? So you have always taught me," said she, pressing his hand, and then, after a pause, and another effort, she said — "And Linda, dear Linda! and my little Charley,—they will comfort you, grandpapa, till we all meet again, where there is no more parting, no more tears. And Aunt Charity, ask her to forgive me for all I have ever done to displease her."

The dying girl then held out her hand to him—and, placing it within the hand of Mary Penrhyn, "God bless you both!" murmured she; "and as soon as I am gone, dearest Mrs Penrhyn, there is a packet you will find in my desk; read it, and—and", but here a slight spasm stopped her speech. When it had passed she once more opened her languid eyes, and said, "God bless you all!" These were her last words, and those deep, loving eyes, which had never opened but to bless or to be blessed, now closed for ever! A piercing shriek escaped from Linda.

"May! May! come back!" cried she, passionately or rather, convulsively, clasping her sister's lifeless form; "come back, for I cannot bear it!"

"Linda!" said the young clergyman—as the tears streamed down his own cheeks—forcibly drawing her away, "do you know that you are blasphemously contending with God? The burdens He imposes we must bear; the blows He deals we must not resist. Kneel down and pray with me, that He may fill up this great void with mercy, even His mercy, which is peace and hope. The

peace which none can trouble, is now hers; let the hope that we may be worthy to rejoin her, be ours."

"God bless you, my darling," said the bereft old man, imprinting a last kiss on the pale beauty of that now rigid face; "it cannot be long, at all events, before we meet again." And he took poor Charley up in his arms, who was not crying, only staring and cold, and looking exceedingly frightened; and as they left the room, the child clasped his grandfather silently round the neck, and his young golden hair mingled caressingly with the silver locks of the other, as he whispered —

"But will May never come back then?"

* * * * *

Typhus.

No.	When and where died	Name and surname	Sex	Age	Occupation	Cause of death	Signature, description and residence of informant	When registered	Signature of registrar
279	Twentyninth April 1848 20 Pelham Terrace Brompton	Emily Elizabeth Bulwer Lytton	Female	19 years	Daughter of Sir Edward George Earle Bulwer Lytton Baronet	Typhus Fever a few days Certified	Charlotte Bruce Present at the death 2 Kings Place St. Johns Fulham	Fourth May 1848	James Stone Registrar

That's what it says on the death certificate. ***Cause of death: Typhus Fever.***

Let's Google it. All the best medical advice is on the internet nowadays. The word ***comes from the Greek typhos meaning smoky or hazy, describing the state of mind of those affected with typhus*** [*Wikipedia*].

Smoky or hazy. I say that extends to the diagnosis.

Like Wikipedia I am no doctor, but the distinguishing features of typhus seem to me to be similar to a number of other conditions. Typhus displays similar symptoms to influenza - with the addition of a body rash, sensitivity to light, evolving into delirium, coma and death through inflamation of meninges, the membranes that protect the brain and the central nervous system - similar to meningitis and encephalitis. So meninfluenza? Certainly not a clear-cut condition outside of the petri dish.

All these diseases kill. Influenza certainly kills - it finishes off Benjamin Disraeli's father Isaac in January of 1848. But Isaac is 81. Typhus has a more deadly reputation, particularly in the young, than influenza.

So - as you've already heard me suspect - is a diagnosis of 'Typhus' simply a serious-sounding catch-all for expensive doctors whose clients' children die unexpectedly on their watch?

* * * * *

The defining element of typhus is the Rickettsia bacteria, which tends to be passed on by lice. It is the lice connection that has helped spin aspersions on the Brompton boarding house in the Emily legend. "Abandoned by her father in a common boarding house in London she dies of an infection caused by bedbugs."

But Brompton is not the Old Kent Road. In Benjamin Disraeli's letters, I read that in March 1848 the exiled French Prime Minister François Guizot (1787-1874) has just moved into No. 21 Pelham Terrace. The French Prime Minister, for goodness sake, is living next door. This is a respectable part of town.

If it is the Rickettsia bacteria, it strikes me as being more likely to have been passed on by a leech, in blood-letting. Was Emily being bled? One hates to think so, but it is likely. Rosina accuses Marshall Hall - Edward choice of doctor - of bleeding Emily, despite Hall's reputation for denouncing the practice early in his career. It could be Hall - but it could also any one of the many other doctors who attend Emily's sickbed, all offering their own solutions.

* * * * *

The 19th Century history of typhus, as spelt out in *Wikipedia,* does give some credence to the diagnosis. It singles out epidemics ***in Ireland between 1816 and 1819***, which is when, you'll recall, Miss Greene come close to death with an illness given the name of 'Typhus Fever'; and also ***during the Great Irish Famine between 1846 and 1849. The Irish typhus spread to England, where it was sometimes called 'Irish fever' and was noted for its virulence. It killed people of all social classes, as lice were endemic and inescapable, but it hit particularly hard in the lower or 'unwashed' social strata.*** [Note Wikipedia's use of Edward Bulwer Lytton's expression - ***the great unwashed*** - from *The Last Days of Pompeii* (1833)]

So, it's the 'Irish fever' that gets her... Let's blame the Irish. There are certainly a number of them involved in this drama.

No. We will come on to blame. Blame is everyone else's game.

Bigger news in London, in 1848, is cholera. In London in 1848 Emily is more likely to have contracted cholera, which claims 14,137 lives in the worst outbreak of the city's history. But Emily's symptoms are not that of cholera.

But then neither, to me, do they sound much like typhus - except for the late-stage delirium.

It confuses me that nobody else in this drama dies of typhus. In my favourite film *Letter From An Unknown Woman* Joan Fontaine's boy gets typhus from a railway carriage, then she gets it too (sorry if I am spoiling it for you, you should have seen it) - it's rampant.

In reality, typhus is not an airborne bacteria - it likes to travel by lice.

But still, No. 29 Pelham Terrace is an intimate family environment. Emily and Natalie are sleeping together; Emily and Robert [from now on I shall call Teddy 'Robert', the middle name he adopts in adulthood, and return to calling his father 'Edward'] are sharing a sick room; Emily, until the end, is receiving regular visitors and being attended by Miss Greene, Madame de Ritter and various servants. Presumably when Robert is sick - and sharing a room with her - he has the same bug as his sister? How come nobody else gets typhus?

* * * * *

Is an autopsy in 1848 going to rigorously pursue the bacteria responsible? Is the coroner getting out a culture dish and a microscope? Emily is not murdered. At least not knowingly. I may be naive, but I imagine the word of an eminent doctor like Marshall Hall is enough for the Kensington coroner to comfortably sign the form and be home in time for Tea.

We will never know - unless some pathological study of her remains in the Knebworth Park Mausoleum solves the mystery one day. But, for all my fascination, I am inclined not to go chipping away at her bones. The Rickettsia bacteria may or may not have been attacking Emily's meninges - but of one thing I am 100% certain, typhus is not the reason Emily Bulwer Lytton died.

* * * * *

Her parents don't think so either. The day before Rosina bribes her way into the upper room at 29 Pelham Terrace, Emily's condition is improving...

Edward believes the shock of Emily being confronted by her mother is what causes her death. Rosina insists she does not enter Emily's room. She believes Edward is responsible for murdering - a word she does not hesitate to use - their daughter through years of neglect, and by putting her in the hands of his pet quack doctors.

Courtesy of Muncaster Castle

Miss Greene takes a pinch of all these reasons, and adds to the mix a physical poison, laudanum, which Emily takes for tooth-ache in Germany. This drug, she believes, and the bad influence of her foreign guardians, poisons Emily's mind.

UNDER HER MAJESTY'S ROYAL LETTERS PATENT.

The best and safest Medicine for Ladies. An eminent Physician says, "Ladies who take No. 1, from 14 to 20, and No. 2, from 20 to 50 years of age, pass through life comparatively free from complaint, and never suffer from the painful diseases of advanced life." Consumption is prevented—Chlorosis—General Weakness, accompanied by weariness and sinking at the pit of the stomach—Feverishness—Indigestion—Constipation—Loss of appetite—Flatulence—Heartburn—Giddiness—Palpitation—Pains in the Head, Stomach, Loins, and all Hysterical Affections are completely removed by their peculiar effects.

Sold by all the London Wholesale Houses: Barclay, Edwards, Sutton, Sanger, Dietrichsen, Prout, at Locock's Female Pill Warehouse, 16, King Street, Covent Garden, and all established Patent Medicine Vendors throughout the kingdom. N.B "Locock's Female Pills" is engraved on the Government Stamp outside each Box.

Quacks and potions are everywhere - this 1850 newspaper advert implies an association with the Queen's doctor - not likely, but even Sir Charles Locock was dishing out poisonous fungus to the Queen after childbirth.

Reverend Green accuses Professor Plum Brandy in the Sick Room with the Laudanum.

Could Emily have been poisoned by the drugs she was taking? At least half a dozen doctors attend Emily in her final months. Each has the previous doctor's prescription to blame, and their own miracle cure to claim. Certainly a doctor's bag in the 1840s rattles with vials of psychotic narcotics and therapeutic poisons long since abandoned by the medical profession.

Queen Victoria's gynecologist [then politely called her 'First Physician Accoucheur'] Sir Charles Lo-

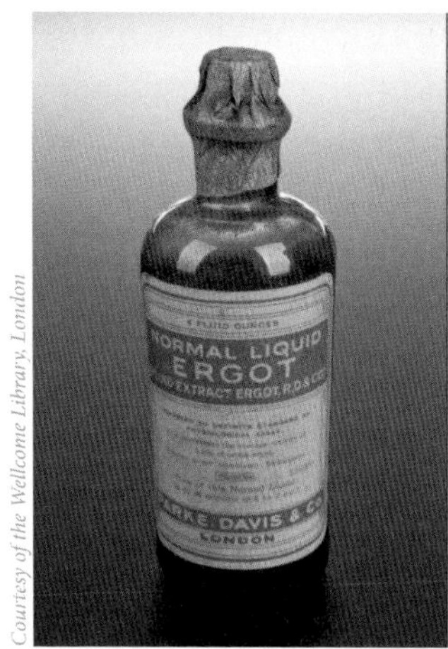

Courtesy of the Wellcome Library, London

cock - whose nephew Dr Cope attends Emily in her final weeks - is known to have prescribed ergot fungus for postpartum and period bleeding. Nowadays we are warned that ***the neurotropic activities of the ergot alkaloids may also cause hallucinations and attendant irrational behaviour, convulsions, and even death*** [Wikipedia]. If laudanum explains Emily's irrational behaviour in Cannstatt, does ergot explain her fevered delusions in Brompton?

In the early days of researching this story I toyed with the idea that Rosina - who we can be sure travels with a bag of potions - might have dosed Emily with laudanum that final night, with every good intention, but fatal consequences. But laudanum, administered, is only a poison over time. And in the 1840s it is ubiquitous, and very likely on her sick room table anyway.

Courtesy of Muncaster Castle

Much more likely, is that Emily quaffed the whole bottle herself.

* * * * *

The first of many things to haunt me about my great-great-great aunt's deathbed is that all of her family and loved ones are near, but none of them are there. All of the people in her life are in the vicinity of Brompton, but none of them are actually living at No. 29 Pelham Terrace with her. At the time she is most sick, she is alone in a boarding house with a landlady and a hired nurse.

Loved ones, loved ones, everywhere, and none to stop and think.

One of the more shocking accusations levelled against Edward is that he does not want family servants at Emily's bedside whilst she is delirious, and therefore could divulge details of his personal indiscretions. Whilst Edward's general wish to shield his private life is certainly a root of Emily's problems, I cannot believe that the Knebworth housekeeper Sophy Tate - indeed all of Edward's servants - don't already know every intimate detail there is to know about him. For goodness sake, Sophy Tate's been emptying his potty since he was a child.

If this is the reason Emily is surrounded by strangers, Edward pays for it dearly. It is the landlady and the nurse - who are not unlikely themselves to know gossip of this celebrity couple - who let Rosina in. Why wouldn't they believe the mother over the father? The nurse - a Mrs Bruce - a year and a half later, still believes she picked the right side.

* * * * *

Most Honoured Lady [December 15th, 1849],***—I cannot find words to express my grateful thanks for your Ladyship's benevolence. Bad and base a man as Sir Edward is, people are not aware of all his villainy to you. Many highly respectable families have heard much from me, amiable lady.***

Mr Rouse made out that he was one of the best of men and fathers, and that he had a medical man in the house all the time your angel daughter was ill of a night; but I soon contradicted that falsehood, and was believed before Mr Rouse.

I informed Sir Edward that she spoke of you in the most dutiful manner, saying, "Oh, my mamma! I reverence my DEAR mamma." He cannot deny it. I hope those words will be a comfort to your Ladyship, knowing that you have an angel to watch over you, who, I am convinced, really loved you, but dared not make it public. Charlotte Bruce.

* * * * *

This note reads as though Mrs Bruce is still for hire, and that Rosina is paying for this letter as therapy as well as evidence. But maybe I am being unfair. I just cannot help but hear different words and emphasis to what, supposedly, the delirious Emily cries out. ***"Oh, my mamma! I reverence my DEAR mamma."*** If Mrs Bruce is telling the truth and Emily genuinely groaned a sentence like this, I argue the verb she heard is much more likely to have been 'resemble'. ***"Oh, my mamma! I resemble my DEAR mamma."***

All the characters in this tragedy bring their own prejudices to Emily's bedside. Gender politics plays a big part, with women tending to side with Rosina - all the madames, Madame de Weling, Madame de Ritter, etc., all suspect Rosina is a wronged wife, a maligned mother; meanwhile the d'evil gentlemen sympathise with the b'devilled husband - the D'Eyncourts, Disraeli, Dickens...

Even the mignon madamoiselle at Edward's side, Marion Waller - the one who says she ***would have gone thro fire & water for him*** - questions his actions regarding Emily. Marion writes to Robert in the 1870s, ***often & often have I wondered at your father's giving you all his love, and keeping so little for his other child, whom I thought so deserving of her share of it, & even of his pride.***

With your father's consent I read some of her letters to him, and never before or since have I read letters so full of genius and loving tenderness; - they touched me so much that I ventured to say something, but was immediately silenced.

When she fell ill, I was so anxious about her, that I have waited hours in the street to hear the sooner how she was.

* * * * *

The image of Edward's mistress, Marion, waiting out in the street, like some mysterious Woman in White, for me, completes the picture of mad melodrama at Pelham Terrace that April in 1848. Chartist revolutionaries marching in the West End. Austrian aristocrats bumping suitcases down the stairs in the middle of the night. A frantic mother banging on the door looking for her missing teenage son. A parade of nervous society doctors humphing at each other and popping to the corner store to buy brandy and port wine. A nervous flushed Irish spinster and a gangly pale Harrow schoolboy shuffling backwards and forwards between No. 20 and No. 29 (with the

French Prime Minister mourning the collapse of his country at No. 21). The indignant neighbouring playwright's daughter marching about defending her friend - the wretched mother, who paces the stairs outside the sickroom, hysterical, cursing the father...

It is a farce. If you were Emily wouldn't you just want to bring the curtain down?

* * * * *

Everybody is there, but nobody is there. Nobody sees Emily's death in its entirety or knows the full truth. Emily takes that with her to her mausoleum.

But the whole cast - including a number of bit players and understudies - all have lines before the Act is over. Emily's death - like Ophelia's in Act 4 of *Hamlet* - is narrated.

Front of stage. Queen Gertrude. Lady Bulwer Lytton to Marshall Hall (whom, we should remember, is her own physician back in the 1820s) [July 17th, 1848] ***Sir,— Now that I am able to hold a pen, painful as it is to me to have any sort of communication with you, yet, as I understand that Sir Edward Bulwer Lytton (that incarnate lie of the nineteenth century) dares to give out that my poor angel child died of 'a natural decay'.***

You, as his accomplice in the last act of this at once awful and disgraceful tragedy, had better warn him to drop this coldblooded falsehood, or I have friends and WITNESSES who are determined to make the TRUTH public, which is, that the primary cause of my poor <u>murdered</u> child's illness was the life of hard labour she led to promote her father's ill-gotten and quacky literary reputation as a German scholar (<u>he not knowing one word of that language</u>), coupled with the terrific seclusion and privations of every sort that she endured. Witness her dying without the <u>commonest</u> necessaries of a sickroom about her, as <u>even</u> the wine poured down her throat (alas! too late) had to be sent for from a common public-house!

The actual cause of her death was your gross ignorance, only to be equalled by the coarse and inhuman brutality of your manner. I shall ever look upon you and proclaim you as her murderer, for when this poor young victim of the parsimony and neglect of a profligate father, and the ignorance of a medical charlatan, was rapidly sinking under TYPHUS, did you not starve and bleed

her as if for nervous fever, and so ensure and hasten her death?

Remember, both you and your employer, that there are too many witnesses to all this for your, or his, falsehoods on the subject to avail. God forgive you both, but I never can. Rosina Bulwer Lytton.

I am aware that he tries to excuse the miserable hole in which she died by giving out that she was on a visit to a German baroness. But was it right to let this poor young girl, without even a maid of her own, traipse about with German baronesses who lived in lodgings at thirty shillings a week, and where a commercial clerk was pacing up and down all night in the garret overhead?

* * * * *

Courtesy of the Wellcome Library, London

Marshall Hall

Rosina elaborates on Hall [quoted in *Life of Rosina, Lady Lytton* by Louisa Devey], ***This inhuman creature pretended that my child's life was at stake if I did not leave the house. In vain I swore she should never know I was there, nor did she. He said his fame as a physician was at stake. 'Which,' said I, 'is of the most import, your fame as a physician or my feelings as a mother?'***

'Oh, my fame as a doctor, to be sure,' said he, with a horse-laugh.

And this indeed is what survives. Hall has a different sort of wife to ensure his legacy. His widow eulogises him in her *Memoirs of Marshall Hall* (1861), even including a tribute from Edward, ***I felt sympathy with Dr Marshall Hall from the first, in the conviction of his earnestness and sincerity... a warm and humane heart, interesting itself immediately in pain and suffering, and unaffectedly anxious to give relief...***[etc.]. No mention of Emily in that book.

But in calling Hall - aged 58 in 1848 - to Emily's bedside, Edward is not skimping on experience or professional eminence. *The Dictionary of National Biography, 1885-1900, Volume 24*, tells us Hall was ***an expert on the nervous system and nervous diseases, denounced the process of blood-letting, open railway carriages*** and the ***cruel flogging of soldiers. The sewage question and slavery in the United States were among the subjects on which he actively exerted himself.*** Hall would be pleased that in the 21st Century all of these inhuman practices are now consigned to history - except, of course, open railway carriages. But on a cramped, spluttering, nose-wiping February morning, who isn't with him on that one?

* * * * *

It is not just Marshall Hall, but all the doctors who are held up for abuse by Rosina. The fact that Emily's other primary doctor, Dr Rouse, is found dead within a year, poisoned by prussic acid - apparently a suicide - is snapped up by Rosina as the result either of the doctor's guilt or divine providence.

Although not as high-profile a doctor as Hall, Robert Rouse is no quack. I have not found his birthdate, but the notices of his death on Friday 25th January 1850 say that the ***eminent surgeon*** had been ***in practice nearly 30 years.*** He starts as a student of the 'Windmill School' founded by the Scottish anatomist William Hunter (1718-1783) in Great Windmill Street (on the current site of the Lyric Theatre) where ***a more attentive pupil than Mr Rouse was not to be found.*** This quote is from ***The Monthly Gazette of Health*** in 1822 and relates to a court case of unpaid fees by an amputee who had ***shattered his left hand*** with an exploding gun shooting ***small birds*** in his garden in Welham Green.

I mention this almost-only-surviving reference to Dr Rouse due to the extraordinary parallel to the circumstances of his own - frankly, suspicious - suicide, which I present for you on the next page in its original newspaper report.

I find this relevant to Emily less in what it says about Dr Rouse, but more in what it says about the ease of suicide with medicinal drugs like prussic acid and laudanum. Prussic acid - which has already seen off Letitia Landon - like laudanum, is widely used and respected for medicinal purposes at this time. Like laudanum and ergot, it could very well be on Emily's bedside table.

MELANCHOLY SUICIDE.—Since Friday last a great sensation has prevailed in Fulham and the surrounding neighbourhood, in consequence of Mr. Robert Rouse, of Walham green, surgeon, who had been in practice nearly 30 years, having destroyed himself by swallowing prussic acid. The deceased had two assistants, Mr. Roland, a visiting assistant, and Mr. Spike, a dispensing assistant. This latter gentleman was in the habit of rising early, and going into the garden, at the rear of the house, to shoot small birds. On Friday morning between eight and nine o'clock Mr. Spike was in the act of reloading his gun whilst at full cock when it went off, and the ramrod entered the wrist of the left arm, passing upwards, and obtruding above the elbow-joint. Mr. Roland succeeded by the application of great force in extracting the ramrod, and as Mr. Rouse had not yet made his appearance, went up to his bedroom to call him, that he might have his opinion as to what further should be done. Mr. Roland having knocked several times and received no answer, became alarmed, and burst the door open, when he discovered Mr. Rouse lying in bed to all appearance dead. On a small table, within the reach of the deceased, was a two ounce bottle, which had recently contained about that quantity of prussic acid (Scheele's strength), and the whole of this powerful poison had evidently been drank by the deceased, who had died ere he could relay his head upon the pillow. The deceased's body was perfectly cold, and life had apparently ceased to exist some hours. No papers were found elucidating the cause of the melancholy act, and deceased had gone to bed at 12 o'clock on the previous night in an apparently comfortable state. Of late he had suffered severely from illness, and was constantly saying he must come to the workhouse. During the prevalence of the cholera the deceased exerted himself very much, and on its subsidence wrote a very intelligent report on the sanitary state of Fulham parish. On Saturday evening a highly respectable jury were empanelled before Mr. M. Wakley, at the George Inn, Walham-green, to inquire into the circumstances, and a verdict of Temporary Insanity was returned.

Report of Robert Rouse's suicide

I am interested to read [in 1908's ***A Practical Treatise On Materia Medica And Therapeutics*** by Robert Bartholow (what were you doing this morning?)] of trials by Dr Kenneth McLeod of the Durham Lunatic Asylum detailed in the *Medical Times Gazette* of 1863, ***To allay cerebral irritation and excitement, prussic acid has been employed with benefit. In forty cases of mental disorder, there was 'slight or temporary amelioration' in ten; a 'more decided and permanent effect', the disease being still stationary or progressive, in nineteen; and in eight cases, six of acute mania, and two of acute melancholia, 'the drug has been a factor, and a very main one, in rapid restoration to reason'. In the treatment of these cases, McLeod used from two to five minims of Scheele's dilute acid...*** [the Swedish pharmacist Carl Wilhelm Scheele (1742–1786) discovers a number of acids including hydrogen cyanide (prussic acid) and arsenic. Arsenic becomes a problem in wallpaper, wax candes and even children's toys with the popular use of paint or dye pigmented with 'Scheele's Green'.]

McLeod's trials are fifteen years after Rouse's death, and still prussic acid is considered a miracle drug. We should not underestimate the innocence of medicine with regard to mania and melancholia in the times Emily is having her crisis.

* * * * *

The very number of different doctors attending Emily's bedside not only increases the likelihood of a varied and potent cocktail of drugs being within her reach, it also makes it easy for the doctors to point the blame - after typhus - at each other. The doctor called by Rosina on the day she is at Pelham Terrace, Alexander Tweedie (1794-1884) of 30 Montague Place, for 38 years physician to the London Fever Hospital, is certainly a respectable choice, but as he writes [May 18th, 1848], ***at the time he saw her daughter medical aid could not possibly be of the slightest service in averting the fatal issue of the malady.*** And, by the way, ***not having received the usual fee for consultation with Dr Hall and Mr Rouse, he begs to name the most moderate sum for consultation—two guineas.***

Rosina can't afford two guineas. She has to turn again to her friend Katherine Planché (the local playwright's daughter whom Miss Greene has mentioned as Rosina's emissary on the fatal day that Rosina is at No. 29 Pelham Terrace). [***Thursday Evening, Seven o'clock, May 18th, 1848***] ***My Poor Little Victim of a Kate... my rudder, chart, and anchor; and who else to turn to in all my difficulties I know not. Here is my present one ...all I possess in the world till July is £1 8s...*** [she presents the dilemma of the bill] ***...believe that had our positions been reversed (which God forbid!), I would with heart, soul, head, and hands do as much for you. I fear you will hardly be able to make this out, but the night is coming on; for that matter, it is in my heart and eyes all day long. God bless you. Ever your grateful and affectionate, Rosina Bulwer Lytton.***

Katherine Planché (1823-1901) - the same age as Edward's companion, Marion - is a companion of Rosina's in the more socially acceptible fashion of such relationships that we have witnessed between Miss Greene and Rosina, Clara D'Eyncourt and Emily, etc. She is the elder of two daughters of the recently widowed, prolific playwright and Brompton-resident, James Robinson Planché (1796-1880), praised at the end of the 19th Century, Wikipedia records, for having ***raised theatrical extravaganza and burlesque to the dignity of a fine art.***

James Robinson Planché

Katherine [Lousia Devey tells us in *Life of Rosina, Lady Lytton*] ***first met Lady Bulwer in July, 1847, at Ashburnham House, Chelsea, at a garden party given by Mrs Leicester Stanhope, afterwards Countess of Harrington*** [Leicester Stanhope (1784–1862) is a Dublin born soldier - in these Doyle circles Rosina retains connections - his wife Elizabeth (1811-1898) is an Irish Green-without-an-e, born in Jamaica]. Katherine is the explanation as to how Rosina discovers where Emily is, and the dangerous condition she is in. A mystery that will cause Edward to cast unhappy aspersions elsewhere.

In the early part of the following year Lady Bulwer invited her [Katherine] ***to East Ham, where she was then residing, when she had ample opportunities for learning the true story of her separation from her husband, and also from her children by his orders. Lady Lytton appears to have formed a strong attachment to this lady, whose sympathy was assured, and to have enlisted her services for obtaining any information respecting her daughter, whose place of residence ever had been carefully concealed from the mother.***

Enquiries among the friends of Sir Edward who were also her own, had no satisfactory result, and she had despaired of success, when an accident procured all the information required; but this had better be explained in her own words, which are quoted as follows:—

* * * * *

[Louisa Devey continues, quoting Katherine Planché] ***Singularly enough, one evening in the month of April, 1848, a friend of my father's came to see us, and said to me immediately on entering the room,***

"Do you know that the young lady you are in search of is living close by here?"

He then explained that while sitting in the shop of a chemist in the Fulham Road, he was shown a prescription, and told that the daughter of Bulwer Lytton was lying dangerously ill at a small lodging house in Pelham Terrace, Pelham Crescent, Brompton, and that Dr Rouse, of Fulham, whom I knew, was attending her. Sad as such news was, I hastened next morning to Pelham Terrace, and seeing a shop-boy knock at a door, I waited till he had been answered, and then hazarded the enquiry,

"How is Miss Lytton to-day?", when immediately came the reply,

"A little better, we think."

Overjoyed at my success, I flew home to the Lodge, Michael's Grove [closed up now by shop fronts a few blocks up the Brompton Road towards Harrods just above Egerton Terrace], *to tell my Father, and to send the information to Lady Bulwer Lytton - but upon further consideration I determined to go myself to East Ham, thinking it better than writing, and never shall I forget the mixed pain and pleasure of my visit.*

It was soon arranged that Lady Lytton should come with her old faithful servant Byrne (who had been Miss Lytton's nurse) to Town, and see if she could possibly gain access to and help to nurse her daughter, under conditions so unsuited to her position and age.

I had soon observed from the style of house that it was let out in separate rooms and apartments, to people in a humble sphere of life, and was therefore most anxious that Lady Lytton should first come to us; but she overruled my objections, and early next morning arrived at Pelham Terrace, where she engaged a room at the top of the same house for herself and Byrne, and then sent me a letter requesting me to come to her after dark. I did so, taking my own maid with me, and on ascending the wretched narrow staircase I passed the second-floor back room, which I then heard was Miss Lytton's, and was soon received by Byrne and the dear and basely wronged wife and Mother.

"She is insensible, Kate," cried Lady Lytton on seeing me, "and I am to see her in half an hour; I have bribed the nurse and landlady." Then tears and sobs broke forth from the overcharged heart, and Byrne had enough to do to calm her preparatory to the interview.

* * * * *

When the time came, I followed Lady Lytton downstairs with Byrne to the door of the bedroom, which was open, impressing on her the importance of keeping very quiet. I had no need, however, to do so: the pitiful sight of this young girl without a relative near her, lying in a room which was almost entirely taken up by the bedstead, which stood nearly filling up the space between the door and the window, was so startling, that she remained for a time speechless, as, almost transfixed, she gazed on the loved form from which she had been so long separated; lying insensible, her features changed by fever, and hardly to be recognised in the darkened room, where only the sheen from her golden hair as it reflected the light of the single candle guided the eye to the pillow and the sufferer.

It was thus, while Lady Lytton stood like a statue just inside the room, that a knock was heard at the door, and lest she should be discovered, Byrne and I hurried her upstairs. The visitors were a Miss Greene (a nursery governess of Lady Lytton's) and the present Earl of Lytton, a youth about sixteen years of age, from Harrow. They came to enquire about the patient, as they were not in the house.

My dear friend had thrown herself on her knees on reaching the top room, and buried her face in the pillow of the wretched bed in which she was to pass the night. No sobs now, only convulsive throbbings of her whole frame, greatly alarming us who were watching her; but after a time she became quiet, and I then took my leave, going home with my servant, and promising to be there early in the morning.

* * * * *

By ten o'clock I was there again, and found everything had been discovered! Dr Rouse and Dr Marshall Hall, the other medical man (both of them are now dead—Dr Rouse soon after committed suicide) were commanded by Sir Edward Lytton to get Lady Lytton out of the house on the plea that her presence had aggravated the disorder (typhoid fever) which we afterwards discovered by our own medical attendant was advancing to its last stage.

Miss Lytton had been delirious, and had spoken of her Mother, who had sat on the stairs outside of the door all night, sending to the room cooling beverages, and any things she had with her which might be of service for her daughter; for Miss Lytton's wardrobe was so scanty that she actually died in a night-dress lent her by the kind nurse, and which was afterwards in my possession.

Dr Rouse knowing me, sent for me on my arrival in Pelham Terrace, and he and Dr Marshall Hall tried to intimidate me into making a promise to them that I would take Lady Lytton away. I told them I should do what Lady

Lytton wished, that she had paid for her room for a week, and no one could turn her out but the landlady.

They declared that Miss Lytton's life was endangered by the knowledge of her mother's presence! a most ridiculous assertion, as the poor girl knew no one, being delirious when not wholly unconscious.

* * * * *

Our interview ended by my telling them I would hear what Lady Lytton herself said. Dr Rouse followed me upstairs immediately, and then Lady Lytton threw herself on her knees to him, and implored him to let her stay to the end. I had in a life, then quite young, seen many stage representations of mental agony, but here was the real anguish, and every phase of it is burnt into my memory.

Dr Rouse himself would have given way, I saw, but he dared not; all he could do was to offer his carriage to take us away. He retired, and then I pointed out to the poor Mother the risk she ran of misrepresentation that she had caused the death of her daughter through excitement, and further attempted to show that she would gain nothing by remaining; but in this I was wrong, and I have since deeply regretted it: she should have stayed, and I with her.

However I prevailed, on assuring her that I would go to Dr Rouse and obtain his promise to send to my father's house, or to come after every visit to his patient, that we might have the latest intelligence of her condition.

* * * * *

I must now mention that the carriages of the two doctors were being driven up and down the little street while this conference was going on; and we had ascertained that Miss Greene lodged only two or three doors further, where the doctors were then in consultation while I was persuading Lady Lytton to return home with me.

So I followed to the house, and was admitted by Miss Greene, who with two men completely blocked the small passage.

"Are the doctors here who attend Miss Lytton?" I said.

They hurriedly answered, "Yes", and made way for me to pass.

I entered the first room on the ground floor, and there sat Sir Edward Bulwer Lytton, Dr Marshall Hall, and Dr Rouse—the latter looking most wretched. I had had the questionable advantage of meeting Sir Edward Lytton in many distinguished houses, the owners of which were good enough to invite me, and of course I knew him; but I addressed myself to the medical men, and told them that Lady Lytton had consented to go with me to my father Mr Planché's house, but that I came to hold Dr Rouse to his promise.

Some remark, on my saying this, fell from this tender husband and father, the great novelist, dramatist, and poet; and I answered it. He kept his seat while I stood, but my reply intimated to him that I knew him, and it is almost amusing to recollect that he sent me an apology for not having risen: 'he was so distressed,'—for I never saw any one less so; he was very deaf, and I regret to say, think he did not hear what I said, for I had no feeling for him but of intense disgust, and he saw it.

I returned trembling with anxiety for my task before me—the removal of this deeply injured innocent woman, wife, mother.

But I need not have doubted her power over herself (of which I saw much more in after days). God alone knows the agony of that Mother's heart as she walked quietly past the closed door of the room where her poor dying girl was so soon to breathe her last.

* * * * *

At ten o'clock I was obliged to accompany my father to a soiree at Mrs Milner Gibson's [Susannah Arethusa Milner-Gibson (1814-1885) of Theberton House Suffolk - society hostess, who assists Dickens with East Anglian dialect for *David Copperfield* (1850)] ***(leaving dear Lady Lytton in my sister's care). I told them what had happened during the day. "It was not possible," people said; but it was not only possible, but true.***

Lady Lytton sent an eminent fever physician, Dr Tweedie, to see Miss Lytton. His first words were, "Too late, too late." He asked for port wine; there was none in the house, and some was procured from a tavern at the end of the street.

On the following evening, Saturday, the 29th of April, 1848, this poor young lady died; Dr Rouse himself coming to announce to me the sad intelligence. The housekeeper from Knebworth was sent up to take possession of the body, which was conveyed to Knebworth and buried there.

In the papers appeared the following :— 'At Knebworth' (mark the veracity of our Colonial Secretary), 'Emily Elizabeth, the only daughter of Sir Edward Bulwer Lytton',

EMILY ELIZABETH BULWER LYTTON.

It is with deep regret that we have to announce the death of this young lady, the only daughter of Sir Edward Bulwer Lytton, Bart., of Knebworth Park, Herts. The melancholy event occurred on Saturday, the 29th ult.

Miss Bulwer Lytton was, through her father, descended from the Bulwers of Norfolk, one of the oldest families in that county, the Robinsons of Gwersylt, and the Norreyses of Speke, as well as from Anne Tudor, sister of Sir Owen Tudor, grandfather of King Henry VII. Through her mother, Rosina Wheeler she deduced descent from the noble house of Massy.

The London Illustrated News' report of Emily's death

I had the satisfaction of putting in the Morning Post, ***and also*** The Britannia, ***a Sunday paper much read in those days, the correction of this mistake:- 'On Saturday, the 29th of April, at a lodging in Brompton, of Typhoid fever, Emily Elizabeth, the only daughter of Sir Edward and Lady Bulwer Lytton, age 20.'*** [Correcting one mistake and making another - Emily is 19 until June]

Sir Edward Bulwer Lytton sent my father a challenge! My father had many grand qualities, but a passage of arms was not at all to his taste (for he fainted at the sight of blood), so in reply he simply threatened to bind him over to keep the peace.

I have letters and papers to corroborate this account, and passed the greater part of my time during [the following] three years - until my marriage in 1851 [to William Curteis Whelan (1817-1869) of Heronden Hall, Tenterden, Kent] - ***in Lady Lytton's company. Seldom has it been the fate of any one to be so maligned and crushed as this woman; it was even said of Lady Lytton that she did not love her children—this I most emphatically deny. I have good reason to know how she loved her daughter, and, as to her son, she scarcely ever spoke of him to me without tears, in the early days of our acquaintance.***

Katherine Curteis Whelan. September 1883.

* * * * *

My dear D'Eyncourt [writes Edward, undated], ***The letter enclosed from Mr Planché relieves you from all further trouble - Tho' it but just comes within the pale of those excuses that are receivable, it does come within it.....And, taking into account the vulgar nature of the man, the influences to which he was subjected - his reference to his solicitor instead of a second - and the domestic character of the discussion - to which Publicity wd be painful - I feel that you have acted perfectly right in accepting it -- & I acquiesce in your opinion that I must rest satisfied.***

I fully appreciate the trouble you must have had in thus completing the matter.....which I think you have done with skill & judgement, more especially as you do not concur with me as to the quality of the offence. Again I must thank you cordially, & again I must say that I am deeply sorry if any ungracious return for your interference in a matter in itself so disagreeable should have been wrung from me in the torture of just resentment at Mr Planchés assault & subsequent implication.

The charge I committed to you is one which belongs truly to the rights of Friendship - And while it is of that nature that Friendship cannot refuse to undertake, it is the more irksome from the keen susceptibilities of a Principal, (as I have found by experience) – which it is seldom easy to content, without that positive encounter for which every brave man wounded in his honour instinctively yearns - & which it is the first duty of the second to avoid...

Hence with that charge must be coupled a generous forgiveness of the very excitement & irritability with which the unhappy Mediator has to contend.... And having first availed myself of the friendship – I now throw myself on the forgiveness. Yrs truly & affectly E.B.L.

* * * * *

It would have been natural in the order of things to have begun this chapter with the expressions of grief of Emily's closest relations, the two Edwards. But you had just heard from Miss Greene of the *most frightful scene of anguish on the part of poor Edward and his father* and I felt a respite from the raw misery was needed. ***She is dead. Dead. Emily, my child. Pity me, I am crushed down.*** Edward writes to John Forster.

It is an unimaginable emotion. Impossible to express.

Edward is a novelist, a romantic, a melancholic, a man we have seen burst into anger both on the page and in life. It should not be surprising that the D'Eyncourt family has to step in to prevent a duel with the father of Rosina's friend and envoy, Katherine Planché, for the gross outrages of her meddling, in particular leading Rosina to Emily's bedside.

But I do find it surprising. This is England. It is the Victorian Era. A time of trains and mills, not pistols at dawn.

But it's the first decade of the Victorian era. My great-great-great-grandfather is a child of the Napoleonic Wars, he shared a lover with Byron, and what is 'civilisation' when Paris and Vienna are in flames - as they are in April 1848?

But if this challenge had escalated into a duel, it would have been unusual. Duelling is not illegal. But murder is. There is uproar seven years before when the Earl of Cardigan (1797-1868) - who is to lead The Charge of The Light Brigade and give his name to a non-bullet-proof vest - is acquitted for shooting one of his former officers of the 11th Light Dragoons (by then renamed Hussars) Captain Harvey Tuckett, purely because the prosecutor gets the full name of the victim wrong. Outraged cries follow that there is one law for the aristocracy and another for everyone else.

The law is thus primed to take a dim view of a successful duel, so the practice has all but died out by 1845. The last recorded fatal duel in England is in 1852 - between two Frenchmen, so nobody minds too much about that.

* * * * *

It is telling that no one contacts the Baroness de Ritter about Emily's death. Not until it dawns that her evidence may be relevant - and so the first letter to reach Vienna is from Katherine Planché. [May 28th, 1848] ***Madam,— Though a perfect stranger, I venture to address you on the part of Lady Bulwer Lytton, whose personal and most intimate friend I have the honor to be. Having heard her repeatedly express a deep anxiety to learn any particulars connected with her much loved and unfortunate daughter, my wish to gratify so natural a desire has emboldened me to write to you, of whose kindness to Miss Lytton I have heard so much.***

I trust I am not the first person to acquaint you with the fatal termina-

tion of her illness, which ended in typhus fever on the 29th of April, two days after the arrival, at my instigation, of her Mother. Her Ladyship hired the room which you had vacated, and remained during the whole night of the 27th on the staircase, listening to poor Emily's continued exclamations about "My Mother", that Mother having given her word of honour to the medical man, Mr Rouse, that nothing should tempt her into her child's room - as he represented that any sudden emotion would endanger her life; at the same time assuring her Mother that there was no danger to be apprehended at that moment, and that the poor young victim's illness was merely an attack of hysteria.

The agony that Lady Lytton suffered during that night, hearing her child's voice for the first time in ten years, in supplication and pain, can easily be understood, Madam, by you, who are a Mother, and the unparalleled control she had over her feelings can only be believed by those who witnessed it... I spare you some of what you have already heard Katherine describe.

...On Sir Edward's first discovery of Lady Lytton's arrival, he suspected that she had been summoned by you to her daughter, which suspicion leads me to hope that you have sympathised with, and pitied, the dear girl's motherless position, and endeavoured to alleviate it as much as possible. I need scarcely say that any little circumstance connected with her beloved child will be vitally interesting to my dear friend, and she is, I know, most grateful to you and your daughter for the affection and kindness you manifested to poor Emily during her life.

Poor child! by this most untimely end she is spared the cruel knowledge of all her Mother has suffered through ten long years of separation from her children.

I must entreat you to pardon my intrusion upon you, Madam, and that you will kindly and charitably throw any light in your power upon the early portion of the poor girl's illness. I shall most anxiously look for an answer from you, and with the assurance of my respect, I have the honor to be, Madam, your obedient servant, Katherine Frances Planché.

* * * * *

The Baroness answers, as Louis Devey tells it in *Life of Rosina, Lady Lytton,*

[From the French] *Madam, yesterday I received your letter of May 29, which contains the first direct news of the death of poor Emily Lytton - my feelings are indescribable, because, I assure you, I loved this sweet and good child like my own daughter - who is now in despair, having lost so unexpectedly, her special friend, whom she adored. My pain is extreme, and I regret with all my heart not having stayed with Emily until her last breath; but having spent all summer and part of the winter with her - and as my family demanded my return - I absolutely could not stay any longer in England.*

I pity, with all my heart, the poor mother of the unfortunate Emily, because I measure her feelings after mine, and I regret the circumstances that did not permit her to be by the bedside of her poor dying child, who frequently called out the name of her mother during her illness. This is a repeated theme of Katherine's and of Rosina's apologist, Louisa Devey's. If truly a line in Madame de Ritter's letter - and for more than reasons of harmless comfort to Rosina - it is odd. I am still of the opinion that Emily calling out her mother's name during her illness is more likely to be about sharing her mother's genes, or her fate.

I can not tell you exactly the cause of her disease, because we were separated for several months - she having accepted a kind invitation from the D'Eyncourts to go to Bayons, where she caught a heavy cold, so continued to cough in a very disquieting way on her return to me in London; I took every care of her, but without success. Finally, she was forced to go to bed because a terrible headache tormented her day and night; I did not leave her bedside for several weeks, and she received every possible care. Finally we took hope that she was getting better, and doctors asked that we not enter her room, fearing that the sight of people she loved would only overexcite her.

I was assured that there was no danger to her life; and after having asked Sir Edward to bring me my sweet Emily after her restoration to Vienna for a change of air, I departed in the hope of receiving good news when I arrived here - that would have been some compensation for the deplorable state in which I found my homeland after an absence of 10 months; and can tell you I spent the first few weeks in tears, and I feel unable to give any consolation to Lady Lytton, who I do not have the honor to know; I can only counsel her to pray to the Good Lord for support over this painful loss, and that she is comforted by the clear thought that our poor Emily leaves a life full of trials, to receive, close to God, rewards for her excellent qualities, to which I have

Revolution in Vienna, March 1848

been witnessed for so long. Accept, although from a stranger, the respectful assurance of your sincere, Amélie de Ritter.

Vienna, Spiegelgasse No. 1,098, le 7 ieme Juin 1848.

* * * * *

Madame de Ritter [writing in French, she uses 'Amélie' rather than the Italian 'Amalia'] has already written to Edward on 25th May [no correlation, but his 45th birthday], and the fact that she is put out that she has not heard the news from him or Teddy suggests that, in her mind, her departure was not intended as a break in relations with the Bulwer Lyttons. Her excuse for leaving - revolution in Vienna - is clearly genuine, but its timing is suspicious and she will do well to tread carefully in her correspondence with the wounded father. She does not.

Sir, I have just read in a German gazette the terrible news of the death of your daughter - our dear Emily! Imagine my grief and that of my poor Natalie, crying day and night, without consolation! I can not believe this terrible blow without seeing it confirmed by a few lines, which I would very much like you to do by return.

I can well imagine your pain and that of your son in losing a daughter of such excellent character and of a heart so pure; but the grief we experience - my daughter and I - can not be less than yours, since Emily has been a daughter to me during the last few months of my separation from my dear Natalie; and if my situation had not been so fraught with the most alarming reports from my homeland - which get worse daily - I could not have brought myself to leave London without awaiting the outcome of the long illness of my poor Emily.

I await with great impatience a few lines of your hand or Edward's. I believe I have merited this attention by my love for Emily. Kindly greet your charming son, who I hope is in good health, and please accept the unerring sentiments of esteem and friendship, your sincerely, Amélie de Ritter

* * * * *

A month later, 30th June, from the same address in Vienna. *Sir,* [from the French] *I received your letter of 11th [June] with the sad confirmation of the death of our poor Emily, which has renewed my pain and that of my poor Natalie, who dearly loved her only friend and whom no other could ever replace; but you <u>have</u> a beloved son, who encompasses all the qualities to make a loving father happy, and that God will take under His protection - which I desire with all my heart, knowing a young man who will one day do his family honour.*

I also received from London three weeks ago a letter from an unknown lady - a friend of Lady Bulwer - which contained the first direct news of the death of our poor Emily, and description of the despair of her unhappy mother, who was sitting in front of the closed door of her daughter and heard the groans of the poor invalid, not daring to enter her room, which touched me to the depths of my heart, for the feelings of a mother can not be understood but by another mother; and I cannot believe that the presence of a mother can be the cause of the acceleration of the death of a daughter, and I beg you not to get carried away with such terrible ideas, which are perhaps suggested to you by people who court discord, to benefit from it.

Be assured, Sir, that I have no motive in talking to you in this way, as I never knew Lady Bulwer nor rarely heard of her, it is simply my sense of jus-

The Austrians fight back against revolting Italians at Vicenza on 10th June 1848

Italy - from an Austrian perspective - having won its independence and completed its unification

tice and fairness that my gives me the courage to make these observations, in begging you to spare the pain of a mother who feels so miserable - as the letter of her friend described to me.

I thank you gratefully for your interest in the fate of my sons, who have been involved in 5 battle sallies, the last of which was the capture of Vicenza. The good Lord has kept them safe for me until now and I hope to see them return one day the victors!

My son Carl joined the National Guard at the commencement of the Revolution, which interrupted his studies, so he is obliged to remain here another year to finish them; I will stay with him and I hope during this time to have the pleasure of seeing you with your son, since I assume you will repeat the Water Cure at Gastein, during which time your son could make a holiday tour to Vienna, where he would be welcome in my house; and my son would be happy to be a cicerone [tour guide] *to our city.*

My address is as above. Yours sincerely Amélie Ritter

Natalie asks me to send you her respects.

* * * * *

Edward keeps a copy of his indignant reply. *Madame* [from the French], *I have the honour of receiving your letter in which you deem it suitable to decry "the terrible ideas" that you think have been "suggested by people who court discord, to benefit from it." You will permit me to point out to you that I have simply cited the opinion of eminent Doctors as to the effect that the presence of Lady Bulwer in the house where my daughter was in an excessively nervous state could not fail to produce.*

As proof, I enclose for you a copy of the note that I received from Dr Hall on the subject. His statement is corroborated by two other doctors consulted, who agree that the sudden change, in the significant improvement in brain inflammation and to the fever, that caused the rapid death of my daughter could not be explained by anything but a mental shock.

You will see from Dr Hall's note that this change dates from the evening that Lady Bulwer entered the house, where she remained despite the strongest warnings of Mr Rouse. The Doctors are not able to doubt the disastrous effect of the only obvious cause.

It is not true, Madame, that the bedroom door was closed, and that Lady Bulwer dared not enter; the door, on the contrary, was open, and Lady B did enter the room.

I am assured of your own good sense, and therefore that you see the wisdom of any reasonably educated doctor that during the crisis of a nervous disease the most absolute tranquility is required and even the sight and sound of voice of the most familiar people should be prohibited. The slightest suspicion of the presence of a person associated with the causes and memory of upset could not fail to produce the most dangerous results.

* * * * *

That you have not responded to the part of my letter telling of the appearance of Lady Bulwer the day after you checked out of the house rented by you, and that your address was known to her friends, gives me the painful impression that you were not ignorant of the intention of Lady Bulwer to break into the house - or as to whether you had communications with people in her confidence, that you never confided to me - to me, the guardian of my daughter - to me, who had so openly delivered to your friendly assurances the care of my most darling treasure, to whom you gave the guarantee of reciprocal hospitality.

It is not my habit to talk about my domestic troubles. I have always believed that the conduct of Lady Bulwer towards me and her children was sufficiently notorious amongst society to save me certain comments in your letter that seriously hurt me as a father and as the head of my family, and excuse me if I add that she almost insults my human dignity.

If it is your opinion that there was not sufficient cause to prevent Lady Bulwer access to her daughter, why do I not have it frankly confessed - before insulting me with the belief that I could submit to the influence of people who love discord, or giving me a lesson on my responsibilities without telling me to my face that I am wrong. I would then certainly not have withheld sufficient evidence to convince you, as a friend of my daughter, as a mother, and as a woman yourself, that to give access was solemnly prohibited to me.

For inexpiable wrongs that I received as a husband I disdained the com-

pensation that laws that could make me, but as a father I could never accept (as is observed in England) that Emily should have contact with the mother that deserted her children to live in open adultery, without compromising the respectability of my daughter, without staining my honour, and without failing in my duties. I have the honor to sign myself, Madame, your very obedient servant.

* * * * *

On whether to trust Madame de Ritter, Miss Greene weighs in from Bonnie's marital home, The Chapel House, Ormskirk, Lancashire, in a letter to Edward on 13th July 1848 ***...I have long had my suspicions of Md de Ritter. She evidently wished to separate me from yourself & all your family; & you may recollect, it was by chance you heard that I was in Brompton, when you followed her & Emily down to my lodging; she was evidently much annoyed at your placing Edward there with me...***

Oh, Miss Greene, even if this is true, don't pin the label to yourself - ***people who court discord, to benefit from it.***

* * * * *

But Madame de Ritter writes a determined reponse from her same Vienna address on 25th July 1848. ***Sir,*** [from the French] ***I am writing again to exonerate myself from the suspicions which you accuse me of in your letter of the 15th, which have caused me extreme pain - because you believe that I was not ignorant of the intention of Lady Bulwer to break into the house rented by me - or that I was in communication with people of her confidence, which is not true at all. On the contrary, when the poor Emily wanted to talk to me about her mother, I asked her not to speak of her parent's relationship, since I was coming to spend time with her and to share her solitude at Knebworth, and I did not want to be party to family secrets that would make me lose my openness with you.***

Believe - as I am a woman of honour, that I never did do or say anything which would have made me lose your esteem and confidence, and I do not think you are wounded so seriously by my letter; but since I did not know un-

til now the real reasons - which made me shudder - that required you to keep separate your daughter from her mother, and the sad letter I received from a friend of Lady Bulwer was the only, and the first, which contained the news of the death of Emily, and the maternal pain of Lady Bulwer, I let myself be carried away by pity, and by my own mother's feelings.

So excuse me if I have offended you, and believe me, I never had relations with anyone who had knowledge of, or was friends of, Lady Bulwer, so I can not conceive as to how she learned my address, and if I ever had the communication that you suspect me of, I would certainly have mentioned them the day before I left London, where you did me the honour of speaking to me as a true friend, which I shall not forget in this life.

I ask you, finally, to be assured of my truly sincere feelings and friendship, with which I say, Sir, I am your devoted Amélie de Ritter

* * * * *

It is a strong response from a woman who knows - whether happily or not - that she has severed, for good, all relations with the Bulwer Lytton family. I don't doubt that Madame de Ritter was looking for the security of a good match for her children, and that the circumstances she witnessed in England were not what she expected - but I don't see treachery. I think Miss Greene is harsh to match this Baroness to the previous Baroness who picked a fight with her.

Dear Miss Greene is her own worst enemy, too, in her admonishments of a hyper-sensitive father. She is not wrong. And no one is more entitled to an opinion on the Bulwer Lytton family than she. But after 20 years of close acquaintance with Edward Bulwer Lytton, she should know by now that he responds best to grace, and not (as authors should) to criticism, however valid. But Miss Greene knows too - as she expresses elsewhere - that her relations with the Bulwer Lytton family are now over, and this is in her mind, I'm sure, when she continues her letter of 13th July (begun above):

...but Emily's having taken a dislike to her [Madame de Ritter] ***& insisting upon my being sent for, gave me the comfort of witnessing the happy state of my dear child's mind upon her death bed, the remembrance of which, that she is taken away from the evil to come, & is now enjoying bliss in Heaven,***

reconciles me to her loss in this sad world.

I wish for your own sake you had for the last 5 years of our acquaintance, trusted in my integrity & faithfulness towards yourself & children, as you did for the first 15, & not have allowed interested whisperers to interrupt the honest confidence which subsisted between us.

I hope Edward is well, he has never written to me since I left Town, tho' I wrote to him directly I came here – pray give him my love. Yours truly, M. L. Greene

* * * * *

What of the other Edward? Teddy, we might expect to have the clearest view of the truth of his sister's death. Whatever his true view, in the tragedy's aftermath, he bottles it.

There is a dearth of letters from his own troubled adolescence. After a disinterested spell at Harrow school - ***We cannot disguise from ourselves that as yet your trial at Harrow has been a complete failure as far as distinction is concerned***, writes his father - Robert is also sent to be tutored in Germany.

Initially he gets on well in Bonn (like Neuwied on the banks of the Rhine) and with his tutor, an Englishman, Dr Perry. Hovever, after an altercation over drinking (primarily, but the accusation is a misunderstanding), smoking, girls and - predictably - debt, Edward (who's been down this river before) cuts Robert's time in Germany short.

Robert is wretched. On leaving Dr Perry, he writes to his tutor, ***Was is Madame de Staël who said, "I sometimes feel the wish to die, as the wakeful feel the wish to sleep." If death were a sleep, who would not wish to die!*** It is either ironic or a subtle suicide note that where he likely remembers this quote is from his father's book, *The Student* (1835), and its description of the tranquility of Knebworth Park Churchyard [and where the originator is given not as Madame de Staël (1766–1817) but Madame de Deffand (1697–1780)]. For, disgraced and admonished, Robert, like his sister, turns to the laudanum bottle - and the stage is set for a exact repeat of the eldest child's fate...

Unlike Emily, however, Robert is blessed with an unofficial 'godparent' who is listened to. John Forster is able to talk sense into both Robert and his father - who is now contemplating consigning his son to military school, in-

Robert, aged 19

dicative of just how addled Edward's parenting judgment is become. Forster encourages sending Robert as an unpaid attaché to join his Uncle Henry's legation in Washington, where Henry is appointed ambassador in April 1849, and so sets Robert on course for the career in foreign service that becomes, in time, his route to worldly success, and full reconciliation with his father.

* * * * *

So why is there not a bundle of letters in a box from Robert's time in Germany? The boy is no doubt less communicative with his father than his sister has been, but I also suspect that he expurgates the correspondence of his youth when it falls back into his possession at his father's death. He prefers to distill its sorrows, and drop its tears into the beautiful poems of his first book, *The Wanderer* (1859).

But Robert does write an account of his sister's death. Ten years after the fact. He is the last of the first hand witnesses to tell the story, and by this time we must accept that his account is as likely tinted as its precursors.

The tragedy of his parents marriage continues its maelstrom spin through the four remaining decades of their lives, descending to a nadir in 1858 in the wake of the Matrimonial Causes Act of 1857 - which makes divorce easier by moving it to the civil courts - and in the swell of a new spell of political success for Edward. Court proceedings continue a constant threat, and evidence continues to be gathered by both sides.

With an election looming, and accusations intensifying in Rosina's writings - including responsibility for their daughter's death - Edward asks his son to commit to paper an account of the circumstances of the family tragedy.

Robert writes from Italy on 20th October 1857, ***My darling Father, Your very dear letter reached me the day before yesterday, and today I enclose you a letter which contains the substance of a short Memoir which I had already put upon paper, for my own satisfaction & for any use it might afterwards avail to serve towards the refutation of public slanders.***

There is but one point, an immaterial one, in which my memory is confused – i.e. whether E died on the night of the day in which we discovered LL [Lady Lytton] ***to be at the house, or on the succeeding Evg. E's last words to me were - "Pray – Pray – Prayer is everything. Promise me that you will." I***

never heard her allude to LL in her delirium.

I must apologise for the slovenly state of the enclosed; but I have written it at an Inn, with bad pens & ink, & do not wish to delay your possession of it by waiting to make a fair copy. I keep none therefore. If it does not answer your purposes let me know how I can alter.....

* * * * *

My dearest Father, Since I had the pain of reading the statements relative to the deathbed of my lost sister, which are contained in the pamphlet sent to me when I was last in England, it has occurred to me that, (as I was present with my sister thro'out her last illness, and as her last words were addressed in my ears) it might perhaps be satisfactory to you if I were to place upon paper my own recollections of circumstances which were too painful not to have been accurately remembered.

I send you at any rate a short statement of facts, which I request you to use in whatever way you may think fit, and of the veracity of which I offer you the greatest pledge in my power, by subscribing my name thereto.....

During her residence in Germany my sister [developed] a strong friendship for a young lady whose family name was 'de Ritter von Zahoney' and whose family was Viennese. Some time after my sister's return to England she received a letter from the mother of this young lady informing her that both herself and her daughter were about to visit England in the intention of passing some months there.

Immediately on learning this, my Father, aware of my sister's friendship for the de Ritters, requested her to invite them to Knebworth, where both he & my sister were staying, and to express to them his wish that they shd consider his house as their home during their visit to England

Mad. de Ritter accepted this invitation and both she & her daughter passed several months at Knebworth, where I became acquainted with them during my holidays, for I was then at school at Harrow.

* * * * *

Subsequently Mad[e] de Ritter wishing to pass some time in London before leaving England, quitted Knebworth with her daughter, and, as my father had not at that time any house in town in which to offer them hospitality, they engaged lodgings in Brompton.

The de Ritters having thus left Knebworth, my Father, my sister and myself also quitted it on a visit to Mr d'Eyncourt, then Member for Lambeth, at Bayons Manor, his country seat in Lincolnshire.

I remember that whilst we were at Bayons the weather there was frequently very severe and the cold exceedingly sharp. My sister had a slight cough - and frequently complained of headache & indisposition. There was nothing in her appearance which could then create alarm, and her spirits, naturally gay, were not less cheerful than usual.

Still, as her cough still continued, my father, rendered uneasy by its duration, brought her with him to London, where he lost no time in consulting a Physician about her health. Her lungs were then examined and declared to be perfectly sound, nor did the medical men whom she then saw consider indisposition to be graver than such as might be caused, in a girl of her age, by the effects of an ordinary cold if not checked in season.

My father however, wishing that she should continue for the present to have medical care and attendance, was anxious that she should not leave town until her health was fully restored, and she having accepted an invitation from the de Ritters to pass with them at Brompton the remainder of their time in England, my father remained in town and took rooms at an hotel in order to be near her.

As the physicians who had held consultation upon my sister's health, had, as I have already stated, concurred in the opinion that there was no symptom of any organic disease, and that ordinary attention & care to avoid exposure to cold for the present was all that was needed to return her to perfect health, my father directed his own medical advisor, Mr Rouse, to visit her daily, and this gentleman's reports continuing to be favourable, I returned to Harrow at the end of the vacation.

* * * * *

I returned however to Town before the operation of the school term, in consequence of my sister's health not having improved, and of her own & my father's anxiety that I should be near her.

As Mad^{e} de Ritter was not able to spare me a bed in her own apartments, I procured one in the house of a Lady who happened to be living within two or three doors of the lodgings occupied by the de Ritters, and who was an old friend of my sister's and of mine. It was, indeed, under the care of this lady that the greater part of our childhood had been passed: altho' now confined to her bed by age and ill health she is still living, I am happy to say, and would, I have no doubt, be able, if necessary, to attest the truth of all that I am now stating.

This arrangement allowed me to pass the whole of every day with my sister. I found Emily much changed. A circumstance of a wholly private character, which is entirely disconnected with the persons concerned in this statement, & which it is quite unnecessary that I should relate, occurring at a time when her health was still feeble, had I think, much shaken her nerves, and she was now agitated by any prolonged conversation and so weak that she was, at last obliged to leave the chair which of late she had so seldom quitted for the bed from which she never rose again.

My father, by whose unmistakable distress and anxiety I was first alarmed into the supposition of a danger greater than I had hitherto suffered myself to anticipate, again called a consultation of physicians, and placed my sister under the care of Dr Marshall Hall, who declared the malady to be entirely on the nerves, and enjoined complete repose.

At this juncture the disturbances which had just broken out at Vienna having alarmed Mad^{e} de Ritter on behalf of her son who was there, she suddenly quitted England.

So soon as my Father was informed by Mad^{e} de Ritter of her intended departure he enquired of the Physicians who were in attendance on my sister, if in their opinion she might, without danger, be removed from the house. And on their stating their belief that in a few days, she would be able to bear a removal, and that a change of air would prove of great benefit to her, he at once hired a small villa not far out of town, & prepared it for her reception.

Meanwhile Dr Marshall Hall declared that, in my sister's present nervous state, it was of the utmost importance that her room should not be entered by any one but the nurse who attended her, and that on the strict adherence to this injunction depended the fulfilment of the expectation which he had confidently expressed, that she would within the day fixed for her removal be able to bear the fatigue of the drive, - my father, myself, Miss Greene (the lady whom I have already alluded to), assembled daily in the room adjoining my sister's sleeping room.

* * * * *

Early in the morning of the day preceding that fixed for my sister's removal, while I was yet dressing to go to her house, I was joined by my father, who, on his way thither, had been informed that Lady Lytton was then in the house.

Dreading the shock which I foreboded that my sister must have suffered had Dr Hall's injunction been already infringed, I hastened to the house in the hope of forestalling a sudden and unexpected interview between Lady Lytton & my sister.

I encountered on the stairs the mistress of the house lodgings, who attempted to prevent me from mounting them, with the assertion that Dr Hall who had been there that morning had declared that altho' Miss Lytton was much better, her room must on no account be entered before his return.

Knowing, that unless my sister's health had suffered some decided change for the worse, it was highly improbable that Dr Hall would have been at the house so early in the morning, I did not believe the assertion to be true, and enquired whether unknown to Miss Lytton's relations she had admitted any one to the house. She replied that she had let one of the rooms left vacant by Mad[e] de Ritter, to a Mrs Johnson.

At the threshold of my sister's door the nurse [he first writes 'again' then replaces it with 'also'] *also attempted to stop me – I entered – unrecognised by my sister – for she was delirious, nor did she recover her mind till during the seconds which preceded her death.*

Lady Lytton was at that moment upstairs.

Upon Dr Hall, who was immediately sent for, declaring to her that unless she left the house he would rather remove my sister from it – ill and in the dangerous condition in which she now was, than leave her top the excitement which, he felt sure, had produced the danger – Lady Lytton left the house in the brougham of Dr Rouse, my father's physician.

* * * * *

Whatever the cause of the terrible change in my sister's health, she did not survive it. She died supported by my father and myself. Her last words were to me, and as they left no light on the mystery of her death, and had no reference but to myself, I shall not repeat them.

From the moment of Lady Lytton's departure to that which was my sister's last, she continued delirious, and never once uttered her mother's name.

These are the circumstances under which my sister died,

In addition to what I have said, I have but one observation to make. From our earliest childhood to the last hour of our intercourse the closest intimacy and confidence existed between my sister and myself. We confided to each other every sentiment and compared every opinion, our friendship was more than the ordinary bond of relationship, and I do not think that there was a secret between us. If there be any truth in the words attributed (in the pamphlet I have mentioned) to my sister in her last illness, then there could have been no truth in the language which she had held to me thro'out the progressive years of intimacy only terminated by her death, and, notwithstanding our unbroken confidence, I must have been deceived as to her feelings. I do not admit this supposition. Ever, my dear Father, Your afft son Robert Lytton. Leghorn. 20th Oct. 1857.

* * * * *

"Pray – Pray – Prayer is everything. Promise me that you will." Not the most convincing advice from a girl about to die - unless she is praying to die. Robert is wrong, I believe, that these last words shed ***no light on the mystery of her death***. They could send me off on paragraphs about the martyr complex and parallels with Julia D'Eyncourt [The eldest D'Eyncourt sister who - having been rejected by Edward - turns Roman Catholic and shuts herself in

a convent for life]... or the comfort in suicide of believing in the afterlife... or perhaps that she has found it a struggle to resist temptation... the fact is, any glimpse into Emily's mind in these final months is invaluable in helping to solve what Robert revealingly calls ***the mystery of her death.***

So where are the thoughts of this voluminous letterwriter? Where are the contents of her busy writing desk after she leaves Knebworth? And why is the great author himself all but silent on these last months of his daughter's life? This, in inself, is a clue to an important element of the mystery that is missing.

Miss Greene writes to Edward [undated] from the Wilkinson's address in Kensington, ***Emily used to keep your letters, tied up in a parcel in a small drawer of the Davenport in her room, next the window. It was the knowledge that she often left it open that made me charge her to take care of her papers on her leaving Knebworth. If she took them to Bayons, Miss Clara d'Eyncourt is likely to know it – when I see her I shall prudently sound her on the subject – after all, it is possible she*** [Emily] ***may have destroyed them... Edward has got the novel, I trust you will not deem it necessary to destroy it – as I shall value it highly. Any personality you may discover in it, she told me, was intended for her mother. I enclose you some letters which I found yesterday.....I hope all unpleasant recollections have been buried with our dear Emily, & that like myself, you never doubt her warm love & attachment to yourself.***

There is a novel?! A novel by the girl who is not impressed by *Jane Eyre*. A novel that will surely shed light on unspoken truths. If only.

But her father does destroy it.

Worse still, he destroys a journal that Emily is keeping until her sickness overwhelms her. Having left us so much, Edward removes the final piece of the puzzle. It is almost technique. The master novelist leaves for his great-great-great-grandson to discover the remakable legacy of Emily's teenage correspondence - then censors and edits the writings of her last few weeks. Why?

Because one subject flares up in those weeks that he is wishes to downplay. A subject born of irrational behaviour.

And even bearing a tradition of suicide.

Romance.

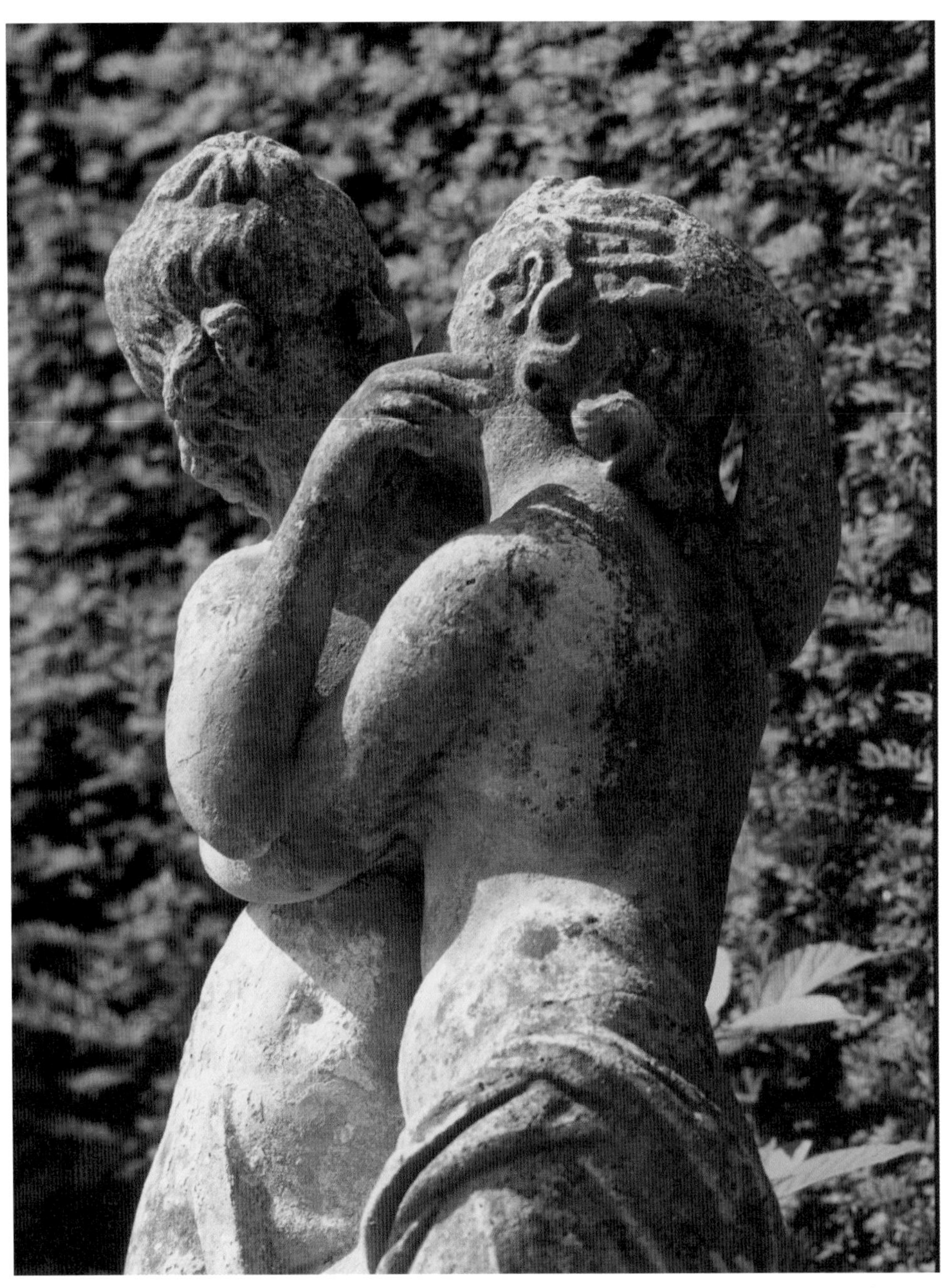

The Lovers *- this statue, which stands today against the yew hedge in the gardens of Knebworth House, Ellen D'Eyncourt reveals in her watercolours (p.765) stood at the very centre of Edward Bulwer Lytton's garden of the 1840s*

CHAPTER 35

~ Last Words ~

By a strange oversight of which I should never have thought you modern ladies - proverbially methodical - guilty, you [posted] a note to Edward without any address than his name. It arrived, after a small circuit round England, to the Athenaeum & - given to me as mine - I opened it.

Happy to find no improper flirtations. [It is Valentine's Day]

Seeing the subject was to visit Edward at Harrow, let me beg of you, if you have not done so, to refrain from it. Mr Harris thinks visits rather unsettle him - & Heaven knows he does not want that – nor am I so pleased with him at present as to wish to step out of the ordinary way to indulge him.

I find that the Ladies at Bayons do not come to Town till Easter [Easter Sunday, in 1848, falls on 23rd April] – ***they have asked Emily much to stay & I believe she will do so, at all events for some time. Be kind eno' to tell this to Mad^e De Ritter with my kind regards tho' I conclude Emily will write herself.***

Edward Bulwer Lytton to Miss Greene, 20 Pelham Terrace, Brompton, Monday, 14th February, 1848.

* * * * *

This letter, written on Valentine's Day, finds Sir Edward in good spirits. Maybe he is in the glow of some kind of positive déjà vu from the early days of his marriage, when his young wife is pregnant and he is having to write himself out of debt having been cut off by his mother. In February 1848, his young paramour Marion is five months pregnant, and he is writing himself out of debt having had his finances cut up by the collapse of Railway shares. But a man can face all calamity if he has someone to love who loves him.

This Valentine's Day, 19-year-old Emily does not, to all appearances, have someone to love who loves her. She loves Natalie - but Natalie is a carefree 16-year-old sprite who is not ready to love anything but life. She loves the idea of Natalie's brother Carl - but this lover she does not appear to have even met. She perhaps fantasises about - and perhaps has received the polite attention of - the bachelors at Bayons, but the D'Eyncourt children are a generation - or at least a decade - older than her. She may have someone who loves her in Cockburn Thomson - but he is just fifteen and whilst fun for a flirtation, not an immediate future for her. The close friend of her past, Bonnie Wilkinson, is already married - at 18, a year younger - and moved to Lancashire. The close friend of her present, Clara D'Eyncourt, is in her thirties and unmarried, almost a worse prospect... for then she will have followed Miss Greene all the way - into spinsterhood and celibacy.

The dreams that gave meaning to the years strapped to a metal stretching bed in Germany have become muddled, misplaced. Knebworth offers her a house but not a home. Her father offers her a weight of terrible family secrets, financial insecurity and worst of all, his absence.

Small, acne-plagued, with a crooked back, Emily, at nineteen, is 'coming out' into a Society that at best, pities her; at least, gossips about her; and at worst, laughs at her, for her funny foreign manners and orphan ways.

* * * * *

Christmas at Bayons is her first real test. She has her gloves and she has her ladies maid, and, as Miss Greene hopes, *the kindness of the d'Eyncourt family and her being in her proper sphere would restore her mind to its proper tone.* Despite being compromised by ill-health, it doesn't appear to go too badly. Miss Greene reports that she is *excited by a Mr Vane falling in love with her and making her an offer, as well as being in the house with Mr G. d'Eyncourt.* But, as mentioned, Charles's eldest son George and both the Vane brothers are almost 20 years older than Emily. The only relationship that appears to flower at Bayons is one with George's then-unmarried sister Clara.

Clara D'Eyncourt is 35-years-old, and here again we see an echo of 19-year-old Rosina's relationship with 35-year-old Miss Greene - a natural attachment of mother-starved child to an elder surrogate.

It should be obvious to me. If Emily is writing her thoughts to anyone once she has moved down to Brompton in March, it is to Clara D'Eyncourt. But it takes Marie Mulvey-Roberts - whilst researching Rosina - to bring to light five letters written by Emily amongst the D'Eyncourt papers in the Lincoln Archives - five letters written in the short time between 17th March and the moment in early April that her sickness prevents her writing. I am straightaway in the car heading up the A1 to Lincoln with master-transcriber Clare Fleck. Here, maybe, we have Emily's 'last words'.

* * * * *

One of the letters is in German. I send it to Joachim in Eichstatt to decipher and translate. In the meantime, Clare sets to work on the other four: ***My dearest Clara*** [undated] ***you will think me very ungrateful in not fulfilling my promise of writing to you upon the morning after my arrival – but till I had something more than mere details to communicate, I thought my letter would be hardly worth reading. You will hear from Mrs d'Eyncourt how, successfully, I arrived at my journey's End. Your parting gift and your kind bright parting smile cheered me upon my somewhat 'lonesome' way – The individuals who started with me from Lincoln were so in love with one another - that I felt but little repugnance at being obliged to part with them at Rugby from which place to London, Maria*** [Madame de Ritter's German maid] ***& I were left in solitude & sweet repose to soothe each other.***

I had a very happy meeting with Natalie, from whom I have gathered a great deal of interesting information with regard to the Revolution. 'My Pa' paid us a visit last night – he told me Mr d'Eyncourt had gone to Paris, for yr sister [Julia, whose rescue by her father from a convent on the unsettled Continent does not bode well for Emily's hopes of escaping there] - ***and that, in the interim, he has been so very kind as to allow my Father the use of his house. I have been appointed to give my Father & Sir J.C*** [another eminent doctor to add to the roll-call of Emily's doctors, James Clark (1788 –1870) Physician-in-Ordinary, i.e. regular physician, to Queen Victoria] ***rendezvous tomorrow morning at 11.***

We were all made rather cross this afternoon by a never ending visit from Dr & M [Mary, aged 20] ***& E*** [Elizabeth, aged 22] ***Thomson!!!! – They wanted to rush upon poor me, & cover me with kisses – but I retreated – and came***

off with a 'genteel' shake hands. Invitations for Thursdays, Fridays, and all the other days in the week (Sunday excepted) were instantly issued, but upon finding them all refused, the young ladies sent a significant look across the table [sounds like a quote from *The Vicar of Wakefield* - it's not, but it is one of many in-jokes and personal references across the four letters, which confirm an intimacy between Emily and Clara, and certain level of conversational fun, at least, over the Christmas holidays].

P.S. Will you kindly address any letters in future 20 Pelham Terrace Brompton, Miss Greene's address – Miss G has left [No. 29] & Madame de Ritter has taken the house

* * * * *

My poor dear Clara [undated] ***...It was very kind of you to write to [Sir James Clark] about me – I assure you I am flayed out of my life with cure – and I consider myself quite well.***

My Father is at Fulham and I cannot say if I shall go to Vienna. I can only hope - tho' perhaps as usual – to be disappointed. Our trio was booked to dine with the T's [Thomsons] ***next Tuesday – but luckily a slight cold Natalie caught in returning from the Theatre furnished us with an excuse for refusing, and we have just [sent] a note to that effect.***

I know my dear Clara how much you have to write, to do & to think of, - and I shall not expect to hear from you -

[The following paragraph is in German] ***But if any moment should appear in which no (other) business constrains your mind and no (other) thoughts constrain your heart, then remember me kindly and write a couple of words that tell me you haven't forgotten me completely. Loving you dearly, Emily Lytton, London, Monday.***

My affectionate regards to Mrs d'Eyncourt

Today Schiller's *Elegie On The Death Of A Youth,* ***amongst his minor poems, is very beautiful.*** *Maria Stuart* [a verse play about the last days of Mary Queen of Scots] ***is interesting, tho' prosy in parts. His minor poems are really beautiful - my favourites are the above mentioned and Die Schale*** [*The Shell]. ***Your much attached, Emily Lytton***

- I fear I shall not go to Vienna

* * * * *

Elegie On The Death Of A Youth - a beautiful sentimental poem about the death of a youth - and *Maria Stuart* - five acts on the impending execution of a young queen - are, in retrospect, not the healthiest reading list for a sick, depressive teenager in winter. The former, as translated by her father, is full of emotions that we can see playing with Emily's mind. The whole poem, in the light of what is to come, has resonance - I give you but a small sample,

Love gilds not for thee all the world with its glow,
Never Bride in the clasp of thine arms shall repose;
Thou canst see not our tears, though in torrents they flow,
Those eyes in the calm of eternity close!

Yet happy--oh, happy, at least in thy slumber--
Serene is the rest, where all trouble must cease;
For the sorrows must die with the joys they outnumber,
And the pains of the flesh with its dust--are at peace!

The tooth of sharp Slander thou never canst feel,
The poison of Vice cannot pierce to thy cell;
Over thee may the Pharisee thunder his zeal,
And the rage of the Bigot devote thee to Hell! ...

Happy thou, happy thou--in the still narrow cell!
To this strange tragi-comedy acted on earth,
To these waters where Bliss is defiled at the well,
To this lottery of chances in sorrow and mirth,

To this rot and this ferment--this sloth and this strife,
To the day and the night of this toilsome repose,
To this Heaven full of Devils--O Brother!--TO LIFE--
Thine eyes in the calm of Eternity close!

* * * * *

My dearest Clara [*Thursday*, undated], *I have just received yr kind letter & thank you very much for it. I am so grieved to hear you are suffering from yr eyes – I am sure it is only from being too good & going too much to see the 'spanging & joumping' old ladies...*

Enclosed is the length and no of stitches of the Boa. I am proud to think anything of mine shld be copied by you. I am afraid when you come to Town you will get some other 'girl for the season' – and forget poor me!

Madame de R. is very uneasy about her friends abroad, more especially for her sons, in the possession of her loved society– The sweetest melodies are floating in my ear – Natalie's small hands are wandering carelessly over the Piano Forte, and the tones they awaken seem to embody the melancholy of her large, sad eye – But I must not speak of Natalie or I shall make a fool of myself –

Madame de Ritter went to a large party at Chevalier Brinsens yesterday evening. Natalie would not go, much to her mother's and my own annoyance – she has my dislike to society – however I have persuaded her to go next Tuesday. I am going to begin a little print piece for you & Mrs d'Eyncourt tomorrow. My life here is very quiet & happy – I of course refuse all invitations – and my only visits are to shops, to help Natalie to select finery –

This letter is very stupid and therefore it is best that I should give over gripping my pen, & in conclusion I assure you, dearest Clara, zu Überfluss [to crown it] of my sincere & grateful affection, Emily Lytton. Turn over

Monday …to the Dr, who satirically expressed a wish to be informed if I was here 'incog' (to use his expression). I think I am on the whole better – much better – since the journey, and Madame de Ritter & dear Natalie are so kind to me, & take so much care of me! –

I often think of you dear Clara, & our long conversations & German readings – how does the Jungfrau get on? Pray do not forget to remember me to Mr Bellamy – I saw a gentlemen very like him in the train & thought of you in course (sic) my dear!

I hope you will not quite forget me, dear Clara, plague as I was to you, I never shall forget all your kindness to me. Pray remember me most affectly to yr mama & master Pullem & believe me ever gratefully & most fondly yours, Emily Lytton.

* * * * *

London Wednesday Evening [undated]. *My dearest Clara. I really cannot tell you what happiness your most kind and welcome letter gave me. There are few thoughts that bring pleasure like that, of having a small place in the memory & regard of those, we love and admire. How often shall I think of the many hours we passed together, in interchange of – thoughts – sentiments – doubts – fears - & hopes – and how happy did it make me to find, at last, in this cold land - amongst this most unenthousiastic[sic] people - one mind that appreciated, one heart that loved & understood, the wild yet lofty beauty of the language of my dear 'Jungenland'* [land of my youth].

The account of your adventures amused me extremely as also your information with regard to the Levee. It was unkind of you to tell me that Mr Robert had come to see you – you know his wit, & 'genteel' appearance made a deep impression upon my youthful heart.

I had an interview with Sir James C[lark] *– on Monday last - he seemed not to think seriously of my case, and indeed I am astonishingly better since my arrival in Town, that it seemed almost needless to have advice at all. My lameness is quite gone, and you may imagine how much better I feel, when I tell you that I walked the whole way with Papa from Pall Mall to Brompton with but little "un heasiness" to my self!! Sir J. C. gave me a receipt for some pills – one of wh I am to take Every night – with this exception I have no medicine to take. I am told the 'tumor' in my neck will go away of itself –*

Mr L. d'Eyncourt [Louis D'Eyncourt (1814-1896), third son] *was kind eno' to call here on Monday, but I am sorry to say I was out with Papa. He was good eno' to repeat his call this afternoon – but we were all out, so missed the pleasure of seeing him. I was truly delighted to hear that Mr d'Eyncourt has gone to fetch your sister, for I long to know you happy, dear Clara, once again.*

* * * * *

[fragment]...*Italy. She is thinking of going soon to Vienna. She is kind eno' to wish me to accompany her which I should be delighted to do if my Father will allow me.*

I am not surprised that yr Brother [Louis] *did not give a flattering acct of Natalie & her mother as neither of them make what is called 'a first impres-*

sion' – They must be known as I know them, before they can be loved or appreciated

You ask me what I eat drink & avoid. I eat: for Breakfast – Bread & butter; for Luncheon – sandwiches, or oranges or biscuits, or eggs; for dinner – soup – meat, vegetables & pudding; & for tea - bread & butter. I drink – tea & delicious cold water - & I avoid the Thomsons! –

'Totengötter' means – the Gods of death – or the malignant fates.

London seems pretty full - & there are some tempting things in the shops qu'on [ne doit] pas regarder [that should not be looked at]. ***I trust yr sister*** [Julia] ***may return to England instead of staying at Boulogne. Forgive my stupidity & ever believe me, Very affectly yrs E. Lytton***

The length of my Boa – is 3 yds. There are 20 stitches in the pink & the same no in the white part.

* * * * *

And that is it. Four cheery letters, full of in-jokes - notably a number about men and romance - one literally discussing what she has for breakfast... ending in a line, telling how many stiches there are in her Boa.

Here, apparently, we have the last surviving thoughts of Emily Bulwer Lytton, who a few weeks later is lying dead in her bed.

Dead, very possibly because she has no wish to live.

So what is missing?

What takes the place of these letters - in what remains to us - are increasingly frantic notes of Madame de Ritter to her father, [undated, from the French] ***Forgive me, sir, that I torment you again regarding your daughter, who has been suffering terribly for two days. The doctor finds no fever or stomach-ache but her pains increase in a very disturbing way and begins occasionally to be delirious; this morning her eyesight was so poor that she could barely distinguish me; I told this to the doctor and he answered me that it was her weakness and her hysterics; he changed the medicine but the pain throughout her body remains the same and brings on fainting.***

I believe her 'medicine' has much to do with it. But something else is at play. Something unspoken. Something that is causing what the doctor - presumably Dr Rouse - describes as 'hysterics'. If Emily has descended into an hysteria, what has triggered it?

* * * * *

Doctors in the 19th Century will spend a lot of time twiddling their stethoscopes, humming and harring, poking and prodding, rubbing and rearranging women to diagnose 'female hysteria'.

They will even, generously, invent the vibrator as a potential cure.

An American physician with the perfect name of George Beard (1839–1883) will writes pages and pages of comedy on the subject: ***My method of counter-irritating nervous patients is, to take one of Alcock's*** [seriously] ***porous plasters and cut off a piece of about the size and shape of my little finger; along the centre of this I place a little Spanish fly ointment, and then apply over the tender spot, and let it stay there until it falls off. Counter-irritation thus used is not very annoying, and is quite effective.*** [*Cases of Hysteria, Neurasthenia, Spinal Irritation and Applied Affections; With Remarks. 1874.*]

There is truth enough (as in comedy), I'm sure, to make all this fun and games worthwhile, but it takes Dr Sigismund Schlomo Freud (1856–1939) to come along at the end of the century and sort most of it out.

I hope doctors and psychiatrists will read this book and throw light on the evidence presented in regard to Emily. As neither, I offer you only my thoughts and comments - and will let you consult on your own the shelves and shelves, web pages and web pages, of historical and hysterical, hippocratic hypothesising on 'hysteria', in all its mental and physical forms.

Dr Rouse indentifies 'hysterics', Miss Greene talks of a subsuming 'madness' - there may be biological reasons; there are likely chemical reasons; but of one thing I am absolutely sure, in my great-great-great-aunt's case, there are overriding metaphysical reasons... take away the hormones for a minute, and consider in their raw form - grief, loneliness, fantasy, shame, horror, and ultimately, despair.

* * * * *

If the beginning of the end is Emily's sickness, whatever it is; and the end of the end is Rosina, whatever effect that has on the final night; the middle of the end, is the breakdown of relations with the de Ritters and the embarrassment caused by this and two silly flirtations which, specifically because they are played out in front of her father, are, literally, mortifying.

The sickness and the last minute appearance of Rosina both play their part in Emily's death, but it is these three excruciating upsets to the sensitive teenager, that, to me, are the bulk of the reason that Emily - I shall say it... takes her own life - either by wilfully succumbing to sickness, or, what will never be proven, taking prussic acid or laudanum or some other poison that her father's doctors are instructed to cover up.

So far, details of the breakdown of her relationship with the de Ritters are sketchy beyond what Miss Greene has told us. The second flirtation is, as yet, unknown to me - it has been so well covered up. We will come to it later. The flirtation that I do know about is pushed to the fore, maybe to dampen gossip about the second. On this subject, even Edward breaks his silence to posterity.

He leaves us a statement of 'Facts', which suggests an interrogation of Emily, and - almost as humiliating to her - of others like her brother and Miss Greene; and that he is preparing for the possibility of a challenge for satisfaction. With the Planché affair soon after, that is two potential 'honour duels' in the space of two months.

If it were a rake or a roué that was threatening his daughter's honour or health, the path would be clearer. Edward is struggling that his insulters are two women called Katherine and a child called Cockburn.

* * * * *

Less than two weeks before Emily's death, 15-year-old (he will 16 in July) J. Cockburn Thomson writes to Sir Edward Bulwer Lytton from the Thomson family home in Wellbeck Street, [Tues. 18th April 1848] ***Dear Sir, Having been informed by your son Edward that my letters to Miss Lytton were annoying and disagreable, and by Mama that you considered them insulting, I cannot refrain from expressing my grief that they should have been so, sincerely asking your forgiveness if they were. But at the same time I must assure you*** *that they were written with far other intentions, and, I meant them anything but insulting.*

That my conduct throughout has been the height of folly, I will not deny, but the blindness and inexperience of boyhood in, at first, mistaking Miss Lytton's kindness for affection may perhaps excuse that. Meanwhile, however, I have kept the whole matter so profoundly secret - and so great was my fear of discovery - that mama has not once been able to give me that advice which would undoubtedly have stopped this folly. I therefore beg that you will pardon it, on the plea of boyhood and ignorance of the world, and enquire not further into the matter.

As regards the letter which I wrote to Miss Lytton to apologise for my conduct, at your son's request, it was written in the heat of a critical moment, and I can neither recollect nor account for what was in it.

Edward's conduct to me has been most kind and reasonable – will you therefore have the kindness to thank him for me and believe me to remain, humbly yours, J. Cockburn Thomson

* * * * *

I would like to give you all of Edward's eleven page 'Facts', as nothing better than its length and detail illustrates how preoccupied and angered Edward is by this contretemps in the days before Emily death. But, like him, in this closing chapter, we should be more concerned with the more pressing matters of the moment. So I cut and paraphrase:

'Facts' [in Edward Bulwer Lytton's hand]

Master George Cockburn aged 14, is asked to Knebworth as a friend of Master Bulwer, last summer. I was absent from Knebworth.

Just before leaving he asked Miss Lytton "to love him better than any one else" & used such expressions implying the foolish fancies common eno' to silly schoolboys towards a grown up girl. Miss Lytton laughed at him good naturedly, treating him as a mere child... Cockburn continues to write to Emily, but on complaining *of his tone* to his mother Mrs Thomson, Emily is asked to humour him, as *he was in a morbid state of mind, & it might seriously affect him.* In both of these two statements, I hear the voice of Emily under interrogation.

...on Miss Lytton's return from Bayons, & while at Madame de Ritter's in a state of great nervous debility, she received a letter of the most offensive character – signed 'Vernon' – with sundry allusions to Mr George D'Eyncourt, Mr Vane & a boy who was Madame de Ritter's son & founded, in part, upon a letter from Miss Lytton to her brother, which Master Thomson had secretly overlooked & a passage of which he had also secretly copied out. This letter was enclosed to Miss Lytton's serving maid, with an intimation to the effect that it should be given to Miss L – or placed on her bed.

Miss Lytton anxious to stop such an impropriety, communicated the insult she had received to her brother – thinking it better that a schoolboy should quietly interfere with [modern: 'challenge' - otherwise an ultra-modern suggestion!] *a schoolboy – & seeing it was useless to complain to Mrs Thomson...*

Robert confronts Cockburn, but is shown letters that Emily has written to Cockburn - letters that Emily says where written as a game the previous summer, when he had asked her *what was the German for 'yours affectionately' & the answer, given in the presence of Miss Greene, was that the equivalent German idiom was 'Deine dich liebende'* - literally, 'yours, you loving'.

The '*morbid*' 15-year-old then runs away from home. *Before daybreak, Madame de Ritter's house in which Miss Lytton was lying on a sickbed was violently knocked up by Mrs Thomson - as if my daughter could know anything of her son's movements, or, as if he could be hid in my daughter's house - my son lodging, as Mrs Thomson knew, in another house.*

The alarm and shock on her nerves at this disturbance at such an hour, threw my daughter, in whose complaint a favourable turn had just declared itself, into a most alarming state of nerves - brought back the worst symptoms, & she has been in great danger ever since.

* * * * *

Meanwhile Master Cockburn Thomson walks down to my house at Knebworth [some 30 miles] *– arrives there late at night, rouses the servants, asks for supper & a bed, & having used my house as an inn, resolves to return home & borrows, I believe, the money for that purpose.*

I say then – that all these facts constitute a great outrage, demanding an unqualified apology & expression of regret from the boy's father. Passing over, wholly as a child's folly, any preposterous notion of affection to my daughter, or conceit that he could be encouraged – no gentleman & no father can deny the misconduct:

1st, of secretly copying out from a confidential letter from sister to a brother, a passage subsequently used to the purpose of annoyance.

2nd, of addressing a letter to a young lady of birth & station, under cover to menial servant & in an assumed name.

3rd, of using as an inn the house of the father whose daughter he had thus insulted.

And besides this apology, it would be natural to express the deepest sorrow at having in a moment of excitement, disturbed an invalid at such an hour & occasioned her so serious an increase of illness.

* * * * *

Instead of such an apology & regret, Mrs Thomson addressed to Sir Edward & to Master Bulwer, letters that insinuate or convey blame to Miss Lytton herself. Mrs Thomson owns, indeed, that she can only blame Miss L – for giving her son encouragement, for not confiding in her *& yet hopes that "it may be a warning to Miss Lytton", [and] that "she is deeply hurt with her".*

At this, smoke needs no long cherrywood pipe to emanate from Emily's father. He writes to Mrs Thomson on 19th April 1848 with fine Bulwerian indignation, *You must allow me to say that your perversion of an insult to my family and myself (as gross as can be well conceived) into a matter of reproach against me & mine is so strange that it is not so that I can suffer the affair to rest. Had you contented yourself with excusing your son and inclosing the apology I have just received from him, I should not have said a word farther* [sic]. *But addressing me in the language of complaint and insinuating blame to Miss Lytton, is really adding outrage to outrage...*

He lists again the facts - so *revolting to all the instincts of a gentleman* - adding to Cockburn's *most impertinent allusions,* that of *brutally telling a Girl on a sickbed that "she would not have long to live"; – and, above all, the crowning insult from one who should know better, of first asking indulgence to the whims of a child, and then seeking to pervert that indulgence into improper encouragement as to a man.* The letter goes on... concluding:

...And for the rest, I am the only person who has a right to blame Miss Lytton in this, and know how thoroughly innocent of all, except romantic exaggeration of language, those expressions really were, referring to one she had not seen since he was twelve years old – and that person two years younger than herself!

He means Carl - who we've heard is the subject of romantic notions in the compromised letter to her brother, and is two years younger than Emily - and if this is a 'Fact', it means that Emily did once meet Carl, presumably on a visit to his sister at the Institute.

Whilst it makes Emily no less fanciful, this does as least make her not quite as cuckoo in her fixation on a future with Carl de Ritter and his family.

Although, again, she is falling in love with a 12-year-old.

* * * * *

Edward is not finished. He now gets nasty. And breaks the fourth wall of civilised parley by saying what everyone is thinking but is too polite to say.

For the rest – Allow me, in reply to assurances of concealment, which, in the spirit they are made, convey an additional insult, to say –

- that while the story, if truthfully told, could only lead persons of the world to suppose that an artful trap had been laid to entangle a Girl of ancient family and large expectations, (deprived of her Mother, and in her Father's absence) into something that might be turned hereafter into worldly advantage (a supposition warranted by your concealment from me and your own advice to Emily); and that the present attempt to justify insolence, to her prejudice, arises from disappointment at the failure of the scheme.....while sure that such would be the interpretation any one acquainted with life would draw from the facts of the case, it is right that I should add not as a threat, but as a caution -

– that the consequences must be infinitely more serious than you seem aware of, if a single word derogatory to Miss Lytton be breathed by a single member of your family. The honor of Women becomes a fearful matter when men are compelled to take it up. And if one of those insinuations which you have made in your letters to me and my son, against Miss Lytton, be repeated elsewhere – your reflexion must shew you that it will become my immediate

duty to place myself in the hands of those who would remove the whole matter from secret gossip & place it in its true light before society. And the same reflexion, (when you think over the whole circumstances of the case) must convince you that that light would be most disastrous to the future career of your son, and be attended with consequences still more grave to those who have not the excuse of his years.

I speak here from long and thoro' knowledge of the world, where most acknowledged usages and most sacred rites have been invaded. And calmly confident of the results, if my caution does not suffice to prevent those verbal liberties of the Drawing room – the consequences of which Ladies do not always sufficiently forsee.

It is for me, whom you so strangely seem to see as the injured party, and of whose position in life you seem so unconscious, to say, that, in spite of all, I am willing to let the matter drop – and thus to close all correspondence with any branch of my family, I am Madam, Yr very obedt servant.

* * * * *

"not as a threat, but as a caution" - It looks like a threat to me. And Mrs Thomson does not take well to it. Another letter is volleyed straight back, and it's looking like pistols. Just as well Edward has included his son as co-offended.

On April 21st - eight days before Emily's death - Edward turns to the Thomson who will have to take up that pistol, Katherine's 70-year-old husband, Dr Anthony Todd Thomson ***...I have just recd the enclosed*** [which sadly - but tellingly - does not survive]- ***& making all allowance for Mrs Thomson's maternal wish to excuse her son, & find anywhere else justification for his conduct, I put it at once to Dr Thomson, as the head of the family, that there is but one view which all honourable men can take of the case – that the apology gentleman owes to gentleman for*** [all the reasons and demands repeated again... and] ***Mrs Thomson charging me "with gross mistatement" & applying to me the word "ungentlemanly".***

Either with this letter or the one before, he includes a note of Madame de Ritter, on Emily's worsening condition: ***The enclosed note explains the cause of my not having earlier replied to your letters; in the anxiety for the alarm-***

ing state of my daughter's health, occasioned by the merciless shock inflicted on her nervous system – and for which no apology in suitable terms has been either made or would be possible She is now attended by two physicians and today has been spitting blood.

* * * * *

Dr Thomson immediately responds, ***Dear Sir Edward, I must add my sincere apology to my sons for the trouble & annoyance occasioned by his foolish conduct, which you can alone excuse by remembering that he is a mere child...*** [then, following some mild excuses for his wife] ***I greatly regret that in a moment of irritation, Mrs Thomson should have written to you her last note, dated April 21st, which I beg in her behalf, entirely to withdraw.***

Equally hastily, Edward responds, ***Dear Sir, I beg to acknowledge your letter & to accept the apology offered in the same spirit in which it is tendered. I will cheerfully view the conduct to which it refers as the inconsiderate folly of a child...*** [then, following some mild disapprobation of the doctor's wife] ***In Mrs Thomson's withdrawal of the note she last wrote to me, all remembrance of it ceases in. Dear sir, yrs faithfully, E.B.L.***

A ***very handsome & gratifying note*** from Mrs Thomson follow, and Edward sends a similar cessation of hostilities to her, on 23rd April - six days before Emily's death.

This complete and instant acceptance by Edward, while his daughter is still traumatised, is odd. It may be that the seriousness of her condition finally overtakes his blustering. But two things suggest that there is something else to it. And here is the curved ball that I am not expecting - and do not fully appreciate until my visit to Lincoln Archive.

Firstly, there is a scribbled draft in our Archive of a letter that Edward does not send in response to Mrs Thomson's penultimate volley. In this is the suggestion that he has actually discovered something that does, in his mind, cast his daughter in a poor light.

Mrs Thomson's letter does not survive because he has given it to George D'Eyncourt. It is George D'Eyncourt who returns with Mrs Thomson's final capitulation. It is Mrs Thomson's mention of Emily in connection with George D'Eyncourt that - in Edward's scribbled draft of a response - gives him

the most painful astonishment and he ***utterly disbelieve***[s] it. ***Such a regard as she*** [Emily] ***might feel for Mr D'Eyncourt [is] perfectly similar to what she might feel for Mr Thomson, Mr Forster or any other of my friends. She stated so openly to me, as no doubt to yourself – and it is not more a cruelty than an insult to pervert or misconceive it.***

Hard indeed, if a man of my own age cannot be received at my House without subjecting my daughter to such interpretations...

He appears genuinely shocked. But for Mrs Thomson - if there's some truth to it - it is an irresistible grenade to throw at Edward's slight of her family seeking ***worldly advantage***.

And if Emily is quizzed over it - in this fragile week - innocent or not, if there has been further concealment from her father, perhaps further lies or purposefully unspoken truths... such an interview with him, we know, could well push Emily over the edge.

* * * * *

George D'Eyncourt has paid the Thomsons a visit, and whether by carefree contradition or carefree confirmation silenced Edward - but it is Lincoln Archive that throws up the proof there is fire to Mrs Thomson's smoke. In looking through other D'Eyncourt letters, Clare and I find the following:

Friday morning, 5th May 1848. Clara D'Eyncourt to George D'Eyncourt, ***My dearest George, You will see I wrote to you last night & have this morning recd yr heartrending letter of yesterday - I guess a great deal & am sorry you have been pained. I know how it wld bruise your kind heart to be in any way connected with the pleasure or pain of those that are yours. We shall meet soon, my dear Brother, in the meantime believe in the true sympathy of one who loved poor Emily like a younger sister. I shall bring your yellow waistcoat all the same, as you will not perhaps remain long in mourning, at least, not so long as you at present imagine. Be comforted my dear George – in these cases we can do nothing but submit – we are not free agents in all the circumstances of our lives, a superintending Providence orders for us better than we could do - & even affliction is beneficial to us. Your letter to me is not revealed & I will burn it as you desire – Adieu till we meet & take care of yourself. Ever your affectionate sister, Clara***

What?! I am quickly digging deeper into what is known about George D'Eyncourt. Apparently, not much. George is very much overshadowed in history by his cousin Alfred. He dies unmarried, aged 62, in 1871. But I do stumble upon upon a note at the bottom of p.62 of *The Letters of Alfred Lord Tennyson, Volume 1 1821-1850,* which in turn quotes from p.184 of *The Tennysons: Background to Genius* by Alfred's grandson Charles Tennyson and Hope Dyson. I give you the whole quote, as it is all of interest, but the bombshell is at the beginning:

It was probably in such moods of depression that he [Charles Tennyson D'Eyncourt] ***coined for his children the opprobrious*** [critical] ***monosyllabic nicknames preserved by family tradition. George Hildyard, the eldest, a man generally beloved - even by the Somersby family*** [Alfred's side] - ***who is said to have been deeply in love with Bulwer Lytton's daughter Emily and driven by her tragic death at 20 years old to seek solace in drink, he nicknamed 'The Sot'; Edwin, who married the daughter of the Duke of Newcastle and became an Admiral was 'The Snob'; Louis, whom Charles thought deficient in filial affection, he called 'The Stone'; Julia, whom everyone loved*** [and whom we are told in another note on p.143 also from *Background to Genius*, ***not being able to marry (her father's friend, Edward Bulwer Lytton) became a Roman Catholic, took the veil and died after many years of seclusion in a convent in Coventry***] ***was 'The Saint'; and Ellen, who had a violent temper, was 'The Shrew'. There is no tradition of any nickname for Clara, whose good nature was always a pacifying influence and who was responsible for bringing the Bayons and Somersby branches together after her father's death; Eustace, whose early death was the great sorrow of his father's life, would, had he lived, no doubt have been canonized with Julia.***

* * * * *

Deeply in love? 38-year-old heir to Bayons Manor finds himself in love with mousey 19-year-old wallflower after winter stay at remote gothic hall? Whether true or not, this spills new light onto the only significant surviving Emily letter from 1848 that is not written to Clara D'Eyncourt. This is the letter I quote at the beginning of this book. Emily's letter to Mrs Thomson, written from Bayons Manor on ***Sunday evening, 30th January, 1848.***

Courtzsy of the Tennyson D'Eyncourt family

The only image of the Tennyson D'Eyncourt siblings I have so far been able to find is of the backs of their heads - as their brother Eustace says a final goodbye in the Great Hall of Bayons Manor in January 1842, before heading to Barbados to die of the Yellow Fever

Whatever the gossip Mrs Thomson has heard from Lincolnshire, she is clearly teasing Emily with parallels to the book that Emily has just read, the recently published *Jane Eyre* by Currer Bell. Emily fires back, ***I do not like the book or the heroine. I felt myself dragged as it were by the roots of the hair thro' the work by an invisible power & form of interest – but all the same I hated the destiny that seemed to impel me. No! I think Jane Eyre disgusting! disgusting as a child, disgusting as a girl – disgusting in her love & disgusting in her happiness!***

SECOND EDITION OF JANE EYRE.
Just published, in 3 vols., post 8vo., price £1 11s. 6d. cloth,
JANE EYRE: an Autobiography. By CURRER BELL.
"A book of decided power. The thoughts are true, sound, and original."—Examiner.
"The most extraordinary production that has issued from the press for years."—Weekly Chronicle.
"Original, vigorous, edifying, and absorbingly interesting."—Jerrold's Newspaper.
"It is a book to make the heart beat, and to fill the eyes with tears."—Atlas.
"Of all the novels we have read for years, this is the most striking, and, we may add, the most interesting."—Economist.
"The characters are strongly marked, the incidents are various, and of a kind which enlist the sympathies; and the style is fresh and vigorous."—Morning Post.
"The book displays considerable skill in the plan, and great power."—Spectator.
"The matter and moral of the book are good, and the style is forcible and impressive."—Observer.
"Reality—deep, significant reality—is the character of this book."—Fraser's Magazine.
London: SMITH, ELDER, and Co., 65, Cornhill.

*Advertisment for **Jane Eyre** in the London Illustrated News - Februrary 1848*

You must hear the beginning of this letter. ***My dearest Mrs Thomson, Notwithstanding your cutting speech at the commencement of your letter, I feel much obliged to you for your thinking of me at all, and am only sorry that I cannot profusely repay you in full measure of interest or amusement for the gratification your epistle afforded me, as I am still excessively stupid and labouring under the wearisome process of convalescence!***

The gay hearted Miss Lomax has departed, her loss being much felt by all more especially by the gentlemen amongst whom perhaps the most ardent of her admirers was Mr G d'Eyncourt.

My Father leaves tomorrow or Monday for London. Mr d'Eyncourt was kind eno' to wish me to remain some little time longer with Clara & Mrs d'Eyncourt. – wh. invitation my Father has allowed me to accept.

My cough has prevented me taking any part in the amusements that have been going forward. I missed the Louth Ball [Louth is a town across the Wolds from Bayons] – ***and was forced to sit with the Dowager-part of the community at some dances that were given in the house.***

I have heard so much of your Friday soireés which indeed must be delightful.

It must be a great triumph for Cockburn to be able anticipate Balliol in the distance. My Father had applied some time since for Edward - but in vain.

You say you are delighted that I like** Jane Eyre **– but I only said I was interested in it. I do not like the book, or the heroine...[etc.]

Thirty-five chapters later you have, I hope, a good idea of the subtext to which I then alluded in Emily's poor review of Charlotte Brontë's novel.

Consider the life, so far, of the girl reading this novel. She is effectively orphaned, exiled to the house of strict Scottish widow with a favoured child, then sent to endure the rigours of distant boarding school, where she finds solace in the sweet love of a little schoolfriend from whom she is separated... As a young woman she finds herself in a remote gothic manor in the Midlands, where she is out of her depth in Society and the handsome heir, who is considerably older than her, is distracted by the ***gay hearted Miss Lomax***... However the troubled, drink-prone hero does notice her - but the girl's prim religious principles hold her back... for, after all else, one thing will always stand in the way of the girl's future - the constant threat to a fragile status quo - the hideous, shameful, mad, secret relation that will inevitably come along and put an end to all hope of happiness... that is, the mad first wife, who will descend the staircase from the room at the top of the house and sit outside on the stairs wailing...

Emily is about as close to the character of Jane Eyre as is humanly possible. Her review of the book is simple self-loathing.

* * * * *

Dear Henry [the email is from Joachim in Eichstatt], ***with usual German efficiency Jürgen*** [Dr Jürgen Reinhard, Joachim's friend and colleague] ***has already sent me an excellent transcript of the excerpts you had attached. As you'll see I've tried to provide an English translation, which may not be in the most elegant language, but I hope it is as close to Emily's original words as possible...***

The fifth letter to Clara. When the translation arrives, it is another bombshell. [The notes are Joachim's. I retain the formality of German expression:]

Dear Clara! Receive my thanks for the letter you sent yesterday. The remarks you made in it did not upset me, for whoever has a good conscience need not be afraid of anybody! The cause of my illness is completely different from the one you fear. I cannot stand there quietly and watch with indifference a girl's corruption [i.e. how she is being corrupted]***! You are older than I am, as a consequence it was not up to me to voice my opinion on the state of things, but I was necessarily surprised when I became aware of the daily visits you paid to a certain Mr B...! And when I noticed your all too visible love for him I lied down*** [to rest/because of the illness]. ***Yes, indeed, my long illness is nothing but the fruit of the vexation I felt with regard to your wrongdoing/crime! Mr B... is a married man and does nothing but play with your emotions*** [***'den Gefühlen of Clara'*** - she mixes German and English], ***eternal damnation or hopeless love is your lot/fate!!***

Yours, who worries/grieves for your sake, Emily Lytton

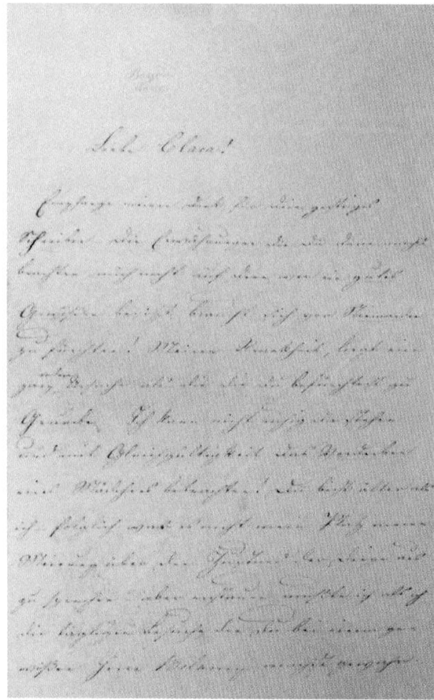

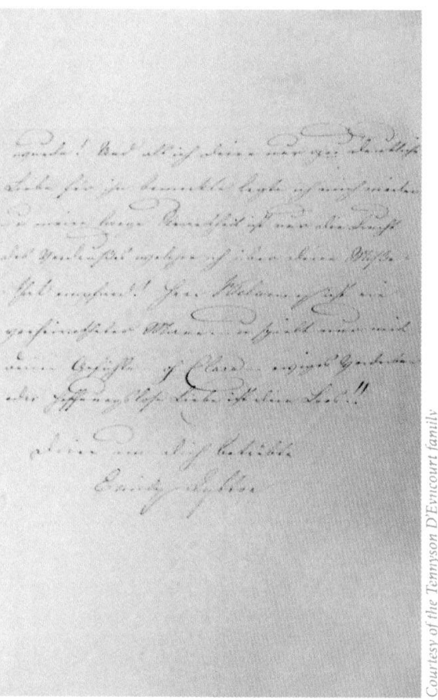

Courtesy of the Tennyson D'Eyncourt family

Written in German for secrecy - but when? The Bayons Manor stamp at the top suggests she is writing at Bayons, but she is in Clara's company until she leaves for Brompton... so is it her first, playful, or - if she takes the paper with her - her last, bitter, letter to Clara?

* * * * *

Bayons, it seems, is a hotbed of sex and intrigue. Whilst Emily is acting out Charlotte Brontë's *Jane Eyre*, Clara it acting out Charlotte Brontë's *The Professor*. Emily looks to have written the name Mr 'Belamy' [last line of the 1st page, and 5th line of the 2nd] – and he is mentioned [with 2 'l's] in another letter to Clara: ***Pray do not forget to remember me to Mr Bellamy – I saw a gentleman very like him in the train & thought of you in course my dear!***

I am now searching for Mr Bellamy – there is an architect based in Lincoln called Pearson Bellamy, whose firm was involved in building Bayons Manor... and also a William Bellamy who rents local land... It is more likely the latter.

So is this letter written in jest? Does it simply reflect the good humour of the other four letters, much of which are also written with playful intrigue?

Or is it Emily's final letter? A bitter, wretched reaction to Clara overstepping Emily's moral boundary - and the break up of a final precious friendship? At this moment, Clara is Emily's only close confidante aside from Natalie. The relationship with Natalie is breaking down at No 29 Pelham Terrace, as the precocious 16-year-old flirts with Robert and is more interested in marching with the Chartists than planning her friend's future. Is Emily, in this letter, scuttling her only remaining friendship - with the 35-year-old lover of a married man? Does she once more feel betrayed? Is this another nail in her stigmata?

As I write this, I can't actually make up my mind. But either way, it is bad.

If it is the former, it is indicative of much mischief - not mischief that I am here to judge, but which, if discovered, and her father confronts her with it, we have seen the effect of such humiliation... The most telling remark of the whole Thomson correspondence is one of Edward's, written within a week of Emily's death, that I have not yet quoted. ***I have spoken unreservedly to Miss Lytton on the subject matter of your letter & remarks...*** Mortified is the word.

If it is the latter, then it piles on yet another reason for Emily's mental and physical descent into suicide-by-any-other-name. The further collapse of her world, as one by one, she is betrayed or deserted (in her eyes) by the only friends she has, her father, her brother, the Thomsons, Clara, Natalie...

What we can safely take from this letter, I think, is the comment, ***my long illness is nothing but the fruit of... vexation.*** Here, I believe, Emily is giving us, in her own words, the answer to the mystery of her death,

* * * * *

I wonder if Edward's 'unreserved' talk with Emily on her sickbed is his last meeting with his daughter before she is delirious or unconcious? I hope not. But it may well be. Edward does not forsee Emily's death. Two days before it, he is still elsewhere than Brompton writing letters - two short notes to his friend the actor/manager William Macready (1793–1873) [who is behind Edward's West End hits ten years before]. They compare notes on sick children - ***I have known Madeira effect such permanent cures in consumptive cases, that I am very sanguine of your son's complete restoration... I too have been much distressed by the long illness of my daughter.***

This suggests he is sanguine too about his daughter. It is misplaced on both accounts. Macready is to lose three of his children in the coming decade - a son, Walter, aged thirteen; another son, Henry (middle name Bulwer), aged nineteen; and a daughter, Lydia, aged sixteen. For all the romance of Victorian costume drama, tell me honestly you would like to live in one.

In the end, Edward is kept away from his daughter's bedside on the doctors' orders. Even this Katherine Planché politicises. She writes in a letter [dated the day itself, April 29th, 1848] to Dr Rouse, that ***Sir Edward not being allowed to see his daughter affords the plausible ultimate assertion that Lady Lytton was not in fact more harshly dealt with as a mother than he was as a father, though in any case there is a wide difference between the feelings of a father and those of a mother.***

* * * * *

Thus scandal, gossip, anger and recriminations are the tawdry circumstances of Emily's final days - and the one thing that isn't tawdry is, as Rosina suggests, the boarding house. I go looking for No. 29 Pelham Terrace today. It is confusing, because the fine corner house at the end of Pelham Place - behind grand Pelham Crescent on the Old Brompton Road - is No.29. But, Victorian 'Pelham Terrace' is not Pelham Place. Pelham Terrace appears to have been buildings that lined what is now Pelham Street, which runs to the side of the Crescent. Much of Pelham Street has long since been carved up by the District Line and mid-rise 20th Century buildings. There is a short stretch of what was Pelham Terrace still in existence, Nos. 51 to 61 Pelham Street - but I choose to believe that this does not include what was No.29. It was a sad place for my family and I am content that it exists no more.

The loss I do mourn is Emily's last writings - her novel, her journal, her last thoughts, the final answers to her state of mind in those final few weeks... all destroyed - for a reason - by her father. The reason, I do not doubt, is nothing more than we have already guessed. But I am spoilt. We have so much of Emily in Box 88, I just want that last, resolving, expression of closure.

And, remarkably, I am to get it.

* * * * *

The fourth - quite unbelievable - piece of serendipity that has blessed this book, I have saved till last to tell.

Throughout my research, I have been growing a family tree of the Greenes of Swords, Ireland. It sits on Ancestry.com, in leaf, and growing thanks to the continued input of Greene descendants around the world. It has been invaluable in understanding the dates, names and relationships that *Miss Greene's Recollections* was not concerned with, because its author already knew them.

Initially this line of research is about discovering what happens to Miss Greene. Her final days - even her death year - prove elusive for many years. Then it becomes about her legacy; who inherits her belongings - does she have other images, writings, memorabilia, of Emily? Her *Recollections* manuscript is brought to Knebworth by Bonnie Wilkinson, and so I am inclined to follow this branch of the family. This is initially confusing because it becomes 'Greene' again, Bonnie Wilkinson marrying her first cousin William Greene.

I continue to follow Bonnie Greene's branch - not through eldest children, but through whichever branch leads to further discoverable branches - to an Alfred D. Greene, born in 1921, but with no death date. Moving to the census website 192.com, I find an Alfred D. Greene registered to vote at an address in Northwood, Middlesex. Northwood is between Knebworth and London, so no more that 45 minutes away from my desk.

I write a letter to this address on 11th July 2012. The very next day I receive a telephone call. It is one of those wonderful warm voices that cushions all news, good or bad. The lady's name is Jean Greene. There is bad news. Alfred has recently died. But hear the rest...

Her husband was indeed a descendant of Grace (Bonnie) Wilkinson. She was his great-grandmother. There is a lovely portrait of Bonnie on her living room wall. What is more, there is a box of Greene heirlooms that she has resisted throwing out, although her husband never showed a great deal of interest in it. She is in her 80s - caring for a disabled son, Paul, with a married daughter Jenny who lives nearby - and is contemplating downsizing, so I haven't written before time. She is off to Norfolk for a couple weeks, but when she gets back, would I like to come for tea?

* * * * *

The day after, I receive an email from Jean. ***I am so excited as this evening, instead of completing my packing, I looked through some of the little books I have had in safe keeping and I found the announcement of the death of Emily. Once I had the date, I looked in two diaries and found quite a long entry written by Grace*** [Bonnie] ***about her friend who she had known and loved as a sister...***

Then in the other Greene family journal the aunt you spoke of [Miss Greene] ***wrote about being with Emily for the last three weeks of her life. I had read all this before but of course it did not mean very much to me, but now these people have almost come to life! It is amazing and I am so glad that I have found all this for you.***

Clare Fleck and I are in Northwood almost the moment Jean steps out of the car from Norfolk. The 'Greene box' is extraordinary. Not only does it contain a wealth of photos, memorabilia and the journals of Bonnie Wilkinson and her subsequent Greene family, it also contains earlier Greene heirlooms passed on by Miss Greene, indeed, left to Bonnie as Miss Greene's natural heir.

But how does this treasure box come to be <u>here</u>, in Northwood, with Jean? The butterfly wings that flapped to make this possible are almost inconceivably random. It passes first to Bonnie's son David William Greene (1848-1890), born five months after Emily's death. David, who lives in South America then Switzerland, marries Maria Loreto Felicia de Medina Y Junquera (1853–1943), the Cuban born niece-by-marriage of his younger sister Rose... you don't have to take this in, I am just stressing how random it is!

Courtesy of the Greene family

Bonnie and her son David in 1850 by John Hayter

The box passes to David's fifth son Felix as, settled in England, he is thought its most appropriate guardian. Felix dies unmarried and passes it - not to his elder nephews, who are all in Australia, but - to the son of the fourth son Christian, whose name is Alfred D. Greene, and who lives 45 minutes from Knebworth...

...and whose widow Jean has just poured me a cup of tea.

It's inconceivable. And it gets better.

* * * * *

Jean doesn't make the connection on our first visit, but having been shown the only image that we have of Miss Greene - a drawing reproduced in my great-grandfather Victor's 1913 biography of Edward Bulwer Lytton, acquired from Bonnie's youngest daughter Helen (a line of enquiry I try early on - unsuccessfully, as Helen, a Derby doctor, never marries) - Jean realises that the drawing is a copy of a beautiful little painting on ivory that she has elsewhere in her home. This is the original - colour - version of this only-known portrait of Miss Greene. It is here in Northwood - and Jean and her family did not know who it was.

* * * * *

Pulling, one by one, more wonderful surprises from this magical tombola, we come to Bonnie's journals. There are two in the box - and what perfect dates, 1845 and 1846-1848!

First, I wish to praise Bonnie Wilkinson for handwriting that I can actually read. Second, how refreshing to read the life of a happy, well-adjusted girl in a happy, well-adjusted family - Bonnie certainly has her dark moments, particularly uncertainties in the first year of her marriage, but when she goes abroad to finish her education (to Brussels, the subject of the first journal) her mother and her 'Aunt Mary' go with her; when she spends time with her father, he is by the parlour fire with her sharing jokes and the stories of the day; or when he is sick, she and the rest of the family are attending to him in the room upstairs. It is a charming father-daughter relationship, within a charming 19th Century family. Here we have Trollope - not Brontë... or Poe.

* * * * *

Then there is the 1848 journal. I cannot believe it. Bonnie has copied into this journal a paragraph in German, under the heading ***April 3rd, 1848, Brompton.*** Beneath the German paragaph she writes, ***These were the last words written in the journal that my dear & first friend kept till within a month of her death. They are true – She was deceived by seeming friends; she was unloved by those who should have nursed and sheltered that delicate & sensitive mind from those cold blasts of the world's breath that withered it, in, what should have been its beauty & its prime.***

There was no happiness on this dark earth for her – And God took her. She suffered through the sins of others, for nearly twenty years, & then through the righteousness of One she was taken to happiness for ever. Who could long weep for her? May God help & pardon her wretched father, & her more wretched mother.

* * * * *

She was my first friend, she was my sister before I had a sister. Since I was two years old I have known & loved her well. Lately, I grieve to say, cir-

Courtesy of the Greene family

The oval frame removed reveals that the little ivory portrait is indeed the original

cumstances & the wishes of others have separated us & I have seen but little of her lately. I fancied her about to enter a sphere so different from mine that it would be impossible for us to be childish friends still & therefore I was almost glad that the separation, which I supposed must come, was being made so gently, so imperceptibly, between us, by circumstances, change of place & a thousand things that I at least could not control.

I was overwhelmed when I heard of her death – I knew she was ill – very

ill. I had not been allowed to see her in London [pregnant Bonnie travels from Lancashire to visit her parents for 5 days from March 21st - just after Emily's arrival in Brompton]. ***I had received a letter from my dearest mother saying that she was very ill - & after dinner I went out into the quiet garden in the cool still evening with my husband.***

We were walking very slowly & a thousand flowers & leaves were closing silently & a thousand birds were singing. We had walked the Linden [lime tree] ***walk when he asked if I had received any news of her. I said I had, & began to read my mother's letter to him. He said nothing till I had finished a passage which said that she was very ill, had received a violent shock from – it was supposed – seeing her mother, & was given up by her Doctors.***

Then he said, quite quietly, "And now she is dead!"

More than a week has now passed & I can say with my whole heart -

Thank God!

* * * * *

Despite the burning of her journal, unbelievably, we do have the final written thoughts of Emily Bulwer Lytton. Because they were copied out - we may guess - by Miss Greene or Mrs Wilkinson or by Bonnie herself, and written down in Bonnie's 1848 journal... which I have just found in a wooden box in Northwood.

The words are in German, Emily's preferred language of secrets. Time to try the patience one last time of my German angel Joachim in Eichstatt. Can he decipher this paragraph?

With Jürgen's help again, this is what Joachim emails back [again, not wishing to pre-judge Emily's thoughts and the meaning of her words, I retain their literal translation from the German:]

Mehrere Tage sind verflossen und ich habe ihren Flug nicht notirt.
Several days have passed and I have not noted down their flight.

Warum diese Nachlässigkeit?
Why this negligence?

Soll ich die Wahrheit sagen?
Am I to tell the truth?

Soll ich gestehen was um mein Herz liegt?
Am I to confess what lies on my heart?

- ***Nein, ach nein!***
- No, oh no!

Denn ich bin getäuscht und Täuschung thut so weh so unendlich weh.
For I've been deceived and deception hurts much, so infinitely.

Genug. Schweige - Ich verzweifle.
Enough. Be silent – I despair.

Keines Glücks für mich mehr - wenigstens auf dieser Welt keines.
No luck/happiness for me anymore – at least none in this world.

* * * * *

These are the last written words of Emily Bulwer Lytton. They are written on Monday 3rd April. Possibly she and her brother have just rowed about Cockburn; possibly Clara has just confessed the reality of her relationship with Mr Bellamy; maybe, even, a secret tryst with an older man is imploding... What I can see, is Emily lying sick in one room of 29 Pelham Terrace, and Madame de Ritter and Natalie joking and laughing with Teddy in the next.

Ultimately, I don't think it matters whether George D'Eyncourt is in love with her. I don't think it matters that Cockburn Thomson is humiliating her. I don't think it matters that Miss Greene is smothering and gauche. I don't think it matters that Carl de Ritter's life is threatened on the barricades of Vienna. I don't think it matters that her mother is a permanent Damocles sword of embarrassment and social disgrace. I don't think it matters that her father is hiding a pack of illegitimate children and is broke. I don't think it matters that she is sick. I don't even think it matters that her mother and father don't love her - I believe they do, in their own peculiar ways...

But I do think it matters if Natalie doesn't love her.

All of the above contributes to Emily giving up on life - but I read these last words as being about Natalie. The Cannstatt letters tell of the deepest love in Emily's life - even beyond her love for her brother - and the realisation that she does not even have a friend in Natalie is the final blow. Her God is all that is left. And in these final weeks, that God is the one in Heaven - not the one in Pimlico.

* * * * *

The best thing, for me, to come out of these seventeen years of exploring Emily's life is the knowledge that Emily did have a family. My own let her down, although they certainly loved her - but, in the Greenes, Emily had a family who unreservedly cared for her, who unreservedly were there for her if she needed a friend, a companion, or a home.

Her parents gave her life, a living, letters - but the Greenes gave her a home.

The last little book to come out of the box in Northwood is a journal of the Greene Family of Swords, Ireland. Started in the late 18th Century by Miss Greene's maternal grandfather Philip O'Dwyer, it is continued by his daughter, Mary Anne Greene, continued by her daughter, Mary Letitia Greene, continued by her niece, Mary Anne Wilkinson, continued by her daughter, Grace 'Bonnie' Greene, and so on... It contains a note on every birth, death and major event in 250 years of the family's history. It is a genealogist's grail.

There are a lot of Greenes. And this journal is, naturally, limited to events in the lives of only Greene family members. There is one exception to this. When the journal is in the care of Mary Letitia Greene, it includes two other members of her family:

June 27th 1828. My dear friend Mrs Bulwer had a daughter born, at Woodcot Hall Oxfordshire, baptized Emily Elizabeth...

Mrs Bulwer had a son born at Hertford Street London on Tuesday Nov 8th 1831 at 4 minutes past two baptized Edward Robert Lytton...

January 1842. My darling Boy E. L. Bulwer left me to go to School at Twickenham, till then I scarcely lost sight of him for 7 years...

Left my darling Emily at Neuweid in Germany Oct 3 1842 – under the care of Mme de Weling... left the dear child miserable...

...[Her father] found her so ill & unhappy that he took her away & placed her with a celebrated Dr near Stuttgart – where thank God she is not so unhappy, but I who know her know how lonely & deserted she feels...

...Mde d'Azzimart left Knebworth – when I was immediately invited - & when I would not have gone, except for Emily's sake. I stayed six months there with her & had an opportunity of coming to the truth of much that had passed whilst she was separated from me, & with great grief that was. The extreme Trials she had met with during our separation had weighed most heavily upon her mind, as she was often very odd - to say the least of it - & often her charming self, & tho she seemed in health she seemed to have a presentiment of death - which she often talked of - & used to say her perfect idea of happiness was Lover to God!

...After nearly five years of indescribable disappointments and unhappiness, my dear Emily Bulwer Lytton died at Brompton April 29th, 1848, at nine o clock in the evening – I had the comfort of being much alone with her for the last three weeks of her life, & witnessing her great piety, and joy at her release from this world of woe, with the certainty of the happiness she was going to, bought for her by the atoning blood of her Saviour.

First, the conviction of her present happiness reconciles me to her loss, & next, seeing that she is taken from the evil to come! The same powerful and good God who has so dealt with her, will I trust guard & guide her dear brother, who still remains.

* * * * *

To that dear brother - my great-great-grandfather - Robert Lytton, I leave the last word about Emily Bulwer Lytton.

It is a poem that I cannot read without weeping.

Eleanor is the princess of the fairy tales spun by Emily to enchant her little brother, Teddy, in the nurseries of their childhood.

His poem is called *Little Ella*.

Robert, Lord Lytton.

CHAPTER 36

~ Little Ella ~

I KNOW now, little Ella, what the flowers
Said to you then, to make your cheek so pale;
And why the blackbird in our laurel bowers
Spake to you only, and the timorous snail
Fear'd less your steps than those of the May shower.
It is not strange these creatures loved you so,
And told you all. 'Twas not so long ago
You were yourself a bird, or else a flower.

And, little Ella, you were pale because
So soon you were to die. I know that now,
And why there ever seem'd a sort of gauze
Over your deep blue eyes, and sad young brow.
You were too good to grow up, Ella, you,
And be a woman, such as I have known !
And so upon your heart they put a stone,
And left you, child, among the flowers and dew.

O thou, the morning star of my sad soul !
My little elfin friend from Faery Land !
Whose memory is yet innocent of the whole
Of that which makes me doubly need thy hand,
Thy guiding hand from mine so soon withdrawn !
Here, where I find so little like to thee,
For thou wert as the breath of dawn to me,
Starry, and pure, and brief, as is the dawn.

Thy knight was I, and thou my Faery Queen,
('Twas in the days of love and chivalry !)
And thou did'st hide thee in a bower of green.
But thou so well hast hidden thee, that I
Have never found thee since. And thou didst set
Many a task, and quest, and high emprize,
Ere I should win from thine approving eyes
My guerdon, –ah! so many, that not yet

My tasks are ended, nor my wanderings o'er.
But some day there will come across the main
A magic barque, and I shall quit this shore
Of care, and find thee in thy bower again ;
And thou wilt say, "My brother, hast thou found
Our home at last ?" . . . Whilst I, in answer, sweet,
Shall heap my life's last booty at thy feet.
And bare my breast with many a bleeding wound.

The spoils of time! the trophies of a world !
The keys of conquer'd towns, and captive kings,
And many a broken sword, and banner furl'd.
The heads of giants, and swart soldan's rings,
And many a maiden's scarf, and many a wand
Of baffled wizard, many an amulet,
And many a shield with mine own heart's blood wet.
And jewels rare from many a distant land !

How sweet with thee, my sister, to renew
The happy search for those ethereal birds
Which back to their own climes thou didst pursue,—
Ah, heedless ! thou, in all whose deeds and words
Unkindness never was till then, nor lack
Of care for others' pain ! Couldst thou but see
How woeful weary is my want of thee,
Methinks that even now thou wouldst come back;

Leaving thy heavenly playmates, for my sake,
To let me lean my head upon thy breast,
And weep away those worst of griefs that ache
And scorch, but cannot turn to tears. Or, best,
The way that leads where thou art gone, contrive
O child, to whisper to me ! Ope the gate,
And help me thro'. Else, I shall die too late
Even for thy consoling to revive.

She pass'd out of my youth at the still time
O' the early light, when all was green and husht.
She passd, and pass'd away. Like broken rhyme
Her sweet short life's few relics are. This crusht
And scatter'd rose, she dropp'd: that page, she turn'd,
And finish'd not: this curl, her gift: this knot
That flutter'd from her . . . Hard world, harm them not !
My right to keep them hath been sorely earn'd.

Robert Bulwer Lytton

The Mausoleum c.1900

CHAPTER 37

~ *Afterwards* ~

In the first days of May 1848, Emily's body is returned to Knebworth Park and placed in the family mausoleum on a side shelf beneath her grandmother, Mrs Bulwer, and her great-grandmother, Mrs Warburton Lytton.

Before the century is played out, she is joined by her brother, Robert, and her nephew, Henry. Her niece Constance joins as ashes in 1923. Like Emily, these Lyttons all live lives shorter than Nature's promise. Last of the current assembled is the sister-in-law Emily will never meet, Edith, in 1936, aged 95.

The letters of her childhood - which only her father has read - are bound and boxed to be discovered in 150 years time. Her sweet short life's few relics are left to blend in amongst the storied treasures that give life to Knebworth House. An embroidered bookmark. The needlepoint of a firescreen. The little portrait on a bedroom wall.

* * * * *

Her father's attention turns to the birth of son, Arthur Edward Gilbert Lowndes, six weeks later at 22 Upper Eaton Street, Pimlico. The parents list themselves on the birth certificate as Arthur Lowndes and Marion Woolstonecraft Godwin Lowndes, formerly Waller. It is the mother's name that looks like a pseudonym, but it is actually her real name. It is the father's name that is not real - and that the mother should take the use of it.

Why 'Lowndes'? Because that is the name of the man the father's mother should have married if love was all that mattered in life. As he writes in the short piece of autobiography included in his son's biography, *The Life, Letters and Literary Remains of Edward Bulwer, Lord Lytton* [1883]:

Poor Mr Milnes Lowndes crept away into the country, and was heard of no more. I confess that, of all the candidates for my mother's hand, he was the

one who most inspires my sympathy; the one with whom, I think, she would have been the most happy, could she have returned his affection.

When, some two years later, a carriage stood at the door of a fashionable London church, when a bride passed from the porch, and the curious by-standers pressed forwards to gaze, a low exclamation made her lift her down-cast eyes, and my mother - that bride - saw amidst the crowd the mournful face of Milnes Lowndes. A year after her marriage he died of a decline.

Marion Lowndes - after the birth of daughters Lucy Augusta Jessie Lowndes in 1851 and Evelyne Grace Elizabeth Lowndes in 1853 (who lives 2 months) - eventually settles in Dorset Square, just up the road from Portman Square where Mrs Bulwer lived. As 'Mrs Lowndes', she becomes a symbol of what might have been, for both Edward and his mother.

* * * * *

Marion remains in Edward's life until the end, although there are further paramours and further children. Marion's letters to Robert are full of stories of women who were in love with his father; and she appears, more than once, to be the one constant companion to get him out of a scrape.

I don't think we need be suspicious of Marion, but it is disturbing that at least three of the further paramours die during, or soon after, their liaisons with Edward.

Marion claims, with annoying delicacy, ***I saved your father from a duel & worse, much worse than a duel*** over Charlotte Lady Glamis, sister-in-law of our present Queen's maternal grandfather. This happens ***at one painful time of my life, when I was suffering such torture (that not for all the gold in this world would I live that time over again).*** We must guess that this is the time of her daughter Evelyne's death in December 1853 - Lady Glamis dies the following November, aged 27, four years into a childless marriage.

In 1870, Edward's 'housekeeper' of a country home closer to London that he keeps in the 1860s - Copped Hall in Totteridge - Eleanor Thomson, is barely out of her 20s when - having given birth to two of Edward's children - she dies in particularly nasty circumstances alone in a boarding house in the Old Kent Road. ***The disease has taken another form, viz that of gangrene in the back - in fact the back bone is exposed and the effluvia thereupon cou-***

pled with other causes is enough to bring fever into the house, writes Edward Savage, keeper of the lodgings. Marion steps in to rescue the two children, adopting the boy, Edward, into her own household and assisting Edward in placing the infant girl, Alice, in an orphanage.

Then, at about the same time, a married American woman, Marie DeRosset, who appears a permanent resident at Edward's London home, 12 Grosvenor Square, dies there of a laudanum overdose, aged 26. ***When Mrs DeRosset's strange death plunged your father in such terrible grief - & he sent for me,*** writes Marion, ***I soon saw that Mr DeRosset was killing him, & that your presence alone could save & console him, that you alone by stepping in your father's house would oblige Mr DeRosset to leave it... Ask your father's housekeeper Mrs Tate. She will tell you, I did all I could at that time (for to my astonishment she & the valet both thanked me before I left that evening) for the good I had done their master.***

* * * * *

If Marion isn't poisoning all these women, it is possible her mother is. A bizarre incident takes place in a hotel in Llangollen, Wales, in the months before Evelyne is born, in Brighton, in October 1853. Rosina becomes ill and believes she is being poisoned by a lady who has befriended her. This lady, Mrs Pyke, makes at least three visits to the hotel where is Rosina is staying, accompanied by her grandson, Arthur.

The lady claims to be American. She pronouces 'daughter', 'darter'. But American is not the only accent that would put that first syllable in a higher register. Italian - or Savoyard - would too. The five-year-old Arthur tells Rosina that he has three papas, who don't live with his mamma - ***but they come and sleep sometimes, but never at the same time... my rich papa, he has such a fine! house in the country – and one in London – but we don't live with him – but he sends us Deers and pheasants – and pineapples, and peaches – and things...***

Mrs Pyke leaves the hotel in a hurry - around the time of Evelyne's birth - saying her son has died & she needs to go to Paris. On 27th Dec 1853, Mrs Pyke writes to Rosina from the Hotel de Provence, Leicester Square, London, ***Pity me - I have lost my son - and my daughter her baby.***

According to Rosina, Mrs Pyke all but confesses, in her remorse, that she has been spying for Edward, and warns Rosina of a further spy to be sent. Her name then becomes one more well-worn curse in Rosina's vitriolic letters to her husband and others - changing to a version closer to the woman's real name four years later, when she hears it from her former landlady in Geneva. Rosina writes that a ***Mme Pianon*** (sic) wants ***to offer me the bribe of a sum of money – to consent to a divorce – that he Sir Liar might marry her niece!!***

* * * * *

The mysterious Mrs Pyke is, clearly, the mysterious Mrs Pian - the inn-keeper's daughter from Dover or Folkestone who was first Jessie Eaglestone, then Jessie Waller of Faversham and Nice, then Jessie Pian of Genova and Geneva. Colonel Ceasar Pian of the Sardinian Army has left her a widow, and none of her seven Waller children, apparently, in a state to which she would like to see them accustomed.

If she is telling the truth about a son in Paris - which Rosina doesn't believe, but is possible, as she has two more sons after the renowned neurophysiologist Augustus Volney - her two youngest, William and Thomas Waller - and supposedly there had been anticipation that the son was on the brink of making a good match. But a clue for us, to Mrs Pian's reduced finances in widowhood, is the fact that she goes to live - and die, 14 years later, of heart disease - in low-cost Geneva, once refuge to Rosina in similar bourgeois penury.

As carer to his son Arthur, Mrs Pian is receiving Edward's financial support whether or not she is spying on Rosina for him. So is malice aforethought in Wales that autumn of 1853? Rosina suspects it is, when she becomes ill from a stomach complaint. If Lady Bulwer were to keel over from food or alcohol poisioning in a hotel in Wales, then the way is clear for Mrs Pian's daughter Marion to become Lady Bulwer and - the continental widow might assume - be set and settled for life. And little Arthur Lowndes, and his sisters Lucy and Evelyne, might secure a more promising future, and their own ***pineapples, and peaches – and things....*** Mrs Pike could disappear and Madame Pian settle quietly in Switzerland.

It is colourfully Agatha Christiesque. If these thoughts are going through Jessie's head, providence steps in and punishes her for them - with the death of the third grandchild, Evelyne, and her daughter's ***torture (that not for all the gold in this world would I live that time over again)***.

But it would be an interesting alternative biography of Edward Bulwer Lytton if all the women and girls close to him are being bumped off, one-by-one, by a Savoyard Colonel's widow looking to make her daughter the only woman at his side.

Do I need to look again at Emily's death? The laudanum and prussic acid theories? I'll leave that to someone else.

* * * * *

The grandson, Arthur Lowndes, in his twenties, is set up in business by Edward, but it is not successful and he emigrates to New York, where he becomes [according to his obituary in *The New York Times*, 3rd January 1917] a clergyman and ***one of the leading scholars of the Protestant Episcopal Church***. My Australian cousin Beth Thomson fills me in, also, on the history of Marion's second child, Lucy Lowndes, who becomes Mrs Lucy Taylor in 1885, second wife of successful businessman Walter Taylor, owner of Taylor's Depository in Pimlico. On his death, childless Lucy moves to Florence, where she joined by Arthur's only child, Jane Lowndes. On Lucy's death in 1910, Jane returns to North America, marries a clergyman Thomas Cracknell, but dies childless in 1926. And so ends the line of 'Arthur/George' and Marion 'Lowndes'.

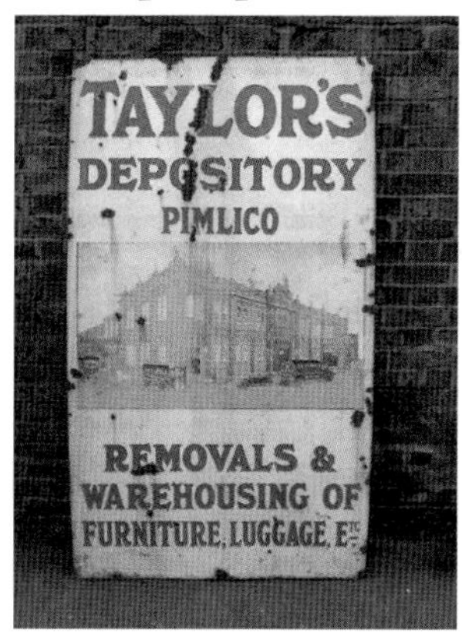

Nor have I found any descendants of Laura Deacon and her surviving daughters. Of Georgina, Gertrude and Violet, only Violet marries and her apparent only son, Richard Caunter, has two daughters, both of whom remain spinsters. It looks as though Eve and Olive Caunter are both living in London suburbs until the 1990s, but this book, sadly, is too late for me to meet them.

Laura Deacon does not appear again in Edward's life. She does appear to die in Paddington in 1886 - with the executor of her Will, Richard Caunter (father of the above Richard Caunter) - as Constance Laura Grant, ***widow of Leonard Archibald Grant, Gentleman.*** But, ever the woman of mystery, the death certificate says Laura Grant is 70 years-old - whereas Laura Deacon would be 81 in early 1886. From what I now know of Laura, this does not surprise me. Nor does the fact that I am yet to find any record of a Leonard Archibald Grant.

* * * * *

There is an unidentified painting that hangs in Knebworth House today that has always been assumed to have been one of Edward's paramours. If it is, Marion Lowndes is the only likely candidate. The age of the woman, the mid-Century hairstyle, the fact that the painting is unnamed, the expression in the woman's eyes, all say Marion Lowndes to me. I have compared it to the photographs that exist of her brother Augustus and detect a similarity in the mouths - and certainty not a dissimilarity as a whole.

An Unknown Woman

Augustus Waller

I am pleased to think it is Marion, and pleased that it hangs in Edward Bulwer Lytton's home. Marion's letters reveal a great tenderness for my great-great-great-grandfather, a man whom even his greatest supporters would admit, could be impassioned, volatile, difficult - creative, if you prefer. No woman in his life - indeed no one in his life - spent as much time with him as Marion did. No one, therefore, knew him as well - and Edward Bulwer Lytton remains to her, to the very end, ***the handsomest & the noblest of beings***.

* * * * *

The D'Eyncourt family remain stalwart friends to Edward during the difficult time of his daughter's death, and he is back staying with them in Bayons in June. Clara marries the following year, aged 37, a John Palmer - but George never marries, and dies before Edward, aged 61, in 1871. Clara writes to

George six days after Emily's death, 4th May 1848, ***poor dear Emily Lytton, so interesting, so young, so formed for the enjoyment of life, cut off so early, just as we had all learnt to love her; whose virtues were most resplendent in private & domestic life & whose talents of a superior order were concealed under a veil of humility & modesty which, once withdrawn, gave light & life to all & every thing she gazed upon. London to me will seem more desolate than ever, for this year I had associated with it the pleasure of sometimes meeting her... Poor Julia has by this time reached Princethorpe (a French Benedictine Convent*** [just south east of Coventry]***) - I wish she & Emily had met; there was something in the latter that reminded me of Julia & made me love her more.***

George does leave a few journals, that are now in Lincoln Archive, but unfortunately nothing that spills more light on the events of 1848. All we know is that he does step in to assist Edward in his contretemps with the Thomsons, which suggests that he did indeed notice the small awkward sick girl who had been staying with them over Christmas, and feels a responsibility to protect her name and her reputation.

My dear Sir Edward, writes Mrs Thomson on 3rd May 1848, ***Mr George d'Eyncourt wished me to write to you last night, & I hope my letter explained all that had pained you yesterday... Mr G d'Eyncourt can tell you that even before, when I wrote to him relative to his kind mediation, all was cancelled in my mind except regret...***

For that moment of error, occurring in a state of anguish in which I was scarcely accountable for what I did, I have sought to make every reparation, & before even that was required of me, I endeavoured to retrace my steps. I trust it is atoned - it will however be expiated by years of regret. You may rest sure that nothing more shall ever trouble you in the conduct of my desponding child. You have ever been kind to him – your displeasure lies heavy at his heart.

Dear Sir Edward, may God bless & sustain you. Your Emily is gone to rejoin your dear Mother – both were high-minded, religious, ready for Heaven. I loved them both - & though we may not meet here, there I trust we may, though through so much sorrow. It will be still my sad privilege here to think of the past, to mourn for the departed – to hope & pray for the living with a sorrowing affection – however uncalled for it may be, Faithfully & ever yours, K. Thomson

* * * * *

After the death of her husband the following year, Mrs Thomson goes abroad for some time, possibly accompanying her son Cockburn on his further education in Bonn, Germany [following just after Robert]. Cockburn does go to Oxford, leaving with a B.A. in 1857 having made a name for himself by translating, from the Sanskrit, the 700-verse Hindu Scripture, the *Bahagavad Ghita*. By 1860, Katherine is living in Dover from where she publishes two books jointly with Cockburn under the pseudonyms Grace and Phillip Wharton - *The Queens of Society* and *The Wits and Beaux of Society.*

Cockburn Thomson

Cockburn's pseudonym Phillip Wharton comes from an ancestor of Katherine's family, Philip, Duke of Wharton (1698–1731), who features in *The Wits and Beaux of Society* as a young prodigy who wastes his talents, ***suffice to say, that when Pope*** [Alexander Pope (1688-1744)] ***wanted a man to hold up to the scorn of the world as a sample of wasted abilities, it was Wharton that he chose -***

Wharton, the scorn and wonder of our days,
Whose ruling passion was love of praise

Cockburn reflects his ancestor in more than just name. The book's description of the Duke of Wharton continues, ***He was precocious beyond measure, and at sixteen was a man. His first act of folly - or perhaps, he thought, of manhood - came off at this early age. He fell in love with the daughter of a Major General Holmes; and though there is nothing extraordinary in that, for nine-tenths of us have been love-mad at as early an age, he did what fortunately very few do in the first love affair, he married the adored one.***

Early marriages are often extolled, and justly enough, as safeguards against profligate habits, but this one seems to have had the contrary effect on young Philip. His wife was in every sense too good for him: he was madly in love with her at first, but soon shamelessly and openly faithless.

* * * * *

Cockburn does not fullfill his young promise, because he drowns, aged 27, swimming off the coast at Tenby, in South Wales, on Saturday 30th May 1860. The papers report that ***the deceased could not resist the temptation [to bathe], and having swam about fifty yards out, his strength suddenly failed him, and being struck by a heavy sea, and probably seized with cramp, he was buried beneath the waves.***

His mother is heartbroken, and is dead only two years later, aged 65. She, however, does not burn his only novel - a gentle romance named *Heart or Head*, which is published in 1864. I can see nothing in it to throw further light on Cockburn's feelings for Emily, although I do notice these lines at the end of the penultimate chapter: ***As for her being four years his senior, that only made her more glorious in his eyes. She was not a girl but a woman; now at three and twenty, one adores a full-blown woman. At thirty, one loves the buds.***

A decade later his old school friend Robert Lytton is to be pilloried - along with his contemporaries the Pre-Raphaelites - by the Scottish (of course) critic Robert Buchanan (1841–1901) for belonging to *The Fleshly School of Poetry*. Cockburn shows early signs of an affinity to this fine company by describing how his heroine's ***long eye-lashes lie on the bosom of her soft cheek.***

It's not Emily. But it's very 1860s.

The only further communication I have found between the Bulwer Lytton family and the Thomson family after Emily's death - until I start a productive correspondence with their descendant Robert Gregg, Professor of History at Stockton University in New Jersey - is the draft of a letter Robert writes to Mrs Thomson after the death of Cockburn, ***There was so much that promised an active and honourable manhood in poor Cockburn...***

* * * * *

Robert's own promise, is better fulfilled - although also threatened in his youth by the incident in Bonn already described. He achieves some early success with - his first love - poetry [under the pseudonym Owen Meredith], but Edward, not wishing on him the money struggles he has known [read jealousy if you wish, but you are being absurd], encourages him to stick to the career in the Foreign Service that begins with his Uncle Henry in Washington. Through the 1850s, 1860s and 1870s, this takes him to almost every capital city in Europe, by good fortune each at its most interesting time - and ultimately lands him the very top job of Viceroy of India. This is the appointment of his father's friend-from-youth and then Prime Minister Benjamin Disraeli (1804–1881), and apparently especially approved by Queen Victoria who particularly enjoys the beautiful turn of phrase in Robert's dispatches.

As a poet rather than a military man, Robert is an unusual Viceroy for the height of British Imperialism. He has to deal with both the Second Afghan War in the north and a desperate famine in the south. Although battles are won in both these unwinnable wars - and robust reasons exist for Robert's decisions in both - Disraeli does him the disservice of dying, and Robert is tarred and feathered by Her Majesty's Opposition. Its then leader, William Gladstone (1809–1898) and subsequent Gladstonian historians, who dominate the 20th Century, leave Robert - in the 21st Century - very much in need of a re-appraisal, along the lines of the one Disraeli is currently enjoying. But I am probably not the person to do this.

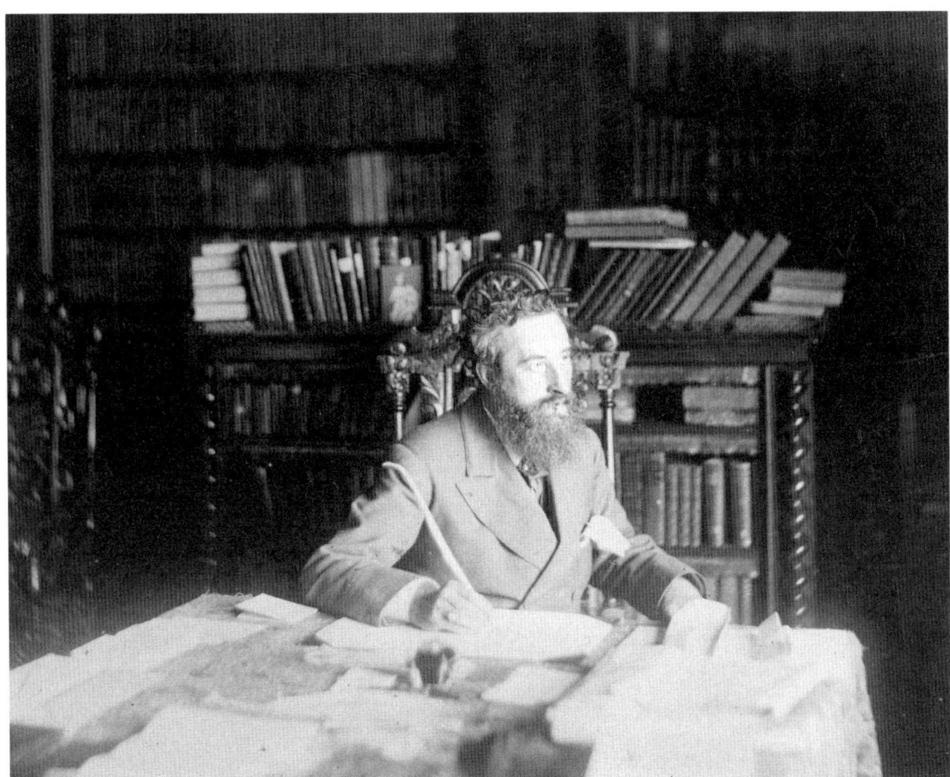

Robert in the Library at Knebworth House

I will, however, brag about my great-great-grandfather's poetry - for which he is better known in the United States than as a diplomat.

His long form poem, *Lucile* [1860], has a place on virtually every parlour table in America at the turn of the 19th Century. According to the University of Iowa's mindboggling website *The Lucile Project* ***during the 78 years 1860-1938, nearly 100 American publishers brought out at least 2000 editions and issues.*** Its sales far outstripped its precursor, his mentor Elizabeth Barrett Browning's *Aurora Leigh*, published four years earlier.

To a New World audience it succeeded as Old World poetry that did not bore or bewilder. If the Americans had paid copyright during Robert's life-time, he might have been able to travel the world, without having to run it.

* * * * *

His poetry is lyrical - often exotic, expressing a lifetime of adventure and travel - and much of it, extremely beautiful. Amongst my favourites is *Sorcery:*

You're a Princess of the water:
I'm a Genius of the air...

You have lain, with linx and lion,
In the jungle and the fen
I have roam'd the wild with robbers,
Pariahs, outlaws, ruined men...

When I head off to Tesco on a Friday evening, I'm usually declaiming its closing lines:

All the ways are wild before us,
And the night is in the skies,
And the dæmons of the desert
Are against us. Yet arise!

There is a humour and lightness of touch to much of Robert's work that is not common amongst his fellow Victorian Romantics. Like his father, he is known for aphorisms that, to this day, adorn tea towels and stationery. The notebook on my desk comes with his declaration on its cover, that ***Genius does what it must; and Talent does what it can.*** And clinging to refrigerators around the world, magnets remind us that,

We may live without poetry, music, and art;
We may live without conscience, and live without heart;
We may live without friends; we may live without books;
But civilized man cannot live without cooks.

* * * * *

On 4th October 1864, Robert ups his grandmother's Lytton family profile by marrying a real aristocrat, Edith Villiers (1841–1936), niece of the 4th Earl of Clarendon. This next generation too suffers the misery of the loss of their eldest child, Rowland, aged six, of whooping cough in Vienna, and also their second son, Henry, aged two - the child's coffin in the Mausoleum at Knebworth. But Robert and Edith are blessed with three daughters, Betty (1867–1942), who marries Gerald Balfour, 2nd Earl of Balfour (1853–1945), nephew of the Prime Minister Lord Salisbury (1830– 1903) and brother of the Prime Minister Arthur Balfour, 1st Earl of Balfour, (1848–1930); Constance (1869–1923), now roundly celebrated as one of the most influential militant suffragettes; and Emily (1874–1964), who marries Britain's foremost architect of the age, Edwin Lutyens (1869–1944).

Two boys follow, my great-grandfather Victor (1876–1947), who marries society beauty Pamela Plowden (1874-1971), first love of Winston Churchill (played by Jane Seymour in the film *Young Winston*); and Neville (1879–1951), who marries Byron's great-granddaughter Judith Blunt (1873–1957).

All five children distinguish themselves as writers, along with a number of their descendants - notably Mary Lutyens (1908–1999) and Jane Ridley (b. 1953), intimidating relations for a screenwriter-hack attempting a biography.

* * * * *

Robert ends his career as a popular British Ambassador to France. The French, like Queen Victoria, appreciate Robert's literary panache and cultured cosmopolitanism, and he is given the rare honour - for a foreigner - of a State Funeral in Paris on his death, in office, in November 1891, from a brain aneurysm, aged just 60. Oscar Wilde, who is at his bedside in the final weeks of his ill-health, dedicates *Lady Windermere's Fan* ***to the dear memory of Robert, Earl of Lytton, in affection and admiration.***

Robert by G. F. Watts

In years only three times as many as his sister's short twenty, Teddy does bring back to his father's hearth ***the spoils of time and the trophies of the world.*** The little boy weeping under the Coventry nursery table because he is not let in to Fairyland, does go out into the world and return with ***the keys of conquer'd towns, and captive kings, and many a broken sword and banner furl'd.*** They are there to see today at his family's home, Knebworth House.

On his return from India in 1880, Robert also adds to the heraldry of his grandmother's ancient family, by topping his father's baronetcy and later peerage (in 1866), with an earldom, becoming Robert, 1st Earl of Lytton.

For the ***many a task, and quest, and high emprize***, little Teddy would indeed have won the ***approving eyes*** of his father, had his father lived to see it. We can know that his father would, in the end, consider Robert, Teddy, worthy of the name - which, but for Miss Greene, he would not have been baptized - Edward Bulwer Lytton.

* * * * *

Rosina lives for longer than both of her two children put together. After a spell in Llangollen, Wales, she settles - a safe distance from her husband - in Taunton in Devon in 1855, where she lives until her husband's death in 1873. The satirical books and vitriolic pamplets continue to fly from her bureau - an endless irritant of buzz and sting to Edward's reputation and career,

His books continue to sell - ***that bundle of bare-face plagiarisms, steeped in brothel-philosophy, which he calls his works*** [*Very Successful,* 1859] - but his political success, in particular joining Lord Derby's Cabinet in 1858 - is curtailed.

VERY SUCCESSFUL!

BY

LADY BULWER LYTTON.

IN THREE VOLUMES.

VOL. I.

"There is a twofold fortune wherewith we are to enter the lists; good and ill, prosperetie and adversetie: these are the two combats, the two dangerous times, wherein it behoveth us to stand upon our guard and to gather our wits about us: for they are the two schooles, essayes, and touch-stones of the spirit of man."—
Of Wisdome, the second booke,—by PETER CHARRON, A.D. 1600.

"Perieramus nisi perissemus."

"Not from the chance of Fortune's wheel,
Nor from the dust—affliction springs;
The troubles that believers feel
Are but GOD's blessings in disguise;
And like Ezekiel's visioned rings,*
The wheels of Providence have *eyes.*—
JOSEPH SNOW's "Churchyard Thoughts."
*Ezek. i. 18.

LONDON:—WHITTAKER & Co., AVE MARIA LANE.
TAUNTON:—FREDERICK R. CLARKE,
AT THE "CAXTON'S HEAD."
1856.

[THE AUTHOR RESERVES THE RIGHT OF TRANSLATION.]

Rosina's 1859 novel

The circumstances of Emily's death become a potent ingredient of the venom.

Physically destroying one child – morally destroying another – kicking his wretched victim of a wife a month before her first child was born till she was nearly dead – turning that poor little martyr out of his house the moment she was born, as he ultimately did, to die [*Very Successful*].

Ten years after the wretched events in Brompton, on the eve of Edward's appointment to Cabinet, the queen wasp attacks Edward's picnic at the hustings in Hertford in June 1858. The poison of this in-person public attack breaks Edward out into the ruddy response that he has been vilified for ever since - the ***EXTRAORDINARY NARRATIVE of an OUTRAGEOUS VIOLATION OF LIBERTY AND LAW in the Forcible Seizure and Incarceration of Lady Lytton Bulwer IN THE GLOOMY CELL OF A MADHOUSE!!!***

[PRICE ONE PENNY.]
EXTRAORDINARY NARRATIVE
OF AN
OUTRAGEOUS VIOLATION OF LIBERTY AND LAW,
IN THE
Forcible Seizure and Incarceration of Lady Lytton Bulwer.
IN THE GLOOMY CELL OF A MADHOUSE!!!
AND THE PROCEEDINGS TO OBTAIN HER RELEASE.

WITH EXCLUSIVE DETAILS OF SIR E. B.'S AMOURS IN THE ALBANY - THE DELICATE DISCOVERY BY HER LADYSHIP,
THE CAUSE OF THE SEPARATION,
LONDON: PUBLISHED BY W. JAMES AND CO., 24, BOOKSELLERS ROW, ST. CLEMENT'S, STRAND,

Pamphlet propaganda in Rosina's cause

With advice from his friend - Robert's unofficial godfather - John Forster, who is conveniently secretary to the Lunacy Commission, Edward obtains the two doctors' signatures necessary to commit his wife into care, on the grounds of diminished responsibility.

* * * * *

Inverness Lodge in Brentford, west of London, where Rosina is taken, is acutally the London address of Dr Robert Gardiner Hill (1811–1878), the former Mayor of Lincoln, Edward's former constituency. Gardiner Hill, who had run the Lincoln Lunatic Asylum, is something of a radical in the lunatic business, decrying the accepted medical practice of the time with works such as *Total Abolition of Personal Restraint in the Treatment of the Insane. A Lecture, with Statistical Tables* (1839) and *A Concise History of the entire Abolition of Medical Restraint in the Treatment of the Insane and of the success of the Non-Restraint System* (1857). Rather like Dr Heine's Institute, this is not a gothic madhouse. It is a clinic and private residence. Even today's The Priory, I imagine, is more gothic madhouse than Inverness Lodge.

One of the few touching passages in Rosina's harsh and uncompromising autobiography *My Blighted Life* is her description of her first morning at Inverness Lodge. The young girl is Gardiner Hill's daughter, Mary (1842-1918) and Rosina's reaction to the teenager is a faint echo of a motherly love that might have been.

I said, "Come in" and a charming little girl of about 14 [Mary is two months shy of 16], ***with a pretty gentle expression of face, soft chestnut hair, and the prettiest and almost dove-like dark hazel eyes I ever saw, came in with some tea and some strawberries. This was Hill's eldest daughter, and how he and his odious vulgar wife came by such a child, I can't imagine, unless the fairies stole theirs and left this one in exchange. This dear little girl, my only consolation while there, conceived a most violent affection for me, which I heartily returned, for she was a perfect star in the desert, and with a big fat magnificent tortoiseshell cat, with the most fascinating manners, a perfect feline Chesterfield!*** [By which Rosina means not a sofa, but Lord Chesterfield (1694-1777), author of *The Art of Pleasing* (1783) - but also relevant in this instance, the most humane and enlighted Lord-Lieutenant of Ireland in the 18th Century, with a deep sympathy for its oppressed and suffering people.]

* * * * *

Much has been written and continues to be written about this 'intervention' - the outcry of the people of Taunton, the campaign in *The Daily Telegraph*, Karl Marx's two articles in *The New York Tribune*, the intercession of Queen Victoria... all go on to form a watershed moment in the history of feminism and the plight of the Victorian wife.

I encourage you to explore the politics of this history, and make your own assessment of my great-great-great-grandmother Rosina's contribution to her mother Anna Wheeler's vocational *Appeal of one Half of the Human Race, Women, against the Pretensions of the other Half, Men* [1825].

I am proud of my pioneering feminist ancestors. Anna Wheeler, Rosina Bulwer Lytton, and in particular Robert's daughter Constance Lytton (1869-1923), are all brave women who win important battles in the tortuous evolutionary struggle towards human equality.

This they do to the honour of their family for all time... but at the expense of their family at the time.

In a sense, Emily is made martyr, also, to this cause.

* * * * *

Rosina spends only a couple of weeks with Dr Gardiner Hill, before her son responds to the negative public opinion weighing heavily on his father. Robert has been party to his mother's detention - and has been receiving letters addressed to ***that white livered little reptile, Robert Lytton.*** He suggests, as an alternative to Inverness Lodge, that he take his mother abroad and [as Victor, his son, expresses it in *Life of Edward Bulwer, First Lord Lytton* 1913] ***bring her to a calmer frame of mind.***

This is the first ray of hope for Edward and Rosina's relationship in twenty years. From the nadir of the conflict comes the one green shoot of hope.

The doctors who three weeks previously had certified Lady Lytton insane now certified that she was fit to be released. In the Lord Warden Hotel in Dover on Saturday Night, July 17th, 1858, Rosina writes on the inside cover of her Prayer Book, ***And shall I indeed once more sleep under the same roof with my poor darling long-estranged boy? That monster's crowning outrage of incarcerating me in a madhouse, for this unhoped-for blessing, I could forgive, but my poor Emily! That he tortured into an early grave, may God forgive him, for I cannot. Oh Lord, wonderful are thy ways!***

It is the first time mother and son have slept beneath the same roof since Mrs Shaw's in St Doloughs, when he was five-years-old. Robert is now 26.

* * * * *

Rosina in miniature, 1858

On their way to Luchon in the Pyrenees, via Paris, mother and son stop in Bordeaux, where on the quayside they have little miniature portraits of themselves made. This is now the only image of Rosina in later life that we know of.

Robert in miniature, 1858

Allowing for the simplicity of the image, 55-year-old Rosina seems a ruddy and portly woman - and I immediately think of Edward's friend Charles Dickens (1812-1870), who in this very year, 1858, trades in his now portly wife, Charlotte (1815–1879), for a thinner, younger, 'Mignon', Ellen Ternan (1839– 1914). Oh, the Predilections of the other Half.

If Edward and Rosina had weathered their differences in the 1830s and found a future with each other, would their relationship have survived beyond middle age and the adulthood of their children? There's a parallel universe to ponder.

* * * * *

Thus placed between Scylla and Charibdis [continues Victor - referencing the sea monsters of Homer's *Odyssey*], ***Robert Lytton tried at first to steer a middle course. In replies to his father he pointed out the partial and one-sided nature of the communications which he received from him, and insisted that peace in the future could only be obtained by a mutual determination to bury the past. To his mother he replied equally emphatically that the only condition on which he would consent to remain in her company was that she should refrain from all abuse of his father. The result*** - for one of the finest international diplomats of his generation - ***was that instead of reconciling either parent to the other he only lost the confidence of both.***

...The son returned to The Hague to resume his official duties, and the

mother returned to Taunton to resume the story of her blighted life.

* * * * *

No doubt your Orthodox English Conventionality is greatly shocked at my 'coarse', 'violent', 'unladylike language'! Rosina resumes her vitriol in *My Blighted Life* [1880]. ***But you must make some allowance (though English people never do, being... only shocked and scandalized by terrible results, while they remain perfectly placid and piano*** [soft] ***upon terrible causes)... for a person writhing under a nearly life-long, unparalleled, ever-recurring, and never-redressed outrages - and suffering from a chronic indigestion of falsehood, hypocrisy, and unscrupulous villainy.***

Mother and son are never to meet again. But on his father's death in 1873, Robert increases his mother's allowance by £200 a year. This is withdrawn when *My Blighted Life* is published in 1880, but renewed when she claims she is not responsible for its publication. This claim is possible, as she does retain loyal and righteous supporters - in the mould of the meddling Katherine Planché - who ***commiserated her neglected and desolate condition, and tried to alleviate her sorrows.*** One such, the author of these words, her biographer Louisa Devey, reveals her final years in *Life of Rosina, Lady Lytton - Published in Vindication of her Memory* [1887]:

For the last seven years of her life Lady Lytton resided at a small house, 'Glenomera', at Upper Sydenham, latterly with only one servant. She rarely left her room, and the house only once during the last five years... She possessed to the last the remains of a beauty that had been so noted in her youth. She was full of anecdote and wit, and although not reticent on the subject of her wrongs, she never failed to leave a feeling of sadness and regret, that so much capacity for all that was loving and affectionate had been so ruthlessly destroyed, successively by neglect, wrong and persecution.

No one can defend some of her published extravagances, but our blame should more justly be laid on those who abused her highly sensitive nature, and induced those feelings of exasperation under the infliction of wrong, which she had no other opportunity to express.

* * * * *

Worn out by sorrow, afflicted with much bodily suffering, and tormented with constant mental distress, this poor lady died rather suddenly on the 12th of March, 1882, in her 80th year. Her funeral was paid for by the present Earl; the only followers were Mr Shakespeare, the solicitor respresenting the Earl of Lytton; the Rev. Freeman Wills, a distant relative of Lady Lytton's; Mr Ancona, a friend; and the Misses Devey, her coexecutries.

Her remains are buried in the pretty churchyard of St. John the Evangelist, at Shirley, in Surrey. There is no monument over the grave.

On Sunday 12th March, 1995, the 113th anniversary of Rosina's death, my father David Lytton Cobbold, puts this right. He organises a further graveside ceremony at which a greater number of supporters turn up - notably feminist historians and academics; however, also notably - as mentioned at the beginning of this book - almost none from the wider Bulwer Lytton family, although all were invited. The wounds run deep across the generations.

My father and my sister Rosina dedicating a grave stone to Rosina in Shirley on 12th March 1995

The stone my father places at the bural plot is inscribed with the words [*Isaiah* XIV. 3] that Rosina requests in her Will, over a century before:

The Lord shall give thee rest from thy sorrow, and from thy fear, and from the hard bondage wherein thou wast made to serve.

* * * * *

In contrast to her husband, the 20th Century is kind to Rosina. As the feminist movement comes to the fore and the balance between 'herstory' and 'history' is redressed, Rosina continues to find champions, and her books at the end of the century are being republished at a greater rate than those of Edward. Her indignant fury - unlike that of many equally worthy Victorian women - never loses that biting and brilliant Regency wit that makes her star shine so bright in the Mayfair salons of her youth. She remains uncompromising and funny, and that combination will always breed disciples.

As she writes, with extraordinary prescience, in *My Blighted Life*: ***when I have been dead some hundred years, how pens will start from their inkstands, like swords from their scabbards, to avenge me!! While Electric Caligraphy will not have left sufficient ink in Christendom to blacken Sir Edward - the Cæsar Borgia of the nineteenth century (with the beauty and the courage left out) - up to his natural hue, Gentlemen of 1964,*** [flip that six over - it takes about 30 years longer (as does Electric Caligraphy)] ***I cannot find words to thank you.....for all I shall have to say then, is what I pray now - Implora Pace!*** [Delicious Peace! - The words Byron desired on his monument]

* * * * *

A figurehead for feminism, Rosina will never be a model for motherhood.

However we justify her conjugal combat, she will always share and bear responsibility for Emily's fate.

The Rosina we remember, I suspect, will never be one of quiet moments - but we may be sure she had them. On the inside cover of her Prayer Book, beneath her one answered prayer of ***once more sleep[ing] under the same roof with my poor darling long-estranged boy***, is a moving tribute to her first born child. These are the first and last four lines of *Dirge* by Quallon [aka Stephen Henry Bradbury (1828-1901), a Nottingham pauper awarded a Civil pension that year, 1858, for his contribution to Literature.]

Young maiden thou hast left the earth,
Too beautiful thou wert to stay;
Till now I never knew thy worth,-
We love things best when past away.
...
Yet so it is, and I must make
Thy absence now one source of thought;
In mourning for some loved one's sake,
We learn from death what life ne'er taught!

Did Rosina learn from Emily's death what Emily's life ne'er taught? No.

But I do believe her daughter was, in absence, more a source of thought that we think she was. Rosina's choice of Quallon's poem for Emily - and its beautiful sentiment - is a touching final tribute from the long-away mother from long-away Tipperary.

* * * * *

To sum up my great-great-great-grandfather, I am astonished to read the following appraisal, which, as literary criticism, could have been written today. It is actually written in only the second decade of his five decade career. In 1838, Edward Bulwer is still yet to receive the recognition of a baronetcy, still, even, not formally separated from his wife.

In spite of [the] honour rendered to him by the world (not the one country) of readers, writes Henry F. Chorley in *The Authors of England (1838)*, ***Mr Bulwer has hardly received fair treatment from the hands of his critics... He has been, for the most part, either insolently flouted, or analyzed with a caution and severity, scarcely less invidious.***

One reason of this may be, that he appeals to the world under a twofold guise... One half of the world, calling itself critical, could understand Pelham's finery, but not discern his philosophy; the other half refused to listen to the latter because it came from one who presented himself before them chained and ringed, and essenced, and who would break off in some subtle digression, to 'sigh like a furnace', under the window of the Cynthia of the minute, or to discuss the fashions of the toilette and the table.

This mixture of the old man and the boy, of wisdom and petulance, of expanded benevolence and lively coxcombry, of sound reason and overmastering passion, was a puzzle to our literary censors... the author was passed over as not deep enough... or he was stigmatized as exaggerated, because he gave free range to passion and fancy, and sometimes to that earnest egotism, that

desire to confess and be absolved, which it is so difficult for one of an ardent and overflowing spirit to repress.

...He has, we sincerely hope, a long and still brightening career before him.

* * * * *

The following words are added, 23 years later, to the same book, *The Authors of England,* 1861 Edition: ***The hopes expressed in the preceding notice have not been disappointed. Her Majesty, on the occasion of her coronation, conferred upon him a baronetcy. Not many years afterwards he re-entered Parliament as member for the county of Herts, accepting in 1858, under the Government of Lord Derby, the office of Secretary of State for the Colonies. In the midst of his arduous parliamentary duties he found time to write*** *The Caxton Family, My Novel,* ***and*** *What will he do with it?* ***— a series of works sufficient of themselves to place him among the greatest writers of English fiction.***

"To be at the head of the novelists of England," says an eloquent writer in the *London Review,* ***"is a proud station"... We can speak of living writers whose fame will go down to posterity as the delight and honour of the present day; but when we glance at the extraordinary extent and diversity of the productions of a Bulwer, and reflect on the fact that they are but emanations floated, as it were, from amidst labours and duties of the most onerous nature, we are lost in astonishment.***

And the more, as nowhere is mediocrity or superficiality to be discovered. Bulwer is far removed from the herd Faciunt nae intelligendo, ut nihil intelligant. [They, so knowing, that they know nothing at all]***; he is sterling throughout, and never can be misunderstood, because he knows what he means, and how to communicate it most intelligibly. His style is always plain, strong, nervous,— when requisite, eloquent, pathetic, passionate. The English language could not furnish quotations more admirable than many we could point out in these Caxton novels.***

* * * * *

It is ironic that the novel *The Caxtons: A Family Picture* (1849), and its follow up *My Novel, or Varieties in English Life* (serialised in 1850) two of Edward's calmest and happiest books, should be written in the wake of Emily's death. I put this down to the positive influence of Marion Lowndes. And the self-confidence that comes with success at, again, writing himself out of financial difficulty.

This time also contains the happy spell of his collaboration with Charles Dickens. Edward writes the play *Not So Bad As We Seem* for Dickens to take on tour in aid of a charity they set up together, The Guild of Literature and Art, for the benefit of impoverished writers and artists. Rosina threatens to disrupt the Royal Performance at Devonshire House and re-dubs the play *Much Worse Than They Seem,* but the play is a success and residue of the Guild today exists as part of the Artists Benevolent Fund.

It is also remarkable that during the open warfare with his wife in 1858, he manages, in his short six months as Secretary of State for the Colonies, to avert open warfare in the gold fields of the north-west coast of North America. It is argued by historians today that it is only because he - rather than his predecessor or successor - is in that Cabinet position, at that very moment in history, that British Columbia is now part of Canada and not part of the United States.

Edward's statue in Victoria

Edward, with fewer ties than others in Parliament to the Hudson Bay Company, works with Governor James Douglas (1803-1877) [pre-empting Barack Obama by 150 years as the first mixed race leader on the North American continent] to forge an alliance with the region's First Nation (then known as Indians) to pose too strong an obstacle for American colonisation. As a result the only statue of Edward Bulwer Lytton that exists in the world today is on the State Capitol building in Victoria, British Columbia.

But the English prefer to remember him for arguing with his wife.

* * * * *

Marion's recollections of him I find the most interesting. Marion's is the closest perspective we have - closer even, as we've seen, than his children's. ***There was I thought an innocence about him & he could be amused with things most men would despise. I often tried to cheer him up & make him forget that oppression on the head - his dizziness & earache. I bought a little Chinese puzzle which appeared rather clever... he spent hours amusing himself & laughing over it just like a school boy...***

When he lived in N°1 Park Lane he occupied himself very much with spirit wrappings & fortune tellers. I often was sent to a very handsome old gypsy woman who lived in a horrid place somewhere beyond the Old Kent Road to question her for him. He tried to get me to interest myself, but I always told him I was too ignorant for them & had not brains enough. He was also very fond of speculating on the future state, and when I used to see him so melancholy & despondent, I used to get so frightened that I have hidden his razors & slept nights at his door. At Nice he suffered very much from earache & the only thing that relieved him was to apply the heart of the Iris bulb or the heart of an onion.

Your image of my great-great-great-grandfather, built up over the pages of this book, is thus complete - a manic depressive peering into a crystal ball with an onion stuck in his ear.

But this description, to me, reveals, at its root, the worst and the best of my great-great-great grandfather. At the root of the worst of Edward is the ill-health that dogs him throughout his life, affects his decision making and bedevils his vanity and his selfishness. At the root of the best of Edward is his endlessly open and interested mind - a mind that embraces all considered philosophy; a mind that remains receptive to an evolving world which everyday reveals new miracles, such as the harnessing of electricity from invisible air; a mind that has the genius, itself, to harness beauty from the seemingly invisible.

In a close-minded age, Edward Bulwer Lytton's mind is beautifully open.

* * * * *

From his first relationship, he loses a daughter Emily. From his second, he loses a son, Ernest - apparently in the Austrian army, at a date I am yet

to discover. From his third, he loses a daughter, Evelyne. In the year of Evelyne's premature death, 1853, he writes to his son Robert [quoted by his grandson Victor, in *Life of Edward Bulwer, First Lord Lytton*] ***I have been interested in the spirit manifestations.*** Is holding seances at Knebworth descending into madness over his lost children? Not to me. To mc, is it a genuine, romantic quest for more things in heaven and earth than are dreamt of in our philosophy.

They are astounding, but the wonder is that they go so far and no farther. To judge by them, even the highest departed spirits discovered seem to have made no visible progress - to be as uncertain and contradicting as ourselves, or more so - still with answers at times that take away one's breath with wonder.

There is no trick, but I doubt much whether all be more than some strange clairvoyance passing from one human brain to another, or if spirits, something analogous to fairies or genii.

This is extraordinary. ***Emily comes often, generally most incoherent, as when, poor thing, she died, but I asked her the last name she thought of, and she answered Carl Ritter. No Medium can know that, and the question was only put in thought.***

Shakespeare has come to me, and gave me the most thrilling advice as to the future and other predictions. Afterwards he came again and flatly contradicted himself; yet I asked him to prove that he was a good spirit sent by God, by telling me the closest secret I have, and he gave it me instantly!

Oh, to be party to this closest secret. But I'm pleased Shakespeare is.

* * * * *

In his final decades Edward becomes the grand old man of English Literature, having held its fame the longest, and continuing to support its causes. In 1859, the *Encyclopaedia Britannica* calls him ***now unquestionably the greatest living novelist of England***. He influences the old - viz Dickens, who changes the ending of *Great Expectations* on Edward's advice in 1861 - and he holds court to the young - viz Algernon Swinburne (1837–1909) who makes a pilgrimage to Knebworth for advice in August 1866.

1866 is the year that he is made the first Lord Lytton - ***my first thought was of my poor mother, and I said, as if she were living still on this earth, or wherever she may be, caring for such matters:- "How it will please her."***

He is writing until the day he dies. His penultimate completed novel is the ground breaking science fiction *The Coming Race* (1871) in which giant wives eat their husbands. It predicts nuclear energy and the Cold War - and even gives the beef flavoured drink in every post-War British pantry its name, Bovril - from 'bovine', of the cow, and 'vril', his name for this future energy source.

BOVRIL.—We beg to draw attention to this non-intoxicating, stimulating beverage. If hard-working literary men, ministers, and others doing mental work, would stir the brain with this instead of tobacco and other more dangerous stimulants, they would *build* as well as boil. We know a popular preacher who every Sunday morning lays the foundation with a good beefsteak. Bovril suits scholars as well as soldiers and sailors.

His final completed novel is the part-autobiographical *Kenelm Chillingly* (1873). ***My father read the manuscript to my wife and myself, and at particular parts of it he could not restrain his tears,*** remembers Robert in *The Life, Letters And Literary Remains Of Edward Bulwer, Lord Lytton*. ***Throughout the day (it was New Year's Eve - the eve of the year of his own death) on which he finished the chapter describing Kenelm's sufferings above the grave of 'Lily,' he was profoundly dejected, listless, broken; and in his face there was the worn look of a man who has just passed through the last paroxysm of a passionate grief.***

We did not then know to what the incidents referred, and we wondered that the creations of his fancy should exercise such power over him. They were not creations of fancy, but the memories of fifty years past.

* * * * *

Edward dies at 2pm on Saturday 18th January 1873, at the age of 69. Also haunting him in the weeks before his death, according to Robert, is his poem *The Tale of A Dreamer,* written in 1824, about the night he contemplates suicide as the graveside of his childhood sweetheart:

Alas ! too soon upon that hideous night
Arose returning reason's wretched light.
Oh, how I long'd, as caged birds for their nest,
For that calm home beneath the grassy sod
Where woe at length hath wept itself to rest,
And, if we dream, our visions are of God.

Edward's funeral in Westminster Abbey as illustrated in ***The Graphic***

I hope my great-great-great-grandfather is finding calm rest in eternity. Despite a professed wish to be interred with this mother and his daughter in the mausoleum at Knebworth, his friends and son saw fit to accept the honour of a burial amongst his literary peers in Westminster Abbey.

Rosina's last words for him are in her *Shells From The Sands of Time* (1876),

Here, still lies, my Lord Lytton, - at last in a fix! Being too stingy to pay, his fare o'er the Styx ...even the devil does not know what to do with him, having no 'Upper House', wherein to shelve him.

And the reality is, the future has been kinder to her, than to him.

The greatest living novelist of England, now dead, is not read.

In *Bulwer and his Wife, a Panorama 1803-1836* (1831), Michael Sadleir (1888–1957) gives the 20th Century's epitaph - ***for Bulwer conquered without a sense of victory, failed where he thought to have achieved; and has become a legend half-impressive, half-absurd, to a posterity which can see his faults and read the satire of his enemies, but cannot appreciate wherein lay his power over his age, nor understand why, if he was the great man he must have been, he was not greater still.***

Today - in the 21st Century - teachers prefer to teach Thackeray, and broadcasters prefer to broadcast Trollope. But Bulwer's hand still carries one trump card in the game of posterity that only a few of his contemporaries share - notably neither Thackeray nor Trollope - and that is, his home.

Edward Bulwer Lytton lives on in Knebworth House His greatest work endures. Dismissed throughout the 20th Century as an ugly piece of Victorian vandalism, it is, in the 21st Century, rated in the top one hundred of Simon Jenkins' *England's Thousand Best Houses* (2001) - one of only two in the county of Hertfordshire.

Photo by Rob Ryder - www.knebworthparkphotographic.com

Fashions change. And history rewrites itself. All things come around.

When modern hero Jimmy Page of Led Zeppelin turns up at Knebworth House to play England's world-famous music venue, he wants to visit the library of the man whose writings played inspiration to one of his heroes, Aleister Crowley (1875–1947).

When drama students from the University of Calgary want to perform plays written by the man who saved the Canadian West - *The Captives* [unpublished in his lifetime] and *The Lady of Lyons* [1838] - they want to do it in the author's own beautiful home... the halls where Charles Dickens himself performed, and where Dickens himself pronounced, ***Ladies and Gentlemen, you know very well that when the health, life and beauty now overflowing these halls shall have fled, crowds of people will come to see the place where he lived and wrote.***

The health, life and beauty has not fled - and will not, whilst his family continues to fight time and taxes to keep its stories alive - but Dickens is not wrong. Crowds of people - a century and half later - do come. Crowds and crowds of them. To see the place where he lived and wrote.

* * * * *

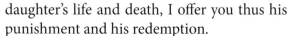

If Edward Bulwer Lytton is still to you the villain of this tragedy of his daughter's life and death, I offer you thus his punishment and his redemption.

My personal feelings, having read it alongside you, match his son's. Teddy shares first hand the agonies and truths of his sister's childhood, and on finishing his father's biography on November 15, 1883, looks back on ***the story of a life, in which all the errors were the errors of a good man, and... in which all the virtues were those of a great one.***

My great-great-great-grandfather's history, I choose to conclude with the final rally of his young meditation on death and grief, *The Tale of A Dreamer*:

And so from days that are no more I turn,
And to thine altars dedicate Tomorrow

* * * * *

In 1869, four years before his death, Edward sends to Robert, then Secretary to the Embassy at Vienna, a letter that has arrived out of the blue from Germany. The letter has a letter of Emily's enclosed, and both are in German. He asks his son to translate them.

Robert replies [28th March 1869] *My dearest Father, The letter of your German correspondent begins by stating that it is 20 years since she first knew your Lordship's daughter. That she was Miss Emily's friend, the letter she encloses will suffice to convince you. She has many more letters from Emily wh she keeps as sacred memories of her friend.*

They were schoolfellows and playmates at Cannstatt, where they slept in adjoining rooms, divided only by an open door and many a night has she passed by the bedside of Miss Emily consoling her – for Miss Emily used often to pass the night long in tears having then a great sorrow which she indeed confided to the writer of the letter. But what this sorrow was is not mentioned.

When Miss Emily returned to England she (the writer) made a sketch – a portrait of Emily – under which Emily subscribed her name – and which being an exact resemblance she has ever since cherished as her only record of the features of lost friend.

Since then she has known the shadowy side of life. She is no longer the merry schoolgirl whom Miss Emily used to call her little bird. But the wife of an Apothecary, by whom she has a daughter ten years old, and called Emily in remembrance of her friend.

She is now impelled to write all this to you, it having occurred to her that you would be glad to have this likeness of your daughter. If so, she will send it to you on condition that you will give her, in exchange for it, some other relic of Miss Emily – anything that once belonged to her. In any case she begs you to return Emily's letter to her, & remains with great respect, etc. etc.

The writer is obviously not Miss de Ritter – for she gives her maiden name. Were this letter written by an English woman, I shd feel certain it was a beg-

ging letter written preparatory to an appeal for pecuniary assistance. But there is such an extraordinary naiveté in German women – especially the South Germans - that the letter may quite possibly mean no more than it says.

* * * * *

Emily's letter (undated) begins by saying how glad she was to hear from her friend who must be sure to write to her often. Then it refers to the great change in her life, and the beauties of Knebworth, which is described as a sort of Aladdin's Palace. She hopes that her brother when he returns will be able to make a sketch of the house wh she can send to her friend. In her bedroom she has a picture of her dear Papa & Uncle when they were babies – one too of her dear brother - & one of herself as a child by wh she sees that she must once have been a very fat little girl.

Among the numerous Family pictures in the house are two wh always remind her of her friend because they are so like somebody & somebody else (German friends named in initials). Does her friend remember how they used to fight for wild strawberries in the Burgwald? Well, every morning she now finds more wild strawberries than she can pick in her walks thro' the Knebworth woods. What a shame that her old friends do not come and fight for them now - & how good the strawberries wd taste if that cd be. But now she eats them greedily, & without pleasure, all alone.

She passes her hours alone thinking of the merry games & romps they used to have together till she bursts out laughing – and yesterday her English waiting woman coming suddenly into the room, found her laughing at one of those fancies, and asked her if she was ill – whereupon she began to abuse the maid in German, wh made the woman think she was stark mad.

Her good dear Uncle has been bidding her goodbye, and says she must come & see him at Madrid. He also wants her Papa & herself to pass the winter with him at Paris, where he has a beautiful house. But whether anything of all that will ever happen she cannot tell.

If some friend of her friends (or relation?) ever comes to England her friend must be sure to let her know. Then follow various messages to various persons, & the letter ends "goodbye little bird, your affectionate camarad" [likely a shortening of the French 'camaraderie' - implying a close comrade].

Probably that is all you will need to know for any purpose of answering the letter – but I will return both letters with translations, as soon as I can make them - & only send this now to satisfy curiosity without delay.

The writer's address is Elise Bohrer (born Reissig, from Nünberg [Nuremberg]***). At present Apothecary's wife, in Rain, near Donauwörth, in Oberbayern (i.e Upper Bavaria).***

There is a wonderful naiveté (peculiar to the German Bourgoise) in this subscription [a signature or short piece of writing at the end of a document] ***– it reads like a description in a Passport.***

Edward does not appear to have taken up this offer, as we have no other image of Emily. But how tantalising that there might be another image of Emily out in the world somewhere.

Unless, of course - not hearing from Edward - the woman sends it to Madame de Ritter instead, and it is the image discovered in Gorizia.

I prefer that that there is another image of Emily out there somewhere.

When I discuss this letter with my friend Joachim of Eichstatt - not very far from Rain in Upper Bavaria - he tells me that Apotheken [pharmacies] in Germany are often long-standing family businesses and we may be able to trace this family and see if they still have Emily's letters.

To date we have had no success... beyond finding a Bohrer family - mother Elisabeth, daughter Emilie - that travel to Brazil in 1877. But this conversation with Joachim inspires the unrequited love story in my screenplay *The Apostasy of Francesco Terremoto*, where a one-chance encounter on a hilltop in Assisi comes to nothing because the German girl feels a duty to return home to run her great-grandfather's Apotheke. Funny how the world spins.

* * * * *

Of most resonance to me in my travels in search of Emily's life is what happened to the two hearts closest to hers. Emily's life is cut short, but today her heart rests at Knebworth, in a mausoleum on a sunny hillside that forever remembers her. Natalie de Ritter and Mary Letitia Greene live long lives, loved by large families and, in Natalie's case, makes a significant impact on her world - so where do their hearts rest?

As with the Thomsons, after Emily's death, the Bulwer Lyttons break off all contact with the de Ritter and the Greene families. The exception is a ***fitful correspondence*** [so described by Robert's daughter Betty in *Personal and Literary Letters of The Earl of Lytton*] between Robert and his "dear Aunt Mary" [Bonnie recalls, at Robert's death, that he always called her this].

Miss Greene certainly writes occasionally to Robert. ***My dear young friend,*** she addresses him from 1 Ebenezer Terrace in Kennington on 31st May 1852, ***I hope most heartily that you may be able to manage to come to see me & now write to beg you will let me know (if possible) the day & the hour when I may expect you in order that I may be at home & meet you, as now that I am getting a little better, I am ordered to be in the fresh air as much as I can, therefore I might be out when you call...*** But I can find no evidence that they met again.

There is a letter written to Bonnie Wilkinson when Robert is quartered as a diplomat in the Hague in 1857. Bonnie's married life takes her to Spain, where her husband William Greene builds the Santander to Madrid railway, the first of a number of pioneering railway engineering projects with which he is involved across Europe.

Your letter was the more welcome to me that I had felt considerable anxiety at the long silence which followed my own letter to our Aunt Mary... It gives me pain to think she should be suffering habitually, as you describe her to be, without the comfort of some familiar face and presence. My profession keeps me in constant exile from England, and my present income allows me but rarely to indulge in the luxury of long journeys; but if you think she could be moved and that she would like to live under my bachelor roof abroad, and share with me if not a 'rusty couch' yet certainly 'frugal fare, my blessing and repose' for the sake of auld lang syne she will be affectionately welcome.

* * * * *

I search everywhere for Miss Greene's final resting place. I look to parish records in Cheltenham, in Kennington, in Swords, even visit the graveyard of the early Greene residence in Stickillen, County Louth. But she is nowhere to be found...

* * * * *

Natalie - in far off Rijeka - should be easier. Natalie's death at 7 o'clock in the morning on 19th May 1895, aged 63, is greeted with a city council order that black flags should be hung on all municipal buildings. Even steam ships and sailing boats off the coast fly black flags. The funeral procession, on the morning of 21st May, seems to involve most of the city - the listing in the newspaper *La Bilancia* goes on for numerous column inches, naming all the dignitaries and community groups involved. The carriage with the coffin is pulled up the hill to the Kozala cemetery by six black horses. The death of the Mayor's wife - ***la consorte del Magnifico Podesta*** - is not a low key affair.

I even have - thanks to the research of Irvin Lukežić - a description of where the coffin is interred. In the Kozala cemetery register it is written that [from the Italian] ***the remains were placed in the tomb of the family of Iginio Scarpa, on the left, 2nd level, 2nd niche.*** That is odd. Since this is the mausoleum of her first husband's family. But it should, at least, be easy to find...

* * * * *

The Scarpa Mausoleum in Rijeka's Kozala cemetery

Sure enough, amidst this extraordinary hilltop city of the dead overlooking Rijeka in Croatia, the Scarpa mausoleum stands at the head of one of the cross streets - a cross street that, a little further down, contains the fine grave and monument to Natalie's husband, the Magnifico Podesta, Giovanni Ciotta, who dies eight years later, on 6th November 1903, having withdrawn from public life soon after her death.

Giovanni Ciotta's grave

But Natalie is not with her second husband. She had been placed in the grander mausoleum of her first husband's family at the head of the street - we may guess, at the wish of her elder Scarpa children. So, I go looking for the 2nd level on the left, 2nd niche... and find that Natalie is long gone.

This is a cemetery that reflects the upheaval of the 20th Century Croatia. If you don't stick around to tend - and pay the rent for - your slot, someone else is going to come along and take it. It doesn't matter whose name in on the door.

Inside the Scarpa Mausoleum - Natalie is long gone, replaced by newcomers

Josipa, my guide, explains that there has probably been two or three bodies in that slot since Natalie was there. Along with any respect for the aristocratic family in whose mausoleum she is shelved, she has long been taken out and dumped. Time moves on in Croatia.

* * * * *

In September 2011, I receive a letter from Dublin. ***Thank you for your enquiry. The Raheny burial registers are here, and I checked both and can confirm the following:***

On 20 November 1825, Mrs Green (sic) ***of the parish of Kilrisk was buried.***

On 29 March 1859 Mary Letitia Green (sic) ***of 2 Upper Gardiner Street, Dublin, was buried, aged 72 years.***

Dr Susan Hood, Archivist / Publications Officer, Church of Ireland, RCB Library, Braemor Park, Churchtown, Dublin 14.

I have found Miss Greene. She is in the Protestant cemetery in Raheny, north Dublin, where her parents Dr Henry and Mary Anne Greene are buried in the company of their joint ancestors the Grace family of Raheny.

It makes sense. I have been distracted by the addresses in England of Miss Greene's later correspondence, her preferred home of Cheltenham, and then in searching for the lost homes of her elder brothers in Swords and County Louth...

At the end of her life she is living with her Shaw niece, Mrs Mary Anne Hayes and her husband, Justice Edmund Hayes, in Mountjoy Square in Dublin. Mrs Hayes has died a few months before, aged 45 - in the same horrific way as Oscar Wilde's half-sisters, Emily and Mary, and too many others ladies of the time - her muslin dress has swept too close to the fire place and ignited. Miss Greene's death, if not pain-free, is at least peaceful, and in her dotage, at the Hayes' townhouse, aged 72.

Another of her Mary Anne nieces, Mrs Wilkinson, writes in the *Greene Family Journal*: ***After more than eight years of extreme agony from nearly universal neuralgia, it pleased God to take my dear Aunt Mary (Mary Letitia) to Himself – she died April 26th 1859 at 11 am firmly trusting in her Saviour, who loved and died for her.***

* * * * *

Emily's niece, Betty Balfour, in her biography of Robert, pays tribute to Miss Greene in words that I can not better ***...Miss Greene had no blood tie with the children; they had no claim upon her, yet she gave them nothing less than her life. She made a home for them; and tended them with a fostering affection which, but for her, their childhood would have lacked... her capacity for devotion was unbounded, and never failed the otherwise homeless children.***

I go to Raheny to find the Protestant cemetery. It is small, on a raised bluff, now encircled by a busy roundbout. There is no apparent way in - only an black iron rail fence sealing it off from the world. I climb the wall of the bluff, and scale the pointed fence.

Stepping over the charred ashes of bonfires, crushed beer cans and fast food wrappers, I look around at the final resting place of Mary Letitia Greene. All there is to see is smashed and shattered grave stones.

This is a cemetery that reflects the upheaval of the 20th Century Ireland. Time has moved on here too.

* * * * *

The final resting place of Miss Greene - Raheny's old Protestant cemetery, Dublin

No trace of Natalie or Miss Greene remains on this earth, and yet dear Emily is still here. Just beyond my study window, out in beautiful Knebworth Park.

I will visit her one last time. But, before I do - I leave for Natalie and Miss Greene a stone that does exist, a stone at which I stop and pause at the edge of the lovely peaceful country - now Catholic - graveyard at Stickillen, once home of the Greene family of County Louth:

GO MBANNAÍ 'DIA DAOIBH, A FHORIREANN,
GO MBEANNAÍ DIA, DAOIBH AGUS MUIRE.
BHÍ SIBHSE TAMALL MAR ATÁ SINNE
BEIMIDNE FÓS MAR ATA SIBHSE...

MAY GOD BLESS ALL THE COMPANY OF SOULS HERE
MAY GOD AND MARY BLESS YOU.
YOU TOO SPENT AWHILE HERE
JUST AS WE ARE NOW
AND WE TOO WILL JOIN YOU SOON...

IN REMEMBERANCE OF
THE FORGOTTEN ONES
WHO LIE HERE IN UNMARKED GRAVES

Oft the sun shall shine down on thy green native hill,
But the glow of his smile thou shalt feel never more!
Oft the west wind shall rock the young blossoms, but still
Is the breeze for the heart that can hear never more!

Elergy On The Death Of A Youth - Friedrich Schiller
translated by Edward Bulwer Lytton

CHAPTER 38

~ *Knebworth - 2016* ~

On 1st December 1891, the Lytton family assemble at Knebworth House to carry Robert's coffin from the Banqueting Hall to the Mausoleum. His daughter Emily writes in her memoir, *A Blessed Girl* (1953):

I have never seen the Mausoleum open before and had always had a horror of it, and it seemed such a cold, dreary place. But instead of that, it looked so cheerful and comfortable. There was not room there for more than ourselves, and it was so nice that in the last part of the service they read alone to us quietly.

There is a slab which hides the coffins of Grandfather's mother [Mrs Bulwer] ***and Grandmother*** [Mrs Warburton Lytton], ***and besides there are only Aunt Emily's and little Teddy's*** [Robert's second son dies in the same year as Edward, 1873, aged 18 months]. ***Father was put beside Teddy and quite close to his sister, and it was so touching, one of father's wreaths fell on the little coffin beside him.***

It made me happy seeing Aunt Emily's coffin, for I have always has a kind of adoration for her, though I don't know much about her life, but when I was a child and very miserable I loved her as I knew she had been treated very unkindly, and I thought I would give her all my love, and I used to hope that I should die young as she did. It makes me happy still to think that I have got her name.

Kipling (the Knebworth gardener) was telling us yesterday that seven years ago Father went alone with him into the Mausoleum and put a wreath of rosebuds on his sister's coffin. The lock of the gate outside was rusty and he could not open it. Father jumped over the railings long before he could get over himself.

* * * * *

Courtesy of the Fondazione Palazzo Coronini Cronberg

Ansicht von Canstadt [view of Cannstatt] *in Amalia's Album*

Former site of Heine's Institute, Bad Strasse (leading off to the right), in 2016

I return to Cannstatt in 2016. I am guest of Stuttgart Archivist Manfred and his wife Margot Schmid, good friends gained of this long adventure. I must be honest and say that Cannstatt is not the town it used to be. You need only compare the picturesque ansicht in Amalia's album to the tarmac and tram lines of my view of the corner of Bad Strasse today, the street on which the Heine Institute once stood. But beyond casually denigrating the over-industrialisation of his home town, it is my intention now to seriously test this new-found friendship by asking Manfred if he will go into the woods with me and pick wildflowers.

I have already reduced my daughter to uncontrollable giggles whilst packing. I respond to her polite inquiry if I have finished - "all but my blotting paper".

"I need to take blotting paper to German to press wildflowers." She is rolling on the bed weeping with laughter. Seventeen years on this project and Dad has completely lost it.

Having finished my book, I am preparing to return to the Mausoleum in Knebworth Park and seal Emily's coffin. As well as a wreath of rosebuds, to echo Robert's, I am inspired by the letter of Elise Bohrer to bring Emily a momento from the Burgwald. ***Does her friend remember how they used to fight for wild strawberries in the Burgwald?***

There's a challenge for Manfred. I have come to Germany to get wild strawberries from the Burgwald to take to my great-great-great aunt in her coffin. Would not lebkuchen and some Ritter chocolate do?

But before we even get to the wild strawberries, where is the 'Burgwald'?

'Burg' is a castle and 'wald' is a wood. I have been looking at the map, but there is no 'Burgwald' today. From one's top floor room at the Heine Institute, looking west across the River Neckar, one would watch the sun setting behing the hill of the Schloss Rosenstein, the impressive summer palace of King Wilhelm I of Württemberg, built between 1822 and 1830. Could the Burgwald be a 'wald' once surrounding the Schloss Rosenstein?

It could - but more likely, it is a 'wald' on the next hill, to the south, where Wilhelm's son, Charles (1823–1891) builds his own summer residence in the year of Emily departure, 1845, and names it after that hill, Villa Berg. 'Berg' means 'mountain' in German, and here we also find the 'Mineral-Bad Berg', and the remains of what was clearly once a larger wood. What Robert has read

Courtesy of the Fondazione Palazzo Coronini Cronberg

Again from Amalia's Album, a view of the Schloss Rosenstein on the opposite side of the River Neckar from Cannstatt, and the beginnings of the Bergwald, the 'mountain wood', on the left

as 'Burgwald', I believe is 'Bergwald'.

The 'wald' that surrounds the Villa Berg today is no more a wood than its hill is a 'berg', but both will have been a much better reflection of their names in the 1840s, before the urban and industrial sprawl of Cannstatt-bei-Stuttgart

Gathering wildflowers in the Bergwald, and placing them in blotting paper for pressing

enveloped them. There is, however, still a small 'wald' - now more of a park - around the Villa Berg.

We'll find no wild strawberries in the Bergwald in 2016, but we will find wild flowers. So, off Manfred and I go... with my blotting paper.

* * * * *

I said I would go back when Emily story is told. I finish this book in the summer of 2016, seventeen years after that gloomy autumn day, last century, when we smashed our way into the bricked up Mausoleum. I did peer in again once, after the restoration was finished, but otherwise I have not been back into the Mausoleum since. I have felt uneasy about the way we left it, caked in the dust of the concrete mixer which it stored during its restoration. Emily's coffin is still in there, open, but for the damaged lid resting on top of it. I assume she remains undisturbed. I hope so.

I want the day to be special. Should it be an anniversary? Perhaps I return on the anniversary of her death, April 29th? Or the anniversary of her funeral, a few days later? No, I want this to be a positive moment. I will visit Emily on her birthday. Her 188th birthday. Monday 27th June 2016.

If my descendents visit me - potentially also in this Mausoleum - on my 188th birthday, it will be the year 2150. Halfway through the next century. I hope they do. I will be delighted to see them. Especially pleased if they walk across from Knebworth House, loving it as their home then as we love it now, and Emily's father and grandmother loved it in the 1840s.

* * * * *

It is a small gathering. On purpose. I don't know how I will feel facing my great-great-great-aunt. I know her now better than I know my own siblings. This is her. Her 19-year-old bones. Her centuries-old dust. All the blood and tears of her life are dried in that coffin, but I bring with me both - her blood in my veins and her tears in my eyes. I feel again that pressure in my chest. Frankly, I am a little overwhelmed.

There will be a doctor on hand. Back in 1999, I tell the events of the first

Monday 27th June 2016. Emily's 188th birthday gathering. From the left: Clare Fleck, David Cobbold, Ken Holmes, Jill Campbell, myself, Mike Watson, Jean Greene, Angie Watson

chapter of this book to the father of a schoolfriend of my daughter. He is one of the top orthapaedic surgeons in the country. At the time, he offers - should I ever look in the coffin - to give a professional opinion on Emily's skelton, it's size, the curve of her spine, etc. My daughter changed schools soon after and I haven't seen Mike Watson since. But my daughter, through the brave new world of Facebook manages to find his email address for me, so I send him a note. Could I, in 2016, take him up on that offer of 1999?

I also want Jean Greene to be there. Miss Greene is not at Emily's funeral, but Mrs Greene will be at her 188th birthday party. Jean joins me in the Rose Garden of Knebworth House on the morning of 27th June and together we pick a beautiful white rose to give to Emily. Adam ('the Knebworth gardener' in 2016) tells me it is called 'Champagne Moment'. Then, it shall represent this book.

We walk to the Mausoleum, where we are joined by the keepers of Emily's short life's few relics, the Knebworth archivists, master transcriber Clare Fleck, bringing a lovely wreath of rosebuds to match Robert's, and master records trawler Jill Campbell, bringing the pressed flowers from Germany.

My father, David, born in 1937, only 89 years after the events of the closing chapters of this book, joins us. He remembers well his grandfather and great-aunts and great-uncle, Emily's nephews and nieces.

No mallet this time. Ken, our Head of Maintenance, has brought the old iron key. I slide it into the lock, and in we go...

* * * * *

Inside the Mausoleum, 27th June 2016

It doesn't look as bad as I remember. It's a little dusty, but I understand my great-great-aunt's comment that she finds it ***cheerful and comfortable.***

There is certainly plenty of room. No problem finding our own spaces in here - in this fine company.

The open floor in front of the shelves has room for a family card table. I imagine midnight games of Racing Demon and plenty of pleasant evenings spent in eternity. Amongst family.

Emily's coffin is as we left it, alone on the right hand side. The loose lid is bowed upwards slightly, show-

Emily's coffin, 27th June 2016

ing a clear gap and the darkness within. It is like she was late home to bed and has just pulled it over her, as any teenager would her duvet.

When all are assembled in the small space, I lift the lid and set it down on the floor. We have a lamp, run from a generator outside. It is held over the coffin.

I lean in. It is awkward, as the stone shelf above means my face has to be closer to the inside of the coffin than I would prefer. The first thing I see is torn, curled pieces of lead lying amongst rotted fabric. I long thought this coffin was broken open in the 1950s for the purpose of stealing lead, but this cannot be the case as there are so many pieces of lead still here. The thieves were looking for precious objects. The fact that they didn't find any, I presume, is why the other coffins are left undisturbed.

I pick out the larger pieces of lead and place them on the shelf above.

And there she is.

* * * * *

And there she is

Her skull has fallen back. The shroud covering it has slipped so that it only covers her eyes. Her raised jaw shows off the top level of her teeth. This is how Herr Bopp, the Stuttgart dentist, knew her. I wonder if he covered her eyes in the same way they are covered now. My dentist covers my eyes when I am in this postition, with big black glasses.

I am looking at my great-great-great-aunt's teeth. The teeth that chewed those collected sugarlumps, then gave her so much trouble that she started taking laudanum. It is as though I have opened her coffin and before we've even been introduced she is showing me the root of her downfall - her teeth - a confirmation of Miss Greene's belief that taking laudanum to ease toothache was the beginning of her losing her mind.

But what of her spine? The reason she was sent to Stuttgart? Dr Watson steps forward to peer into the past with me.

Mike's first comment is that her skeleton is not especially small, as the builder in 1999 had suggested. He points straight to the twist in her spine, "There's her scoliosis". It is clear to see. A simple, slight curve of the spine bone lying on the floor of the coffin. "We wouldn't bother to do anything with that now. Slight curvature like that is relatively common and not too problematic to live with."

"So Dr Heine did some good?"

"Very possibly." This is what I want to hear.

Later, when I raise the question of exposure to Heine-Medin disease - i.e. polio - Mike supposes it is possible she could have suffered a mild variation of polio as a child, but she went to Dr Heine with a pre-existing condition. It's as likely for her bone growth to have been affected by a variant of extrapulmonary tuberculosis, picked up from, amongst other things, unpasturised milk. So should I be worrying - along with Miss Greene - about Emily's over-suckled wetnurse, Mrs Parr, the farmer's wife...? The Victorians were poisoning themselves every day with the products of diseased animals and toxic food additives - alum in the bread, lead in the mustard, the scroll rolls on and on - but plenty of them made it to a ripe old age.

No. I have been given the answer. Emily's skelton does not look like a child's or a monkey's, as I was told in 1999. It is a relatively normal 19-year-old girl's skelton, with a mild curvature of the spine. Emily's death, as you have read in the preceding chapters, is about what was going on inside that tipped back skull... behind the row of teeth that I am now staring at.

* * * * *

Jean Greene steps forward and she and I place the white rose in Emily's hand. I remember Lillian Gish in her last film *The Whales of August* (1987),

The Flower Plucked

celebrating an anniversary with her deceased husband with roses, red for passion and white for truth. Emily's rose from the Knebworth House garden is white speckled with red. Even more I associate the rose with this book.

Happy Birthday, Emily.

Before saying a final goodbye, I scatter the wildflowers from the Bergwald in Cannstatt at her feet... and we place the lid back on the coffin.

The coffin is sealed. Clare places the beautiful handmade wreath upon it.

We lock the door of the Mausoleum, and walk back up the hill, beneath grey English skies, to Knebworth House.

We are shadowed by a single red kite, that circles above. It circles three times. Will Miss Emily still want escorting out this evening... to ***soar above*** (as dreamt in her little childhood story, *The Flower Plucked*) ***with myriads of happy spirits like herself***?

Wildflowers at her feet

Yes! I believe so. ***Happily in the bosom of her God.***

And her father?

He could be this red kite. For all we know.

Joachim Mathieu and David Cobbold

Serenella Ferrari

Christa and Hans Hekler

Manfredo Ritter de Záhony

Beth Thomson *Ivo Lazzari*

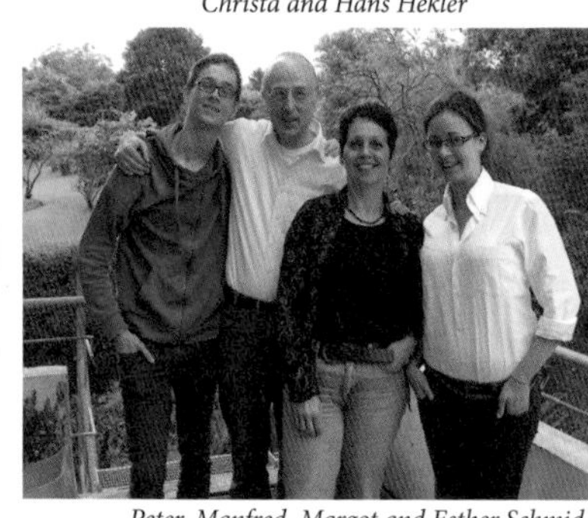

Peter, Manfred, Margot and Esther Schmid

Jill Campbell

Josipa Santini

Irvin Lukežić

Jean and Paul Greene, Jenny, Peter and Nick the Greene family returns to Knebworth

Stefan Töpfer contemplates the centre of the universe

Richenda van Laun of the Tennyson D'Eyncourt family

Jean Greene and Bonnie Wilkinson (on the wall)

Clare Fleck at the gateway to Bayons

CHAPTER 39

~ Angels ~

I am persuaded that if my father's biography is written, as I have tried to write it, honestly and faithfully, no clumsiness on the part of its writer can render it wholly uninteresting, nor even wholly uninstructive.

Robert Lytton. Knebworth. November 15, 1883.

I am persuaded of the same by the many angels who have made these volumes possible, probable, and finally, printable. For all the naiveties and nonsense of my prose (greener than Miss Greene's, and verdant in my genes), I know this book - my first - could never be ***wholly uninteresting*** or ***wholly uninstructive,*** as it includes the rally and wisdom of angels on every page.

Angels all - thank you for watching over this story across three decades, three centuries and a couple of millennia. The flutter of your wings has dissolved the degrees of separation and revealed a tale that wished to be told. You are the story, so I simply offer you the thanks already included in the book's text and photos, the august company of the Index that follows, some fine memories opposite, a few personal additions below... and if you still don't find your name, here it is to fill the unforgiving minutes of future researchers: _____ _____[indecipherable].

You have your own chapter because 39 is my lucky number.

Henry Lytton Cobbold. Knebworth. November 8, 2016.

[Robert's 185th birthday]

A special thank you to all whose words and images I have used; to those closest to their presentation - Clare, Jill, Marie, Steve, Joachim, Jürgen, Sam, Rob (photos), Dean at Aitch Creative (cover), Daniel and Jamie at Jarrolds (publishing); Johnson to my Boswell, Rosemarie Jarski (who has already written a 100-page book on this book); and my guardian and archangel, Martha.

INDEX

Emily's immediate family is marked as *passim* [which, appropriately, means 'scattered' - but here denotes that their appearance in the text is too regular to index]. Along with her brother, father and mother I have included in this definition her grandmother and - I hope you agree, also appropriately - Miss Greene, the Wilkinsons and myself... then after p.535, Natalie de Ritter.

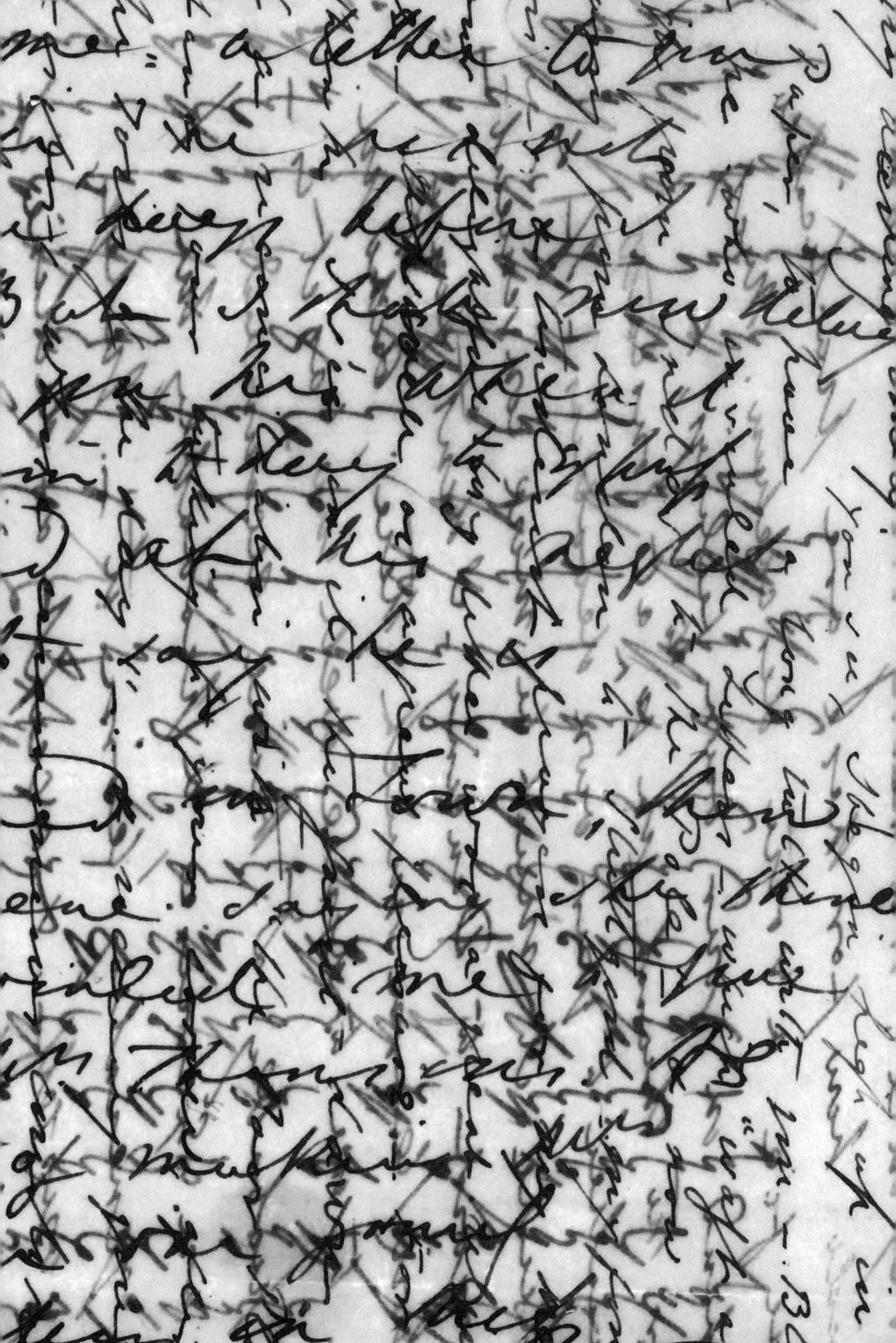